How to find what you need in

1. **Consult the table of contents.** The table of contents (pages v–xvi) offers a comprehensive list of the *Handbook*'s parts, sections, and subsections. Parts are designated with Roman numerals, from I to VIII. Sections, numbered consecutively without regard to parts, are designated with Arabic numerals, from 1 to 79. Subsections are designated with letters within each section (for example, 1a, 1b). The book ends with an appendix of checklists.

2. **Look over the list of exercises.** Exercises found on the companion website (www.oupcanada.com/CCWH3e) are listed by section number on pages xvii–xx. Sections and subsections with corresponding online exercises are identified in the text with a symbol.

3. **Use the running heads.** The running heads, at the top of each page, identify parts and sections by number and title. They also feature the subsection number and letter so you can tell at a glance what section and subsection are being discussed on each page.

4. **Check the index.** The detailed index (pages 487–505) will direct you to the pages where you will find information on specific topics (for example, dangling modifiers) and words and phrases (for example, *although, though*).

5. **Refer to the list of marking symbols.** The list of marking symbols, located on the inside back cover, will direct you to the sections that discuss specific writing problems, such as faulty parallelism or dangling modifiers.

THE CONCISE CANADIAN WRITER'S HANDBOOK

Third Edition

William E. Messenger
Jan de Bruyn
Judy Brown
Ramona Montagnes

OXFORD
UNIVERSITY PRESS

OXFORD
UNIVERSITY PRESS

Oxford University Press is a department of the University of Oxford.
It furthers the University's objective of excellence in research, scholarship,
and education by publishing worldwide. Oxford is a registered trade mark of
Oxford University Press in the UK and in certain other countries.

Published in Canada by
Oxford University Press
8 Sampson Mews, Suite 204,
Don Mills, Ontario M3C 0H5 Canada

www.oupcanada.com

Copyright © Oxford University Press Canada 2017

The moral rights of the authors have been asserted

Database right Oxford University Press (maker)

First Edition published in 2009
Second Edition published in 2013

Library and Archives Canada Cataloguing in Publication

Messenger, William E., 1931-2003, author
The concise Canadian writer's handbook / William E. Messenger,
Jan de Bruyn, Judy Brown, Ramona Montagnes. -- Third edition.

Includes index.
ISBN 978-0-19-902109-3 (spiral bound)

1. English language--Composition and exercises. 2. English
language--Grammar. 3. Report writing. I. De Bruyn, Jan, 1918-,
author II. Brown, Judy, 1954-2013, author III. Montagnes, Ramona,
author IV. Messenger, William E., 1931-2003. Canadian writer's
handbook. V. Title. VI. Title: Canadian writer's handbook.

PE1408.M5837 2016   808'.042   C2016-907242-8

Cover: images © iStock/pialhovik, composite by Laurie McGregor

Oxford University Press is committed to our environment.
Wherever possible, our books are printed on paper which
comes from responsible sources.

Printed and bound in the United States of America

3 4 5 — 21 20 19

CONTENTS

Contents

PART III | Parts of Speech 83

13. Nouns 86

14. Pronouns 89

Contents

Contents

Contents

Contents

List of Online Student Exercises

The exercises listed below can be found on the companion website for this book (www.oupcanada.com/CCWH3e).

PART II | Understanding Sentences

List of Online Student Exercises

PART III | Parts of Speech

PART IV | Writing Effective Sentences

PART V | Punctuation

Common Mechanical and Spelling Errors

When you prepare a piece of writing for an academic or professional environment, you are expected to follow certain conventions of mechanics and spelling. To make a good impression, you should format your document with care and ensure that you spell words correctly and consistently. You should also follow standard conventions for abbreviating, capitalizing, and italicizing words, and for enclosing words in quotation marks.

The following list is a quick guide to the sections in this handbook that will help you avoid those mechanical and spelling errors most common in student essays and reports. Students who have difficulties with spelling will find sections #61 (a detailed discussion of spelling rules and common causes of error) and #62 (a list of commonly misspelled words) particularly helpful. Note that the parenthetical abbreviations used in this list are explained on the inside of the back cover.

PART VI | Mechanics and Spelling

#58b (*Q*)	Mishandled quotation marks for titles of short works and parts of longer works
#58c (*ital*) or (*Q*)	Needed or incorrect use of italics or quotation marks for titles within titles
#59c (*ital*)	Needed or incorrect use of italics for words referred to as words
#60b (*num*)	Numeral needed or misused for dates
#60e (*num*)	Numeral needed or misused for parts of a written work
#60f (*num*)	Numeral needed or misused for numbers of more than two words
Tip on page 291 (*num*)	Improper use of a numeral at the beginning of a sentence
Tip on page 298 (*sp*)	Incorrect or inconsistent spelling of *practice* vs *practise* and of *licence* vs *license*
#61f (*sp*)	Spelling error due to not knowing when to double the final consonant before a suffix
#61h (*sp*)	Spelling error due to confusion with other words
#61i (*sp*)	Spelling error due to confusion between homophones and other words that are similar
#61k (*sp*)	Spelling error due to misplaced or missing hyphen
#61-l (*sp*)	Spelling error due to incorrect plural form
#61n (*sp*)	Spelling error due to incorrect possessive form
#62 (*sp*)	Spelling error in a commonly misspelled word

Important Topics for EAL Students

The following list is a quick guide to the sections in this handbook that discuss issues of particular importance to students who have English as an additional language (EAL). Whether you are relatively new to writing in English or you are more experienced and looking to master the finer points of the written language, these sections of the text—in combination with a learner's dictionary—will help you improve your writing skills. Note that the entries in this list correspond to the EAL symbol found throughout the text: **EAL** .

PART II | Understanding Sentences

PART III | Parts of Speech

PREFACE

The third edition of *The Concise Canadian Writer's Handbook* is designed to help you in what we see as the ongoing (even lifelong) project of improving written communication. We know that the improvement of our own writing is a work in progress, and we believe that the same may be true for our readers. Whether you are a long-time writer of English seeking to refresh and refine your abilities or one who is writing in English as an additional language, we hope that the suggestions, examples, and guidelines in this new edition will provide a trustworthy resource that will enable you to write with greater confidence and skill.

This handbook has a three-part organization that opens and closes with an emphasis on the larger units of writing. We begin with a section on principles of composition, ranging from the design of paragraphs to the design of the whole essay and the principles of effective planning and argument; we close with a section on current practices in research-based writing. In the middle parts of the book, we explore principles of grammar, syntax, and usage at the word and sentence level. We devote considerable space to examination of sentence patterns, parts of speech, and sentence structure and variety; we also include parts devoted to punctuation, mechanics and spelling, and diction. The appendix of this book provides comprehensive checklists designed for use at the planning and revising stages of your writing projects.

Overview

This handbook is intended for you to use as a reference work, to consult on particular issues arising from the everyday writing activities, challenges, and questions you encounter. It may also be used as a class text for discussion and study in writing courses, programs, and workshops. We suggest that you begin by considering the ways you will be using this book. Then, start to familiarize yourself with it by seeing what it has to offer you. Browse through the table of contents and the index. Look up some sections that arouse your interest. Flip through the pages, pausing now and then for a closer look. Note the numbered running heads at the tops of pages and the tabbed inerts at the beginning of each new part. These features, together with the guide at the end of this preface, can help you find things in a hurry.

Organization

Notice how the material is organized. We have arranged the parts of this handbook to reflect the natural order in which most students think about, prepare, and polish a written essay or assignment. Part I offers broad coverage of the principles of composition in order to get you started on the writing process. This part examines the larger units of communication: the essay as a whole and the paragraphs that form the essay. Part II narrows the focus to provide a basic overview of the sentences that constitute paragraphs, and Part III narrows the focus further to examine the components of sentences: the parts of speech. With this foundation in place, Part IV offers more advanced advice on how to construct *effective* sentences—that is, sentences that achieve their intended purpose, add variety to a piece of writing, and are free from common problems with structure, logic, and unity. Parts V, VI, and VII offer guidance on the finer details of punctuation, mechanics and spelling, and diction, respectively, all of which are important for a writer to consider while revising her or his work. Part VIII discusses topics of concern to students preparing a research essay, with useful coverage of how to find resources, develop a research plan, take notes, write the essay, acknowledge sources, quote from secondary sources, and document sources. Finally, the appendix provides checklists for use as you revise, edit, and proofread your work.

Once you understand how the parts of this book fit together, you should begin to think about how you can best approach the material. You may want to start at the beginning and proceed slowly and carefully through each section. Or, if you are struggling with a particular aspect of writing, you may want to skip to the relevant section and then consult other sections as your needs change. As you progress, you can test yourself by trying some of the exercises available on the companion site (www.oupcanada.com/CCWH3e) and checking your answers with your instructor or against the online answer key.

For Readers and Writers of English as an Additional Language

Our experience as university instructors has given us the opportunity to work with a number of writers engaged in the challenging project of reading and writing in English as an additional language (EAL). Because English is a third, fourth, or fifth language to many such students, we have long felt that the term *ESL* (English as a second language), used to describe or even to label these writers, is something of a misnomer. Still, at several points in this handbook, we offer information and direction of particular importance to those of you who are approaching English as a relatively new language, and have designated those relevant sections with the symbol `EAL`.

Checking Your Work Before Submitting It

When you finish a piece of writing, go through the omnibus checklists in the Appendix. If you find you're not sure about something, follow the cross-references to the sections that will give you the help you need.

Correcting and Revising Returned Work

When you get a piece of writing back with marks and comments, first look it over alongside the list of marking symbols and abbreviations on the book's inside back cover. The information there may be enough to help you make the appropriate changes. But if you need more than a reminder about a specific issue or pattern—if you don't understand the fundamental principles—follow the cross-references and study the sections that discuss and illustrate those principles in greater detail. (See the sample pages on page xxviii.) You should then be able to edit and revise your work with understanding and confidence.

An important feature of this book is that it discusses and illustrates various issues in several places. If the information you find in one place isn't enough to clarify a point, remember that you may not yet have exhausted the available resources: consult the index to see if it will lead you to still other relevant places.

Marking Symbols and Abbreviations

Numbers refer to handbook sections.

abbr	incorrect or inappropriate abbreviation *#56*	**log**	illogical *#10e–h, #38, #41, #42*
ack	acknowledgement of sources missing or incorrect *#77–79*	**mix**	mixed construction *#37*
ad	misused adjective or adverb *#19, #20*	**mm**	misplaced modifier *#35*
agr	faulty agreement: pronoun–antecedent *#15, subject–verb #18*	**ms**	improper manuscript form *#55*
		nsw	no such word
al	illogical or incongruous alignment *#38*	**num**	numeral needed or misused *#60*
ambig	ambiguous, clarity lacking *#16b* (pronoun reference), *#31–42, Pt. VII, EAL Checklist*	**org**	weak or faulty organization *#4, #8a–j, #10d*
apos	missing or misused apostrophe *#61m–n*	**p**	punctuation error *Pt. V*
art	missing or misused article *#19c*	**pam, ¶**	paragraph needed, or weak paragraphing *#1–7*
awk	awkward *EAL Checklist*	**pas**	weak passive voice *#17-i, #29f*
ca	incorrect case of pronoun *#14e*	**passim**	an error occurs throughout
cap	missing or faulty capitalization *#57*	**pred**	faulty predication (alignment) *#38*
cl	clarity lacking *#31–42, Pt. VII, EAL Checklist*	**pron**	error in pronoun use *#14–16*
cliché	cliché, trite *#71e*	**pv**	inconsistent point of view *#39*
coh	coherence lacking *#3–5, #8b, #31*	**Q**	mishandled quotation or quotation marks *#52, #78*
colloq	colloquial, too informal *#64b*		
comp	faulty or incomplete comparison *#42*	**red**	redundant *#71c*
conc	insufficient concreteness *#66*	**ref**	weak or faulty pronoun reference *#15, #16*
coord	coordination needed *#23a, #41*	**rep**	weak or awkward repetition *#71b*
cs	comma splice *#33, #54b*	**run-on**	run-on (fused) sentence *#34, #54a*
d	weak or faulty diction *Pt. VII*	**shift**	unwanted shift in point of view or perspective *#39*
dev	development needed *#1b, #4b, #7b, #66*		
dm	dangling modifier *#36*	**sp**	spelling error *#61, #62* (and *#63*, on dictionaries)
doc	faulty documentation *#78–79*		
emph	weak or unclear emphasis *#6, #8c, #29, #41*	**split**	unnecessary split infinitive *#21c*
euph	weak euphemism *#68*	**squint**	squinting modifier *#35c*
fc	faulty coordination *#41*	**ss**	faulty sentence structure, or faulty sense *#12, Pt. IV, EAL Checklist*
fig	inappropriate or confusing figurative language *#65, #71e*	**stet**	let it stand as originally written
fp, //	faulty parallelism *#40*	**sub**	subordination needed *#12n–o, #23c, #29, #41*
frag	unacceptable fragment *#12w–x, #32*	**t**	error in verb tense *#17g–i*
fs	fused (run-on) sentence *#34, #54a*	**tr**	weak or missing transition *#4, #6c–d, #8b*
gen	weak generalization *#66b*	**trite**	trite, cliché
id	unidiomatic *#70*	**u**	weak uni
inc	incomplete comparison *#42*	**uc**	uppercase
inf	too informal, colloquial *#64b*	**us**	incorrect
ital	italics needed or incorrect *#58, #59*	**var**	lack of va
jarg	inappropriate or unnecessary jargon *#71h*	**vb**	incorrect
lc	no caps; lowercase letter needed *#57*	**w**	wordines
leg	illegible (handwritten work)	**ww**	awkward *#20d, #2*
lev	inappropriate level of diction *#64*	**ww**	wrong w

39e Shifts in Number of Pronoun (see #14a)

shift: **If the committee wants its recommendations followed, they should have written their report more carefully.**

The committee changed from a collective unit (*it*) to a collection of individuals (*they, their*); the committee should be either singular or plural throughout. See also *#15e* and *#18f*. (The errors in *#39d* and *#39e* could also be marked *agr*: see *#15*.)

40 Faulty Parallelism

fp, // Parallelism, the balanced and deliberate repetition of identical grammatical structures (words, phrases, clauses), can be a strong stylistic technique. Not only does it make for vigorous, balanced, and rhythmical sentences, but it can also help develop and tie together paragraphs (see *#5a*). Like any other device, parallelism can be overdone, but more commonly it is underused. Of course, if you're writing an especially serious piece, like a letter of condolence, you probably won't want to use lively devices like parallelism and metaphor (see *#65*). But in most writing, some parallel structure is appropriate. Build parallel elements into your sentences, and now and then try making two or three successive sentences parallel with each other. Here is a sentence from a paper on computer crime. Note how parallelism (along with alliteration) strengthens the first part, thereby helping to set up the second part:

Although one can distinguish the malicious from the mischievous or the harmless hacker from the more dangerous computer criminal, security officials take a dim view of anyone who romps through company files.

Be careful as you experiment, for it is easy to set up a parallel structure and then lose track of it. Study the following examples of **faulty parallelism**. (See also *#23a–b*.)

221

Numbering and Cross-Referencing

This handbook is subdivided into sections and subsections that are numbered consecutively throughout, without regard to parts. Cross-references are to section and subsections, or, occasionally, to parts. In the index, references are to page numbers.

Key Terms

The first one or two times an important term occurs, it is set in **bold-face**. Pay attention to these terms, for they make up the basic vocabulary necessary for the intelligent discussion of grammar, syntax, and style.

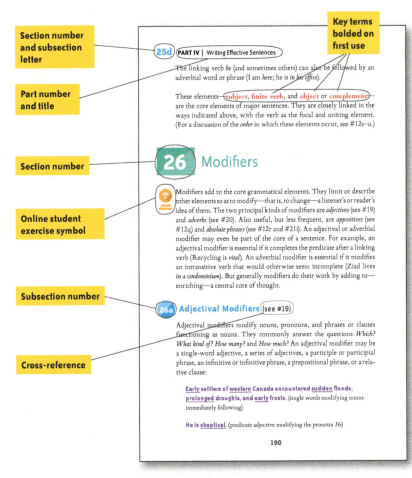

Section number and subsection letter

Part number and title

Section number

Online student exercise symbol

Subsection number

Cross-reference

Key terms bolded on first use

25d PART IV | Writing Effective Sentences

The linking verb *be* (and sometimes others) can also be followed by an adverbial word or phrase (I am *here*; he is *in his office*).

These elements—*subject*, *finite verb*, and *object* or *complement*—are the core elements of major sentences. They are closely linked in the ways indicated above, with the verb as the focal and uniting element. (For a discussion of the *order* in which these elements occur, see #12s–u.)

26 Modifiers

Modifiers add to the core grammatical elements. They limit or describe other elements so as to modify—that is, to change—a listener's or reader's idea of them. The two principal kinds of modifiers are *adjectives* (see #19) and *adverbs* (see #20). Also useful, but less frequent, are *appositives* (see #12q) and *absolute phrases* (see #12r and #21i). An adjectival or adverbial modifier may even be part of the core of a sentence. For example, an adjectival modifier is essential if it completes the predicate after a linking verb (Recycling is *vital*). An adverbial modifier is essential if it modifies an intransitive verb that would otherwise seem incomplete (Ziad lives *in a condominium*). But generally modifiers do their work by adding to—enriching—a central core of thought.

26a Adjectival Modifiers (see #19)

Adjectival modifiers modify nouns, pronouns, and phrases or clauses functioning as nouns. They commonly answer the questions *Which? What kind of? How many?* and *How much?* An adjectival modifier may be a single-word adjective, a series of adjectives, a participle or participial phrase, an infinitive or infinitive phrase, a prepositional phrase, or a relative clause:

Early settlers of **western** Canada encountered **sudden** floods, **prolonged** droughts, and **early** frosts. (single words modifying nouns immediately following)

He is **skeptical**. (predicate adjective modifying the pronoun *He*)

190

Other Features

42 **PART IV** | Writing Effective Sentences

WRITING TIP

Effective Workplace Writing

In today's competitive job market, the ability to prepare effective proposals, reports, memos, emails, and other forms of written communication is a highly valued skill. To get your message across successfully, you must not only understand your audience and your purpose in writing but also be able to construct sentences that are clear, concise, and free of the sorts of problems outlined in the preceding sections (#31–42). Moreover, you must be able to avoid common mistakes in grammar (see Part III), punctuation (see Part V), mechanics and spelling (see Part VI), and diction (see Part VII). Think of mistakes in these areas as static on the radio. Static can garble your message, making it difficult—and often frustrating—for your audience to understand what you are trying to say. The following tips should help you keep your workplace writing free of static:

1. Be specific, but don't provide more detail than your reader requires.
2. Make sure you are certain about the meaning of all words that you use. If you need help, consult a dictionary.
3. If you have difficulty composing complex and compound-complex sentences without errors, use mostly simple and compound sentences (see #12z).
4. Always proofread your work. Go slowly, and try to read your work from your reader's perspective. Look carefully for typos and errors you know you're prone to making.

Aim to produce clear, courteous, error-free writing in all workplace contexts. After all, even a short, quickly written email to a colleague may eventually find its way to your boss or even the head of [...] you consistently make errors in your writing, your [...] visors will question your professionalism and your [...] a good job. Think of every piece of writing as an [...] good impression.

230

Numerous boxes to highlight important information

61c **PART VI** | Mechanics and Spelling

ent, ently, ence, ency; ant, antly, ance, ancy

-en-		*-an-*	
apparent	independent	appearance	flamboyant
coherent	permanent	blatant	irrelevant
consistent	persistence	brilliant	maintenance
excellent	resilient	concomitant	resistance
existence	tendency	extravagant	warrant

tial, tian; cial, cian

-tia-		*-cia-*	
confidential	influential	beneficial	mathematician
dietitian	martial	crucial	mortician
existential	spatial	commercial	physician

ce; se

-ce		*-se*	
choice	fence	course	expense
defence	presence	dense	phrase
evidence	voice	dispense	sparse

PROOFREADING TIP

practice, practise; licence, license

Canadian writers tend to follow the British practice of using the -ce forms *practice* and *licence* as nouns and the -se forms *practise* and *license* as verbs:

> We will **practise** our fielding at today's slo-pitch **practice**.

> Are you **licensed** to drive?
> Yes, I've had my driver's **licence** since I was sixteen.

American writers tend to favour the -ce spelling of *practice* and the -se spelling of *license* regardless of whether each is being used as a noun or a verb.

Note also that Canadian as well as British writers generally prefer the -ce spelling for *offence* and *defence*, while American writers tend to use the -se spellings of these words

298

Canadian advice for Canadian users

79b **PART VIII** | Research, Writing, and Documentation

79b **The Name–Date Method (APA Style)**

The name–date system is detailed in the sixth edition of the *Publication Manual of the American Psychological Association* (2010). Using this system, you provide a short parenthetical reference in the text, and you list all sources in a reference list at the end of your paper:

sample in-text citation	sample reference-list entry
Our understanding of national identity must allow for "the expression of diverse types of identities within the public space" (Winter, 2011, p. 3).	Winter, E. (2011). *Us, them, and others: Pluralism and national identity in diverse societies.* Toronto, ON: University of Toronto Press.

Here are some examples of name–date parenthetical references, followed by some examples of reference-list entries.

In-Text Citations

In-text citations generally begin with the author's last name followed by a comma and the date the source was published. If the reference is to a general argument or evidence presented by the entire work, list only the author's last name and the year of publication:

> **National identity is deeply connected to a sense that there is a boundary between those who belong to a nation and those who do not (Winter, 2011).**

But if you refer to a particular part of the source, or if you quote from it, supply the relevant page number or numbers, preceded by the abbreviation "p." (for a single page) or "pp." (for a page range):

> **As Elke Winter (2011) notes, "a pluralist 'natio** opposition to a real or imagined 'Others' with a

As the above example shows, you do not need name in the parenthetical citation if you have pr elsewhere in the sentence.

Author   Title   Publication information

434

Detailed, up-to-date guidelines for documenting in MLA, APA, Chicago, and CSE (number) styles

Checklists for planning and revising your work

APPENDIX

Omnibus Checklist for Planning and Revising

The checklists presented below are designed to help you produce an appealing, complete, well-polished essay. The questions are based on the kinds of questions we ask ourselves in reading and evaluating students' writing. If you can answer all of the questions in the affirmative, your essay should be not just adequate, but very good.

1. **During and after planning the essay, ask yourself these questions:**

Subject	❑ Have I chosen a subject that sustains my interest? (#9a)
	❑ If I am writing a research essay, have I formulated a researchable question? (#9a, #74)
	❑ Have I sufficiently *limited* my subject? (#9b)
Audience and Purpose	❑ Have I thought about audience and purpose? (#9c)
	❑ Have I written down a statement of purpose and a profile of my audience? (#9c)
Evidence	❑ Have I collected or generated more than enough material/evidence to develop and support my topic well? (#9d)
Organization and Plan	❑ Does my *thesis* offer a focused, substantive, analytical claim about the subject?
	❑ Is my *plan or outline* for the essay logical in its content and arrangement? (#9e–j)
	❑ Considering my plan or outline, do I have the right number of *main ideas*—neither too few nor too many—for the purpose of my essay?
	❑ Are my main ideas reasonably *parallel* in content and development?
	❑ Have I chosen the best *arrangement* for the main parts? Does it coincide with the arrangement of ideas in the thesis?

479

ACKNOWLEDGEMENTS

As with the previous editions of *The Canadian Writer's Handbook*, this third concise edition owes much to the contributions of reviewers, colleagues, friends, fellow writers, and talented and committed editors.

For their determination to strengthen and polish their work and their commitment to grow and change as thinkers and writers, we thank our students. We are especially grateful for their generosity in allowing us to use their questions and insights about writing in this book.

We would like to thank the following reviewers, as well as those who wish to remain anonymous, whose comments and suggestions helped shape this book:

Bob Ackroyd, Northern Alberta Institute of Technology
Karen Bamford, Mount Allison University
A.E. Christa Canitz, University of New Brunswick
Hugh Hodges, Trent University
Ken Jacobsen, Memorial University
Matt Kavanagh, University of British Columbia
Sherry Klein, University of Regina
Julie Morris, Sheridan College
Howard F. Muchnick, Ryerson University
Dennis R. Nighswonger, Lakehead University
Cindy Soldan, Lakehead University
Ron Srigley, University of Prince Edward Island
Janice Stewart, University of British Columbia

We deeply appreciate the encouragement, advice, and support we receive from the talented and enthusiastic staff of Oxford University Press—especially from Phyllis Wilson, Dave Ward, Peter Chambers, and Leah-Ann Lymer. Special appreciation goes out to Janice Evans, our meticulous editor whose input helped to shape the new edition.

To all of you, many thanks.

Kinds of Paragraphs

A paragraph can be classified in two ways:

1. according to its function in its larger context, or
2. according to the kind of material it contains and the way that material is developed.

1a Functions of Paragraphs

Introductory, **concluding**, and **transitional paragraphs** are especially designed to begin or end an essay or to provide links between major sections of a longer essay. Other paragraphs in an essay, the **body paragraphs**, contribute to the development of a topic.

1b Kinds of Paragraphs: Methods of Development

Body paragraphs can be classified according to the way their material is developed. There are several **methods of development** to choose from. The method(s) you use for any given paragraph or essay will depend on the nature of your topic, your audience, and your purpose. Principal methods include *description, narration, definition, classification, analysis into parts, process analysis, comparison and contrast, cause and effect*, and *example and illustration*. The following questions can help you approach essay topics with these methods in mind. In each question, "X" represents the topic being developed.

- *description:* What are the physical features of X?
- *narration:* What is the story/history of X?
- *definition:* What is X?
- *classification:* Into what categories or types can X be divided?
- *analysis into parts:* What are the parts of X and how do they contribute to the whole of X?
- *process analysis:* What are the steps of X, or what are the steps leading to X?

- *comparison and contrast:* How is X similar to Y? How is X different from Y?
- *cause and effect:* What are the causes of or reasons for X? What are the effects or consequences of X?
- *example and illustration:* What are some concrete/specific examples or instances of X?

These methods of development are seldom mutually exclusive. Two or more are often combined in a single paragraph, and a whole essay may use several. Even narration can be used in an expository (explanatory) essay: for example, a case study may provide narrative evidence to support an observation.

To demonstrate the ways in which the questions we have listed would operate in the development of a topic, consider the following scenario.

Suppose that you were asked to write a short paper of 500 words or so on the broad subject area of contemporary air travel. At first, you might draw a blank in thinking about ways in which to focus the topic to allow you to write something distinctive—something to engage your own interest and to earn the respect and interest of your potential readers. Applying the questions we have listed would very likely help you to open up the possibilities for development.

The process would look something like this:

SUBJECT: **air travel today**

narration: **What is the story? Tell the story of recent air travel to the United States.**

analysis: **What were the steps in the process of the journey?**

effect: **What are the consequences of air travel?**

- **the stress of travelling**
- **the boredom of spending hours in the boarding lounge, the aircraft cabin, and the baggage claim area**
- **cramped quarters and claustrophobia for those travelling economy class**

comparison: **What are the essential differences between travel to the US by air and travel to the US by car, train, or bus?**

description: **What might I describe to enhance my paper?**

- **the terminal building**
- **the security gate or customs desk**
- **the cramped quarters in the aircraft cabin**
- **the noise of the aircraft, of fellow passengers**

In this stage of the process, you might see the methods of definition, classification, process analysis, and example/illustration as being less promising. Keep in mind that you may return to them at a later point, for the process of thinking your way through a topic is *recursive*—back and forth—rather than linear.

The following is an example of a paragraph that might result from this process:

My most recent trip to New York City brought home to me the many inconveniences of air travel today. When we arrived at the security gates at Vancouver Airport, we were required to undergo several lengthy and uncomfortable procedures. Passengers were asked to remove coats, belts, and shoes; they were required to dispose of items prohibited in carry-on luggage; their photo identification was studied carefully; several adult passengers were subjected to invasive full-body computer scans. After a four-hour delay in our departure time, armed air marshals quietly boarded the aircraft with us, and the cockpit was locked. These measures put many of us passengers on edge and added a dose of nervousness to the boredom and claustrophobia long associated with cross-border flights.

narrative opening

analysis: the steps in the security process

time transition: "after a four-hour delay"

effects of the process

2-7 Unity, Coherence, and Emphasis in Paragraphs

To be effective, all paragraphs, but especially body paragraphs, require **unity**, **coherence**, and well-controlled **emphasis**. Writing a paragraph involves designing the best possible package to contain and convey your ideas. You have a sense of what point you wish to convey (your topic), and, usually early in the process, you have an array of items to include as well (your supporting ideas and evidence). You arrange your ideas and evidence in the package by ordering them logically, linking them to one another using strategies for coherence. You may well spend some time rearranging to make the package look the way you want it to—to give each item the appropriate emphasis.

2 Paragraph Unity

An effective body paragraph ordinarily deals with one main idea; its singleness of purpose engages its readers by focusing their attention on that main idea. If a paragraph is disrupted by irrelevant digressions or unnecessary shifts in point of view or focus, readers will lose sight of the main idea. In other words, a paragraph has unity when every sentence in it contributes to its purpose.

3 Paragraph Coherence

Though a paragraph is unified because every sentence contributes to the development of its single theme or idea, it could still come apart if it doesn't have another essential quality: coherence. Coherence can be defined as the connection of ideas. Some inexperienced writers assume that simply placing one sentence after another guarantees coherence. In fact, coherence is achieved only by carefully packing the contents of a paragraph and linking the ideas to one another. You can ensure coherence in your writing in two ways:

1. by carefully organizing your material, and
2. by using a variety of transitional devices that create structural coherence.

Coherence Through Organization: Beginning, Middle, and Ending

A body paragraph has a *beginning*, a *middle*, and an *ending*. Good organization means rational order. Typically, the beginning introduces the main idea; the middle clearly and logically follows from and develops the statement of that idea, and the ending unobtrusively closes the discussion or provides a hook for the next paragraph. (But see the **writing tip** on positioning transitional material in #4a.)

 ## The Beginning: Topic Sentences

Body paragraphs typically open with a statement of the main idea, called a **topic sentence**.

1. Functions of Topic Sentences

A good topic sentence indicates what the paragraph will be about. It is, in effect, a promise that the rest of the paragraph fulfills. If the paragraph is part of a larger context, such as an essay, the topic sentence will usually perform two other functions:

1. It will refer to the subject of the essay and at least suggest the relation of the paragraph to that subject.
2. It will provide a transition so that the new paragraph flows smoothly from the preceding paragraph.

WRITING TIP

Positioning Transitional Material

It is sometimes possible, but often difficult, to provide forward-looking material at the end of a paragraph. Don't struggle to get something transitional into the last sentence of a paragraph. The work of transition should be done by the first sentence of the next paragraph. In other words, tampering with a paragraph's final sentence merely for transitional purposes may diminish that paragraph's integrity and effectiveness. See #4c.

2. Efficiency of Topic Sentences

Since it has so much to do, a good topic sentence, even more than other sentences, should be efficient. Here is one that is not:

> **The writer uses a great deal of good imagery throughout the article.**

The sentence indicates the topic—the article's imagery—but promises nothing more than to show that the article contains a lot of it. But offering a long list of images wouldn't develop an idea; it would merely illustrate what is self-evident. Trying to revise this weak topic sentence, the writer inserted the adjective *good* before *imagery*; now the paragraph must at least try to show that the numerous images are good ones. But the focus is still largely on the quantity of imagery, which is not where the focus should be. What is most important is the function of the imagery: What does the writer do with the imagery? Further thought might lead to a revision like this—a topic sentence that not only has more substance in itself but also suggests the approach the paragraph will take:

> **The article's imagery, most of it drawn from nature, helps to create not only the article's mood but its themes as well.**

The same essay also contained the following inefficient topic sentence:

> **In the second paragraph, the writer continues to use images.**

Again, what is needed is something sharper, more specific, such as an assertion that provides a significant idea that can be usefully developed. For example,

The imagery in the second paragraph contrasts vividly with that of the first.

A good topic sentence should be more than just a table of contents; it should be a significant part of the contents of the paragraph. Pay close attention to the formulation of your topic sentences, for they can help you achieve both unity and coherence not only in individual paragraphs but also in an essay as a whole (see #8a–b).

3. Placement of Topic Sentences

In many paragraphs, the development fulfills the promise made in an opening topic sentence. Or, by conscious design, a topic sentence may be placed at the end or elsewhere in a paragraph. Sometimes delaying a topic sentence can increase readers' interest by creating a little mystery to get them to read on. And stating a topic at the end of a paragraph takes advantage of that most emphatic position (see #6).

A paragraph's topic, though single, may consist of more than one part. Similarly, it may not be stated all in one sentence. In this paragraph and the one preceding, for example, note that not until the end of the second sentence is the topic fully clear. It is not uncommon for a paragraph to have a second topic sentence, one that partly restates the topic and partly leads into the body of the paragraph.

And, rarely, a paragraph's topic may not be stated at all because the focal idea of the paragraph is clearly and strongly implied. This kind of paragraph occurs most often in narratives, where paragraphs begin in such a way that their relation to the preceding paragraph is sufficiently clear—perhaps indicated by no more than an opening *Then* or *When*.

See also the notes on beginnings in #9-l.

 ## The Middle

1. Coherence Through Orderly Development

A well-developed body paragraph fulfills the promise of its topic sentence by providing details that are sufficient to support what is stated. While there are often several different ways to structure this supporting material coherently, the organization you choose should make sense: one idea should lead logically to another until you reach your goal.

2. Patterns of Development

Orderly development sometimes occurs automatically as one works through one's ideas in composing paragraphs and essays. But most writers must give some conscious thought to how a particular paragraph (or essay) can best be shaped. The most common *patterns of development* writers use to make their paragraphs orderly and coherent are the following:

- *spatial* (moving through space, such as top to bottom or left to right; used in describing physical space),
- *chronological* (moving through time; used in narration and process analysis),
- *climactic* (moving from the least important to the most important point; often used in academic writing),
- *inverse pyramid* (moving from the most important to the least important point; used in reportage/print journalism),
- *inductive* (moving from data to assertions; often used in writing for sciences and social sciences),
- *deductive* (moving from assertions to supporting data or premises; often used in writing for the humanities),
- *block* (in a comparison of two items, a full discussion of the first item followed by a full discussion of the second item), and
- *alternating* (in a comparison of two items, a back-and-forth discussion of the first and second items).

Further, some of the *methods of development* discussed above (see #1b) themselves impose patterns on the arrangement of ideas in a paragraph. In addition to using narration and process analysis (which focus on chronological order) or description (with its focus on spatial order), one can move from cause to effect or from effect to cause, or from a statement about a whole to a division of the whole into parts (analysis), or from a statement about one thing to a comparison of that thing with another. As with the methods of development, these patterns are not mutually exclusive within a paragraph or an essay.

4c The Ending

As you compose and revise your drafts, the endings of your paragraphs will sometimes come naturally. But they are likely to do so only if, when you begin a paragraph, you know just where it is going. The final sentence of a paragraph, like all the others, should be a part of the whole (and see the **writing tip on positioning transitional material in #4a** on page 8). In other words, the final sentence of a paragraph will most often be a statement growing out of the substance of the paragraph, a sentence that rounds off the paragraph in a satisfying way.

Some Advice for Ending Paragraphs

If a paragraph doesn't seem to be ending naturally, you may have to stop and think consciously about it. Here are a few pointers to help you do that:

1. A good ending may point back to the beginning, but it will not merely repeat it; if it repeats something, it will do so in order to put it in the new light made possible by the development of the paragraph.
2. A good ending sentence doesn't usually begin with a stiff "In conclusion" or "To conclude." In fact, sometimes the best way to end a paragraph is simply to let it stop, once its point is made. A too-explicit conclusion might damage the effectiveness of an otherwise good paragraph that has a natural quality of closure at its end.
3. A good ending might have a slight stylistic shift that marks a paragraph's closing, perhaps no more than an unusually short or long sentence. Or an ending might be marked by an allusion or brief quotation, as long as it is relevant and to the point.
4. Avoid ending a paragraph with a direct quotation. Such an ending will leave a feeling that you have abandoned your paragraph to someone else. If you use a quotation near the end of a paragraph, follow it with a brief comment that explains, justifies, or re-emphasizes it in your own words.

5 Structural Coherence

Careful organization and development go a long way toward achieving coherence. But you will sometimes need to use other techniques as well, providing links that ensure a smooth flow of thought from one sentence to another.

The main devices for structural coherence are parallelism, repetition, pronouns and demonstrative adjectives, and transitional words and phrases. Like the methods and patterns of development, these devices are not mutually exclusive: two or more may work together in the same paragraph, sometimes even in the same words and phrases.

5a Parallelism (See #28c and #40.)

Parallel sentence structure is a simple and effective way to bind successive sentences. Similar structural patterns in clauses and phrases work like a call and its echo. (Clauses and phrases are groups of words that function as grammatical units within sentences but—except for independent clauses—cannot stand alone as sentences; see #12m–r.) But don't try to maintain a series of parallel elements for too long—the echoes will diminish in power as they get farther from the original.

5b Repetition

Like parallelism, repetition of words and phrases effectively links successive sentences. But the caution against overdoing it is also applicable here. Repetition properly controlled for rhetorical effect can be powerful (as in Martin Luther King's famous "I have a dream" speech), but repetition, especially on paper, can also give the impression of limited vocabulary or lack of ingenuity. Structure your repetitions carefully; don't put too many too close together. And generally use the device sparingly.

5c Pronouns and Demonstrative Adjectives

By referring to something mentioned earlier, a pronoun (e.g., he, him, she, her, I, me, they, them, you, it; see #14) or a demonstrative adjective (this, that, these, those; see #19a) constructs a bridge within the paragraph between itself and its antecedent or referent (i.e., the word it is replacing or referring to). For example,

> **I enjoyed reading the book. It was about dinosaurs.**

Here, the pronoun *It* in the second sentence refers back to the word *book* in the first sentence.

WRITING TIP

Using Pronouns and Demonstrative Adjectives to Create Unity and Coherence

It is also possible to use pronouns and demonstrative adjectives to create links between paragraphs, but avoid using them when

  a. the antecedent is ambiguous (e.g., *The book is on the table. It is blue*. Here, *It* could refer to the book or to the table), or
  b. the antecedent is too distant to be clear.

And make it a point to use demonstrative adjectives rather than demonstrative pronouns. While demonstrative adjectives are clear and can add emphasis, demonstrative pronouns are often weak and ambiguous. (Compare *Those manuscripts* are priceless to *Those* are priceless; see #14f, #16c, #19a, and #41.)

5d Transitional Terms

Used strategically, transitional words and phrases can create coherence and a logical flow from one part or idea to another. Here are some of the more common and useful transitional terms:

- terms showing addition of one point to another

and	also	another	in addition
further	besides	moreover	

- terms showing similarity between ideas

again	equally	in other words	in the same way
likewise	similarly		

- terms showing difference between ideas

but	although	conversely	despite
even though	however	yet	though
in contrast	whereas	nevertheless	in spite of
still	otherwise	on the contrary	on the other hand

- terms showing cause and effect or other logical relations

as a result	because	consequently	for
hence	of course	since	then
therefore	thus		

- terms introducing examples or details

for example	in particular	namely	specifically
for instance	to illustrate	that is	

- terms expressing emphasis

chiefly	especially	more important
indeed	mainly	primarily

- terms showing relations in time and space

after	afterward	at the same time	before
earlier	in the meantime	later	meanwhile
simultaneously	then	while	subsequently
behind	beyond	farther away	here
nearby	in the distance	next	there
to the left			

These and other such words and phrases, occurring usually at or near the beginnings of sentences, help hold paragraphs together. But if the paragraph isn't unified in its content, and if its parts haven't been arranged to fit with one another, then even these explicit transitional terms won't give much structural coherence to your writing.

WRITING TIP

Avoiding Overuse of Transitions

Don't overuse transitional terms. If your paragraph already contains structural elements that make it coherent, it won't need any of these. Adding a transitional word or phrase to nearly every sentence will make your writing stiff and mechanical sounding.

6 Emphasis in Paragraphs

Just as in a sentence, so in a paragraph the most emphatic position is its ending, and the second most emphatic position is its beginning (see #29a). That is another reason the opening or topic sentence is such an important part of a paragraph. And an ending, because of its emphatic position, can make or break a paragraph.

But structure and diction are also important. Parallelism and repetition create emphasis. Independent clauses are more emphatic than subordinate clauses and phrases. (Subordinate clauses and phrases cannot stand by themselves as complete sentences.) Precise, concrete, and specific words are more emphatic than vague, abstract, and general ones. A long sentence will stand out among several shorter ones; a short sentence will stand out among longer ones. Keep these points in mind as you compose and revise your paragraphs; let emphasis contribute to the effectiveness of your writing.

7 Length of Paragraphs

There is no optimum length for a paragraph. The length of a paragraph will be determined by its particular function. In narration or dialogue, a single sentence or a single word may constitute a paragraph. In a complex exposition or argument essay, a paragraph may go on for a page or more—though such long paragraphs are rare in modern writing. Most body paragraphs consist of at least three or four sentences, and seldom more than nine or ten. Transitional paragraphs are usually short, sometimes only one sentence. Introductory and concluding paragraphs will be of various lengths, depending on the complexity of the material and on the techniques of beginning and ending that the writer is using.

7a Too Many Long Paragraphs

If you find that you are writing many long paragraphs, you may be overdeveloping, piling more into a paragraph than its topic requires. Or you may not be weeding out irrelevant material. Or you may be dealing in one paragraph with two or more topics that should be dealt with in separate paragraphs. Any of these tendencies can damage the coherence of your writing. Keep in mind that paragraphs are at least as much for readers as they are for writers. Generally, you should give your reader regular breaks to pause and consider your main claims and evidence, which means providing one or two paragraphs per page of your writing.

7b Too Many Short Paragraphs

If you find yourself writing many short paragraphs, you may not be adequately developing your main ideas. The body of a paragraph should be long enough to develop a topic satisfactorily. Merely restating or summarizing the topic is not enough. An excess of short paragraphs can also endanger coherence by splintering your discussion into small parts: when you revise, check to see if two or more related short paragraphs can be integrated to form one substantial paragraph. Generally, a body paragraph in a piece of academic writing should set out a claim and provide well-integrated evidence. It should also comment on and explain the significance of the evidence using several sentences.

7c Variety

Try to ensure that any extended piece of writing you produce contains a variety of paragraph lengths: long, short, medium. The reader may become unengaged if the essay has a constant similarity of paragraph lengths. (The same is true of sentences of similar length; see #28a). You should also try to provide a variety of patterns (#4b.2) and methods (#1b) of development in your paragraphs. For example, parallelism, however admirable a device, would likely lose its effect if it were the basic pattern in several successive paragraphs.

Normally, then, the paragraphs that make up an extended piece of writing will vary in length. Ensure that each of your paragraphs is as long or as short as it needs to be to achieve its intended purpose. See also #8c.

1-7 Review: A Sample Paragraph with an Analysis

The paragraph that follows illustrates principles discussed in the preceding sections of this part. The writer has gone on to analyze her handling of the paragraph. Consider analyzing several paragraphs of your own writing in the same way to assess your strengths and weaknesses in this important aspect of writing.

> [1] Can child characters be heroic? [2] Some adult readers might argue that heroism is something beyond the reach of a child. [3] Such readers might add that children lack the experience, the knowledge, and the power required to separate themselves from the adult-dominated communities they know and to embark on the quest into the unsafe, unpredictable world identified with the hero's quest. [4] But consider characters as different as Lewis Carroll's Alice and, more recently, Philip Pullman's Will Parry. [5] Alice quite happily chooses to enter the bizarre world of Lewis Carroll's *Through the Looking Glass*, and she holds her own in encounters with lions, twin boys, bad-tempered eggs, and transmogrifying monarchs. [6] Will Parry, for his part, leaves Oxford to seek his missing father and, with Lyra Silvertongue as his companion, leads other children as well as adults through adventure, suffering, and turmoil to establish a Republic of Heaven on Earth.

Analysis of the Paragraph

Function

- The paragraph is from the body of the essay as far as a reader can determine without the context of the whole essay.
- It deals with substantial ideas about child heroism in literature.

Methods of Development

- The principal method is argument.
- There is also an element of comparison in sentence 4.
- The writer gives examples to support the argument. See sentences 5 and 6.

Unity

- The paragraph focuses in each of its sentences on how child protagonists can be heroic.

Coherence and Emphasis

- The topic sentence of this paragraph is sentence 1.
- Sentence 1 starts with a question to engage the reader's attention.
- Sentence 2 picks up the key words *child* and *heroism*.
- Sentence 3 picks up the words *readers* and *children*.
- Sentence 4 starts with a strong coordinating conjunction, *but*, that indicates a reversal in thought.
- Sentences 5 and 6 follow parallel structure in content and form.

Length and Development

- With six sentences, the paragraph can be said to be of average length.
- Its development is sufficient for its purpose.

8-11 The Whole Essay

8 Unity, Coherence, and Emphasis

The principles of composition apply with equal validity to the essay as a whole and to each of its parts: what holds true for the sentence and the paragraph also holds true for the essay as a whole.

8a Unity

Like a sentence or a paragraph, an essay should be unified. That is, everything in it should be about one topic. If your paragraphs are themselves unified and if you make sure that the opening sentences of each paragraph refer explicitly (or implicitly but unmistakably) to your overall subject as indicated by your title (see #4a.1), your essay will be unified.

8b Coherence

Coherence is important not only between words in a sentence and between sentences in a paragraph, but also between paragraphs in an essay. If the beginning of each paragraph provides transition from the preceding paragraph, the essay will almost surely be coherent. The transitional words and phrases listed above (#5d) and others like them are often useful for establishing the necessary connections between paragraphs, but don't overdo it by using them to begin every paragraph. Often you can create the link by repeating a significant word or two from the preceding paragraph, usually from somewhere near its end, and sometimes you can make or strengthen the link with a demonstrative adjective, or even a pronoun (but see the **writing tip** in #5c). (See also #4a, on topic sentences.)

8c Emphasis

Just as in a sentence or a paragraph (see #29a and #6), the most emphatic position in an essay is its ending, and the second most emphatic is its beginning. That is why it is important to be clear and to the point at the beginning of an essay, usually stating the thesis explicitly (see #9-l.3), and why the ending of an essay should be forceful. Don't, for example, conclude by repeating your introduction or, in a short essay, by summarizing your points. And since the last thing readers see is usually what sticks most vividly in their minds, essays often use climactic order, beginning with simple or less elaborate points and ending with more important or complex ones (see #4b.2).

Further, the length of a paragraph automatically suggests something about the importance of its contents. Although a short, sharp paragraph can be emphatic in its own way, generally a long paragraph will deal with a relatively important part of the subject. As you look over your work, check to make sure you haven't skimped on an important point, and also that you haven't gone on for too long about a relatively minor point (see #7).

9 The Process of Planning, Writing, and Revising

No effective essay can be a mere random assemblage of sentences and paragraphs. It needs a shape, a design, even if only a simple one. How does one get from the blank page to the desired finished product? By taking certain steps, because a piece of writing, like any other product, is the result of a process. The usual steps that a writer takes, whether consciously or not, fall into three major stages:

- **STAGE I: PLANNING**
  - finding a subject and formulating questions about it
  - limiting the subject
  - determining audience and purpose
  - gathering reliable data
  - classifying and organizing the data
  - outlining

- **STAGE II: WRITING**
  - writing the first draft
  - integrating evidence
  - commenting on the significance of the evidence

- **STAGE III: REVISING**
  - revising
  - preparing the final draft
  - editing and proofreading

Sometimes one or more steps may be taken care of for you; for example, if you are assigned a specific topic, finding and limiting a subject, and perhaps even determining audience and purpose, will already be taken care of. And often several parts of the process will be going on at the same time; for example, there is often a good deal of interaction among the activities in the planning stage. Sometimes the order will be different; for example, you may not be clear about your purpose until you have finished gathering and then classifying and organizing data. And sometimes in the revising stage, you may want to go back and rethink your purpose, or dig up more material, or even further limit or expand your topic.

Finding a Subject and Pre-writing

1. For Writing Situations That Are Discipline-Specific

When you are enrolled in a course of study for a particular discipline, writing topics will not necessarily be assigned to you. Instead, an essential part of the process will involve you designing topics and projects relevant to your studies. Develop topics around researchable questions of current interest in the field, and narrow them to fit the time allotted to the assignment and the length expected by your reader.

You might consider some of the following when developing the proposal or statement of purpose that is often called for in such circumstances:

- a question of definition, a key term with a history of changing denotations over time (for a cultural geography course, "What is gendered space?")
- a central debate evidenced in the scholarly writing produced in the discipline (for a Canadian studies course, "How do scholars of the 1970's and those of today differ on the evaluation of Pauline Johnson's poetry?")
- a review of the scholarly literature surrounding a particular question in the field (for a children's literature course, "How can theories of ecocriticism be applied to the reading of Canadian children's literature set on the Prairies?")
- a question or issue that crosses disciplinary boundaries (e.g., a question preoccupying linguists and sociologists, or economists and geographers) (for a human geography course, "How will global climate change affect birth rates in Central and South America?")
- an idea raised incidentally in lectures or seminars that deserves further investigation (for a film studies seminar course, "Do images of children in recent Canadian films provide clues to the way Canadian culture has constructed ideas of childhood?")

Such possibilities should make it possible for you to produce a paper distinctive in its approach—something more and better than a cutting and pasting of the views of two or three major sources.

In working out your research and preparing a plan for the paper, devise a reasonable timeline for research, planning, writing, revising, and editing. Consider the needs and expectations of your reading audience and the availability of a variety of electronic and non-electronic sources that are both scholarly and current. Keep in mind that the use of Canadian sources may be important to your objectives and to your readers.

2. For Writing Situations That Are Not Discipline-Specific

If you are enrolled in a writing course that involves writing papers in a variety of forms and for a range of audiences, you may be working outside a particular discipline or area of study. In such circumstances, a specific subject area or discipline will not likely be attached to your writing assignments, and you will be seeking one for yourself. Some writers think this is among the most challenging parts of composing an essay, but it needn't be, for subjects are all around us and within us. A few minutes of free-associating in an empty word-processing file or with a pencil and a sheet of paper, jotting down and playing around with questions and any ideas that pop into your head, will usually lead you at least to a subject area if not to a specific subject. Scanning the pages of a magazine, a newspaper, or a scholarly website or journal is another way to stimulate a train of thought; editorial and letters pages are usually full of interesting subjects to write about, perhaps to argue about. Or think about the questions or problems you may have about the course for which you are writing the essay. Often the very thing that puzzles you provides a good topic. The possibilities are almost endless.

Try to find a subject that interests you, one that you will enjoy working with and living with for an extended period of time. Formulate a question or series of questions worth investigating and researching. Don't, in desperation, pick a subject that bores you, for you may handle it poorly and end up boring your readers as well. If you are assigned a topic that doesn't particularly interest you, try to make it a learning experience: immerse yourself in it; you may be surprised at how interesting it can become.

Whether your assignment is discipline-specific or more general, consider producing in the initial stages a proposal or statement of purpose that you can discuss with your instructor or prospective readers. Following is a preliminary statement of purpose for a 1,000-word paper on nineteenth-century immigrant experiences in Canada.

Kevin Cheung   History 222/010
10 September 2017

Paper is due: 8 November 2017 (approximately two months)

Target length: 1,000 words

Audience: fellow students and my instructor, all with an interest in the subject

Subject: nineteenth-century immigrant experiences contrasting

Topic: the responses of Catharine Parr Traill and Susanna Moodie to their first years in Canada

Questions:
Why did these two individuals—sisters close in age and living close to one another in their first days in Upper Canada—react so differently to their new homeland?
How is it that Traill celebrates the land, the people, even the winter weather?
How is it that Moodie is so critical of the land, the people (especially her neighbours), and the conditions of life?

Major sources so far:
Charlotte Gray's *Sisters in the Wilderness*, Anne Cimon's *Susanna Moodie*, Pioneer Author Traill's *The Backwoods of Canada*, Moodie's *Roughing It in the Bush*

9b Limiting the Subject

Once you have a subject, limit it: narrow it to a topic you can develop adequately within the length of the essay you are writing. More often than not, writers start with subjects too big to handle. Seldom do they come up, right away, with a topic like what people's shoes reveal about their characters, or a contradiction in a philosopher's argument, or the inefficiency of the cafeteria; they're more likely to start with some vague notion about footwear, or about how interesting the article was, or about campus architecture. To save both time and energy, to avoid frustration, and to guarantee a better essay, be disciplined at this stage. If anything, overdo the narrowing, for at a later stage it's easier to broaden than it is to cut.

For example, let's say you wanted to write about "travelling"; that's obviously far too broad. "National travel" or "international travel" is narrower, but still too broad. "Travelling in Asia?" Better, but still too large, for where would you begin? How thorough could you be in a mere 500 or even 1,000 words? When you find yourself narrowing your subject to something like "How to survive on $20.00 a day in Tokyo" or "What to do if you have only twenty-four hours in Hong Kong" or "Why I don't travel with my mother" or "The day my passport got stolen," then you can confidently look forward to developing your topic with sufficient thoroughness and specificity. (See also #66.)

Considering Audience and Purpose

1. Audience

When you write a personal letter or email, you naturally direct it to a specific reader. If you write a "Letter to the Editor" of a newspaper, you have only a vague notion of your potential readership, namely anyone who reads that newspaper, but you will know where the majority of them live, and knowing only that much could give you something to aim at in your letter. The sharper the focus you can get on your audience, the better you can control your writing to make it effective for that audience. Try to define or characterize your audience for a given piece of writing as precisely as possible.

Some of the writing you do for school may have only one reader: the instructor. But some assignments may ask you to address some specific audience; sometimes an instructor will ask you to write "for an audience of your peers." In the absence of any other guideline, writing for your peers is not a bad idea. Your tone and language and the definitions and explanations you provide will often be appropriate if you keep an interested and serious but not fully informed audience in mind.

2. Purpose

All writing has the broad purpose of communicating ideas. In a course, you write for the special purpose of demonstrating your ability to communicate your knowledge to your audience. But you will write more effectively if you think of each essay as having one or more of the following purposes:

1. to inform,
2. to convince or persuade, and/or
3. to enter into discussion or debate.

Few essays, however, have only one of these purposes. For example, a set of instructions will have the primary purpose of informing readers how to do something, but it may also be trying to convince them that this is the best way to do it. And to interest readers more, the instructions may also be written in a stimulating style. An analysis of a piece of legislation may seem to be pure exposition, explaining how the legislation works and the changes it introduces, but in a sense it will also be trying to persuade readers that this interpretation is an accurate one. An argument will then necessarily include exposition. An entertaining or even whimsical piece may well have a satiric tone or some kind of implicit "lesson" calculated to spark debate. Usually one of the three purposes will dominate, but one or both of the others will often be present as well. (And see #10 on writing arguments.)

The clearer your idea of what you want to do in an essay, and why, and for whom, the better you will be able to make effective rhetorical choices. You may even want to begin by writing, as a memo to yourself, a detailed description or "profile" of your audience and as clear a statement of your purpose as you can formulate. Tape this memo to the wall over your desk. If your ideas become clearer as the work proceeds, you can refine these statements. In any event, as you go through the process of writing, keep sight of your audience and your purpose.

9d Gathering Evidence

An essay can't survive on just vague generalizations and unsupported statements and opinions; it must contain specifics: facts, details, data, examples. Whatever your subject, you must gather material by reading and researching, conducting formal interviews, talking to others, or thinking about your personal experience. And don't stop when you think you have just enough; collect as much information as you can within the time you have allotted for evidence gathering, even two or three times what you can use; you can select the best and bank the rest for future use.

1. Brainstorming

If you are expected to generate material from your own knowledge and experience (instead of through formal research), you may, at first, have difficulty coming up with ideas. Don't be discouraged. Sit down for a few minutes at the computer or with a pencil and a sheet of paper, write your topic in the centre or at the top, and begin writing ideas. Put down everything that comes into your head about your topic. Let your mind run fast and free. Don't bother with sentences; don't worry about spelling; don't even pause to wonder whether the words and phrases are going to be of any use. Just keep writing. It shouldn't be long before you've filled the page with possible ideas, questions, facts, details, names, examples. It may help if you also brainstorm your larger subject area, not just the narrowed topic, since some of the broader ideas could prove useful.

2. Using Questions

Another way to generate material is to ask yourself questions about your subject or topic and write down the answers. Start with the reporter's standard questions—*Who? What? Where? When? Why? How?*—and go on from there with more of your own: *What is it? Who is associated with it? In what way? Where and when is it, or was it, or will it be? How does it work? Why is it? What causes it? What does it cause? What are its parts? What is it a part of? Is it part of a process? What does it look like? What is it like or unlike? What is its opposite? What if it didn't exist?* Such questions and the answers you develop will make you think of more questions, and so on; soon you'll have more than enough material that is potentially useful. You may even find yourself writing consecutive sentences, since some questions prompt certain kinds of responses. For example, asking *What is it?* may lead you to begin defining your subject; *What is it like or unlike?* may lead you to begin comparing and contrasting it, classifying it, thinking of analogies and metaphors; *What causes it?* and *What does it cause?* may lead you to begin exploring cause-and-effect relations; *What are its parts?* or *What is it a part of?* could lead you to analyze your subject; *How does it work?* or *Is it part of a process?* may prompt you to analyze and explain a process.

Classifying and Organizing the Evidence

1. Classifying

As you brainstorm a subject and jot down notes and answers, you'll begin to see connections between one idea and another and start putting them in groups or drawing circles around them and lines and arrows between them. It is important to do this kind of classification when you have finished gathering material. You should end up with several groups of related items, which means that you will have classified your material according to some principle that arose naturally from it. During this part of the process you will probably also have discarded the weaker or less relevant details, keeping only those that best suit the topic as it is now beginning to take shape; that is, you will have selected the best.

For a tightly limited topic and a short essay, you may have only one group of details, but for an essay of even moderate length, say 750 words or more, you will probably have several groups.

The map below was created by a student to classify and organize her ideas for an 800-word paper on the effects of war on the child characters in Joy Kogawa's novel *Obasan*.

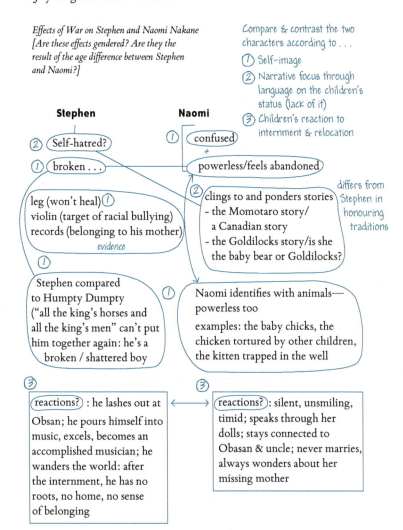

Effects of War on Stephen and Naomi Nakane
[Are these effects gendered? Are they the
result of the age difference between Stephen
and Naomi?]

Compare & contrast the two characters according to . . .
① Self-image
② Narrative focus through language on the children's status (lack of it)
③ Children's reaction to internment & relocation

Stephen   **Naomi**

② Self-hatred?   ① confused
① broken . . .   +
                                powerless/feels abandoned

differs from Stephen in honouring traditions

leg (won't heal) ①
violin (target of racial bullying)
records (belonging to his mother)
evidence
①

② clings to and ponders stories
- the Momotaro story/ a Canadian story
- the Goldilocks story/is she the baby bear or Goldilocks?

Stephen compared to Humpty Dumpty ("all the king's horses and all the king's men" can't put him together again: he's a broken / shattered boy

① Naomi identifies with animals—powerless too

examples: the baby chicks, the chicken tortured by other children, the kitten trapped in the well

③ (reactions?) : he lashes out at Obsan; he pours himself into music, excels, becomes an accomplished musician; he wanders the world: after the internment, he has no roots, no home, no sense of belonging

③ (reactions?): silent, unsmiling, timid; speaks through her dolls; stays connected to Obasan & uncle; never marries, always wonders about her missing mother

2. Organizing

Once you have classified your material into groups, put the groups into some kind of order. Don't necessarily accept the first arrangement that comes to mind; consider as many different arrangements as the material will allow, and then select the best one for your purpose and audience. (For the most common arrangements, see #4b.2.) The order should be logical rather than accidental or arbitrary. Ideally, the groups and their details should fall into order naturally, resulting in an arrangement that is the most effective way of presenting the material.

9f The Thesis Statement and the Outline

The most crucial parts of the planning or "pre-writing" stage are the formulation of a **thesis statement** and the construction of an **outline**.

During the early stages, you gradually increase your control over your proposed essay: you find and narrow a subject, you think about audience and purpose, you gather evidence and generate ideas, and you classify and arrange your material. At some point while you are doing all this you will probably have formulated at least a tentative thesis, a statement that identifies your topic and points the way to what you want to say about it.

This *thesis statement* or *thesis sentence* performs the same function for an essay that a *topic sentence* does for a paragraph. It leads off the outline; the ordered groups become *main headings*, and the details that make up each group, if they aren't simply absorbed by the main heading, become subdivisions of it in various levels of *subheadings*. And though tentative sketches of a possible beginning and ending aren't essential to an outline, it's usually worth trying to think of something of the sort at this stage; you can easily make a change later if you think of something better. Here is an example, a student's outline for a short essay:

Thesis Statement: Students who have a social life are happier, smarter, and better prepared for the workforce than students who concentrate only on their studies.

Beginning: All work and no play makes a dull student. Although many people, including my parents, believe that students should spend all their time studying, I believe students are better off socializing in moderation at university. Why?

I. They are happier.
   A. develop friendships
   B. develop maturity and a more balanced perspective toward life

II. They are smarter.
   A. receive academic support in study groups
   B. receive academic support from friends who are strong in certain disciplines

III. They are better prepared for the workforce.
   A. develop an effective network of contacts
   B. develop interpersonal skills
   C. develop communication skills

Ending: So the next time my parents tell me to put away my phone because I should be studying, I will be ready with my answer. I will tell them I am leading a balanced life, improving academically, and getting ready for my future.

Note the layout of an outline: numerals and letters are followed by periods and a space or two; subheadings are indented at least two spaces past the beginning of the first word of a main heading. Few outlines will need to go beyond one or two levels of subheading (see #9j.5), but if further subdivision is necessary, here is a way to clearly indicate successive levels:

I.
II.
    A.
    B.
       1.
       2.
          a.
          b.
             (1.)
             (2.)
                (a.)
                (b.)

9g The Importance of Outlining

An outline drawn up before you write a major essay will save you both time and effort at later stages. Writing the draft will be easier and smoother because it follows a plan: you know where you're going. You can avoid such pitfalls as unnecessary repetition, digression, and illogical or otherwise incoherent organization. In other words, a good outline can be like a map that keeps the writer from taking wrong turns, wandering in circles, or getting lost altogether.

Keep in mind, too, that an outline should not be binding. If as you write and revise you think of a better way to organize a part of your essay, or if some part of the outline proves clumsy when you try to set it down in paragraphs, or if you suddenly think of some new material that should be included, by all means go with your instincts and revise accordingly. And as you proceed, you may want to refine your thesis to reflect changes in your ideas.

9h Kinds of Outlines

Outlining of some kind is necessary for a good essay. The more complicated the essay, the more important the outline. A short, relatively simple essay can sometimes be outlined in your head or with a few informal jottings, but even a shorter essay can be easier to write if you've made a blueprint first.

The method of outlining you use may be your own choice or it may be set by your instructor or by the nature of a project. Some people like the *topic outline* with its brief headings and subheadings, as in the example above (#9f). Sometimes a *paragraph outline* will work well, one that simply lists the proposed topic or opening sentences of the successive paragraphs that will eventually form the essay. Probably the most useful outline is the *sentence outline*, for it helps to establish the foundation of your essay.

9i Sentence Outlines

A sentence outline resembles a topic outline except that brief headings and subheadings are replaced by complete sentences. The advantage of having to phrase each item as a complete sentence is that you are unlikely to fool yourself into thinking you have something to say when in fact you don't. For example, imagine you are planning an essay on various cuisines and, in a topic outline, you put down the heading "the new trends." But if you haven't been eating out recently, you might find when you sit down to write your draft that you have little or nothing to say. In a sentence outline, you are compelled to make a statement about the topic, in this case perhaps something like "Although people have their favourite meals at home, when it comes to eating out, they are willing to try different foods." With even such a vague sentence before you, you can more easily begin supplying details to develop your idea; the act of formulating the sentence guarantees that you have at least some ideas about whatever you put down.

Another benefit of a sentence outline is that, when properly handled, it is self-constructing. In a topic or other relatively informal outline, the thesis statement should set up or contain the main headings, as it does in the example in #9f. In a sentence outline, the headings and subheadings work the same way, but their connection to the thesis statement is more explicit. Our earlier example—"Although people have their favourite meals at home, when it comes to eating out, they are willing to try different foods"—automatically leads into two subheadings: "A. People have their favourite meals" and "B. When it comes to eating out, they are willing to try different foods." Such partial repetition is natural to a good sentence outline; it may seem stiff and clumsy, but it is a strength, since it fosters coherence and unity within each part of an essay and in an essay as a whole.

As an illustration, here is a student's sentence outline on the topic of the environment:

Thesis Statement: Certain corporations get away with crimes against the environment because profits are all important, our society cannot easily measure the crimes committed, and when the company is prosecuted, the penalties are weak.

Beginning: Although corporate crimes against the environment are profound in their impact, corporations are not held accountable or are mildly prosecuted. Three important reasons seem to stand out.

I. There is a conflict between making a profit and protecting the environment.
    A. The strength of economics outweighs ideological or political views.
    B. There is the perception that corporate crime against the environment is not real crime, as the people involved are often professional and respectable.

II. It is difficult to determine or measure the extent of crimes against the environment.
    A. Government and regulatory bodies resist releasing facts.
    B. Records and comments from officials that are released are not always consistent.
    C. As corporate crime against the environment is often outside the scope and the know-how of traditional investigative journalism, the media does not always uncover the extent of the activity.

III. Weak penalties and lax enforcement do not deter corporations.
    A. The wording of environmental laws is ambiguous.
    B. Sanctions and penalties are weak.
    C. Prosecution involves expense and political repercussions private citizens' groups may wish to avoid.

Ending: (Sum up the main points and point to implications for the future or suggest possible solutions?)

 ## **Constructing Sentence Outlines**

The following are some guidelines for putting together a good sentence outline:

1. Make every item from the thesis statement down to the last subheading a single complete major sentence.
2. Use only simple or complex sentences; do not use compound sentences. (A simple sentence consists of a single independent clause; a complex sentence consists of one independent clause and one or more dependent [or subordinate] clauses; a compound sentence combines two independent clauses. See #12z.) Since the independent clauses

of a compound sentence could themselves be written as separate sentences, having a compound sentence in your outline may mean that two or more headings are masquerading as one; consider making each clause a separate heading.

3. In any kind of outline you need to supply at least two subheadings if you supply any at all. A subheading, by definition, implies division. For this reason, a heading cannot be subdivided into only one part as a subheading. If under "I" you have an "A," then you must also have at least a "B"; if you have a "1," you must also have at least a "2," and so on. If you find yourself unable to go beyond one subheading, it probably isn't a subdivision at all but an integral part of the main heading that should be incorporated into it.

4. The headings or subheadings at each level should be reasonably parallel with each other; that is, I, II, III, etc. should have about the same level of importance, as should subheadings A, B, C, etc. under a given main heading, and 1, 2, 3, etc. under each of these. One way to help achieve this balance is to make the sentences at any given level, as much as possible, grammatically parallel.

5. Few outlines need to go beyond one level of subheading for the average essay. If an essay is unusually long or complicated, you may find it helpful or necessary to break things down to a second or even third level of subheading. But remember that headings and subheadings should mostly state ideas, propositions, generalizations; the supporting facts can be supplied at the writing stage and don't need to go into the outline. If you find yourself including several levels of subheading, you may already be itemizing your facts and details.

WRITING TIP

Managing the Number of Subheadings in an Outline

As with the major sections of an essay, having more than six or seven subheadings under any one heading risks being unwieldy.

9k **Writing the First Draft**

Once you have a good outline to follow, the work of drafting becomes smoother and more purposeful. With the shape of the whole essay laid out, you can concentrate on the main tasks of drafting: finding the right words, generating effective sentences, and constructing good transitions and strong paragraphs.

> ### WRITING TIP
>
> *Going from an Outline to a Draft*
>
> (1) Sometimes a main heading and its subheading from the outline will become a single paragraph in the essay; sometimes each subheading will become a paragraph; and so on. The nature and density of your material will determine its treatment.
>
> (2) It may be possible to transfer the thesis statement from your outline to the essay unchanged, but more likely you will want to change it (perhaps several times) to fit the actual essay. The thesis is the statement of your purpose or of the position you intend to defend in the essay, so it should be as polished as possible. The kind of basic or mechanical statement that is suitable in an outline may be inappropriate in the essay itself.

Notes on Beginnings

1. Postponing the Beginning

Starting the actual writing can be a challenge: most writers have had the experience of staring at a computer screen while trying to think of a good way to begin. If you have no beginning in mind at this point, don't waste time trying to think of one. Plunge right into the body of the essay and write it as rapidly as you can. Once you have finished writing the first draft, you'll have a better idea of what it is that needs to be introduced; you can then go back and do the beginning with relative ease. In fact, writers who write a beginning first often discard the original version and write a new one, either because the essay that finally took shape demands a different kind of beginning or because in the midst of composing they thought of a better one.

2. Beginning Directly

Just as it isn't always a good idea to begin a final paragraph with "In conclusion," so it's generally not good practice to open routinely with something mechanical like "In this essay I will discuss" or "This essay is concerned with." On occasion, such as when your essay is unusually long or complicated or when you are presenting it as part of a seminar, conference, or panel, it may be helpful to explain in advance what your essay is about, to provide readers with what amounts to a brief outline. But most essays don't require this kind of beginning and won't engage an audience with such a stiff introduction. As a rule, then, don't talk about yourself and your essay; talk about your topic. Rather than begin by informing readers of what you are going to say (and then at the end reminding them of what you have said), start with something substantial and, if possible, attention-getting. Try to end with something similarly sharp and definitive.

3. Determining Subject and Thesis

However you begin, it is necessary to identify your subject and to state your thesis somewhere near the beginning—usually not later than the first or second paragraph. For example, even if your title is something like "Imagery in Shakespeare's Sonnet 65," you should still, preferably in your first sentence, mention both the author and the title of the poem. The title of your essay is not a part of its content; the essay must be able to stand on its own.

Special circumstances may, on occasion, call for you to delay the full statement of your thesis to near the end, for example as part of a strategy of building to a climax. Even then, you will probably provide at least some indication of your thesis near the beginning, perhaps in general terms. Or sometimes a thesis can be broken into several parts to be stated at intervals in the course of an essay. On rare occasions, you may want to be mysterious, but readers generally don't like being kept in the dark. (See also #10d.2.)

4. Being Direct, Smooth, Economical: Some Examples

Begin as directly, smoothly, and economically as you can. Here, for example, are three ways an essay with the title "Imagery in Shakespeare's Sonnet 65" might begin; note how differences in order, punctuation, and wording make each succeeding one better and shorter than the one before:

(1) **In Sonnet 65 by William Shakespeare, there is a great deal of imagery.**

(2) **William Shakespeare in his Sonnet 65 uses imagery to . . .**

(3) **The imagery in Shakespeare's Sonnet 65 . . .**

Here is the beginning of a student's essay on Shakespeare's Sonnet 65. The writer can't seem to get the engine warmed up:

> **William Shakespeare, famous English poet and writer of plays, has always been known for the way he uses imagery to convey the point he is making in a particular piece of work. Shakespeare's Sonnet 65 is no exception to this, and this is one of the better examples of his work that I have studied, for illustrating his use of imagery.**
>
> **The best example in the sonnet comes in lines five and six, where Shakespeare compares a "summer's honey breath" and a "wrackful siege of battering days."**

Compare this with another student's beginning on the same topic:

> **In Sonnet 65, Shakespeare appeals to a person's knowledge of visible properties in nature in an attempt to explain invisible properties of love and time.**

The second writer has taken control of the material immediately. Even though no particular image has yet been mentioned, the second writer, in one crisp sentence, is far beyond where the first writer, well into a second paragraph, is.

Here is another example of an ineffective beginning. That the writer was in difficulty is shown by the redundancy in the first sentence, the illogicality in the second sentence, and the vague reference and wordy emptiness of the third:

> **Nowadays, in these modern times, different cultures celebrate different holidays in many different ways. Thanksgiving is filled with a seemingly endless variety of memories and emotions. I would imagine this is experienced by almost every family and mine is most certainly not an exception.**

The writer's own revision proves that the difficulties were merely the result of floundering, trying too hard to make a beginning; had the beginning been written after the body of the essay was complete, it might have taken this form:

> **Holidays help define a family. In my family, where expectations are great, Thanksgiving brings out the best and worst of our individual characteristics.**

The Final Steps

The product of rapid composition is a first draft. Although some first drafts may come close to being acceptable finished products, don't gamble that your draft can pass for a polished essay. There are three tasks to undertake before you should consider an essay finished: *revising, preparing the final draft,* and *proofreading.*

Revising

Revision (re-vision, literally "scrutinizing again") is an extremely important stage of writing, far too often neglected by less experienced writers. Experienced writers revise a piece of writing at least two or three times. Many writers revise five or even ten or more times before they consider a piece to be finished.

Revise carefully and slowly, looking for any way to improve what you've written. Aim not only to correct errors made in haste but also to remove clutter and improve diction, sentence structure, punctuation, coherence, paragraphing, organization, and so on. Some writers find that going through a draft for one thing at a time is effective—for example, going through it looking only at paragraphing, then going through it again looking only at the structure and variety of sentences, then at punctuation, then at diction, and so on. And you will want to proofread carefully for those errors you know you tend to make.

Adopt the role of an observant and alert reader looking for strengths and pinpointing weaknesses and errors. To do this effectively, try to allow yourself a cooling-off period; wait as long as possible between the drafting and the revising—at least two or three days—so that you can look at your own work with more objectivity, as a dispassionate third-party reader would. If you're having trouble, you may find the Omnibus Checklist (see the appendix) helpful during your revisions.

Preparing the Final Draft

When you are through revising a piece of writing, carefully prepare the final draft, the one that will be presented to your reader or readers. Once the work is out of your hands, it's too late to change anything; make sure it's in good shape when it leaves your hands. It should be neat, and it should be in the appropriate format for the kind of writing it is. For most of your academic writing, heed the requirements of your particular audience, and follow carefully the manuscript conventions listed and discussed in #55.

 ## Proofreading

Proofreading will have been taking place during revision, of course, and also during drafting, but go over what you consider to be the final copy of your essay when you believe it is ready. This final proofreading will prove worthwhile; despite earlier careful scrutiny, you will probably discover not only typographical errors but also previously unnoticed slips in spelling, punctuation, and grammar.

Do your proofreading with exaggerated care. Read each sentence, as a sentence, slowly (and aloud whenever possible); but also read each word as a word; check each punctuation mark, and consider the possibility of adding some or removing some or changing some. Particularly when you proofread for spelling errors, do so as a separate process. You might consider doing this by starting at the end of your work and reading backward, one word at a time, so that you won't get caught up in the flow of a sentence and overlook an error.

Do not put full trust in any of the spelling, grammar, and style checks that are part of, or designed to be used with, word-processing programs. They can't possibly cover all the matters that require attention. And remember that spell-checkers can't spot a misspelled word that happens to be the same as some other correctly spelled word—for example, *form* instead of *from*, or *through* instead of *though*; nor can they tell you that you've mistaken, say, *your* for *you're*, or *principal* for *principle*.

10 Argument: Writing to Convince or Persuade

Most of the principles of composition are even more important in argument than in other kinds of writing, though as we have suggested earlier (#9c.2), other kinds of writing, especially exposition, often include an element of argumentation. But when your principal purpose is to convince or persuade, there are several additional points and principles to keep in mind. Here are some brief suggestions and some practical advice to help you write effective arguments.

Subject

When you are focusing on your subject for an argumentative essay, keep in mind that there is no point in arguing about easily verifiable facts or generally accepted assumptions (2 + 2 = 4; the sky looks blue; good nutrition promotes good health; oil is a non-renewable energy source). One cannot argue about facts, only about what the facts mean. Since an argument depends on logical reasoning, when you argue about opinions based on facts you will necessarily use factual data to support your contentions. A collection of unsupported opinions is not an argument but merely a series of assertions.

Similarly, one cannot logically argue about matters of taste. You can't argue that blue is a prettier colour than green; you can only assert that *you* find it prettier, for whatever reason. The subject of an argument should be something that is capable of verification.

Audience

When your *purpose* is to convince or persuade, your knowledge of your *audience* and your constant awareness of that audience are crucial. Consider, for example, how differently you would have to handle your material and your tone depending on whether you were writing to an audience of (a) people basically sympathetic to your position, or (b) people likely to be hostile to your position. Since the effectiveness of an argument depends partly on your gaining or holding the confidence of your readers, or at least getting them to listen to you willingly and with a reasonably open mind, it is important that you avoid presenting anything that might keep them from listening.

The more you know about your potential readers and their attitude toward your topic, the better you will know what choices to make so that you can clearly communicate your position and its value as an argument worth thinking about.

10c Evidence

When you are gathering material for an argument, look especially for concrete, specific, precise, factual data that you can use to support your generalizations (see #66b). The effectiveness of your argument will, in part, depend on the quality and the quantity of the evidence you provide both to support your position and to counter your opposition. For example, try to find some statistics you can cite, or some expert you can quote (the appeal to authority), or some common experience or assumption about life that you can remind your readers of (the appeal to common sense). You may be able to make good use of your own experience or that of someone you know well. But be sure that the evidence you gather and use is both reliable and relevant.

10d Organization

Consider audience and purpose when laying out your material. You will find that an outline will often help you. Here are some specific points to keep in mind:

1. Emphasis

Usually, you will want to save your strongest point or points for the end, the most emphatic position of your argument. But since the beginning of your essay is also emphatic, don't open with a weak or minor point. It is usually best to begin with strength and then deal with minor points and proceed to the end in the order of climax. (See also #6, #8c, and #29.)

2. Thesis

In an argument, your thesis statement is in effect a proposition that you intend to support; you want to prove it, at least to the satisfaction of your readers. For that reason, it usually appears at the beginning, just as a formal debate begins with a reading of the proposition to be debated. Occasionally, however, you can delay your statement of the thesis until near the end, letting a logical progression of reasoning lead up to it. But don't try for this dramatic effect unless it will work better than stating your proposition up front; for example, consider whether your readers might be put off, rather than drawn in, by being kept in the dark about just what your proposition is. (See also #9-l.3.)

3. Methods of Development

Arguments can make use of any of the methods of development: narration (an illustrative anecdote), description (a detailed physical description of something it is important for readers to visualize clearly and perhaps feel emotion toward), comparison and contrast, analysis, and so on (see #1b). But be careful with analogy: using an analogy as the central pillar of an argumentative structure is risky, for opponents can too easily challenge it and pull it apart (see #10h.9); use analogy as an extra illustration or as one of several minor props. Definitions help establish a common ground between you and the reader. And give strong consideration to cause-and-effect analysis (*What caused it? What does it cause? What will it cause?*), often a mainstay of argument: you argue for or against something because of what has happened or is happening or will happen as a result of it.

4. Patterns of Development

Similarly, an argument can use any one or more of the common patterns of development (see #4b.2). An argument is likely, for example, to follow a logical progression, to move from general to specific or from specific to general, and to rise to a climax. But there is one further pattern that often occurs in argument: like a formal debate, many arguments move back and forth between *pro* and *con*, between statements supporting your proposition and statements refuting your opponent's position (see #10f).

How to Argue: Reasoning Logically

Being Reasonable

Appeal to common sense; appeal to authority; above all, appeal to reason. Demonstrate your respect for your reader's intelligence by appealing to it; a reader is then more likely to respect you and your arguments. If you appeal to prejudices and baser instincts you may get through to a few, but thoughtful readers won't respond favourably to such tactics. Appeals to people's emotions (sympathy for the poor or sick, love of children, feelings of patriotism, fear of injury) can be effective additions to an appeal to reason, but they are not a valid substitute for it. Similarly, if you're conducting a reasoned argument you will usually want to adopt a moderate tone. Stridency and sarcasm will win you points only with readers who are already thoroughly in agreement with your position.

10f Including the Opposition

Be fair: bring in and address any major opposing points of view. Your readers are likely to be aware of these and will expect you to address them. If you try to sway your readers by mentioning only what favours your side, you will lose their confidence because they will conclude correctly that you are unfairly suppressing unfavourable evidence. By raising opposing points and doing your best to refute them convincingly, you will not only strengthen the logic of your argument but also present yourself as a reasonable person, willing to concede that there is another side to the issue. Moreover, by taking on the discussion of both sides in a debate, you can often impart a useful back-and-forth movement to your argument, and you can see to it that after refuting the final opposition point, you end on your own strongest points.

10g Using Induction and Deduction

The two principal methods of reasoning, *induction* and *deduction*, occur both separately and in combination in argument. You should know how each works, and it sometimes helps to be aware of which one you are using at any given point so that you can use it effectively.

1. Induction

Inductive reasoning argues from the particular to the general. That is, it uses specific examples to support a general proposition. A team of chemists will argue that their new theory is correct by describing the results of several experiments that point to it. If you want people to vote for mayoral candidate A rather than B, you could point to A's positive actions on city council and also perhaps point to several instances of B's harmful decisions. If you wanted to argue against a proposal to cut back on funding for the athletic program at your school, you could cite the major ways in which the program benefits the school and its students; you could also interview other students to show that many of them agree with you.

Inductive reasoning cannot prove anything; it can only establish degrees of probability. Obviously the number of examples affects the force of such arguments. If the chemists could point to only two successful experiments, the claim for their theory would remain weak; if they could cite a hundred consecutive successes, their argument would be convincing; there would be a strong likelihood that the experiment would work again if tried for the hundred-and-first time.

Be rigorous in presenting your data, but also consider how much detail your audience really needs. If, in a speech or a written argument, you detailed fifty noble acts of candidate A and fifty ignoble acts of candidate B, you would probably lose your audience and turn them against you and your proposition. You would do better to describe a few actions on each side and try to establish that those actions were representative of the two candidates' behaviour.

Similarly, if you interviewed students about the athletic program at your university or college, you would need to talk to enough of them for your sampling to be considered representative; if you polled only elite athletes, you could hardly claim that their opinions were typical. And though the sampling would have to be large for the results to be convincing, it would be the total number that would carry weight, not the detailed opinions of each individual student.

In addition, you must be able to explain any notable exceptions among your examples, for these form the bases of possible opposition arguments. For example, if one of their experiments failed, the chemists would need to show that at that time their equipment was faulty, or that one of their ingredients had accidentally become adulterated. If candidate A had once voted to close a useful facility, you could try to show that financial exigency at that time left no choice, or that the facility, though generally perceived as beneficial, was in fact little used and therefore an unnecessary drain on the city's resources. If you explicitly acknowledge such exceptions and show that they are unimportant or atypical, they can't easily be used against you by a reader who disagrees with you.

2. Deduction

Deductive reasoning argues from the general to the particular. It begins with facts or generally accepted assumptions or principles and applies them to specific instances. For example, we know that oil and other fossil fuels are non-renewable energy sources that will someday be depleted, and we also know that the world's energy needs are increasing exponentially. Basing their argument on those two facts, energy experts have concluded that it is increasingly important for us to discover or develop alternative sources of energy.

The standard way of representing the process of deductive thinking is the *syllogism*:

> major premise: **All mammals are warm-blooded animals.**
> minor premise: **Whales are mammals.**
> conclusion: **Therefore, whales are warm-blooded animals.**

Syllogistic reasoning is a basic mode of thought, though commonly in everyday thinking and writing one of the premises is omitted as "understood"; for example, if a student says "This term paper is due tomorrow, so I'll have to finish it tonight," the assumed second premise ("I don't want to hand the paper in late") goes without saying.

Deductive reasoning, unlike inductive reasoning, can establish proof, but only if the premises are correct and you follow the rules of logic. For example, if one of the premises is negative, the conclusion must be negative—and two negative premises cannot lead to a conclusion at all. The term common to both premises—called the "middle" term (in the foregoing example, *mammals*)—cannot appear in the conclusion. Most important, if the conclusion is to be an absolute certainty, this "middle" term must, in at least one of the premises, be all-inclusive, universal, or what is called "distributed"; that is, it must refer to all members of its class, usually with an absolute word like *all, every, no, none, always, never.* If instead it is qualified by a word like *some, most,* or *seldom,* the conclusion can only be a probability, not a certainty (and if both premises include such a qualifier, they cannot lead to a conclusion):

> **Most mammals are viviparous.**
> **Whales are mammals.**
> **Therefore, whales are probably viviparous.**

Here, one could reason further that since whales are not among the oviparous exceptions (platypus, echidna), they are indeed viviparous.

For a conclusion to amount to certainty both premises must be true, or accepted as true:

> No mammals can fly.
> Whales are mammals.
> Therefore, whales cannot fly.

Here, the conclusion is *valid* (the reasoning process follows the rules), but it is not *sound*, since the first premise with its categorical *no* excludes the bat, a flying mammal. Such a conclusion, even if true (as this one is), will be suspect because it is based on a false premise.

Consider the following argument:

> All mammals are four-legged animals.
> Whales are mammals.
> Therefore, whales are four-legged animals.

The conclusion, however valid, is not only unsound but untrue as well. To be accurate, the first premise would have to refer to *some* or *many*; the conclusion would then have to be something like "whales may be four-legged animals." Here, the absurdity is obvious. But it is not uncommon to hear something like "X must be anti-business; after all, he is in favour of preserving the rain forests." In such a case the absurdity may not appear so obvious, but in the syllogism underlying this reasoning the first premise would read something like "Anyone who argues for preserving the environment is against business"; again, changing "Anyone who argues" to the correctly qualified "Some people who argue" renders the conclusion unsound.

Be skeptical whenever you find yourself using—or thinking—absolute terms like *all* and *everyone* and *no one* and *must* ("Everyone benefits from exercise"; "All exams are unfair"; "[All] Scots are charming"; "No one cares about the elderly"; "Vitamin E must be good for you"): you may be constructing an implicit syllogism that won't stand up, one that an opponent can turn against you. Use such qualifiers as *most* and *some* and *sometimes* when necessary; you won't be able to establish absolute proof or certainty, but you may still have a persuasive argument.

3. Combining Induction and Deduction

Induction and deduction often work together. For example, when you cite instances from candidate A's record, you use induction to establish the general proposition of your candidate's worthiness. But then you implicitly turn to deduction, using that generalization as the basis for a further conclusion: "Candidate A has done all these good things for our city in the past; therefore when elected mayor he or she will do similar good things." (But would the unstated second premise—"A person who behaved in a certain way in the past will continue to behave that way in the future"—require some qualification?)

10h Detecting and Avoiding Fallacies

If you are mounting a counter-argument, it often pays to look for flaws in your opponent's reasoning, such as hidden assumptions and invalid syllogisms. There are several other kinds of recognized, and recognizable, logical fallacies to look for—and, of course, to guard against in your own writing. Most of them amount to either avoiding or distorting evidence, or both, and some are related to or overlap with others. Here are the main ones to watch for:

1. *Argumentum ad Hominem*

Argumentum ad hominem means "argument directed at the person." It refers to an attempt to evade the issue by diverting attention to the person at the centre of the argument: "Mozart lived an amoral life; therefore his music is bound to be bad." Mozart's morality is irrelevant to a discussion of the aesthetic quality of his music. "My opponent is obviously not fit to be mayor; she never goes to church, and her daughter was arrested last year for shoplifting." Neither the candidate's non-attendance at church nor her daughter's arrest—whether or not she was guilty—necessarily has any bearing on the candidate's fitness for office. Such tactics, according to their degree of directness or nastiness, are referred to as innuendo or name-calling or mud-slinging.

A similar tactic, known as guilt (or virtue) by association, is an attempt to tarnish (or enhance) someone's or something's reputation through an association with another person or thing. This kind of argument often takes the form of an endorsement: "I always take my car to Caesar's Garage because my friend Manuel says they're great, and he knows a lot about cars." Many instances of this kind of argument turn out to be fallacious because the stated connection between the two things is either not real or irrelevant. A brand of soft drink is not necessarily better because a famous actor is paid to say it is, nor is a politician necessarily evil because he once had his picture taken with someone later convicted of a crime.

2. *Argumentum ad Populum*

Argumentum ad populum is an "argument directed at the people"—an attempt to evade the issue by appealing to mass emotion. Like *argumentum ad hominem*, this technique uses appeals to prejudices, fears, and other feelings not—or not clearly—relevant to the issue. Often by using what are called "glittering generalities," it calls upon large and usually vague, unexamined popular feelings about religion, patriotism, home and family, tradition, and the like. One version of it, called the "bandwagon" approach, associates mass appeal with virtue: if so many people are doing this or thinking that or drinking this or wearing that, it must be right or good.

3. Red Herring

A red herring is a false or misleading issue dragged across the trail to throw the dogs off the scent. The new matter may be interesting, but if it is fundamentally irrelevant to the question being argued, it is a red herring. For example, *ad hominem* arguments are red herrings, since they divert a reader's or listener's attention from the main question by injecting the issue of personality.

4. Hasty Generalization

A hasty generalization is a generalization for which there is insufficient evidence. It occurs when an arguer jumps to a conclusion that is based on relatively little proof, for example when a team of chemists formulates a theory with only two successful experiments to point to (see #10g.1). Consider another example: just because you and a friend didn't like the food you were served once at a particular restaurant, you aren't justified in asserting that the food is always bad at that restaurant; maybe the regular chef was away that day. But if you've had several such experiences and can find other people who've had similar ones, you'll be closer to establishing that those experiences were typical and therefore sufficient to generalize upon.

5. Begging the Question

Begging the question is assuming as true something that needs to be proved: "The government should be voted out of office because the new tax they've just imposed is unfair to consumers." The arguer here is guilty of begging the question of the tax's unfairness, which needs to be established before it can be used as a premise.

Similar to question-begging is circular reasoning, in which a reason given to support a proposition is little or no more than a disguised restatement of the proposition: "Her consistently good cooking is easy to explain: she's an expert at all things culinary." This is the same as saying she is a good cook because she is a good cook.

6. Post Hoc Ergo Propter Hoc

Post hoc ergo propter hoc means "after this, therefore because of this." It refers to oversimplifying the evidence by assuming that merely because B follows A in time, B must be caused by A. It's true that thunder is caused by lightning, but the subsequent power failure may have been caused not by the lightning but by a tree blown down across the power line. Think about common superstitions: if you always wear your green socks during an exam because once when you wore them you wrote a good exam and so you think they bring you good luck, you are succumbing to the *post hoc* fallacy. Consider another example: "As soon as the new government took office, the price of gasoline went up"; the price hike might have nothing to do with the new government, the timing being coincidental.

7. Either-or

The either-or fallacy, also called "false dilemma," refers to an oversimplification of an issue by presenting it as consisting of only two choices when in reality it is more complex than that. Some questions do present two clear choices: one either gets up or stays in bed; either one is pregnant or one is not; either one votes in an election or one doesn't. But most arguable issues are not matters simply of black and white; there is often a large area of grey between the extremes. One doesn't have to vote for either A or B; one can perhaps find a third candidate, or one can stay home and not vote for anyone. "If you aren't for us, then you must be against us!" This common cry is false; one could be neutral, impartial, uninterested, or committed to a third option. "If I don't pass this course, my life will be ruined." This can be seen as an exaggeration. "The administration at work is either indifferent to employees' needs or against employees in general." Neither unpleasant alternative is likely to be true. This insidious pattern of thinking underlies a good deal of what we think of as prejudice, bigotry, and narrow-mindedness: "If you don't attend a recognized religious institution, then you're not really religious," or "If you don't support the war, you're unpatriotic." Although it is sometimes tempting, don't oversimplify; acknowledge the rich complexity of most issues.

8. Exaggerating the Trivial

When you exaggerate the trivial, you distort the evidence by treating a minor point as if it were a major one. If the point is your own, discerning readers will infer that you lack substantial evidence and have had to fall back on weak arguments. If the point is an opposing one, the audience will infer that you can't refute major points and are trying to make yourself look good by demolishing an easy target. "We should all give more to charity because being generous can give us a warm feeling inside" may be worth mentioning, but not worth dwelling on. On the other hand, don't distort the evidence by trivializing opposition points that are important.

9. False or Weak Analogy

A false or weak analogy occurs when one oversimplifies the evidence by arguing that because two things are alike in some features, they are necessarily alike in one or more others as well. You can say that learning to ride a bicycle is like learning to play the piano: once you learn, you seldom forget; but you would not go on to argue that one should have a bicycle tuned periodically or that one should mount a tail light on a piano for safety while playing at night. Analogies can provide interesting and concrete illustrations; by suggesting similarities they can help define, clarify, explain, or emphasize something; see, for example, the analogy comparing an outline to a map in #9g. We would not expect our analogy to convince you of the importance of an outline, but we hope that, by adding its concrete touch, we help you to understand and perhaps to accept our assertions.

One fairly common argument claims that because city or provincial or other governments are in some ways similar to large business organizations, they need experienced business people to run them. The more similarities you can point to, the stronger the argument. The trouble with this and other arguments from analogy is that no matter how many specific similarities you can come up with, your opponents can usually keep ahead of you by citing an even greater number of specific and significant differences. After all, leading a government may be *like* running a business, but it is not the same thing.

10. Equivocation

Equivocation involves using a term in more than one sense; being ambiguous, whether accidentally or intentionally: "It is only natural for intelligent people to reject this idea. And as science tells us, natural law is the law of the universe; it is the law of truth and must be obeyed." Aside from the appeal to snobbery and self-esteem (we all like to think we are "intelligent," but just what is "intelligence"?) and the appeal to the prestige of "science" in the modern world (but just how infallible is science?) and the imposing but vague term *universe* and the glittering abstraction *truth*, do the two occurrences of the word *natural* correspond with each other? And is a natural *law* comparable to legislation passed by a government and enforced by police and the courts? Don't let the meanings of words shift as you move from one phrase or sentence to the next. Choose and use your words ethically and carefully.

11. Non Sequitur

Non sequitur means "it does not follow." When for whatever reason a general proposition does not follow logically from the particular examples cited to support it, or a conclusion does not logically follow from its premises, it is a *non sequitur.* The term would apply to any of the fallacies discussed above and also to such leaps of logic as "She can French braid hair; she'd make a good mother," and "I've had singing lessons for two years; I should get the lead role in the opera."

11 Writing In-Class Essays and Essay Examinations

Writing an essay in class or during an examination is much like writing an essay in your own room, in the library, or anywhere else—except that you may have to do it faster: you don't have time to think and plan at leisure and at length. Therefore, you need to make the best use of the time you have. All the principles discussed earlier in this part still hold, but here is some additional advice to help you work quickly and efficiently:

1. **At the beginning of an examination, read through the whole test right away.** If it has more than one part, budget your time:

before you start thinking and writing, decide just how much time you will need or can afford to spend on each part. Make decisions about time allotment based on the mark value of each section of the examination.

2. **Read the topics or questions carefully.** Don't, in haste, misread or misinterpret. Don't read wishfully, finding in a question what you want to find instead of what is actually there.

3. **Follow instructions.** If you're asked for an argument, *argue*. If a question asks you to *analyze* a text, don't simply give a summary of it. If it asks you to *justify* or *defend* your opinions or conclusions, don't simply assert them. If it asks for *comparison and contrast*, don't spend too much time on one side of the matter. If it asks you to *define* a term or concept, don't simply describe it or give an example of it, and don't ramble on about your feelings about it or your impressions of it.

4. **Take time to plan.** Don't panic and begin writing immediately. Think for a few minutes. The time you spend planning will ensure that the job of writing is easier and the result is clearer. Do a little quick brainstorming. Take the time to make at least a sketch outline, with a thesis or proposition and a list of main points and supporting details; you will then be less likely to wander off the topic or change your thesis as you proceed. It's often a good idea to limit yourself to three or four main points, or parts (in addition, that is, to a beginning and an ending).

5. **Get started.** Once you've drawn up your plan, start writing. If necessary, leave several lines or a page blank at the beginning and plunge right into your first point. Don't waste time trying to think of a beginning if one doesn't occur to you quickly; you can come back and fill it in later. Quite possibly you won't need to supply a separate "beginning" at all. Get to the point quickly and stay with it. Make your thesis clear early on; that may be all you need by way of a beginning. Often you can pick up some significant words or phrases from the question or topic and use them to help frame a thesis and get yourself going.

6. **Write carefully.** Whereas in an essay written at home or in a research essay you may write your draft hurriedly and spend most of your time revising and editing, in an exam you have to make most of your changes as you go. (This is another reason it's important to have a plan: without one, you could, as you pause to tinker with a

sentence, forget your line of argument.) You won't have time to do much revising; your first efforts at sentences will often have to do.

7. **Aim for quality, not quantity.** More is not necessarily better. Your essay should be of reasonable length, and sometimes a required minimum length will be specified. What is most important is that you adequately develop your subject by developing each of your main points. But don't try to impress by going on and on, for then you will likely ramble, lose control of your thesis and your organization, and not give yourself time to edit and proofread.

8. **Be specific.** Provide examples, illustrations, and evidence. By all means generalize, but support your generalizations with specific and concrete details.

9. **Conclude effectively.** Refer to, or restate, your thesis, and if necessary refer again to your three or four main points, but do so in a way that adds something new. Sometimes a single concluding sentence can make a good clincher, especially if it suggests or underscores some result or effect growing out of what your discussion has said. If possible, echo an idea you had in your introduction.

10. **Proofread carefully.** Leave yourself enough time to look for the kinds of mistakes and slips we all make when writing fast. Don't just run your eyes over your sentences, assuming that any errors will leap out at you, even though that may give you the illusion that you've checked your work. Read carefully. If you know that you're prone to certain kinds of errors, look specifically for them.

12 Sentence Patterns and Conventions

All sentences have this purpose: to communicate ideas and/or feelings. There are conventional ways to convey these ideas and feelings. For example, if someone tells you,

I am designing an experiment to collect data on colony collapse disorder.

you know that the sentence is stating a fact, or a supposed fact. If the same person then says,

Are you familiar with "colony collapse disorder"?

you know that you are being asked a question and that you are expected to give an answer. If your friend says,

Tell me what you think of my research proposal.

you know you are being asked to do something, being given a mild command. And when your fellow student says,

What an ambitious project!

you know you are hearing an emphatic expression of strong feeling.

We know how to interpret these different kinds of utterances because we understand and accept the *conventions* of the way sentences communicate. Sentences are classified according to the kind of purpose each has. Sentences that *make statements of fact or supposed fact* are declarative:

Anne of Green Gables **is tremendously popular in Japan.**

Iqaluit is the capital of Nunavut.

Sentences that *ask questions* are **interrogative**; in speech, they often (but not always) end with a rise in the pitch of one's voice; in writing, they end with a **question mark**:

Do you have that app on your phone?

Why? What's the reason?

Sentences that *give commands* or *make requests*, that expect action or compliance, are **imperative**:

Please print the document.

Edit your email message carefully before sending it.

Sentences that *exclaim*, that express strong feeling with vigour or emphasis, are **exclamatory**; they customarily end with an **exclamation point**:

That was an unforgettable trip!

Not if I can help it!

Like many other traditional categories, however, the ones we've described aren't always so simple or obvious. A sentence may include a mixture of elements:

"Will the Albert Memorial Bridge take me downtown?" the driver asked. (interrogative and declarative)

Please contact me about your project: I have information that's relevant. (imperative and declarative)

Slow down! (imperative and exclamatory)

Sometimes the same basic sense can be expressed in all four ways:

I need your help.
Will you help me?
Help me with this.
Help!

Your awareness of the *conventions* guides you in understanding the purposes of sentences you hear, read, speak, or write: you know almost instinctively how to frame a sentence to make it do what you want.

A more conscious grasp of the way sentences work will help you frame them even more effectively. It will help you when you're in doubt. And it will help you not only to avoid weaknesses and errors but also to revise and correct them when they do occur.

Since most sentences in written and academic discourse are *declarative*, their patterns are the ones you need to understand first. The rest of Part II, for the most part, then, deals with the basic elements and patterns of declarative sentences. (See #25 and #26 for an expanded discussion of basic sentence elements and their modifiers.)

Subject and Predicate, Noun and Verb

A standard declarative sentence consists of two parts: a **subject** and a **predicate**. The subject is what acts or is talked about; the predicate is what the subject does or what is said about it. For example:

subject	predicate
Birds	fly.
I	sing.

The essential element of the subject part of a sentence is a **noun** (*Birds*) or a **pronoun** (*I*). (Nouns name persons, places, things, classes, concepts, qualities, or actions; see #13. Pronouns stand in place of nouns; see #14.) The essential element of the predicate part of a sentence is a **verb** (*fly*, *sing*). (Verbs express actions, occurrences, processes, or states of being; see #17.)

Articles and Other Modifiers

Few sentences, however, consist of only a one-word subject and a one word predicate. Frequently, for example, nouns are preceded by articles (*a, an, the*; see #19c):

subject	predicate
The child	chattered.

And both subject and predicate often include **modifiers**, words that change or limit the meaning of nouns and verbs (see #26). Nouns are modified by **adjectives**, which generally answer the questions *Which? What kind of? How many?* and *How much?* (see #19):

subject	predicate
The <u>young</u> child	chattered.
A <u>caged</u> bird	will sing.

Verbs are modified by adverbs, which generally answer such questions as *How? When? Where? Why?* and *To what degree?* (see #20):

subject	predicate
The young child	chattered <u>happily</u>.
A bird	flew <u>south</u>.

Basic Sentence Patterns

ONLINE
EXERCISES

Single-word modifiers account for only part of the richness of many sentences, which may feature impressive arrays of modifying phrases and clauses (see, for example, the sentences discussed in #26). Almost all English sentences follow one of a few basic patterns, or combinations of them. If you can recognize and understand the sentence patterns indicated in the chart below and elaborated on in the following pages, you will be well on your way to being able to analyze any sentences you write or read.

Sentence Pattern #	Description
1	Subject + Verb
2A	Subject + Verb + Direct Object
2B	Subject + Passive Voice Verb
3	Subject + Verb + Indirect Object + Direct Object
4A	Subject + Linking Verb + Subjective Complement (predicate adjective)
4B	Subject + Linking Verb + Subjective Complement (predicate noun)
5A	Subject + Verb + Direct Object + Objective Complement (adjective)
5B	Subject + Verb + Direct Object + Objective Complement (noun)
6	*There* or *It* + Linking Verb (+ complement) + Subject

12c Sentence Pattern 1

SUBJECT + VERB

This is the pattern you've already looked at and imitated. The subject, consisting of a noun (with its modifiers) or a pronoun, is followed by the predicate, consisting of a verb (with its modifiers):

subject	predicate
The Cheshire cat	smiled mysteriously.
These large, ungainly birds	can fly quite gracefully.
They	dance exuberantly.

12d Sentence Pattern 2A

SUBJECT + VERB + DIRECT OBJECT

This pattern expands the basic sentence core by adding a **direct object** to the predicate. (A direct object answers the question consisting of the verb and *what?* or *whom?* For example, in the first example below, *landscapes* answers the question, *I paint what?*) A direct object, like a subject, must be either a noun or a pronoun, and the verb must be transitive—that is, it must be able to take a direct object (see #17a):

subject	predicate	
noun or pronoun	*transitive verb*	*direct object*
I	paint	urban landscapes.
Bahaar	is reading	poems.
Impatient journalists	pursue	tight-lipped celebrities.

In this pattern the subject acts, the verb indicates the action, and the direct object is the product (*landscapes*) or the receiver (*poems, celebrities*) of the action. Note that direct objects can, like subject-nouns, be modified by adjectives (*urban, tight-lipped*).

12e Sentence Pattern 2B (passive voice)

ONLINE EXERCISES

> SUBJECT (receiver of the action) + PASSIVE VOICE VERB
> (+ *by*-phrase: agent/performer of the action)

Here, the order of the main elements of Pattern 2A is reversed. The former direct object becomes the subject, and the former subject moves to the end of the sentence, after the **preposition** *by*. (Prepositions are structure words that link nouns or pronouns to other words in the sentence, thereby establishing meaningful relations between them; see #12-l and #22.) The verb stays in the middle but changes to the passive voice—a form of the verb *be* followed by a **past participle**. (Past participles are past-tense verb forms used in the passive voice, in the perfect tenses, and as adjectives; see #17b–c, #17g, and #21d.) Use the passive voice strategically—that is, when you want to emphasize the receiver rather than the performer of an action. Make your choice knowing that overuse of the passive can sometimes make writing wordy and unclear (see #17-l). Consider a crime scenario in which a detective might say, using Pattern 2A,

Gunfire killed him. (active voice)

But in the circumstances it would be more natural to say

He was killed by gunfire. (passive voice)

Similarly, you can write some of the sentences under Pattern 2A according to Pattern 2B:

subject	predicate	
noun or pronoun	*verb*	*prepositional phrase*
Urban landscapes	are painted	by me.
Poems	are read	by Bahaar.
Tight-lipped celebrities	are pursued	by impatient journalists.

But you can see that such alternatives would be preferable only in unusual circumstances, for example if you wanted special emphasis on *urban landscapes* or *poems* or *tight-lipped celebrities* (see #29f). Note that in this pattern the *by*-phrase is often omitted as unnecessary or unknown:

He **has been shot** **(by someone).**

12f Sentence Pattern 3

ONLINE
EXERCISES

SUBJECT + VERB + INDIRECT OBJECT + DIRECT OBJECT

A sentence with a direct object sometimes also includes an **indirect object**. An indirect object is a noun or pronoun identifying the recipient of an action.

subject		predicate	
noun or pronoun	*transitive verb*	*indirect object*	*direct object*
He	sent	his adviser	an email message.
Grace	lent	Ari	her lecture notes.
Rishad	offered	his guests	sushi.

You can usually vary this pattern, and still say essentially the same thing, by changing the indirect object to a prepositional phrase that comes after the direct object:

subject		predicate	
noun or verb	*transitive verb*	*direct object*	*prepositional phrase*
He	sent	an email message	to his adviser.
Grace	lent	her lecture notes	to Ari.
Rishad	offered	sushi	to his guests.

12g Sentence Pattern 4A

ONLINE
EXERCISES

SUBJECT + LINKING VERB + SUBJECTIVE COMPLEMENT (predicate adjective)

Linking verbs (see #17a) require something other than an object to complete the idea, something called a **complement**. And since the complement is linked to the subject, it is sometimes called a **subjective complement**. The principal linking verb is *be* in its various forms (see #17f); others include *become, seem, remain, act, get, feel, look, appear, smell, sound,* and *taste.* In Pattern 4A, the verb links the subject with an adjectival modifier in the predicate part of the sentence; the modifier is called a **predicate adjective**:

subject	predicate	
noun or pronoun	*linking verb*	*subjective complement (predicate adjective)*
She	is	curious.
Cellphones	have become	indispensable.
That	sounds	difficult.

12h Sentence Pattern 4B

> **SUBJECT + LINKING VERB + SUBJECTIVE COMPLEMENT**
> **(predicate noun)**

In this pattern, a verb links the subject with a noun or pronoun acting as a subjective complement and called a **predicate noun**:

subject	predicate	
noun or pronoun	*linking verb*	*subjective complement (predicate noun)*
This	is	it.
Madeleine Thien	is	a gifted writer.
Fresh fruits	make	healthy snacks.

12i Sentence Pattern 5A

> **SUBJECT + VERB + DIRECT OBJECT + OBJECTIVE**
> **COMPLEMENT (adjective)**

Such verbs as *appoint, believe, call, consider, declare, designate, elect, find, judge, make, name, nominate, select,* and *think* are sometimes followed by a direct object and an objective complement—a complement describing the object rather than the subject. In Pattern 5A, as in 4A, the complement is an *adjective*:

subject	predicate		
noun or pronoun	*transitive verb*	*direct object*	*objective complement (adjective)*
Wareesha	declares	the field	unsafe.
The jury	found	them	guilty as charged.
They	made	themselves	comfortable.

12j Sentence Pattern 5B

ONLINE
EXERCISES

> SUBJECT + VERB + DIRECT OBJECT + OBJECTIVE
> COMPLEMENT (noun)

In this variation, the objective complement that completes the meaning of the direct object is a *noun*:

subject			predicate
noun or pronoun	*transitive verb*	*direct object*	*objective complement (noun)*
The party	named	her	interim leader.
Jamal	considers	sports	a distraction.
We	judged	the party	a success.

12k Sentence Pattern 6 (expletive)

ONLINE
EXERCISES

> *THERE* or *IT* + LINKING VERB (+ complement) + SUBJECT

This final pattern is, like the passive voice in Pattern 2B, something to use judiciously: the **expletive** pattern. In such sentences the word *There* or *It* appears at the beginning, in the place usually occupied by the subject; then comes a linking verb, usually a form of the verb *be*; and then comes the subject. When used strategically, *There* and *It* enable you to make certain kinds of statements in a more natural way or with a different emphasis than you could otherwise. For example, instead of having to say

subject	predicate
That life begins at forty	may be true.
No solutions	existed.
No plumbing	was in the cabin.

you can, using Pattern 6, say

expletive	linking verb	complement	subject
It	may be	true	that life begins at forty.
There	were		no solutions.
There	was		no plumbing in the cabin.

Here are some further examples of Pattern 6:

> **There was one reason for the army's defeat.**
>
> **It is challenging to study Sanskrit.**
>
> **There wasn't a cloud in the sky.**

See also #18e, #29f, and #71a.

 ## Other Elements: Structure Words

Most declarative sentences use one or more of patterns 1 to 6. The elements in those patterns—subjects, verbs, modifiers, objects, and complements—make up the substance of all sentences.

Many sentences also include words like *and, but, for, of, under, with.* Such words are important because they connect other elements in various ways that establish meaningful relations between them. Such words are sometimes called **structure words** or **function words**; most of them belong to two other classes of words, or "parts of speech": **conjunctions** and **prepositions**. (Conjunctions join together words, phrases, clauses, and sentences; see #23. Prepositions were introduced in #12e and are discussed more fully in #22.) These and the other parts of speech are covered in Part III.

 ## Clauses and Phrases

 To master sentence structure and punctuation, you need to understand the differences between **clauses** and **phrases** and how they work in sentences. Clauses and phrases are groups of words that function as grammatical units or elements *within* sentences but—except for **independent clauses**—cannot stand alone *as* sentences.

 ## Independent (Main) Clauses

A clause is a group of words containing both a *subject* and a *predicate.* If it is an **independent clause**, it can, as the term indicates, stand by itself as a sentence. Each of the sample sentences in the preceding sections is an independent clause, since each contains the minimum requirement: a noun or pronoun as subject and a verb functioning as the predicate; each is a **simple sentence** (see #12z.1).

But an independent clause can also function as only part of a sentence. For example, if you start with two separate independent clauses—that is, two simple sentences:

The exam ended.

The students submitted their papers.

you can combine them to form a **compound sentence** (see #12z.2):

The exam ended; the students submitted their papers.

The exam ended, and the students submitted their papers.

The exam ended; therefore the students submitted their papers.

Each of the two halves of these sentences is an independent clause; each could stand alone as a sentence.

Subordinate (Dependent) Clauses

A **subordinate clause**, unlike an independent clause, usually cannot stand by itself. Even though, as a clause, it contains a subject and a predicate, it is by definition *subordinate*, *dependent* on another clause—an *independent* one—for its completion or meaning. It therefore must be treated as only part of a sentence, as in the following examples (the subordinate clauses are underlined); these are called **complex sentences** (see #12z.3):

<u>When the exam ended</u>, the students submitted their papers.

The students submitted their papers <u>as the exam ended</u>.

The students submitted the papers <u>that they had written during the exam</u>.

The exam ended, <u>which meant that the students had to submit their papers</u>.

Note that subordinate clauses often begin with such words as *when*, *as*, *that*, and *which*, called subordinators, which clearly signal the presence of a subordinate clause as opposed to an independent clause (see #23c).

(Subordinate clauses can be used separately, for example in dialogue or as answers to questions, where the context is clear: Why did the students submit their papers? *Because the exam had ended.* Except in such circumstances, a subordinate clause should not stand by itself as if it were a sentence. See #12w and #12x.)

Functions of Subordinate Clauses

Like a phrase (see #12p), a subordinate clause functions as a grammatical unit in its sentence. That is, a subordinate clause can occupy several of the slots in the sentence patterns illustrated just above.

A noun clause can serve as the subject of a sentence:

<u>What he taught his students</u> inspired the movement. | Pattern 2A |

as a direct object:

Azin knows <u>that democracy is important</u>. | Pattern 2A |

or as a predicate noun:

The question is <u>what we should do next</u>. | Pattern 4B |

Adjectival clauses (also called relative clauses; see #14d) modify nouns or pronouns, such as a direct object:

She left her teacher a note <u>that explained her absence</u>. | Pattern 3 |

or a subject:

The critic <u>who wrote the article</u> confused the facts. | Pattern 2A |

Adverbial clauses usually modify main verbs:

We left <u>because we were utterly bored</u>. | Pattern 1 |

12p Phrases

A **phrase** is a group of words lacking a subject and/or predicate but functioning as a grammatical unit within a sentence. For example, a **verb phrase** (see #17e) acts as the verb in this Pattern 1 sentence:

Most of the wedding guests will be arriving in the morning.

A **prepositional phrase** (see #22) can be an adjectival modifier:

Most of the wedding guests will be arriving in the morning.

or an adverbial modifier:

Most of the wedding guests will be arriving in the morning.

The words *Most of the wedding guests* constitute a **noun phrase** functioning as the subject of the sentence. Any noun or pronoun along with its modifiers—so long as the group doesn't contain a subject–predicate combination—can be thought of as a noun phrase. Similarly, a **gerund phrase** can function as a subject. (A gerund phrase is introduced by a gerund—a verb form that ends in *ing* and functions as a noun; see #21f):

Slicing vegetables is easy. | Pattern 4A |

A gerund phrase can also function as a direct object:

She tried bungee jumping. | Pattern 2A |

A **participial phrase**—always adjectival—can modify a subject. (A participial phrase is introduced by a past or present participle; see #21d):

Trusting her instincts, Jane gave the candidate her support. | Pattern 3 |

A participial phrase can also modify a direct object:

I am reading an article discussing human cloning. | Pattern 2A |

An **infinitive phrase** can function as a direct object (noun). (An infinitive phrase is introduced by an infinitive—a verb form consisting of *to* followed by the basic form of a verb and functioning as a noun, an adjective, or an adverb; see #21a):

This organization wants <u>to eradicate poverty</u>. Pattern 2A

An infinitive phrase can also function as a subject (noun):

It may be impossible <u>to eradicate poverty</u>. Pattern 6

or as an adjective, for example one modifying the subject:

Their desire <u>to eradicate poverty</u> is idealistic. Pattern 4A

or as an adverb, for example one modifying the verb:

They arranged the agenda <u>to highlight the anti-poverty campaign</u>.

Pattern 2A

Adverbial infinitive phrases can also act as **sentence modifiers** (see #20a and #20d.4), modifying not the verb or any other single word but rather all the rest of the sentence:

<u>To be honest</u>,
<u>To tell the truth</u>, } **I rarely attend my brother's dance recitals.**

12q Appositives

An **appositive** is a word or group of words that renames or restates, in other terms, the meaning of a neighbouring word. For example, if you start with two simple sentences,

Suzanne is our accountant. She looks after our business dealings.

you can turn the first into an appositive by reducing it and combining it with the second:

Suzanne, <u>our accountant</u>, looks after our business dealings.

The noun phrase *our accountant* is here said to be **in apposition to** *Suzanne*.

Most appositives are nouns or noun phrases that redefine, usually in more specific terms, the nouns they follow. But occasionally an appositive precedes the other noun:

<u>**A skilful accountant**</u>**, Suzanne looks after our business dealings.**

And occasionally another part of speech can function as an appositive, for example a participial (adjectival) phrase:

Searching frantically, <u>tossing books and papers everywhere</u>, they failed to find the missing passport.

or a verb phrase:

Document <u>(provide details of your sources for)</u> this argument.

An appositive can also be a single word, often a name:

Our accountant, <u>Suzanne</u>, looks after our business dealings.

And, rarely, even a subordinate clause can function as an appositive:

How she travelled—<u>whether she journeyed alone or not</u>—remains a mystery.

Note that an appositive is grammatically equivalent to the term it defines and could replace it in the sentence:

Our accountant looks after our business dealings.

A skilful accountant looks after our business dealings.

Suzanne looks after our business dealings.

Tossing books and papers everywhere, they failed to find the missing passport.

Provide details of your sources for this argument.

Whether she journeyed alone or not remains a mystery.

(For the punctuation of appositives, see #43f.2 and #54i.)

12r Absolute Phrases

An **absolute phrase** has no direct grammatical link with what it modifies; it depends simply on juxtaposition, in effect modifying the rest of the sentence by hovering over it like an umbrella. Most absolute phrases amount to a sentence with the verb changed to a participle (see #21d). Instead of using two sentences,

> **The site had crashed. She could not access her account.**

you can reduce the first to an absolute phrase modifying the second:

> **The site having crashed, she could not access her account.**

If the original verb is a form of *be*, the participle can sometimes be omitted:

> **The thunderstorm (being) over, the tennis match resumed.**

Sometimes, especially with certain common expressions, the participle isn't preceded by a noun:

> **There were a few rough spots, but generally speaking the rehearsal was a success.**

> **Judging by the population statistics, we have become a multicultural nation.**

And sometimes infinitive phrases (see #12p and #21a) function as absolutes:

> **To say the least, the campaign was not a success.**

You can also think of many absolutes as *with*-phrases from which the preposition has been dropped:

> **(With) the thunderstorm over, the tennis match resumed.**

> **Careful measurement is a must, (with) the results dependent on this kind of due attention.**

And you can think of most absolute phrases as functioning much like an adverb modifying the rest of the sentence (see #20a and #20d.4):

absolute: <u>**All things considered**</u>**, it was a fair exam.**

adverb: <u>**Unfortunately**</u>**, I hadn't studied hard enough.**

See also #21i.

12s Order of Elements in Declarative Sentences

Even if you didn't know the names of some of the bits and pieces, chances are that the samples presented in earlier sections to illustrate the basic sentence patterns felt natural to you; they're the familiar kinds of sentences you use every day without even thinking about their structure. Note that the natural order of the elements in almost all the patterns is the same:

subject—verb

subject—transitive verb—object(s)—(objective complement)

subject—linking verb—subjective complement

The only exception is Pattern 6, the expletive, in which the subject follows the verb (see #12k).

This conventional order of *subject—verb—object or complement* has proven itself the most direct and forceful pattern of expression:

War is hell.

Humpty Dumpty had a great fall.

We are such stuff as dreams are made on.

We shall defend every village, every town, and every city.

But this order can be altered to create special stylistic effects or special emphasis, and to introduce pleasing variations:

direct object	subject	transitive verb
Their generosity	I	have never doubted for a moment.

subjective complement	linking verb	subject
Long	was	the introduction to this otherwise short speech.

Such inversions aren't wrong, for conventions (or rules) are made to be broken as well as followed; but their very unconventionality demands that they be used judiciously. They are most at home in poetry or highly oratorical prose:

> **Thirty days hath September . . .**

> **And now abideth faith, hope, and charity, these three; but the greatest of these is charity.**

> **Never in the field of human conflict was so much owed by so many to so few.**

Elsewhere such variations are rare, since any unusual pattern almost automatically calls attention to itself, something seldom appropriate in expository prose. But used occasionally, and appropriately, they can be highly effective.

12t Order of Elements in Interrogative Sentences

The conventional order used in interrogative sentences usually differs from that used in declarative sentences. It is, of course, possible to use the declarative order for a question—for example in speaking, when one can use stress and end with the rising or falling intonation that usually indicates a question:

> **They're getting married tomorrow?**

thereby conveying a meaning something like

> **Do you mean to tell me that they are actually getting married so soon rather than waiting and planning a more formal ceremony? How surprising!**

Unless you're recording or imitating dialogue, you won't use this technique too often in your writing.

Usually, an interrogative sentence, besides ending with the conventional question mark, will take one of the following patterns. If the verb is a single-word form of *be*, it precedes the subject:

verb	subject	subjective complement
Is	Nunavut	a province?

With all other single-word verbs, it is necessary to supply a form of the auxiliary verb *do* before the subject; the main part of the verb then follows the subject in the normal way:

auxiliary verb	subject	main verb	direct object
Does	Nunavut	have	provincial status?

If the verb is already a verb phrase, the first auxiliary comes before the subject:

auxiliary verb	subject	second auxiliary	main verb
Are	you		daydreaming?
Will	Max		speak first?
Have	you	been	meditating?

If the question includes a negative, the *not* goes before or after the subject, depending on whether one uses the less formal, contracted form:

Aren't you going?   **Are you not going?**

With questions using expletives (Pattern 6; see #12k), the expletive and the verb are reversed:

Were there many people at the orientation?

Was it easy to follow her argument?

With so-called "tag" questions, a statement is followed by a verb-pronoun question; note also that a *not* appears in one or the other of the two parts:

Shulpa has been running, hasn't she?

Shulpa hasn't been running, has she?

All the above questions invite a *yes* or *no* answer, perhaps extended by a short clause made up of the appropriate pronoun (or expletive) and auxiliary, such as

Yes, she was.	**Yes, I am.**	**No, I haven't.**
Yes, there were.	**No, it wasn't.**	**No, he hasn't.** **No, he has not.**

Note that the negative answers include a *not* in the clause.

The only other common form of question begins with a **question word**, one of the interrogative adverbs (*where, when, why,* or *how;* see #20a.2) or interrogative pronouns (*who, whom, which, what,* or *whose;* see #14c); these invite answers beyond a mere *yes* or *no.* When a question begins with an interrogative adverb, a form of *do* or another already present auxiliary comes before the subject:

How did he write that?

Where (When) are you going?

If an interrogative pronoun functions as the subject, the sentence retains standard declarative word order:

Who will speak first?

If the opening pronoun is the *object* of the verb or a preposition, it is followed by the added auxiliary *do* or the first part of a verb phrase, the subject, and the rest of the verb, just as in the *yes* or *no* pattern:

Whom did you invite?

To whom did you address the invitation?

A similar reversal occurs when an interrogative pronoun functions as a possessive or other adjective (see #19a):

Whose (Which, What) political platform do you favour?

To what (which, whose) problems will the speaker address herself?

See also #22b, on the placement of prepositions in questions.

The Structure of Imperative Sentences

It is possible, especially with emphatic commands, to use the full structure of a declarative sentence:

subject	predicate
You	take that back!
You two in the corner	please join the rest of the group.

Still, the conventional form of an imperative sentence uses only the *predicate*, omitting the *subject* (an understood *you*):

Come into the garden, Maud. (Maud is not the subject, but a noun of address—that is, the name of a person being directly addressed; see #13b.)

For instance, examine the opening line of her speech.

Stretch before you run.

Edit carefully.

Enjoy.

Sometimes, especially in dialogue or informal contexts, even the verb can be omitted; a complement alone does the job:

Careful. Easy, now. Steady.

You may think you'll have little use for imperative sentences in your writing. But if you ever want to write a set of instructions, you'll need to use a great many of them. And they can provide useful variety in other contexts as well, just as questions can. *Declarative* sentences are the mainstay of written expression, but *interrogative* and *imperative* sentences are also useful. Consider using them.

 ## What Is a Sentence?

Now for a different kind of look at these groups of words called sentences. First, just what is a sentence? Most standard definitions are unsatisfactory and unrealistic because they leave out the kinds of sentences we use more often in speech than in formal writing. One definition, for example, says that a sentence is a group of words with a subject and a verb. But the first sentence of this section, just above, lacks a subject-verb combination. And here are some more sentences that lack one or the other or both:

Yes. No. When? Now or never. Oh my goodness! Wow!

Who, me? Well, I never! John. Coffee.

Come here. Never mind. Call me Ishmael. Sink or swim.

Out of context, such sentences don't tell us much, but they are clearly acceptable units. Moreover, some groups of words do contain a subject-verb combination but are still not sentences: an opening capital letter and a closing period don't make a subordinate clause a sentence:

I decided to make a list. Before I went shopping.

They bought me the bike. Which I had stared at in the store the week before.

The second clause in each of these is a fragment . (A fragment is a phrase or a subordinate clause that is incorrectly punctuated as if it were a sentence; see #12x.)

Another common definition claims that a sentence is a complete thought. But *Yes* and *No* aren't satisfyingly complete without the questions that prompted them, nor are some of the other examples without their respective contexts. Nor is there anything necessarily "incomplete" about such words as *dog, hand, chair, freedom, love*—yet these words are not normally thought of as sentences.

Remember that language is primarily spoken. It is more realistic to define a sentence as *a satisfyingly complete pattern of intonation or expression*: that is, a complete utterance. Your voice and natural tone should tell you whether a certain group of words is or is not a sentence. Make it a practice to read your written work aloud, or at least to sound it out in your mind. Doing so will help you avoid ambiguity.

Minor Sentences, Fragments, and Major Sentences

ONLINE
EXERCISES

Sentences—that is, acceptable patterns of expression—are of two kinds, which we call **minor** and **major**. Though this and similar books deal almost exclusively with *major* sentences, and though you won't have much use for *minor* sentences in academic writing, you should understand what minor sentences are so that you can use them occasionally for emphasis or other rhetorical effects, or when you are writing a piece of dialogue. And you need to be able to distinguish between the minor sentence, which is acceptable in some academic writing, and the fragmentary expression, which is not.

Minor Sentences

A **minor sentence** is an acceptable pattern of expression that nevertheless lacks either a subject or a finite verb, or both. But it is easy to supply the missing element or elements from context; for whereas major sentences can usually stand by themselves, most minor sentences need a context of one or more nearby sentences in order to make sense—most obviously, for example, as answers to questions. The minor sentence, however, like the major, is grammatically independent.

Minor sentences are usually one of the following four kinds:

1. Exclamations:

    Oh! No problem!   **So good!**
    Wow!   **Incredible!**

2. Questions or responses to questions:

    When? Tomorrow.   **How many? Seven.**
    Why? What for?   **How come? Really?**
    Yes.   No.   **Perhaps.   Certainly.**

3. Common proverbial or idiomatic expressions:

    Easy come, easy go.   **Now or never.**
    Better late than never.   **Down the hatch.**

4. Minor sentences used for rhetorical or stylistic effect: These are more common in narrative and descriptive writing, but they can be effective in other contexts as well. Here is how Charles Dickens begins *Bleak House*:

> **London. Michaelmas Term lately over, and the Lord Chancellor sitting in Lincoln's Inn Hall. Implacable November weather. As much mud in the streets, as if the waters had but newly retired from the face of the earth, and it would not be wonderful to meet a Megalosaurus, forty feet long or so, waddling like an elephantine lizard up Holborn Hill.**

And so on, for three long paragraphs: not a major sentence in sight.

Clearly the beginning of a piece of writing is a good place to try the effects of a minor sentence or two. A writer might begin an essay this way:

> **Time, time, time. It is our constant companion and our greatest nemesis.**

And here is a paragraph from another essay:

> **One of the best times of the year in Vancouver is the spring. Gardens and parks filled with crocuses, cherry trees in bloom, newborn birds in their nests.**

12x Fragments

Don't mistake an unacceptable fragment for an acceptable minor sentence:

> frag: **I didn't see the film. Because I felt that it would be too violent for my taste.**

The *Because*-clause is a fragment. The period after *film* should be deleted so that the subordinate clause can take its rightful place in the sentence. (But note that this *Because*-clause, like many other fragments, would be acceptable as an answer to a question just before it.)

> frag: **It was a hilarious moment. One that I'll never forget.**

The clause beginning with *One* should be linked to the preceding independent clause with a comma, not separated from it by a period. It can then take its rightful place as a noun clause in apposition to *moment*.

frag: **He gave me half his sandwich. <u>Being of a generous nature.</u>**

The participial phrase beginning with *Being* is not a separate sentence but an adjective modifying *He*; it should be introduced by a comma, or even moved to the beginning of the sentence:

revised: **Being of a generous nature, he gave me half his sandwich.**

Note that fragments tend to occur after the independent clauses that they should be attached to.

12y Major Sentences

A major sentence is a grammatically independent group of words containing at least two essential structural elements: a subject and a finite verb (see #12a and #17b, Note). Major sentences constitute 99 per cent or more of most college and university writing. They are the sentences whose basic patterns are illustrated in sections #12c to #12k.

12z Kinds of Major Sentences

Sentences can be classified grammatically as simple, compound, complex, and compound-complex.

1. Simple Sentences

A simple sentence has one subject and finite verb unit, and therefore it contains only one clause, an independent clause:

    s   **v**
<u>The boat leaks</u>.

      s   **v**
<u>The new website launched</u> last week.

The subject or the verb, or both, can be compound—that is, consist of more than one part—but the sentence containing them will still be simple:

Claude and Qian left early. (compound subject)

She watched and waited. (compound verb)

The sergeant and his troops moved down the hill and crossed the river. (compound subject, compound verb)

2. Compound Sentences

A **compound** sentence consists of two or more simple sentences—that is, independent clauses—linked by coordinating conjunctions (see #23a), by punctuation, or by both:

S   V   S   V
The guitarist's amp overheated, and the show abruptly ended.

S   V   S   V
The clouds massed thickly against the hills; soon the rain fell in torrents.

S   V
The government considered new legislation in the past, but
S   V
the public now demands it.

S   V   S   V
Gabriel's patience and persistence paid off; he not only won
V
the prize but also earned his competitors' respect.

S   V   S   V   S   V
The day was mild, the breeze was warm, and everyone went for a swim.

3. Complex Sentences

A complex sentence consists of one independent clause and one or more subordinate clauses; in the following examples, the subordinate clauses are underlined:

> We believe <u>that we have some original plans for the campaign</u>. (noun clause as direct object)

> The strike was averted <u>before we reported for picket duty</u>. (adverbial clause modifying *was averted*)

> This course is the one <u>that calls for the most field research</u>. (adjectival clause modifying *one*)

> Marco Polo, <u>who left his native Venice as a teenager</u>, returned home after twenty-five years of adventure. (adjectival clause modifying *Marco Polo*)

> <u>When the film ended</u>, the audience burst into applause <u>which lasted several minutes</u>. (adverbial clause modifying *burst*, adjectival clause modifying *applause*)

> <u>Although it seems premature</u>, the government is proceeding with third reading of the legislation. (adverbial clause of concession, in effect modifying the rest of the sentence)

Note that when the meaning is clear, the conjunction *that* introducing a noun clause, or the relative pronouns *that* and *which*, can be omitted:

> He claimed <u>he was innocent</u>.

> . . . the suitcase <u>he had brought with him</u>.

But see the proofreading tip near the end of #43f.1.

4. Compound-Complex Sentences

A compound-complex sentence consists of two or more independent clauses and one or more subordinate clauses:

> **Because the architect knows that the preservation of heritage buildings is vital, she is consulting widely, but as delays have developed, she has grown impatient, and therefore she is thinking of pulling out of a project that represents everything important to her.**

We can analyze this example as follows:

Because the architect knows (adverbial clause)

that the preservation of heritage buildings is vital (noun clause)

she is consulting widely (independent clause)

but (coordinating conjunction)

as delays have developed (adverbial clause)

she has grown impatient (independent clause)

and (coordinating conjunction)

therefore (conjunctive adverb)

she is thinking of pulling out of a project (independent clause)

that represents everything important to her (adjectival clause)

English words fall traditionally into eight categories called **parts of speech**. Five of these can be inflected in one or more ways:

- noun
- pronoun
- verb
- adjective
- adverb

The other three are not inflected:

- preposition
- interjection
- conjunction

Note that the term *inflection* applies only to the change of a word's form within its part of speech. That is, when the noun *girl* is inflected to make it plural, the new form, *girls*, is still a noun; when the pronoun *they* is inflected to *them* or *theirs*, the new forms are still pronouns.

Many words can be changed so that they function as different parts of speech. For example, the noun *centre* can be made into the adjective *central*, or the noun *meaning* into the adjective *meaningful*, or the verb *vacate* into the noun *vacation*. Such changes, however, are not inflections but **derivations**; a word can be *derived* from a word of a different part of speech, often by the addition of one or more suffixes: *trust, trustful, trustfully, trustfulness*. And many words, even without being changed, can serve as more than one part of speech; for example:

She is <u>cool</u> under pressure. (adjective)

Keep your <u>cool</u> in a crisis. (noun)

Relations between the leaders may <u>cool</u> after the debate. (verb)

The word *word* itself can be a noun ("Use this *word* correctly"), a verb ("How will you *word* your reply?"), or an adjective ("*Word* games are fun"). Or consider the versatility of the common word *over*:

The awning hung <u>over</u> the storefront. (preposition)

The battle is <u>over</u>. (adjective)

Write that sentence <u>over</u>. (adverb)

"Roger. Message received. <u>Over</u>." (interjection)

The *form* of a word, then, doesn't always determine its function. What part of speech a word is depends on its *function* in a particular sentence.

The rest of Part III discusses the eight parts of speech—their inflections (if any) and other grammatical properties; their subcategories; how they work with other words in sentences; and some of their important derivatives (verbals)—and calls attention to some of their potential trouble spots, such as **agreement** and a verb's **tenses**.

13 Nouns

A **noun** is a word that names or stands for a person, place, thing, class, concept, quality, or action: *queen, country, river, citizen, freedom, silence, investigation*. **Proper nouns** are names of specific persons, places, or things and begin with a capital letter: *Jessica, Canada*, the *Titanic*. All the others, called **common nouns**, are capitalized only if they begin a sentence:

> **Freedom is a precious commodity.**

> **Investigation leads to discovery.**

or form part of a proper noun:

> **Queen's University**

> **Peace Arch**

> **Red River**

or are personified or otherwise emphasized, most often in poetry:

> **Our noisy years seem moments in the being
> Of the eternal Silence. . . .**
>
> (Wordsworth, "Ode: Intimations of Immortality")

(See #57, on capitalization.)

One can also classify nouns as either **concrete**, for names of tangible items (*doctor, elephant, book*), or **abstract**, for names of intangible things or ideas (*friendship, happiness, history*). (See #66.)

Collective nouns are names of collections or groups often considered as units: *committee, family, flock.* (See #15e and #18f.)

13a Inflection of Nouns

 Nouns can be inflected in two ways: for **number** and for **possessive case**.

1. For Number

Most common concrete nouns that stand for **countable** things are either **singular** or **plural**. And though proper nouns generally name specific persons, places, or things, they too can sometimes logically be inflected for the plural; for example, there are many *Lams* in the telephone book, there are several *Londons*, and since 1948 there have been two *Koreas.* Most singular nouns are inflected to indicate the plural by the addition of *s* or *es*: *boy, boys; box, boxes.* But some are made plural in other irregular ways: *child, children; stimulus, stimuli.* (For more on the formation of plurals, see #61-l.)

Some concrete nouns, however, called **mass** nouns, name materials that are measured, weighed, or divided, rather than counted—for example, *silver, oxygen, rice, soil.* As **uncountable** or **noncountable** nouns, these are not inflected for the plural. Also **uncountable** are **abstract** nouns and nouns that stand for ideas, activities, and states of mind or being—for example, *honour, journalism, skiing, happiness.*

Some nouns, however, can be either countable or uncountable, depending on the context in which they are used. For example:

Plants need <u>soil</u> to grow. (uncountable)

Experienced gardeners know the properties of various <u>soils</u>.
(countable, equivalent to *kinds of soil*)

They insisted on telling the truth as a matter of <u>honour</u>. (uncountable)

Many <u>honours</u> were heaped upon the returning hero. (countable, since honours designates specific things like medals or praises)

(See also #15c, #18g, and #19c.5.)

2. For Possessive Case

As we saw earlier, in English, whether a noun is a *subject* (**subjective** case) or an *object* (**objective** case) is shown by word order rather than inflection. But nouns are inflected for **possessive** case. By adding an apostrophe and an *s*, or sometimes only an apostrophe, you inflect a noun so that it shows possession or ownership: *my mother's job, the children's toys, the students' grades.* (For more on inflecting nouns for possessive case, see #61n.)

13b Grammatical Function of Nouns

Nouns function in sentences in the following ways:

- as the subject of a verb (see #12a):

  Students work hard.

- as the direct object of a verb (see #12d):

  The chef roasted the vegetables.

- as the indirect object of a verb (see #12f):

  Professor Jansen gave the class an assignment.

- as the object of a preposition (see #12e, #12f, and #22):

  Giselle had to write a personal essay about hobbies.

- as a predicate noun after a linking verb (see #12h):

  Quartz is a mineral.

- as an objective complement (see #12j):

  The judges declared Aiden the winner.

- as an appositive to any other noun (see #12q):

  Omar, the author, stood up and introduced *They Made You Want It*, his book on the history of advertising.

Nouns in the *possessive case* function as adjectives (see #19a):

Yoko's project is groundbreaking. (Which project? Yoko's.)

I did a day's work. (How much work? A day's.)

or as predicate nouns, after a linking verb (see #12h):

The expensive-looking coat is Maria's.

Even without being inflected for possessive case, many nouns can also function as adjectives within noun phrases: the *school* mascot, the *automobile* industry, the *dessert* course, and so on (see #71g).

A noun (or pronoun) referring to someone being directly addressed, as in dialogue or in a letter, is called a *noun of address*. Such nouns, usually proper names, are not directly related to the syntax of the rest of the sentence and are set off with punctuation:

Soon, Lea, you'll see what I mean.

14 Pronouns

ONLINE EXERCISES

A pronoun is a word that stands in place of a noun or that functions like a noun in a sentence. Most pronouns refer to nouns that come earlier, their **antecedents**:

Joshua offered an opinion, but he didn't feel confident about it.

Here, *Joshua* is the antecedent of the pronoun *he*, and *opinion* is the antecedent of the pronoun *it*. Occasionally an antecedent can come after the pronoun that refers to it, especially if the pronoun is in a subordinate clause and if the context is clear—that is, if the pronoun couldn't refer to some other noun (see also #16d):

Although he offered an opinion, Joshua didn't feel confident about it.

There are eight different pronoun types:

- personal
- impersonal
- interrogative
- relative

- demonstrative
- indefinite
- reflexive (or intensive)
- reciprocal

Like nouns, pronouns perform several functions: they are most often subjects of verbs, direct and indirect objects, and objects of prepositions; some can also function as appositives and predicate nouns. Some pronouns are inflected much more than nouns, and some require closer proofreading for case, reference, and agreement than you might think.

The following sections discuss the different kinds of pronouns; their inflections; their grammatical functions in phrases, clauses, and sentences; and the special problems of **case** (#14e), **agreement** (#15), and **reference** (#16).

14a Personal Pronouns

Personal pronouns refer to specific persons or things. They are inflected in four ways:

1. For Person

- **First-person** pronouns (*I*, *we*, etc.) refer to the person or persons doing the speaking or writing.
- **Second-person** pronouns (*you*, *yours*) refer to the person or persons being spoken or written to.
- **Third-person** pronouns (*he*, *she*, *it*, *they*, etc.) refer to the person(s) or thing(s) being spoken or written about.

2. For Number

- **Singular** pronouns (*I*, *she*, etc.) refer to individuals.

  I am writing. She is writing.

- **Plural** pronouns (*we*, *they*, etc.) refer to groups.

  We are writing. They are writing.

(Note that the second-person pronoun *you* can be either singular or plural.)

3. For Gender (2nd- and 3rd-person pronouns)

- **Masculine** pronouns (*he*, *him*, *his*) refer to males.
- **Feminine** pronouns (*she*, *her*, *hers*) refer to females.
- The **neuter** pronoun (*it*) refers to ideas or things, and sometimes to animals.

(Note that in the plural forms—*we*, *you*, *they*, etc.—there is no indication of gender.)

4. For Case (see also #14e)

- Pronouns that function as **subjects** must be in the **subjective** case:

  I paint. She paints. They are painting.

- Pronouns that function as **objects**—whether direct or indirect—must be in the **objective** case:

  The idea hit them. Tell her the idea. Tell it to me.

- Pronouns that indicate possession or ownership must be in the **possessive** case:

  That turtle is his. This turtle is mine. Where is yours?

(Note that pronouns in the possessive case—*yours*, *theirs*, *its*, *hers*, etc.—do not take an apostrophe before the *s* to indicate possession.)

The following chart shows all the inflections of personal pronouns:

		subject	object	possessive pronoun	possessive adjective
singular	1st person	I	me	mine	my
	2nd person	you	you	yours	your
	3rd person	he	him	his	his
		she	her	hers	her
		it	it		its
plural	1st person	we	us	ours	our
	2nd person	you	you	yours	your
	3rd person	they	them	theirs	their

Possessive (or **pronominal**) **adjectives** always precede nouns (*My* car is in the shop); **possessive pronouns** may function as subjects, objects, or predicate nouns (Let's take *yours*).

Note that *you* and *it* are inflected only for possessive case, that *his* serves as both possessive pronoun and possessive adjective, and that *her* serves as both object and possessive adjective.

 ## Impersonal Pronouns

Especially in relatively formal contexts, the **impersonal pronoun** *one*, meaning essentially "a person," serves in place of a first-, second-, or third-person pronoun:

> <u>One</u> must be careful when choosing course electives.

> <u>One</u> must keep <u>one</u>'s priorities straight.

The pronoun *it* is also used as an impersonal pronoun in such sentences as the following; note that the impersonal *it* is usually the subject of some form of *be* (see #17f) and that it usually refers to time, weather, distance, and the like:

> <u>It</u> is getting late. <u>It</u>'s almost four o'clock.

> <u>It</u>'s warm. <u>It</u> feels warmer than <u>it</u> did yesterday.

> <u>It</u> is two kilometres from here to the station.

PROOFREADING TIP

Using the Impersonal Pronoun *It*

Edit your work to avoid overuse of the impersonal pronoun *it*. Sentences formed using this pattern are known as weak expletives and sometimes delay unnecessarily the true subject of the sentence. The last example could easily be revised to read *The station is two kilometres from here.*

14c Interrogative Pronouns

Interrogative pronouns are *question words* used usually at or near the beginning of *interrogative sentences* (see #12t). *Who* is inflected for objective and possessive case, *which* for possessive case only:

subjective	objective	possessive
who	whom	whose
which	which	whose
what	what	

Who refers to persons, *which* and *what* to things; *which* sometimes also refers to persons, as in *Which of you is going?* The compound forms *whoever* and *whatever*, and sometimes even *whichever* and *whomever*, can also function as interrogative pronouns. Here are some examples showing interrogative pronouns functioning in different ways:

- as a subject:

  Who said that?

  Which of these experts are you citing?

  What is the expert's name?

- as the direct object of a verb:

  Whom do you suggest for the position?

  What did you give Marcus for his birthday?

- as the object of a preposition (see also #22):

  To whom did you recommend the film?

  To what do I owe this honour?

- as an objective complement:

  What did you call me?

  You've named the baby what?

In front of a noun, an interrogative word functions as an **interrogative adjective**:

> **Whose bag is this?**

> **Which car shall we take?**

For more on *who* and *whom,* see #14e.

 ## Relative Pronouns

A **relative pronoun** usually introduces an *adjectival clause*—called a **relative clause**—in which it functions as subject, object, or object of a preposition. The pronoun links, or *relates*, the clause to an antecedent in the same sentence, a noun, pronoun, or noun phrase that the whole clause modifies.

The principal relative pronouns are *who*, *which*, and *that*. *Who* and *which* are inflected for case:

subjective	objective	possessive
who	whom	whose
which	which	whose
that	that	

Who refers to persons (and sometimes to animals thought of as persons), *which* to things, and *that* to either persons or things. Consider some examples of how relative pronouns function:

> **Ruby, who is playing the drums, is going to be a star.** (*who* as subject of verb *is*; clause modifies *Ruby*)

> **Joel contacted the reporter whom he had met at the crime scene.** (*whom* as direct object; clause modifies *reporter*)

> **At midnight Sula began to revise her essay, which was due in the morning.** (*which* as subject of verb *was*; clause modifies *essay*)

> **She avoided working on the report that she was having trouble with.** (*that* as object of preposition *with*; clause modifies *report*)

A relative clause is either **restrictive** and unpunctuated, or **nonrestrictive** and set off with punctuation. It is **restrictive** if it gives us information that is essential to identifying the antecedent (e.g., *whom he had met at the crime scene*); it is **nonrestrictive** if the information it gives us is not essential to identifying the antecedent and could be left out of the sentence (e.g., *which was due in the morning*). (See also #43f.) If the relative pronoun in a restrictive clause is the object of a verb or a preposition, it can usually be omitted:

> **Joel contacted the reporter** [**whom** or **that**] **he had met.**

> **She avoided working on the report** [**that** or **which**] **she was having trouble with.**

But if the preposition is placed before the relative pronoun (e.g., *with which*), the relative pronoun cannot be omitted:

> **She was working on the report with which she was having trouble.**

And sometimes the relative pronoun is necessary to prevent misreading:

> incorrect: **Different varieties of tea shops sell are medicinal.**

A *that* after *tea* prevents misreading the subject of the verb as *different varieties of tea shops*.

When *whose* precedes and modifies a noun in a relative clause, it functions as what is called a **relative adjective**:

> **Jana was the one whose advice he most valued.**

And sometimes a **relative adverb**, often *when* or *where*, introduces a relative clause (see also #20a):

> **Here's an aerial photo of the town where I live.** (The clause *where I live* modifies the noun *town*.)

> **My parents told me about the time when I ate a crayon.** (The when-clause modifies the noun *time*.)

Sometimes *what* and the *ever*-compounds (*whatever, whoever, whomever, whichever*) are also considered relative pronouns, even though they introduce noun clauses (e.g., "Remember *what I said*." "Take *whichever one you want*."). *Who*, *whom*, and *which* may also introduce such noun clauses.

For more on *who* and *whom*, see #14e. For more on adjectival clauses, see #19 and #26a.

14e Case (see also #14a.4)

ca Determining the correct case of personal, interrogative, and relative pronouns is sometimes challenging. In writing particular sentences and in formal writing generally, the challenge may be to determine whether a pronoun should be in the subjective or objective case. In everyday speech and informal writing, things like "*Who* did you lend the book to?" and "It's *me*" and "That's *her*" are widely accepted. But in formal writing and strictly formal speech, you should use the correct forms: "To *whom* did you lend the book?" and "It is *she*." If you know how a pronoun is functioning grammatically, you will know which form to use. Here are some guidelines to help you with the kinds of sentences that sometimes cause problems:

1. A pronoun functioning as the *subject* should be in the *subjective* case. Be particularly careful whenever you use a pronoun as part of a *compound subject* (see #12z.1). Someone who wouldn't say "*Me* am going to the store" could slip and say something like "Susan and *me* studied hard for the examination" instead of the correct

   Susan and I studied hard for the examination.

   If you're not sure, remove the other part of the subject; then you'll know which pronoun sounds right:

   ~~**Susan and**~~ **I studied hard for the examination.**

   But even a one-part subject can lead someone astray:

   ca: **Us students should stand up for our rights.**
   revised· **We students should stand up for our rights.**

   The pronoun *We* is the subject; the word *students* is an appositive (see #12q) further identifying it, as if saying "We, the students, should . . ."

2. A pronoun functioning as a direct or indirect *object* should be in the *objective* case. Errors most often result from the use of a two-part structure—here, a *compound object*. Someone who would not say "The club asked *I* for my opinion" could slip and say "They asked Ingrid and *I* to take part in the play." When you use a pronoun as part of a compound object, make sure it's in the *objective* case. Again, test by removing the other part:

> They asked ~~Ingrid and~~ <u>me</u> to take part in the play.

PROOFREADING TIP

Hypercorrection of Pronouns

Speakers and writers who have learned that it is incorrect to use *me* as part of a compound subject sometimes mistakenly believe that they should use *I* in the objective case as well. Do not fall into this trap of "hypercorrection."

> My aunt taught Ana and me [not *I*] to fish.
> The new ball was for Jake and me [not *I*].

---

3. A pronoun functioning as the *object* of a preposition should be in the *objective* case:

> ca: This secret is between <u>you</u> and <u>I</u>.
> revised: This secret is between <u>you</u> and <u>me</u>.

Don't be confused by the two-part object; *me* is correct in this instance because it is the object of the preposition *between*.

4. A pronoun functioning as a *predicate noun* (see #12h and #25d) after a linking verb should be in the *subjective* case. In other words, if the pronoun follows the verb *be*, it takes the subjective form:

> It is <u>they</u> who must decide, not <u>we</u>.

> The swimmer who won the prize is <u>she</u>, over there by the pool.

> It is <u>I</u> who will carry the greater burden.

If such usages sound stuffy and artificial to you—as they do to many people—find another way to phrase your sentences; for example:

They, not we, must decide.

The swimmer over by the pool is the one who won the prize.

I will be the one carrying the greater burden.

Again, watch out for compound structures:

ca: **The nominees are Yashmin and me.**

revised: **The nominees are Yashmin and I.**

5. Pronouns following the conjunctions *as* and *than* in comparisons should be in the *subjective* case if they are functioning as subjects, even if their verbs are not expressed but left "understood":

Roberta is as bright as they [are].

Aaron has learned less than I [have].

If, however, the pronouns are functioning as objects, they should be in the *objective case*:

I trust her more than [I trust] him.

See also **so . . . as** in the Usage Checklist, #72.

6. Use the appropriate case of the interrogative and relative pronouns *who* and *whom*, *whoever* and *whomever*. Although *who* is often used instead of *whom* in speech and informal writing, you should know how to use the two correctly when you want to write or speak more formally.

a. Use the *subjective* case for the *subject* of a verb in a question or a relative clause:

Who is your favourite hockey player?

Maurice Richard was a player who was extremely popular in his own time.

b. Use the *objective* case for the *object* of a verb or a preposition:

> **Whom do you prefer in that role?**
>
> **He is the candidate whom I most admire.**
>
> **She is the manager for whom the employees have the most respect.**

If such usages with *whom* seem to you unnatural and stuffy, avoid them by rephrasing:

> **She is the manager that the employees respect most.**

c. In noun clauses, the case of the pronoun is determined by its function in its clause, not by other words:

> **How can you tell who won?** (subjective case)
>
> **I'll give the trophy to whomever the judges declare the winner.** (objective case, object of preposition)

For the possessive case of pronouns with *gerunds*, see #21h.

14f Demonstrative Pronouns

Demonstrative pronouns, which can be thought of as pointing to the nouns they refer to, are inflected for *number*:

singular	plural
this	these
that	those

This and *these* usually refer to something nearby or something just said or about to be said; *that* and *those* usually refer to something farther away or more remote in time or longer in duration; but there are no precise rules:

> **The clerk was helpful; this was what pleased her the most.**
>
> **These are the main points I will cover in today's lecture.**
>
> **That was the story he told us the next morning.**
>
> **Those were his exact words.**

These pronouns also often occur in prepositional phrases with *like* and *such as*:

> Someone who wears a shirt like <u>that</u> has no fashion sense.

> I need more close friends like <u>those</u>.

> A cute house such as <u>this</u> will sell immediately.

PROOFREADING TIP

Avoiding Vagueness in Using Demonstrative Pronouns

Useful as demonstrative pronouns can be, employ them sparingly in writing, for they are often vague in their reference. If you think a demonstrative pronoun is too vague, follow it with a noun to turn it into a *demonstrative adjective*: *this* belief, *that* statement, *these* buildings, *those* arguments. See #16c and #41.

 ## Indefinite Pronouns

 Indefinite pronouns refer to indefinite or unknown persons or things, or to indefinite or unknown quantities of persons or things. The only major issue with these words is whether they are *singular* or *plural*. Think of indefinite pronouns as falling into four groups:

- GROUP 1: compounds ending with *body*, *one*, and *thing*. These words function like nouns—that is, they need no antecedents—and they are almost always considered *singular*:

anybody	everybody	nobody	somebody
anyone	everyone	no one	someone
anything	everything	nothing	something

- GROUP 2: a few other indefinite pronouns that are almost always *singular*:

another	each	either	much
neither	one	other	

- GROUP 3: a few that are always *plural*:

  both   few   many   several

- GROUP 4: a few that can be either *singular* or *plural*, depending on context and intended meaning:

  all   any   more   most
  none   some

For discussions of grammatical agreement with indefinite pronouns, and examples of their use in sentences, see #15c and #18d.

Only *one* and *other* can be inflected for number, by adding *s* to make them plural: *ones*, *others*. Several indefinite pronouns can be inflected for possessive case; unlike personal pronouns, they take *'s*, just as nouns do (or, with *others'*, just an apostrophe):

anybody's   anyone's   everybody's   everyone's
nobody's   no one's   somebody's   someone's
one's   other's   another's   others'

The remaining indefinite pronouns must use *of* to show possession; for example:

That was the belief <u>of many</u> who were present.

When in the possessive case, indefinite pronouns function as adjectives. In addition, all the words in groups 2, 3, and 4, except *none*, can also function as adjectives (see #19a.1):

<u>any</u> boat   <u>some</u> people   <u>few</u> people
<u>more</u> money   <u>each</u> day   <u>either</u> direction

The adjective expressing the meaning of *none* is *no*:

Send <u>no</u> attachments.

Sometimes the cardinal numbers (*one*, *two*, *three*, etc.) and the ordinal numbers (*first*, *second*, *third*, etc.) are also classed as indefinite pronouns, for they often function similarly, both as pronouns and as adjectives:

Do you see any geese? I see <u>several</u>. I see <u>seven</u>.

Do you like these stories? I like <u>some</u>, but not <u>others</u>. I liked the <u>first</u>, but not the <u>second</u> or <u>third</u>.

14h **Reflexive and Intensive Pronouns**

Reflexive and intensive pronouns are formed by adding *self* or *selves* to the possessive form of the first- and second-person personal pronouns, to the objective form of third-person personal pronouns, and to the impersonal pronoun *one* (see #14a and #14b).

singular	plural
myself	ourselves
yourself	yourselves
himself	themselves
herself	themselves
itself	
oneself	

A **reflexive pronoun** is used as an object when that object is the same person or thing as the subject:

> **He treated <u>himself</u> to bubble tea.** (direct object)

> **One should pamper <u>oneself</u> a little.** (direct object)

> **She gave <u>herself</u> a break.** (indirect object)

> **We kept the idea to <u>ourselves</u>.** (object of preposition)

These pronouns are also used as **intensive pronouns** to emphasize a subject or object. An intensive pronoun comes either right after the noun it emphasizes or at the end of the sentence:

> **Although he let the others leave, Ethan <u>himself</u> will stay.**

> **The professor told us to count up our scores <u>ourselves</u>.**

Intensive pronouns are also used in prepositional phrases with *by* to mean "alone" or "without help":

> **I can solve this problem by <u>myself</u>.**

PROOFREADING TIP

Use of Intensive and Reflexive Pronouns

Do not use an intensive or reflexive pronoun as a substitute for a personal pronoun:

The team and I [not *myself*] **played a great game tonight.**

Especially don't use *myself* simply to avoid having to decide whether *I* or *me* is correct in a compound subject or object (see #14e).

14i Reciprocal Pronouns

 Like a reflexive pronoun, a **reciprocal pronoun** refers to the subject of a sentence, but this time the subject is always plural. The two reciprocal pronouns themselves are singular and consist of two words each:

each other (referring to a subject involving two)

one another (referring to a subject involving three or more)

They can be inflected for possessive case by adding *'s*:

each other's **one another's**

These pronouns express some kind of mutual interaction between or among the parts of a plural subject:

The president and the prime minister praised <u>each other's</u> policies.

The computers in this office speak to <u>one another</u>, even though the employees never do.

15 Agreement of Pronouns with Their Antecedents

agr Any pronoun that refers to or stands for an *antecedent* (see #14) must **agree** with—that is, be the same as—that antecedent in **person** (first, second, or third), **number** (singular or plural), and **gender** (masculine, feminine, or neuter). For example:

> **Olivia is learning about social networking so that <u>she</u> will be prepared to make <u>her</u> mark in the world of online marketing.**

Since the proper noun *Olivia*, the antecedent, is in the third person, singular, and feminine, any pronouns that refer to it must also be third-person, singular, and feminine: *she* and *her* thus "agree" grammatically with their antecedent.

The following sections (#15a–f) point out the most common sources of trouble with pronoun agreement. Note that these errors all have to do with *number*—whether a pronoun should be *singular* or *plural*. Mistakes in gender and person also occur, but not as frequently (but see #39d, on shifts in person).

15a Antecedents Joined by *and*

When two or more singular antecedents are joined by *and*, use a *plural* pronoun:

> **Farah and Chloe launched <u>their</u> new magazine.**

If such a compound is preceded by *each* or *every*, however, the pronoun should be *singular*:

> **Each article and editorial has <u>its</u> own title.**

15b Antecedents Joined by *or* or *nor*

When two or more antecedents are joined by *or* or *nor*, use a *singular* pronoun if the antecedents are singular:

Either David or Jonathan will bring <u>his</u> notes.

Neither Maylin nor her mother gave <u>her</u> consent.

If one antecedent is masculine and the other feminine, rephrase the sentence (see #15d).

Use a *plural* pronoun if the antecedents are plural:

Neither the players nor the coaches did <u>their</u> jobs properly.

If the antecedents are mixed singular and plural, a pronoun should agree with the nearest one. But if you move from a plural to a singular antecedent, the sentence will almost inevitably sound awkward; try to construct such sentences so that the last antecedent is plural:

awkward: **Neither the actors nor the director could control <u>his</u> temper.**

revised: **Neither the director nor the actors could control <u>their</u> tempers.**

Note that the awkwardness of the first example extends to gender: if the actors included both men and women, neither *his* nor *her* would be appropriate; see #15d. For more information on agreement of verbs with compound subjects joined by *or* or *nor*, see #18c.

15c Indefinite Pronoun as Antecedent

If the antecedent is an *indefinite pronoun* (see #14g), you'll usually use a *singular* pronoun to refer to it. The indefinite pronouns in Group 1 (the compounds with *body*, *one*, and *thing*) are singular, as are those in Group 2 (*another*, *each*, *either*, *much*, *neither*, *one*, *other*):

<u>Each</u> of the men worked on <u>his</u> own project.

<u>Either</u> of these women is likely to buy that sports car for <u>herself</u>.

<u>Everything</u> has <u>its</u> proper place.

Indefinite pronouns from Group 3 (*both*, *few*, *many*, *several*) are always plural:

> Only a <u>few</u> returned <u>their</u> ballots.

The indefinite pronouns in Group 4 (*all*, *any*, *more*, *most*, *none*, *some*) can be either singular or plural; the intended meaning is usually clear:

> <u>Some</u> of the food on the menu could be criticized for <u>its</u> lack of nutrients.

> <u>Some</u> of the ships in the fleet had been restored to <u>their</u> original beauty.

Here, the mass noun *food* demands the singular sense for *some*, and the countable noun *ships*, in the plural, demands the plural sense. But confusion sometimes arises with the indefinite pronoun *none*. (See also #18d.) Although *none* began by meaning "no one" or "not one," it now commonly has the plural sense:

> <u>None</u> of the boys knew how to fix <u>their</u> bicycles.

With a mass noun, or if your intended meaning is "not a single one," treat *none* as singular:

> <u>None</u> of the food could be praised for <u>its</u> quality.

> <u>None</u> of the boys knew how to fix <u>his</u> bicycle. (Here, you could perhaps even change *None* to *Not one*.)

When any of these words function as *adjectives*, the same principles apply:

> <u>Each</u> man worked on <u>his</u> own project.

> <u>Either</u> woman may buy the car for <u>herself</u>.

> Only a <u>few</u> people returned <u>their</u> ballots.

> <u>Some</u> food can be praised for <u>its</u> nutritional value.

> <u>Some</u> ships had been restored to <u>their</u> original beauty.

Note: The word *every* used as an adjective requires a *singular* pronoun:

Every man has his own project.

15d Pronouns and Inclusive Language: Avoiding Gender Bias

Several indefinite pronouns and indefinite nouns like *person*, as well as many other nouns used in a generalizing way, present an additional challenge: avoiding gender bias.

In centuries past, if a *singular antecedent* had no grammatical gender but could refer to one or more males or females, it was conventional to use the masculine pronoun *he* (*him*, *his*, *himself*) in a generic sense, meaning any person, male or female:

biased: **Everyone present at the lecture raised his hand.**

biased: **A writer should be careful about his diction.**

Today this practice is widely regarded as inappropriate and inaccurate, since it implies, for example, that no women were present at the lecture and that there are no women writers. Merely substituting *she* or *her* in all such instances is no solution, since it represents gender bias as well.

All of us can and should avoid biased language. Colloquially and informally, many writers simply use a plural pronoun:

agr: **Anyone who doesn't pay their taxes is asking for trouble.**

But this practice is grammatically incorrect. In this example, the plural pronoun *their* clashes with the singular verb *is*.

Here are five solutions you can use when writing in a formal context:

1. If you are referring to a group or class consisting entirely of either males or females, use the appropriate pronoun, whether masculine or feminine:

    Everyone in the room raised his hand.

    Everyone in the room raised her hand.

If the group is mixed, try to avoid the problem, for example by using the indefinite article:

Everyone in the room raised a hand.

2.   Often the simplest technique is to make the antecedent itself plural:

All those in the room raised their hands.

Writers should be careful about their diction.

3.   If your purpose and the formality of the context permit, you can use the impersonal pronoun *one*:

One should be careful about one's diction.

If this sounds too formal, consider using the second-person pronoun *you* (but see #16e; you need to be careful when you address the audience directly):

You should be careful about your diction.

4.   Another option is to revise a sentence so that no gendered pronoun is necessary:

Everyone's hand went up.

Sometimes the pronoun can simply be omitted:

A writer should be careful about diction.

5.   But if a sentence doesn't lend itself to such changes, or if you want to keep its original structure for some other reason, you can still manage. Don't resort to strings of unsightly devices such as *he/she*, *him/her*, *her/his*, *him/herself*, or *s/he*. But an occasional *he or she* or *she or he* and the like is acceptable:

If anyone falls asleep, he or she will be asked to leave.

A writer should be careful about her or his diction.

But don't do this too often, as such repetitions can become tedious and cluttering.

See also **man, woman, –ess, etc.** in the Usage Checklist, #72.

 ### Collective Noun as Antecedent

If the antecedent is a *collective noun* (see #13), use either a singular or a plural pronoun to refer to it, depending on context and desired meaning. If the collective noun stands for the group seen as a unit, use a *singular* pronoun:

> The <u>team</u> worked on <u>its</u> power play during the practice.

> The <u>committee</u> announced <u>its</u> decision.

If the collective noun stands for the members of the group seen as individuals, use a *plural* pronoun:

> The <u>team</u> took up <u>their</u> starting positions.

> The <u>committee</u> had no sooner taken <u>their</u> seats than <u>they</u> began chatting among <u>themselves</u>.

 ### Agreement with Demonstrative Adjectives

Demonstrative adjectives must agree in number with the nouns they modify (nouns such as *kind* or *kinds* often cause the most difficulty):

> agr: <u>These kind</u> of snakes are very rare.

> revised: <u>This kind</u> of snake is very rare.

> revised: <u>These kinds</u> of snakes are very rare.

16 Reference of Pronouns

ref

A pronoun's **reference** to an antecedent must be clear. The pronoun or the sentence will not be clear if the antecedent is remote, ambiguous, vague, or missing.

ONLINE EXERCISES

16a Remote Antecedent

An antecedent should be close enough to its pronoun to be unmistakable; your reader shouldn't have to pause and search for it. An antecedent should seldom appear more than one sentence before its pronoun within a paragraph. For example:

ref: **People who expect to find happiness in material things alone may well discover that the life of the mind is more important than the life filled with possessions. Material prosperity may seem fine at a given moment, but in the long run its delights have a way of fading into inconsequential boredom and emptiness. <u>They</u> then realize, too late, where true happiness lies.**

The word *People* is too far back to be a clear antecedent for the pronoun *They*. If the second sentence had also begun with *They*, the connection would be clearer. Or the third sentence might begin with a more particularizing phrase, like "Such people . . ."

16b Ambiguous Reference

A pronoun should refer clearly to only one antecedent:

ref: **When Lea's sister told her that <u>she</u> had won a trip to France, <u>she</u> was very excited.**

Each *she* could refer either to Lea (*her*) or to Lea's sister. When revising such a sentence, don't just insert explanatory parentheses; rephrase the sentence:

weak: **When Lea's sister told her that she (her sister) had won a trip to France, she (Lea) was very excited.**

clear: **Lea was very excited when her sister told her about winning a trip to France.**

clear: **Lea's sister had won a trip to France, and she was very excited when she told Lea about it.**

clear: **Lea was very excited when her sister said, "I won a trip to France!"**

Another example:

> ref: **His second film was far different from his first. It was a war story set in Belgium.**

A pronoun like *it* often refers to the subject of the preceding independent clause, here *second film*, but *it* is also pulled toward the closest noun or pronoun, here *first*. The problem is easily solved by combining the two sentences, reducing the second to a subordinate element:

> clear: **His second film, a war story set in Belgium, was far different from his first.**

> clear: **His second film was far different from his first, which was a war story set in Belgium.**

 ## Vague Reference

Vague reference is usually caused by the demonstrative pronouns *this* and *that* and the relative pronoun *which*:

> ref: **The doctors are overworked, and there are no beds available. This is an intolerable situation for the hospital.**

Another way of writing this would be to change *This*, after a comma, to *which*:

> ref: **The doctors are overworked, and there are no beds available, which is an intolerable situation for the hospital.**

In both sentences there is a problem with vague reference. *This* in the first example and *which* in the second seem to refer to the entire content of the preceding sentence, but they also seem to refer specifically to the fact that there are no beds available in the hospital. Revision is necessary:

> clear: **The overworked doctors and the lack of available beds make for an intolerable situation for the hospital.**

> clear: **The doctors are overworked, and there are no beds available. These two circumstances make for an intolerable situation for the hospital.**

This or *which* can be adequate if the phrasing and meaning are appropriate:

> clear: **It is not only the overworked doctors but also the lack of beds which makes the situation intolerable for the hospital.**

Another example:

> ref: **Othello states many times that he loves Iago and that he thinks he is a very honest man; Iago uses <u>this</u> to his advantage.**

The third *he* is possibly ambiguous, but more problematic is the vague reference of *this*. Changing *this* to *this opinion*, *these feelings*, *this attitude*, *these mistakes*, *this blindness of Othello's*, or even *Othello's blindness* makes the reference clearer. Even the *his* is slightly ambiguous: *Iago takes advantage of* would be better.

And don't catch the "this" virus; sufferers from it are driven to begin a large proportion of their sentences and other independent clauses with a *this*. Whenever you catch yourself beginning with a *this*, look carefully to see

- if the reference to the preceding clause, sentence, or paragraph is as clear on paper as it may be in your mind;
- if the *this* could be replaced by a specific noun or noun phrase, or otherwise avoided (e.g., by rephrasing or subordinating);
- whether, if you decide to keep *this*, it is an ambiguous demonstrative pronoun; if so, try to make it a demonstrative adjective, giving it a noun to modify—even if the result is no more specific than "This idea," "This fact," or "This argument" (see #14f and #41).

And always check if an opening *This* looks back to a noun that is in fact singular; it may be that "These ideas," "These facts," or "These arguments" would be more appropriate.

16d Missing Antecedent

Sometimes a writer may have an antecedent in mind but fail to write it down:

> ref: **After the mayor's speech <u>he</u> agreed to answer questions from the audience.**

The implied antecedent of *he* is *mayor*, but it isn't there, for the possessive *mayor's* functions as an adjective rather than a noun. Revise the sentence to include a clear antecedent:

clear: **When <u>the mayor</u> finished <u>his</u> speech, he agreed to answer questions from the audience.**

clear: **At the end of <u>his</u> speech, <u>the mayor</u> agreed to answer questions from the audience.**

Note that in this last version, *his* comes before its supposed "antecedent," *mayor*—an unusual pattern, but one that is acceptable if the context is clear (e.g., if no other possible antecedent for *his* occurred in the preceding sentence) and if the two are close together.

ref: **Whenever a student assembly is called, <u>they</u> are required to attend.**

Since *student* here functions as an adjective, it cannot serve as an antecedent for *they*. It is necessary to replace *they* with *students*—and then one would probably want to omit the original *student*. Or one could change "student assembly" to "an assembly of students" and retain *they*.

16e Indefinite *you*, *they*, and *it*

In formal writing, avoid the pronouns *you*, *they*, and *it* when they are indefinite:

informal: **In order to graduate, <u>you</u> must have at least 120 course credits.**

formal: **In order to graduate, a student must have at least 120 course credits.**

informal: **In some cities <u>they</u> do not have enough recycling facilities.**

formal: **Some cities do not have enough recycling facilities.**

formal: **Some cities' recycling facilities are inadequate.**

Although it is correct to use the expletive or impersonal *it* (see #12k and #29f) and say "*It* is raining," "*It* is seven o'clock," and so on, avoid such indefinite uses of *it* as the following:

informal: **It states in our textbook that we should be careful how we use the pronoun *it*.**

formal: **Our textbook states that we should be careful how we use the pronoun *it*.**

17 Verbs

Verbs are core parts of speech. A verb is the focal point of a clause or a sentence. Standard sentences consist of subjects and predicates: every subject has a predicate, and the heart of every predicate is its verb.

Verbs are often called "action" words; yet some verbs express little or no action. Think of verbs as expressing not only *action* but also *occurrence*, *process*, and *condition* or *state of being*. All verbs *assert* or *ask* something about their subjects, sometimes by *linking* a subject with a complement. Some verbs are single words; others are phrases consisting of two or more words. Here are some sentences with the verbs underlined:

He **makes** gourmet cupcakes.

Zarmina **is** a perfectionist.

I **am running** a marathon.

The CN Tower **was completed** in 1976.

By the end of the year, I **will have written** more than thirty essays.

Did you **knit** that scarf?

The two columns of figures **came out** even.

(For a discussion of such two-part verbs as *come out* and *set out*, see #22d.)

Kinds of Verbs: Transitive, Intransitive, and Linking

Verbs are classified according to the way they function in sentences.

A verb normally taking a *direct object* is considered a **transitive verb**. A transitive verb makes a transition, or conveys a movement, from its subject to its object:

> I <u>invited</u> Noam to the party.

> She <u>expresses</u> her ideas eloquently.

> He <u>stuffed</u> himself with marshmallows.

A direct object answers the question consisting of the verb and *what* or *whom*: Invited *whom*? Noam. Expresses *what*? Ideas. Stuffed *whom*? Himself. (See also #12d, #12f, #12i, and #12j.)

A verb that normally occurs without a direct object is considered **intransitive** (see also #12c):

> The earthquake <u>occurred</u> during the night.

> He <u>gossiped</u> with his roommate.

> What <u>has happened</u> to the aquarium's whale?

Many verbs can be either transitive or intransitive, depending on how they function in particular sentences:

> I <u>ran</u> my school's newspaper. (transitive)

> I <u>ran</u> to the store. (intransitive)

A third kind of verb is called a **linking** or copulative verb. The main one is *be* in its various forms. Some other common linking verbs are *become*, *seem*, *remain*, *act*, *get*, *feel*, *look*, *appear*, *smell*, *sound*, and *taste*.

Linking verbs don't have objects, but they are yet incomplete; they need a **subjective complement**. A linking verb is like an equal sign in an equation: something at the right-hand (predicate) end is needed to balance what is at the left-hand (subject) end. The complement will be either a *predicate noun* or a *predicate adjective* (see also #12g and #12h). Here are some examples:

Angela <u>is</u> a lawyer. (predicate noun: *lawyer*)
Angela <u>is</u> not well. (predicate adjective: *well*)

Mikhail <u>became</u> a pilot. (predicate noun: *pilot*)
Mikhail <u>became</u> uneasy. (predicate adjective: *uneasy*)

Verbs such as *act, sound, taste, smell,* and *feel* can also function as transitive verbs: She *acted* the part. He *sounded* his horn. He *smelled* the hydrogen sulphide. I *tasted* the soup. He *felt* the bump on his head.

Similarly, many of these verbs can also function as regular intransitive verbs, sometimes accompanied by *adverbial* modifiers (see #20): We *looked* at the painting. Santa *is* on the roof. Teresa *is* at home. We *are* here. But whenever one of these verbs is accompanied by a predicate noun or a predicate adjective, it is functioning as a linking verb.

 ## 17b Inflection of Verbs: Principal Parts

 As well as being important in spoken and written communication, verbs are also the most complex, the most highly inflected, of the eight parts of speech. Verbs are inflected

- for **person** and **number**, in order to agree with a subject (#17d);
- for **tense**, in order to show an action's time—present, past, or future—and aspect—simple, perfect, or progressive (#17g);
- for **mood**, in order to show the kind of sentence a verb is in—indicative, imperative, or subjunctive (#17k); and
- for **voice**, in order to show whether a subject is active (performing an action) or passive (being acted upon) (#17-l).

Every verb (except some auxiliaries; see #17e) has what are called its **principal parts**:

1. its **basic form** (the form a dictionary uses in headwords, see #63c),
2. its **past-tense form**,
3. its **past participle**, and
4. its **present participle**

Verbs regularly form both the *past tense* and the *past participle* simply by adding *ed* to the basic form. If the basic form already ends in *e*, however, only *d* is added:

basic form	past-tense form	past participle
push	pushed	pushed
move	moved	moved
agree	agreed	agreed

Present participles are regularly formed by adding *ing* to the basic form. For verbs ending in an unpronounced *e*, the final *e* is usually dropped before *ing* is added:

basic form	present participle
push	pushing
move	moving
agree	agreeing

Some verbs double a final consonant before adding *ed* or *ing*:

grin	grinned	grinning
stop	stopped	stopping

For more on these and other irregularities, see #61d–f. Further, good dictionaries list any irregular principal parts, ones not formed by simply adding *ed* or *ing* (and see #17c).

It is from these four parts—the basic form and the three principal inflections of it—that all other inflected forms of a verb are made.

Note: The basic form of a verb is sometimes called the **infinitive** form, meaning that it can be preceded by *to* to form an infinitive: *to be, to push, to agree*. Infinitives, participles, and gerunds are called **non-finite verbs**, or **verbals**; they function not as verbs but as other parts of speech (see #21a–g). **Finite verbs**, unlike non-finite forms, are restricted or limited by person, number, tense, mood, and voice; they function as the main verbs in sentences.

17c Irregular Verbs

 Some of the most common English verbs are **irregular** in the way they make their past-tense forms and their past participles. Whenever you aren't certain about the principal parts of a verb, check your dictionary, or use the following list, which contains most of the common irregular verbs with their past-tense forms and their past participles. If you're looking for a verb that is a compound or that has a prefix, look for the main verb: for *misread*, *proofread*, or *reread*, look under *read* instead. (For the inflection of the irregular verbs do, be, and have, see #17f.)

basic form	past-tense form	past participle
arise	arose	arisen
awake	awoke	awoken
bear	bore	borne (*born* for "given birth to")
beat	beat	beaten
become	became	become
begin	began	begun
bend	bent	bent
bet	bet	bet
bid	bid	bid
bind	bound	bound
bite	bit	bitten
bleed	bled	bled
blow	blew	blown
break	broke	broken
breed	bred	bred
bring	brought	brought
build	built	built
burn	burned, burnt	burned, burnt
burst	burst	burst
buy	bought	bought
cast	cast	cast
catch	caught	caught
choose	chose	chosen
cling	clung	clung
come	came	come
cost	cost	cost

basic form	past-tense form	past participle
creep	crept	crept
cut	cut	cut
deal	dealt	dealt
dig	dug	dug
dive	dived, dove	dived
draw	drew	drawn
dream	dreamed, dreamt	dreamed, dreamt
drink	drank	drunk
drive	drove	driven
eat	ate	eaten
fall	fell	fallen
feed	fed	fed
feel	felt	felt
fight	fought	fought
find	found	found
fit	fit, fitted	fit, fitted
flee	fled	fled
fling	flung	flung
fly	flew	flown
forbid	forbade, forbad	forbidden
forget	forgot	forgotten
forgive	forgave	forgiven
forgo	forwent	forgone
forsake	forsook	forsaken
freeze	froze	frozen
get	got	got, gotten
give	gave	given
go	went	gone
grind	ground	ground
grow	grew	grown
hang	hung (*hanged* for "executed")	hung (*hanged* for "executed")
hear	heard	heard
hide	hid	hidden
hit	hit	hit
hold	held	held
hurt	hurt	hurt
input	input, inputted	input, inputted
keep	kept	kept

basic form	past-tense form	past participle
kneel	knelt, kneeled	knelt, kneeled
knit	knitted, knit	knitted, knit
know	knew	known
lay	laid	laid
lead	led	led
leap	leaped, leapt	leaped, leapt
leave	left	left
lend	lent	lent
let	let	let
lie ("recline")	lay	lain
light	lit, lighted	lit, lighted
lose	lost	lost
make	made	made
mean	meant	meant
meet	met	met
mimic	mimicked	mimicked
mow	mowed	mowed, mown
panic	panicked	panicked
pay	paid	paid
prove	proved	proven, proved
put	put	put
quit	quit	quit
read	read (changes pronunciation)	read (changes pronunciation)
rid	rid	rid
ride	rode	ridden
ring	rang	rung
rise	rose	risen
run	ran	run
say	said	said
see	saw	seen
seek	sought	sought
sell	sold	sold
send	sent	sent
set	set	set
sew	sewed	sewn, sewed
shake	shook	shaken
shed	shed	shed
shine ("glow")	shone	shone
shoot	shot	shot

basic form	past-tense form	past participle
show	showed	shown, showed
shrink	shrank, shrunk	shrunk
shut	shut	shut
sing	sang	sung
sink	sank, sunk	sunk
sit	sat	sat
sleep	slept	slept
slide	slid	slid
sling	slung	slung
slit	slit	slit
sneak	snuck, sneaked	snuck, sneaked
sow	sowed	sown, sowed
speak	spoke	spoken
speed	sped, speeded	sped, speeded
spend	spent	spent
spin	spun	spun
spit	spat, spit	spat, spit
split	split	split
spread	spread	spread
spring	sprang, sprung	sprung
stand	stood	stood
steal	stole	stolen
stick	stuck	stuck
sting	stung	stung
stink	stank, stunk	stunk
stride	strode	stridden
strike	struck	struck
string	strung	strung
strive	strove, strived	striven, strived
swear	swore	sworn
sweep	swept	swept
swell	swelled	swollen, swelled
swim	swam	swum
swing	swung	swung
take	took	taken
teach	taught	taught
tear	tore	torn
tell	told	told
think	thought	thought

basic form	past-tense form	past participle
thrive	throve, thrived	thriven, thrived
throw	threw	thrown
thrust	thrust	thrust
traffic	trafficked	trafficked
tread	trod	trodden, trod
understand	understood	understood
wake	woke, waked	woken, waked
wear	wore	worn
weep	wept	wept
wet	wet, wetted	wet, wetted
win	won	won
wind	wound	wound
withdraw	withdrew	withdrawn
wring	wrung	wrung
write	wrote	written

Inflection for Person and Number

 In order to agree with its subject (see #18), a verb is inflected for *person* and *number*. To illustrate, here are two verbs inflected for person and number in the *present tense*, using personal pronouns as subjects (see #14a):

singular

1st person	I walk	I fly
2nd person	you walk	you fly
3rd person	he walks	he flies
	she walks	she flies
	it walks	it flies

plural

1st person	we walk	we fly
2nd person	you walk	you fly
3rd person	they walk	they fly

Note that the inflection occurs *only in the third-person singular*, and that you add *s* or *es* to the basic form (first changing the final *y* to *i* where necessary; see #61e).

Auxiliary Verbs

 Auxiliary or helping verbs go with other verbs to form verb phrases indicating tense, voice, and mood. The auxiliary *do* helps in forming questions (see #12t), forming negative sentences, and expressing emphasis:

> **Do** you go to class every day?
>
> I **did not** know the answer.
>
> I **did** do my homework!

Modal Auxiliaries

There are also what are called **modal auxiliaries**. The principal ones are *can*, *could*, *may*, *might*, *must*, *should*, and *would*. They combine with main verbs and other auxiliaries to express such meanings as ability, possibility, obligation, and necessity.

The following chart illustrates the principal modal verbs currently in use:

the modal	used to express ...
can	ability
could	ability, possibility
may	permission, possibility
might	
ought to	obligation
should	
must	
shall	probability, prediction, intention
will	
should	condition
would	

Consider the following examples:

> I **can** study tonight.
>
> There **could** be a quiz tomorrow.
>
> I **would** tell you the answer if I **could**.
>
> The instructor **may** decide to cancel the quiz.

Note that the equivalent phrases *able to* (*can*), *ought to* (*should*), and *have to* (*must*) also function as modal auxiliaries. In addition, note the following:

- *Could*, *might*, *would*, and *should* also serve as the past-tense forms of *can*, *may*, *will*, and *shall*, respectively. These past-tense forms appear most often when demanded by the sequence of tenses after a verb in the past tense (see #17h.2):

  He <u>was</u> sure that I <u>could</u> handle the project.

  She <u>said</u> that I <u>might</u> watch the rehearsal if I <u>was</u> quiet.

  I <u>hoped</u> that I <u>would</u> (or <u>should</u>) win.

  (For the distinction between *can* and *may*, see can, may in the Usage Checklist, #72.)

- *Might* and *may* are sometimes interchangeable when expressing possibility:

  She <u>may</u> <u>(might)</u> challenge the committee's decision.

  He <u>may</u> <u>(might)</u> have finished the job by now.

  But usually there is a difference, with *may* indicating a stronger possibility, *might* a somewhat less likely one. To express a condition contrary to fact (see #17k), *might* is the right word:

  If you had edited your essay, you <u>might</u> [not may] have received a higher grade.

  That is, you *didn't* edit carefully, and you *didn't* get a higher grade. *Might* is necessary for clear expression of a hypothetical as opposed to a factual circumstance.

  Like forms of *do*, modal auxiliaries can join with the contraction *n't*: *can't*, *couldn't*, *shouldn't*, *wouldn't*, *mustn't*. In addition, *can* can join with the word *not*: *cannot*. Unlike other verbs, modal auxiliaries are not inflected for third-person singular (see #17d):

He or she or it can go.

Nor do these verbs have any participial forms, or an infinitive form (one cannot say *to can*; instead, one must use another verb phrase, *to be able*). But modal auxiliaries can work as parts of certain tenses (see #17g). (For more on modal auxiliaries, see #17k.)

17f Inflection of *do*, *be*, and *have*

Do, *be*, and *have* are different from the other auxiliaries in that they can also function as main verbs. As a main verb, *do* most often has the sense of "perform, accomplish":

I <u>do</u> my job. He <u>did</u> what I asked. She <u>does</u> her best.

Have as a main verb most often means "own, possess, contain":

I <u>have</u> enough money. July <u>has</u> thirty-one days.

And *be* as a main verb can mean "exist" or "live" (I think; therefore I *am*), but most often means "occur, remain, occupy a place":

The exam <u>is</u> today. I won't <u>be</u> more than an hour. The car <u>is</u> in the garage.

(See your dictionary for other meanings of these verbs.)

Even when functioning as auxiliaries, these verbs are fully inflected. Here are the inflections for *do* and *have*, which, as you can see, are irregular:

singular

1st person	I do	I have
2nd person	you do	you have
3rd person	he does	he has
	she does	she has
	it does	it has

plural

1st person	we do	we have
2nd person	you do	you have
3rd person	they do	they have
past-tense form	did	had
past participle	done	had
present participle	doing	having

The most common verb of all, *be*, is also the most irregular:

singular	present tense	past tense
1st person	I am	I was
2nd person	you are	you were
3rd person	he / she / it is	he / she / it was

plural		
1st person	we are	we were
2nd person	you are	you were
3rd person	they are	they were
past participle	been	
present participle	being	

For a fuller discussion of tense, see the next section.

17g Time and the Verb: Inflection for Tense

 Even though verbs must agree with their subjects in person and number (see #17d and #18), they are still the strongest elements in sentences because they not only indicate action but also control time. The verb by its inflection indicates the *time* of an action, event, or condition. Through its **tense** a verb shows *when* an action occurs:

past tense: **Yesterday, I <u>practised</u>.**

present tense: **Today, I <u>practise</u>.**

future tense: **Tomorrow, I <u>will practise</u>.**

Here, the adverbs *yesterday*, *today*, and *tomorrow* emphasize the *when* of the action, but the senses of past, present, and future are clear without them.

Following are brief descriptions and illustrations of the main functions of each tense. Although these points are sometimes oversimplifications of very complex matters, and although there are other exceptions and variations than those listed, these guidelines should help you to use the tenses and to take advantage of the possibilities they offer for clear expression.

tense		verb form
1. Simple Present	I / you	dance
	he / she / it	dances
	we / you / they	dance
2. Simple Past	I / you / he / she / it / we / you / they	danced
3. Simple Future	I / you / he / she / it / we / you / they	will dance
4. Present Perfect	he / she / it	has danced
	I / you / we / you / they	have danced
5. Past Perfect	I / you / he / she / it / we / you / they	had danced
6. Future Perfect	I / you / he / she / it / we / you / they	will have danced
7. Present Progressive	I	am dancing
	you	are dancing
	he / she / it	is dancing
	we / you / they	are dancing
8. Past Progressive	I	was dancing
	you	were dancing
	he / she / it	was dancing
	we / you / they	were dancing
9. Future Progressive	I / you / he / she / it / we / you / they	will be dancing
10. Present Perfect Progressive	I / you	have been dancing
	he / she / it	has been dancing
	we / you / they	have been dancing
11. Past Perfect Progressive	I / you / he / she / it / we / you / they	had been dancing
12. Future Perfect Progressive	I / you / he / she / it / we / you / they	will have been dancing

1. Simple Present

Generally, use this tense to describe an action or condition that is happening now, at the time of the utterance:

The pitcher <u>throws</u>. The batter <u>swings</u>. It <u>is</u> a high fly ball.

But this tense has several other common uses. It can indicate a general truth or belief:

Ottawa <u>is</u> one of the coldest capitals in the world.

or describe a customary or habitual or repeated action or condition:

I plant trees as a hobby.

or describe the characters or events in a literary or other work, or what an author does in such a work (see #17j):

In the novel, owls deliver the mail to the school.

or even express future time, especially with the help of an adverbial modifier of time (see also number 7 on the present progressive below):

He arrives tomorrow. (adverbial modifier: tomorrow)

2. Simple Past

Use this tense for a single or repeated action or condition that began and ended in the past (compare number 4 on the present perfect below):

She earned a lot of money last summer.

I was happy yesterday.

3. Simple Future

Although there are other ways to indicate future time (see, for example, number 1 on the simple present above and number 7 on the present progressive below), the most common and straightforward is to use the simple future, putting *will* or *shall* before the basic form of the verb:

She will arrive tomorrow morning.

I shall be happy tomorrow.

4. Present Perfect

Use this tense for an action or condition that began in the past and that continues to the present (compare number 2 on the simple past above); though commonly considered "completed" as of the moment, some actions or conditions referred to in this tense could continue after the present:

I have earned a lot of money this summer.

James Bond has just entered the casino.

You can use this tense for something that occurred entirely in the past, if you intend to imply the sense of "before now" or "so far" or "already":

I have painted a picture; take a look at it.

I have visited Greece three times.

5. Past Perfect

Use this tense for an action completed in the past before a specific past time or event. Notice that there are at least two actions taking place in the past:

Though I had seen the film twice before, I went again last week.

6. Future Perfect

Use this tense for an action or condition that will be completed before a specific future time or event:

I will already have eaten when you arrive.

7. Present Progressive

Use this tense for an action or condition that began at some past time and is continuing now, in the present:

Global warming is causing a significant rise in sea levels.

Sometimes the simple and the progressive forms of a verb say much the same thing:

We hope for snow. We are hoping for snow.

But usually the progressive form emphasizes an activity, or the singleness or continuing nature of an action, rather than a larger condition or general truth:

A tax hike hurts many people.

The tax hike is hurting many people.

Like the simple present, the present progressive tense can also express future time, especially with adverbial help:

They <u>are arriving</u> early tomorrow morning.

You can also express future time with a form of *be* and *going* before an infinitive (see #21a):

They <u>are going</u> to walk around Stanley Park on New Year's day.

Stative verbs—verbs that express senses or cognitive or emotional states—don't often appear in the progressive form. Unless the stative verb is expressing an action, do not use it in the progressive tense.

incorrect: **After being sprayed by the skunk, the dog is smelling bad now.** (condition)

correct: **After having its nose injured, the dog is smelling poorly.** (activity)

Here is a short list of some common stative verbs:

appear	**appreciate**	**be**	**believe**	**dislike**
feel	**hear**	**imagine**	**know**	**like**
look	**love**	**remember**	**resemble**	**seem**
smell	**understand**	**want**	**wish**	

8. Past Progressive

Use this tense for an action that was in progress during some past time, especially if you want to emphasize the continuing nature of the action:

I remember that I <u>was painting</u> a picture that day.

Sometimes the past progressive tense describes an interrupted action or an action during which something else happens:

When the telephone rang I <u>was making</u> tempura.

9. Future Progressive

Use this tense for a continuing action in the future or for an action that will be occurring at some specific time in the future:

I <u>will be painting</u> pictures as long as I can hold a brush.

10. Present Perfect Progressive

Use this tense to emphasize the continuing nature of a single or repeated action that began in the past and that has continued at least up to the present. This tense is suitable for showing trends in the sense of showing changes over time.

I <u>have been working</u> on this sketch for an hour.

The profits <u>have been increasing</u> in the last quarter.

11. Past Perfect Progressive

Use this tense to emphasize the continuing nature of a single or repeated past action that was completed before or interrupted by some other past action:

We <u>had been expecting</u> something quite different.

I <u>had been pondering</u> the problem for an hour when suddenly the solution popped into my head.

12. Future Perfect Progressive

This tense is seldom used in academic writing. Use it to emphasize the continuing nature of a future action before a specific time in the future or before a second future action:

If she continues to dance, by the year 2020 she <u>will have been dancing</u> for over half her life.

17h Sequence of Tenses

When two or more verbs occur in the same sentence, they will sometimes be of the same tense, but often they will be of different tenses.

1. Compound Sentences

In a compound sentence, made up of two or more independent clauses (see #12z.2), the verbs can be equally independent; use whatever tenses the sense requires:

> **I am leaving** [present progressive] **now, but she will leave** [future] **in the morning.**

> **The polls have closed** [present perfect]; **the clerks will** soon **be counting** [future progressive] **the ballots.**

2. Past Tense in Independent Clauses

In complex or compound-complex sentences, if the verb in an independent clause is in any of the past tenses, the verbs in any clauses subordinate to it will usually also be in one of the past tenses. For example:

> **I told her that I was sorry.**

> **They agreed that this time the newly elected treasurer would not be a gambler.**

Refer to a time *earlier* than that of the verb in the simple past tense by using the *past perfect* tense:

> **We had left the party before they arrived.**

But there are exceptions. When the verb in the subordinate clause states a general or timeless truth or belief, or something characteristic or habitual, it stays in the present tense:

> **Einstein showed that space, time, and light are linked.**

And the context of the sentence sometimes dictates that other kinds of verbs in subordinate clauses should not be changed to a past tense. If you feel that a tense other than the past would be clearer or more accurate, use it; for example:

> I <u>learned</u> yesterday that I <u>will be able</u> to get into the new program in the fall.

The rule calls for *would*, but *will* is logical and clear. Notice that the adverbial marker "in the fall" tells us the action will occur in the future.

Here is an example of a sentence in which the "sequence of tenses" rule is best ignored:

> The secretary <u>told</u> me this morning that Professor Barnes <u>is</u> ill and <u>will</u> not <u>be teaching</u> class this afternoon.

17i Verb Phrases in Compound Predicates

When a compound predicate consists of two verb phrases in different tenses, don't omit part of one of them:

> t: **The leader has never and will never practise nepotism.**

Rather, include each verb in full or rephrase the sentence:

> revised: **The leader has never practised and will never practise nepotism.**

> revised: **The leader has never practised nepotism and will never do so.**

17j Tenses in Writing About Literature

When discussing or describing the events in a literary work, it is customary to use the present tense (see also #17g.1):

> While he <u>is</u> away from Denmark, Hamlet <u>arranges</u> to have Rosencrantz and Guildenstern put to death. After he <u>returns</u> he <u>holds</u> Yorick's skull and <u>watches</u> Ophelia being buried. He <u>duels</u> with Laertes and <u>dies</u>. Without a doubt, death <u>is</u> one of the principal themes in the play.

For the tenses of infinitives and participles, see #21b and #21e.

It is also customary to speak even of a long-dead author in the present tense when one is discussing his or her techniques in a particular work:

In *Pride and Prejudice,* Jane Austen shows the consequences of making hasty judgments of others.

17k Mood

English verbs are usually considered to have three moods. The most common mood is the indicative, which is used for statements of fact or opinion and for questions:

The weather forecast for tomorrow <u>sounds</u> promising.

The **imperative** mood is used for most commands and instructions (see #12u):

<u>Put</u> the extra suitcase in the trunk.

The **subjunctive** mood in English is less common, and it presents some challenges. It is discussed below.

Using the Subjunctive

The subjunctive is fading from contemporary English. You need consider only two kinds of instances where the subjunctive still functions.

1. Use the subjunctive in a *that*-clause after verbs expressing demands, obligations, requirements, recommendations, suggestions, wishes, and the like:

   The doctor recommended that she <u>take</u> a sea voyage.

   I wish [that] I <u>were</u> in Paris.

2. Use the subjunctive to express conditions that are hypothetical or impossible—often in *if*-clauses or their equivalents:

   He looked as if he <u>were</u> going to explode. (But he didn't explode.)

   If Lise <u>were</u> here she <u>would</u> back me up. (But she isn't here.)

An *as if*– or *as though*–clause almost always expresses a condition contrary to fact, but not all *if*-clauses do; don't be misled into using a subjunctive where it's not appropriate:

> incorrect: **He said that if there <u>were</u> another complaint he would resign.**

The verb should be *was*, for the condition could turn out to be true: there may be another complaint.

Since only a few subjunctive forms differ from those of the indicative, they are easy to learn and remember. The third-person-singular subjunctive form loses its *s*:

> indicative: **I like the way she <u>paints</u>.**
> subjunctive: **I suggested that she <u>paint</u> my portrait.**

The subjunctive forms of the verb *be* are *be* and *were*:

> indicative: **He <u>is</u> friendly. (I <u>am</u>, you / we / they <u>are</u>)**
> subjunctive: **The judge asked that she <u>be</u> excused. (that I / you / we / they <u>be</u>)**

> indicative: **I know that I <u>am</u> in Edmonton.**
> subjunctive: **I wish that I <u>were</u> in Florence.**

Note that both *be* and *were* function with either singular or plural subjects. Note also that the past-tense form *were* functions in present-tense expressions of wishes and contrary-to-fact conditions. Other verbs also use their past tense as a subjunctive after a present-tense wish:

> **I wish that I <u>shopped</u> less.**

After a past-tense wish, use the standard past-perfect form:

> **He wished that he <u>had been</u> more attentive.**

> **She wished that she <u>had played</u> better.**

Using Modal Auxiliaries and Infinitives Instead of Subjunctives

The *modal auxiliaries* (see #17e) offer common alternatives to many sentences using subjunctives; they express several of the same moods:

> **The doctor told her she <u>should</u> [<u>ought to</u>] live in a less polluted area.**

> **I wish that I <u>could</u> be in Paris.**

> **He looked as if he <u>might</u> explode.**

Another alternative uses the *infinitive* (see #21a):

> **It is necessary for us <u>to be</u> there before noon.**

> **The judge ordered Ralph <u>to attend</u> the hearing.**

17-l Voice: Active and Passive

pas

ONLINE EXERCISES

There are two voices, **active** and **passive**. The active voice is direct: *I made this toy boat.* The passive voice is less direct, reversing the normal subject–verb–object pattern: *This toy boat was made by me* (see #12e). The verb uses some form of *be* followed by a past participle: *was made*. What in active voice would be a direct object (*boat*) in passive voice becomes the subject of the verb. And passive constructions often leave unmentioned the agent of the action or state they describe: *The toy boat was made* (by whom isn't specified).

Using the passive voice, some people can promise action without committing themselves to perform it, and they can admit error without accepting responsibility:

> passive: **An error has been made in your account, but be assured that action will be taken.**

Who made the error? Who is doing the assuring? Who will take action? The details are unclear. When possible, use the direct and more vigorous active voice:

> active: **<u>We</u> made an error in your account, but <u>I</u> can assure you that <u>I</u> will look into the matter and correct it immediately.**

Passive constructions can also lead to a *dangling modifier* (see #36):

passive: **Mixing the chemicals, hydrogen sulphide was formed.**

In this sentence, there is no subject to explain who is doing the mixing. The active voice eliminates the grammatical error:

active: **By mixing the chemicals, the chemist produced hydrogen sulphide.**

When to Use the Passive Voice (See also #29f)

Use the passive voice when the active voice is impossible or when the passive is for some other reason clearly preferable or demanded by the context. Generally, use the passive voice

- when the agent, or doer of the act, is indefinite or not known;
- when the agent is less important than the act itself; or
- when you want to emphasize either the agent or the act by putting it at the beginning or end of the sentence.

For example:

It was reported that there were two survivors.

Here, the writer doesn't know who did the reporting. To avoid the passive by saying "Someone reported that there were two survivors" would oddly stress the mysterious "someone." And the fact that *someone reported* it is less important than the content of the report.

The meteor's descent was witnessed by more than thirty people.

Here, the writer emphasizes the large number of witnesses by putting them at the end of the sentence, the most emphatic point in the utterance.

Note: Don't confuse passive constructions with the past tense just because the past participle is used. Passive constructions can appear in any of the tenses.

18 Agreement Between Subject and Verb

agr A verb should agree with its subject in number and person. Here are the main circumstances to watch out for while editing a first or subsequent draft:

18a Words Intervening Between Subject and Verb

When something plural comes between a singular subject and its verb, the verb must still agree with the subject:

> Far below, a <u>landscape</u> of rolling brown hills and small trees <u>lies</u> among the small cottages.

> <u>Each</u> of the plans <u>has</u> certain advantages.

> <u>Neither</u> of the parties <u>was</u> willing to compromise.

Similarly, don't let an intervening singular noun affect the agreement between a plural subject and its verb.

> The <u>contents</u> of the bag—an assortment of spoons—<u>were</u> surprising.

18b Compound Subject: Singular Nouns Joined by *and*

A compound subject made up of two or more singular nouns joined by *and* is usually plural:

> A personal trainer and a Pilates instructor <u>are</u> hosting the event.

> Coffee and tea <u>were</u> served with dessert.

Occasional exceptions occur. If two nouns identify the same person or thing, or if two nouns taken together are thought of as a unit, the verb is singular:

> A common-law spouse and father <u>has</u> an obligation to share the domestic responsibilities.

> Macaroni and cheese <u>is</u> a student favourite.

18c Compound Subject: Parts Joined by *or* or a Correlative

When the parts of a subject are joined by the coordinating conjunction *or* (see #23a) or by the correlative conjunctions *either . . . or, neither . . . nor, not . . . but, not only . . . but also, whether . . . or* (see #23b), the part nearest the verb determines whether the verb is singular or plural:

> One or the other of you <u>has</u> the winning ticket. (both parts singular: verb singular; note that the subject is *one or the other*, not *you*)

> Neither my parents nor I <u>was</u> to blame. (first part plural, second part singular: verb singular)

Try to avoid the construction in the previous example, since it usually sounds incorrect (see also #15b). It's easy to rephrase:

> Neither I nor my parents <u>were</u> to blame.

18d Agreement with Indefinite Pronouns
(see also #14g and #15c)

Most indefinite pronouns are almost always singular, while a few are always plural (see #14g). And a few—*all, any, more, most, none, some*—can be either singular or plural, depending on whether they refer to a single quantity or to a number of individual units within a group:

Some of the pasta **is** eaten. (a single amount—*pasta* is singular, a mass noun)
Some of the cookies **are** missing. (a number of cookies—*cookies* is plural)

Most of the champagne **was** drunk. (a single mass—*champagne* is singular)
Most of the cases of champagne **have been** exported. (a number of cases—*cases* is plural)

None of the work **is** finished. (a single unit—*work* is singular; but note that *is* is also correct if the meaning of *none* is "not a single one")
None of the reports **are** ready. (a number of reports—*reports* is plural)

All of this novel **is** good. (a whole novel—*novel* is singular)
All of his novels **are** short. (a number of novels—*novels* is plural)

18e Subject Following Verb

When the normal subject–verb order is reversed, the verb still must agree with the real subject, not some word that happens to precede it:

There **is** only one **answer** to this question.
There **are** several possible **solutions** to the problem.

Here **comes** the **judge**.
Here **come** the **clowns**.

When compounded singular nouns follow an opening *there* or *here*, most writers make the verb agree with the first noun:

There **was** **a computer** and **a scanner** in the next room.

There **was** still **an essay** to be revised and **a play** to be studied before he could think about sleep.

But others find this kind of syntax awkward sounding. By rephrasing the sentence you can easily avoid the issue and save a few words as well:

> **A computer and a scanner were in the next room.**

> **He still had an essay to revise and a play to study before he could think about sleep.**

In expletive patterns, *it* takes a singular verb—usually a linking verb (see #17a):

> **It <u>is</u> questions like these that give the most trouble.**

For more on the expletives *it* and *there*, see #12k and #71a.

18f Agreement with Collective Nouns

Collective nouns (see #13) are collections or groups that are considered as units and therefore usually take singular verbs:

> **The government <u>has</u> passed the legislation.**

> **The company <u>is</u> planning several events to celebrate <u>its</u> centennial.**

But when such a noun denotes the individual members of a group, the verb must be plural:

> **His family <u>comes</u> from Korea.** (singular)

> **His family <u>come</u> from Jamaica, India, and Southern Europe.** (plural)

Such words as *number, half,* and *majority* can also be considered collective nouns and either singular or plural. In the following examples, notice how the article—*a* or *the*—changes the verb agreement:

> **A number of optimistic skiers are heading to the slopes.** (*a number of*: plural)

> **The number of skiers here is quite large.** (*the number of*: singular)

(See also **amount, number** in the Usage Checklist, #72.)

18g Nouns That Are Always Singular or Always Plural

[EAL] Some nouns, because of their meanings, cannot be inflected for number and will always be either singular or plural. Do not be fooled by some singular nouns that look plural because they end in *s.* Some examples of uninflectable nouns include the following:

> **The gold comes from the Yukon.** (always singular)

> **Oxygen is essential to human life.** (always singular)

> **Economics is difficult for some people.** (always singular)

> **The scissors are in the kitchen.** (always plural)

> **His glasses are fogged up.** (always plural)

> **Her clothes are very stylish.** (always plural)

For more on *mass* and *countable* nouns, see #13a and #19c.6.

18h Plurals: *criteria, data, media,* etc.

Words of Greek and Latin origin ending in *a* look like singular words but are in fact plural. The following words are plural; they can't be used with singular verbs (see #61-l.7):

criteria (singular is *criterion*)

phenomena (singular is *phenomenon*)

strata (singular is *stratum*)

While *criteria*, *phenomena*, and *strata* should always be treated as plural forms, some similar nouns may take either a singular or a plural verb, depending on the context. For instance, *data* should be treated as a plural noun in scientific contexts (the singular form is *datum*); in non-scientific practice, it may take a singular verb:

Some meteorological data <u>are</u> collected by satellites. (plural)

Data from the poll <u>has been</u> tabulated and entered in the system. (singular)

Media can be regarded in some contexts as a collective noun and thus followed by either a plural or a singular verb, depending on whether it's being used to mean TV, print, radio, and Internet sources of information collectively or individually.

Some argue that the media <u>is</u> responsible for making health care the primary concern among voters. (singular)

A local newspaper broke the story, but other media <u>were</u> quick to report it. (plural)

18i Agreement with Relative Pronouns

Whether a relative pronoun is singular or plural depends on its antecedent (see #15). Therefore, when a relative clause has *who*, *which*, or *that* as its subject, the verb must agree in number with the pronoun's antecedent:

Her success is due to her intelligence and perseverance, which <u>have</u> overcome all obstacles. (The antecedent of *which* is *intelligence and perseverance*.)

Questions about agreement most often occur with the phrases *one of those . . . who* and *one of the . . . who*:

> He is one of those people who <u>have</u> difficulty reading aloud.

> He is one of the few people I know who <u>have</u> difficulty reading aloud.

Have is correct, since the antecedent of *who* is the plural *people*, not the singular *one*. The only time this construction takes a singular verb is when *one* is preceded by *the only*; *one* is then the antecedent of *who*:

> He is the only one of those attending who <u>has</u> difficulty reading aloud.

You can avoid the problem by simplifying:

> He has difficulty reading aloud.

> Of those attending, he alone has difficulty reading aloud.

18j Titles of Works and Words Referred to as Words

Titles of literary and other works and words referred to as words should be treated as *singular* even if they are plural in themselves:

> *The Adventures of Sherlock Holmes* <u>is</u> one of Doyle's best-known collections.

> Vivaldi's *Four Seasons* <u>is</u> a superb example of Baroque music.

> *Nervous Nellies* <u>is</u> an out-of-date slang term.

19 Adjectives

ad An **adjective** modifies—limits, qualifies, particularizes—a noun or pronoun. Adjectives generally answer the questions *Which? What kind of? How many?* and *How much?*

> <u>The</u> <u>black</u> cat was <u>hungry</u>; he ate <u>five</u> sardines and drank <u>some</u> milk.

Kinds of Adjectives

Adjectives fall into two major classes: **non–descriptive** and **descriptive**.

1. Non-descriptive Adjectives

The several kinds of non-descriptive adjectives include some that are basically *structure words* (see #12-l):

- **articles** (see #19c):

  <u>a</u> melon   <u>an</u> apple   <u>the</u> strawberry

- **demonstrative adjectives** (see also #14f):

  <u>this</u> lamp   <u>that</u> table   <u>these</u> pictures   <u>those</u> books

- **interrogative and relative adjectives** (see also #14c–d):

  <u>Which</u> book is best?   <u>What</u> time is it?

  <u>Whose</u> opinion do you trust?   She is the one <u>whose</u> opinion I trust.

- **possessive adjectives**—the possessive forms of personal and impersonal pronouns (see #14a–b) and of nouns (see #13b):

  <u>my</u> book   <u>her</u> car   <u>its</u> colour   <u>their</u> heritage
  <u>one's</u> beliefs a <u>man's</u> coat   the <u>river's</u> mouth
  <u>Hamlet's</u> ego <u>Shirley's</u> job the <u>car's</u> engine

  (Note: People who think of *form* rather than *function* prefer to call these "possessive pronouns" and "possessive nouns.")

- **indefinite and numerical adjectives** (see #14g):

  <u>some</u> money   <u>any</u> time   <u>more</u> fuel   <u>several</u> keys
  <u>three</u> ducks <u>thirty</u> ships the <u>fourth</u> act <u>much</u> sushi

2. Descriptive Adjectives

Descriptive adjectives give information about such matters as the size, shape, colour, nature, and quality of whatever a noun or pronoun names:

> a <u>hybrid</u> car   a <u>delicate</u> balance
> an <u>Impressionist</u> painting   a <u>brave</u> woman
> a <u>tempting</u> dessert   a <u>well-done</u> steak
> a <u>once-in-a-lifetime</u> chance   <u>Canadian</u> literature
> an <u>experimental</u> play   <u>composted</u> leaves
> a <u>fascinating</u> place <u>to visit</u> <u>kitchen</u> towels
> a <u>dictionary</u> definition   <u>looking refreshed</u>, he …
> the festival <u>to exceed all others</u>   the man <u>of the hour</u>
> the rabbits <u>who caused all the trouble</u>
> a <u>large</u>, <u>impressive</u>, <u>three-storey</u>, <u>grey</u>, <u>Victorian</u> house

As these examples illustrate, adjectival modifiers can be single (*hybrid, delicate, Impressionist,* etc.), in groups or series (*large, impressive, three-storey, grey, Victorian*), or in compounds (*three-storey, well-done, once-in-a-lifetime*); they can be proper adjectives, formed from proper nouns (*Victorian, Canadian, Impressionist*); they can be words that are adjectives only (*delicate, large*) or words that can also function as other parts of speech (*hybrid, brave, tempting,* etc.), including nouns functioning as adjectives (*kitchen, dictionary*); they can be present participles (*tempting, fascinating*), past participles (*composted*), or infinitives (*to visit*); they can be participial phrases (*looking refreshed*), infinitive phrases (*to exceed all others*), or prepositional phrases (*of the hour*); or they can be relative clauses (*who caused all the trouble*). For more examples see #26a. On the overuse of nouns as adjectives, see #71g; on infinitives and participles, see #21a and #21d; on prepositions, see #22; on relative clauses, see #14d.

19b Comparison of Descriptive Adjectives

ONLINE EXERCISES

Most descriptive adjectives can be inflected or supplemented for *degree* in order to make *comparisons*. The basic or dictionary form of an adjective is called its **positive** form: *high, difficult, calm*. Use it to compare two things that are equal or similar, or with qualifiers such as *not* and *almost* to compare two things that are dissimilar:

> This assignment is <u>as difficult as</u> last week's.

> It is <u>not nearly so difficult as</u> I expected.

To make the **comparative** form, add *er* or put *more* (or *less*) in front of the positive form: *higher, calmer, more difficult, less difficult.* Use it to compare two unequal things:

> **My grades are <u>higher</u> now than they were last year.**

> **Your part is <u>more difficult</u> than mine.**

For the **superlative** form, add *est* or put *most* (or *least*) in front of the positive form: *highest, calmest, most difficult, least difficult.* Generally, use it to compare three or more unequal things:

> **Whose talent is the <u>greatest</u>?**

> **He is the <u>calmest</u> and <u>least pretentious</u> person I know.**

You can usually follow these guidelines:

- For adjectives of one syllable, add *er* and *est*:

positive	comparative	superlative
short	shorter	shortest
large	larger	largest
dry	drier	driest
grim	grimmer	grimmest

You can also use *more* and *most, less* and *least* with many of these positive forms. (And note the spelling changes in the last three examples; see #61d–f.)

- For adjectives of *three or more* syllables, use *more* and *most* (or *less* and *least*):

beautiful	more beautiful	most beautiful
tiresome	more tiresome	most tiresome

- For most adjectives of two syllables ending in *al, ect, ed, ent, ful, ic, id, ing, ish, ive, less,* or *ous* (and any others where an added *er* or *est* would sound wrong), use *more* and *most* (or *less* and *least*):

formal	more formal	most formal
direct	more direct	most direct
polished	more polished	most polished
potent	more potent	most potent
tactful	more tactful	most tactful

- For other adjectives of two syllables, you have a choice; for example:

gentle	gentler, more gentle	gentlest, most gentle
lively	livelier, more lively	liveliest, most lively

When there is a choice, the forms with *more* and *most* will usually sound more formal and more emphatic than those with *er* and *est*.

However, adjectives of three or more syllables, and even shorter ones ending in *ous* and *ful* and so on, almost always require *more* and *most*.

Because of their meanings, some adjectives should not be compared: see unique in the Usage Checklist, #72. See also #42 and #38, on faulty comparison.

PROOFREADING TIP

Avoiding "Doubling-Up" Errors in Adjective Forms

Don't double up a comparative or superlative form as in *more better* or *most prettiest*. If you want emphasis, use the adverbial intensifiers *much* or *far* or *by far*:

much livelier	much more lively
far livelier	far more lively
livelier by far	by far the liveliest
much the liveliest	much the livelier of the two

PROOFREADING TIP

Irregular Comparative and Superlative Adjective Forms

A few commonly used adjectives form their comparative and superlative degrees irregularly:

good	better	best
bad	worse	worst
far	farther; further	farthest; furthest
little	littler; less, lesser	littlest; least
much, many	more	most

(And see **farther, further** in the Usage Checklist, #72.)

Good dictionaries list all irregular forms after the basic entry, including those in which a spelling change occurs.

Articles: a, *an*, and *the*

Articles—sometimes considered separately from parts of speech—can conveniently be thought of as kinds of adjectives. Like adjectives, they modify nouns. Like demonstrative and possessive adjectives, they are also sometimes called *markers* or *determiners* because an article indicates that a noun will soon follow.

The definite article (*the*) and the indefinite article (*a* or *an*) are used idiomatically, and they often challenge people whose first language doesn't include articles. An advanced learner's dictionary can be invaluable in helping you decide which article, if any, to use. For example, this entry from the *Oxford Advanced Learner's Dictionary* (*OALD*) indicates contexts in which the word *democracy* is countable (and would most likely need an article in its singular form) or uncountable (and would probably not take the indefinite article but might take the definite).

---

dem·oc·racy /dɪˈmɒkrəsi; *NAmE* -ˈmɑːk/ *noun* (*pl.* **-ies**)
1 [U] a system of government in which all the people of a country can vote to elect their representatives: *parliamentary democracy* ◊ *the principles of democracy.* **2** [C] a country which has this system of government: *Western democracies* ◊ *I thought we were supposed to be living in a democracy.* **3** [U] fair and equal treatment of everyone in an organization, etc., and their right to take part in making decisions: *the fight for justice and democracy.*

Reproduced by permission of Oxford University Press from *Oxford Advanced Learner's Dictionary*, 9th ed. © Oxford University Press 2015.

It is almost impossible to set down all the rules for article use, but here are some guiding principles.

1. Using the Indefinite Article

The form *a* of the indefinite article is used before words beginning with a consonant (*a dog, a building, a computer, a yellow orchid*), including words beginning with a pronounced *h* (*a horse, a historical event, a hotel, a hypothesis*) and words beginning with a *u* or *o* whose initial sound is that of *y* or *w* (*a useful book, a one-sided contest*). The form *an* is used before words beginning with a vowel sound (*an insect, an opinion, an ugly duckling*) and words beginning with an unpronounced *h* (*an honour*).

Generally, a person or thing designated by the indefinite article is not specific:

> **He wants to buy <u>a</u> horse and <u>an</u> emu for his farm.**

The indefinite article is like *one*: it is often used before singular countable nouns.

2. Using the Definite Article

Generally, the definite article designates one or more particular persons or things whose identity is established by context (familiarity) or a modifier (clauses, phrases, superlative adjectives, ordinal numbers). Also, the definite article is used with some proper nouns.

> **Go past <u>the</u> bookstore and you will see <u>the</u> Avon Theatre.**

In this example, the definite article is used because the **context** is understood or your reader is familiar with the nouns being modified.

If the noun is followed by a **modifying clause** or **phrase**, the definite article is often used:

> **My parents gave me <u>the</u> scooter I wanted.** (*scooter* is particularized by the modifying clause *I wanted*)

Compare to the use of the indefinite article:

> **My parents gave me <u>a</u> scooter.** (unspecified)

The definite article can also be used to indicate exclusiveness; *the* is then equivalent to *the only* or *the best*. In fact, we often use *the* in front of **superlative adjectives**:

> **He is <u>the</u> happiest person I know.**

> **She is <u>the</u> most diligent student.**

We also can indicate exclusiveness with the use of ordinals (*first*, *second*, *third*, etc.), which are numerical adjectives:

The first act of the play takes place in Montreal.

No one enjoyed **the** third sequel.

3. Using Articles with Proper Nouns

Definite articles go with some **proper nouns** but not with others. Strangely, *the* often goes with place names that are plural. Others have modifying phrases that begin with "of."

we say	but also
Great Britain	the United Kingdom
Gabriola Island	the Thousand Islands
Mount Baker	the Rockies
Western University	the University of Saskatchewan

4. Using Articles with Uncountable Nouns or Plural Nouns

Uncountable nouns, whether mass nouns or abstract nouns, take no article if the mass or abstract sense governs:

art: **The poem features a simple praise of nature.**

Here, *a* must be removed because *praise* in this context is uncountable. But notice the difference if the concrete noun *hymn* is inserted:

The poem features a simple hymn of praise to nature.

In addition, plural countable nouns rarely take indefinite articles:

art: **She wanted a writing notebooks.**

revised: **She wanted writing notebooks.**

However, you can use the definite article with plural nouns if they are particularized by a modifier.

revised: **She wanted the writing notebooks that are made in Italy.**
(Here, *notebooks* is particularized by *that are made in Italy*.)

5. Using Articles with Abstract Nouns

If a usually abstract noun is used in a countable but not particularized sense, the indefinite article precedes it; if in a particularized way, the definite article:

This is <u>an</u> honour. (countable)

He did me <u>the</u> honour of inviting me. (uncountable, specific)

6. Using the Definite Article in Front of Nouns That Represent Groups

The definite article usually precedes an adjective functioning as a noun that represents a group (see #19f):

<u>The</u> young should heed the advice of <u>the</u> elderly.

This rule can also be applied to species of animals or inventions when emphasizing the class:

<u>The</u> computer facilitates various modes of communication.

7. Using the Definite Article with Titles of Artistic Works

Titles of artistic works are not usually preceded by articles, but usage is inconsistent, and some idiomatically take the definite article. It would be incorrect to say:

art: **Donne's poetic power is evident in the Sonnet X.**

Either omit *the* or change *the* to *his*. It would be natural to refer to "the *Adventures of Huckleberry Finn*."

8. Using Articles with Names of Academic Fields and Courses

With names of academic fields and courses, whether proper nouns or abstract common nouns, no article is used:

She is enrolled in Psychology 301.

He reads books on psychology.

9. Using the Definite Article Before Names of Ships, Trains, and Planes

Use the definite article before the names of individual ships, trains, planes, and other vehicles:

the *Beagle*   the *Titanic*   the *Royal Canadian Pacific*
the *Orient Express* the *Enola Gay*   the *Discovery*

19d Placement of Adjectives

Adjectival modifiers usually come just before or just after what they modify. Articles always, and other determiners almost always, precede the nouns they modify, usually with either no intervening words or only one or two other adjectives:

Trying to save <u>some</u> money, <u>the</u> manager decided to close <u>his</u> store early.

<u>The wise</u> manager decided not to hire <u>his scatterbrained</u> nephew.

Predicate adjectives (see #12g) almost always follow the subject and linking verb:

The forest is <u>cool</u> and <u>green</u> and <u>full of mushrooms</u>.

Shortly after his operation he again became <u>healthy</u>.

Adjectives serving as *objective complements* usually follow the subject–verb–direct object (see #12i):

I thought the suggestion <u>preposterous</u>.

Most other single-word adjectives, and many compound adjectives, precede the nouns they modify:

The <u>tall</u>, <u>dark</u>, and <u>handsome</u> hero lives on only in <u>romantic</u> fiction.

The <u>weather</u> map shows a <u>cold</u> front moving into the <u>well-prepared</u> <u>northern</u> prairies.

Judiciously, if you want a certain emphasis or rhythm, you can put a predicate adjective before a noun:

> **<u>Frustrated</u> I may have been, but I hadn't lost my wits or my passport.**

or a regular adjective after a noun:

> **She did the only thing <u>possible</u>.**

> **There was food <u>enough</u> for everyone.**

Compound adjectives and adjectives in phrases are often comfortable after a noun:

> **His friend, always <u>faithful and kind</u>, came at once.**

> **Elfrida, <u>radiant and delighted</u>, left the room, <u>secure</u> in her victory.**

Relative clauses and various kinds of phrases customarily follow the nouns they modify:

> **He is one detective <u>who believes in being thorough</u>.**

> **The president <u>of the company</u> will retire next month.**

The only adjectival modifier not generally restricted in its position is the participial phrase (see #21d):

> **<u>Having had abundant experience</u>, Kenneth applied for the job.**

> **Kenneth, <u>having had abundant experience</u>, applied for the job.**

> **Kenneth applied for the job, <u>having had abundant experience</u>.**

This movability makes the participial phrase a popular way to introduce variety and to control emphasis (see #29e). But be careful: such phrases can be awkward or ambiguous, especially in the form of a *dangling modifier*:

dm: **Having had abundant experience, the job seemed just right for Kenneth.** (This sentence implies it is the job, not Kenneth, that has the abundant experience.)

See #36; see also #35, on misplaced modifiers.

19e Order of Adjectives

EAL Adjectives usually follow an idiomatic order: a determiner (an article, possessive, or demonstrative) comes first, then numbers, then adjectives that express a general description, then physical-state adjectives, then proper adjectives, and then noun adjuncts before the main noun.

The following chart shows the common order of adjectives:

determiner	number	general description	physical state including age, size, shape, colour, and temperature	proper adjectives	noun adjuncts including adjectives ending in "ic(al)" or "al"	main noun
the	one	talented	young	Canadian	vocal	star
Alex's	seventh	expensive	orange		impractical	lamp
a		trendy	small	Indian		restaurant
your	four	new	square		coffee	mugs
their		richest	warm		chocolate	cake
her	two	funny, daring		Australian	theatrical	friends

Note that adjectives expressing an inherent quality or a general description can be reversed in order. For example, you could write: *her two daring, funny Australian theatrical friends*. Notice that *daring* and *funny* are separated by a comma because they are interchangeable in order (see #43d).

19f Adjectives Functioning as Nouns

If preceded by *the* or a possessive, many words normally thought of as adjectives can function as *nouns*, usually referring to people, and usually in a plural sense (see #19c.6); for example:

the Swedish   **the British**   **the Chinese**   **the Lebanese**

(but Canadians, not *the* Canadians)

the free	the brave	the poor	the sick and dying
the powerful	the wealthy	the uneducated	the more fortunate
the starving	the enslaved	the deceased	the badly injured
the abstract	the metaphysical	the good	the true

20 Adverbs

Adverbs are often thought of as especially tricky. This part of speech is sometimes called the "catch-all" category, since any word that doesn't seem to fit elsewhere is usually assumed to be an adverb. Adverbs, therefore, are a little more complicated than adjectives.

20a Kinds and Functions of Adverbs

ad

ONLINE
EXERCISES

Whereas adjectives can modify only nouns and pronouns, adverbs can modify *verbs* (and *verbals*; see #21), *adjectives*, other *adverbs*, and *independent clauses* or whole *sentences*. Adverbial modifiers generally answer such questions as *How? When? Where? Why?* and *To what degree?* That is, they indicate such things as *manner* (How?); *time* (When? How often? How long?); *place* and *direction* (Where? In what direction?); *cause*, *result*, and *purpose* (Why? To what effect?); and *degree* (To what degree? To what extent?). They also express affirmation and negation, conditions, concessions, and comparisons. Here are some examples:

<u>For many years</u> they lived <u>very happily together in Yellowknife</u>.

How? *Happily* and *together*: the adverbs of manner modify the verb *lived*. To what degree? *Very*: the intensifying adverb modifies the adverb *happily*. Where? *In Yellowknife*: the adverbial prepositional phrase modifies the verb *lived*. How long? *For many years*: the prepositional phrase functions as an adverb of time or duration modifying the verb—or it can be thought of as modifying the whole clause *they lived very happily together in Yellowknife*.

<u>Fully</u> expecting to fail, he slumped <u>disconsolately</u> <u>in his seat</u> and began the examination.

To what degree? *Fully*: the adverb of degree modifies the participial (verbal) phrase *expecting to fail*. How? *Disconsolately*: the adverb of manner modifies the verb *slumped*. Where? *In his seat*: the prepositional phrase functions as an adverb of place modifying the verb *slumped*.

Fortunately, the cut was not deep.

To what effect? *Fortunately*: a sentence modifier. To what degree? *Not*: the negating adverb modifies the adjective *deep*.

Because their budget was tight, they eventually decided not to buy a car.

Why? *Because their budget was tight*: the adverbial clause of cause modifies the verb *decided* or, in a way, all the rest of the sentence. When? *Eventually*: the adverb of time modifies the verb decided. The negating *not* modifies the infinitive (verbal) *to buy*.

Last November it seldom snowed.

When? *Last November*: the noun phrase functions as an adverb of time modifying the verb *snowed*. How often? *Seldom*: the adverb of time or frequency modifies the verb *snowed*.

Driving fast is often dangerous.

How? *Fast*: the adverb of manner modifies the gerund (verbal) *driving*. When? *Often*: the adverb of time or frequency modifies the adjective *dangerous*.

If you're tired, I will walk the dog.

The conditional clause modifies the verb *will walk*.

Although she dislikes the city *intensely*, she agreed to go there in order to keep peace *in the family*.

Intensely (degree) modifies the verb *dislikes*. *There* (place) modifies the infinitive *to go*. *Although she dislikes the city intensely* is an adverbial clause of concession. The prepositional phrase *in order to keep peace in the family* is an adverb of purpose modifying the verb *agreed*. The smaller adverbial prepositional phrase *in the family* modifies the infinitive phrase *to keep peace*, answering the question *Where?*

> Meredith was <u>better</u> prepared <u>than I was</u>.

The adverb *better* modifies the adjective *prepared*; the combination of *better* and the clause *than I was* expresses comparison or contrast.

1. Adverbs as Condensed Clauses

Some single-word adverbs and adverbial phrases, especially sentence modifiers, can be thought of as reduced clauses:

> <u>Fortunately</u> [It is fortunate that], **the cut was not deep.**

> <u>When possible</u> [When it is possible], **let your writing sit <u>before proofreading it</u>** [before you proofread it].

2. Other Kinds of Adverbs: Relative, Interrogative, Conjunctive

- The **relative adverbs** (*where, when,* and *why*) are used to introduce relative (adjective) clauses (see #14d):

  > She returned to the town <u>where she had grown up</u>.

  > Adam looked forward to the moment <u>when it would be his turn</u>.

- The **interrogative adverbs** (*where, when, why,* and *how*) are used in questions:

  > <u>Where</u> are you going? <u>Why</u>? <u>How</u> soon? <u>When</u> will you return?

- **Conjunctive adverbs** usually join whole clauses or sentences to each other and indicate the nature of the connection:

  > Only fifteen people showed up. <u>Nevertheless</u>, the promoter didn't let his disappointment show.

  > The tornado almost flattened the town; <u>however</u>, only Dorothy and her dog were reported missing.

For more on conjunctive adverbs, see #44a.

Forms of Adverbs

1. Adverbs Ending in *ly*

Many adverbs are formed by adding *ly* to descriptive adjectives—for example, the adjective *rough* becomes *roughly*, *happy* becomes *happily*, *fundamental* becomes *fundamentally*, and *curious* becomes *curiously*. Don't use an adjectival form where an adverbial form is needed:

She is a <u>careful</u> driver. (adjective modifying driver)

She drives <u>carefully</u>. (adverb modifying drives)

Some common adjectives end in *ly*, among them *burly, curly, early, friendly, holy, homely, leisurely, likely, lively, lovely, lowly, orderly, silly, surly,* and *ugly.* Adding another *ly* to these inevitably sounds awkward. And though some dictionaries label some of these words as adverbs as well (he walked *leisurely* toward the door; she behaved *friendly* toward the strangers), that usage also often sounds awkward. You can avoid the problem by adding a few words or rephrasing:

He walked toward the door in a <u>leisurely</u> manner. (adjective)

She behaved in a <u>friendly</u> way toward the strangers. (adjective)

She was <u>friendly</u> toward the strangers. (adjective)

In a few instances, however, the *ly* adjectives do also serve idiomatically as adverbs—for example, "He spoke *kindly* of you," "She rises *early*," "He exercises *daily*," "The tour leaves *hourly*," "Most magazines are published *weekly* or *monthly*."

2. Adverbs Not Ending in *ly*

Some adverbs don't end in *ly*—for example, *ahead, almost, alone, down, however, long, now, often, quite, since, soon, then, there, therefore, when,* and *where*. Others without the *ly* are identical in form to adjectives—for example, *far, fast, little, low, more, much,* and *well*:

> **He owns a <u>fast</u> car.** (adjective)
> **He likes to drive <u>fast</u>.** (adverb)

> **They have a <u>low</u> opinion of him.** (adjective)
> **They flew <u>low</u> over the coast.** (adverb)

Well as an adjective means "healthy" (I am quite *well*, thank you) or sometimes "satisfactory," "right," or "advisable" (all is *well*; it is *well* you came when you did). When someone asks you about your health, don't say you are *good* (unless you want to imply you are the opposite of *bad* or *evil*). You should say "I am well." Otherwise, *well* is an adverb and should be used instead of the frequently misused *good*, which is an adjective. Similarly, *bad* is an adjective, *badly* an adverb. Be careful with these often misused forms:

> **She did a <u>good</u> coaching job. The team played <u>well</u>.**

They felt <u>bad</u> for the child, who had played <u>badly</u> in the game. (*Felt* is a linking verb here and requires a predicate adjective—*bad*—as its subjective complement.)

See also **good, bad, badly, well** in the Usage Checklist, #72.

3. Adverbs with Short and Long Forms

Some common adverbs have two forms, one with *ly* and one without. (The form without *ly* is identical to the adjective.) With some of these pairs, the two forms do not mean the same thing:

even, evenly	fair, fairly	hard, hardly	high, highly
just, justly	late, lately	near, nearly	right, rightly

With others, the shorter form is equivalent to the longer form:

Don't talk so <u>loud</u>. Don't talk so <u>loudly</u>.

Look <u>deep</u> into my eyes. Look <u>deeply</u> into my eyes.

In these examples, the shorter forms sound more natural because the longer forms have fallen out of common usage. But in most cases, the form without *ly* is considered to be informal. Therefore, while words such as *cheap, clear, close, direct, loose, quick, quiet, sharp, smooth, strong, tight,* and *wrong* are often used as adverbs, in formal contexts you should use the *ly* form.

PROOFREADING TIP

Using Adverbs and Adjectives in the Imperative Mood

When you're writing instructions in the imperative mood (see #17k), be careful not to use an adverbial form where an adjectival form is required. It's right to tell readers to "stir the sauce *slowly,*" but wrong to tell them to "slice the onion *thinly.*" The correct instruction would be "slice the onion *thin,*" meaning "slice the onion *until it is* thin." Similarly, you wouldn't tell someone to "sand the wood *smoothly,*" but *smooth*—that is, until it is smooth. In such phrases, the modifier goes with the noun, not the verb; therefore an adjective, not an adverb, is required.

20c Comparison of Adverbs

Like descriptive adjectives, most adverbs that are similarly descriptive can be inflected or supplemented for degree (see #19b). The following are some guidelines on how adverbs are inflected:

- Some short adverbs without *ly* form their comparative and superlative degrees with *er* and *est*; for example:

positive	comparative	superlative
fast	faster	fastest
hard	harder	hardest
high	higher	highest
late	later	latest
low	lower	lowest
soon	sooner	soonest

Less and *least* also sometimes go with the positive form of these adverbs; for example:

They still ran fast, but <u>less fast</u> than they had the day before.

Students work <u>least hard</u> on the days following an exam.

- Adverbs of three or more syllables ending in *ly* use *more* and *most*, *less* and *least*; for example:

happily	**more happily**	**most happily**
stridently	**less stridently**	**least stridently**

- Most two-syllable adverbs, whether or not they end in *ly*, also use *more* and *most*, *less* and *least*, though a few can be inflected with *er* and *est*; for example:

slowly	**more slowly**	**most slowly**
grimly	**less grimly**	**least grimly**
fully	**more fully**	**most fully**
alone	**more alone**	**most alone**
often	**more often, oftener**	**most often, oftenest**
early	**earlier**	**earliest**

- Some adverbs form their comparative and superlative degrees irregularly:

badly	worse	worst
well	better	best
much	more	most
little	less	least
far	farther, further	farthest, furthest

- A few adverbs of place use *farther* and *farthest* (or *further* and *furthest*; see farther, further in the Usage Checklist, #72); for example:

down	farther down	farthest down
north	farther north	farthest north

- As with adjectives, the adverbs *much*, *far*, and *by far* serve as intensifiers in comparisons:

    Angelo and Felix live <u>much</u> more comfortably than they used to.

    They flew <u>far</u> lower than they should have.

    He practises harder <u>by far</u> than anyone else in the orchestra.

 ## 20d Placement of Adverbs

1. Adverbs Modifying Adjectives or Other Adverbs

An intensifying or qualifying adverb almost always goes just before the adjective or adverb it modifies:

<u>almost</u> always	<u>strongly</u> confident	<u>very</u> hot
<u>only</u> two	<u>most</u> surely	

2. Modifiers of Verbs

Whether single words, phrases, or clauses, most modifiers of verbs are more flexible in their position than any other part of speech. Often they can go almost anywhere in a sentence and still function clearly:

Proudly, he pointed to his photo in the paper.

He proudly pointed to his photo in the paper.

He pointed proudly to his photo in the paper.

He pointed to his photo in the paper proudly.

But notice that the emphasis (and therefore the overall effect and meaning) changes slightly. Here is another example; note how much you can control the emphasis:

Because she likes live music, Sue often goes to the jazz club.

Sue, because she likes live music, often goes to the jazz club.

Sue often goes to the jazz club because she likes live music.

And in each version, the adverb *often* could come after *goes* or after *jazz club*.

3. Adverbs of Place

The preceding example also illustrates the only major restriction on adverbial modifiers of the verb. A phrase like *to the jazz club*, like a direct object, almost has to follow the verb immediately or with no more than an *often* or other such word intervening. But sometimes an adverb of place or direction can come first if a sentence's usual word order is reversed to emphasize place or direction:

Off to market we shall go.

There she stood, staring out to sea.

Where are you going? (but: Are you going *there*?)

Downward he plummeted, waiting until the last moment to pull the rip cord.

4. Sentence Modifiers

Sentence modifiers usually come at the beginning, but they, too, can be placed elsewhere for purposes of emphasis or rhythm:

<u>**Fortunately**</u>**, the boxer was able to stand.**

The boxer, <u>fortunately</u>, was able to stand.

The boxer was, <u>fortunately</u>, able to stand.

The boxer was able to stand, <u>fortunately</u>.

With longer or more involved sentences, however, a sentence modifier at the end loses much of its force and point, obviously; obviously it works better if placed earlier, as this sentence demonstrates.

See also #35, on misplaced modifiers.

Verbals: Infinitives, Participles, and Gerunds

ONLINE
EXERCISES

Infinitives, participles, and gerunds are called **verbals**, forms that are derived from verbs but that cannot function as main or finite verbs. Verbals are **non-finite** forms, not restricted by person and number as finite verbs are (see #17d, and the note at the end of #17b). They function as other parts of speech yet retain some characteristics of verbs: they can have objects, they can be modified by adverbs, and they can express tense and voice. Verbals often introduce *verbal phrases*, groups of words that themselves function as other parts of speech (see #12p). Verbals enable you to inject much of the strength and liveliness of verbs into your writing even though the words are functioning as adjectives, adverbs, and nouns.

21a Infinitives

We sometimes use a form called the **infinitive** to identify particular verbs. An infinitive usually consists of the word *to* (often called "the sign of the infinitive") followed by the basic form: *to be*, *to live*. Infinitives can function as *nouns*, *adjectives*, and *adverbs*.

1. Infinitives as Nouns

To save the wolves was Mowat's primary intention.

The infinitive phrase *To save the wolves* is the subject of the verb *was*. The noun *wolves* is the direct object of the infinitive *To save*.

She wanted to end the game quickly.

The infinitive phrase *to end the game quickly* is the direct object of the verb *wanted*. The infinitive *to end* is modified by the adverb *quickly* and has the noun *game* as its own direct object.

2. Infinitives as Adjectives

His strong desire to be a doctor made him studious.

The infinitive phrase *to be a doctor* modifies the noun *desire*. Since *be* is a linking verb, the infinitive is here followed by the predicate noun *doctor*.

The rarest coins are the ones to collect.

The infinitive *to collect* modifies the pronoun *ones*.

3. Infinitives as Adverbs

She was lucky to have such a friend.

The infinitive phrase *to have such a friend* modifies the predicate adjective *lucky*. The noun phrase *such a friend* is the direct object of the infinitive *to have*.

He went to Niagara-on-the-Lake to experience the Shaw Festival.

The infinitive phrase *to experience the Shaw Festival* is an adverb of purpose modifying the verb *went*; *the Shaw Festival* is the direct object of the infinitive *to experience*.

EAL

PROOFREADING TIP

Verb Idioms That Omit to Before the Infinitive Verb Form

After some verbs, an infinitive can occur without the customary *to*; for example:

<u>Let</u> sleeping dogs <u>lie</u>.　　　　It <u>made</u> me <u>cry</u>.

We <u>saw</u> the man <u>jump</u>.　　　He <u>felt</u> the house <u>shake</u>.

I <u>helped</u> her (to) <u>decide</u>.

Of particular note here are the verbs *make* and *let*, as well as verbs of perception (e.g., *see*, *feel*, *hear*, *watch*).

21b　Tense and Voice of Infinitives (see #17g and #17-l)

Infinitives may be either *present* (to indicate a time the same as or later than that of the main verb):

She wants me <u>to go</u> to the pyramids with her.

I was hoping <u>to cruise</u> along the Nile.

or *present perfect* (to indicate a time before that of the main verb); the *to* then goes with the auxiliary *have*, followed by the verb's past participle:

I was lucky <u>to have met</u> the manager before the interview.

Each of these may also take the *progressive* form, using the auxiliaries *be* and *have*:

I expect <u>to be travelling</u> in Europe this summer.

He was said <u>to have been planning</u> the takeover for months.

Infinitives may also be in the *passive voice*, again putting *to* with the appropriate auxiliaries, then adding a past participle:

The children wanted <u>to be taken</u> to see Cirque du Soleil.

He was thought <u>to have been motivated</u> by sheer ambition.

21c   Split Infinitives

split   Since an infinitive is a unit, separating its parts can weaken it and often results in lack of clarity:

split: **He wanted <u>to</u> quickly <u>conclude</u> the business of the meeting.**

split: **She claimed that it was too difficult <u>to</u> very accurately or confidently <u>solve</u> such a problem.**

You can usually avoid such splits by rephrasing or rearranging so the adverbs don't interrupt the infinitive:

He wanted <u>to conclude</u> the business of the meeting quickly.

She claimed that it was too difficult <u>to solve</u> such a problem with any degree of accuracy or confidence.

Occasionally, it is better to split an infinitive than to sound overly formal:

The space crew vowed <u>to</u> boldly <u>go</u> where no one has gone before.

This split sounds more natural than the formal *boldly to go*, and *boldly* can't be moved to the end of the sentence.

If the infinitive includes a form of *be* or *have* as an auxiliary, an adverb before the last part is less likely to sound out of place:

The demonstration was thought <u>to have been</u> carefully <u>planned</u>.

21d   Participles

ONLINE
EXERCISES

The **past participle** and **present participle** work with various auxiliaries to form a finite verb's *perfect* and *progressive* tenses (see #17g–h). But without the auxiliaries to indicate *person* and *number*, the participles are non-finite and cannot function as verbs. Instead they function as *adjectives*, modifying nouns and pronouns:

<u>Beaming</u> happily, Josef examined his freshly <u>sanded</u> bench.

Present participles always end in *ing*, regular past participles in *ed* or *d*. Irregular past participles end variously: *made, mown, broken*, etc. (see #17b–c). A regular past participle is identical to the past-tense form of a verb, but you can easily check a given word's function in a sentence. In the example above, the past-tense form *examined* clearly has *Josef* as its subject; the past participle *sanded*, with no subject, is an adjective modifying *bench* and is itself modified by the adverb *freshly*. Here are some more examples:

<u>**Impressed**</u>**, she recounted the film's more** <u>**thrilling**</u> **episodes.**

The past participle *impressed* modifies the subject *she*; the present participle *thrilling* modifies the noun *episodes* and is itself modified by the adverb *more*.

The subject <u>**discussed**</u> **most often was the message behind the song.**

The past participle *discussed* modifies the noun *subject* and is itself modified by the adverbial *most often*.

Suddenly <u>**finding**</u> **himself alone, he became very** <u>**flustered**</u>**.**

The present participle *finding* introduces the participial phrase *finding himself alone*, which modifies the subject, *he*; *finding*, as a verbal, has *himself* as a direct object and is modified by the adverb *suddenly*. The past participle *flustered* functions as a predicate adjective after the linking verb *became*; it modifies *he* and is itself modified by the adverb *very*.

21e **Tense and Voice of Participles** (see #17g and #17-l)

ONLINE
EXERCISES

The standard present or past participle indicates a time the same as that of the main verb:

<u>**Being**</u> **the tallest, Luzia played centre.**

Strictly speaking, a past participle by itself amounts to passive voice:

<u>**Worried**</u> **by what he'd heard, Joe picked up the phone.**

With *ing* attached to an auxiliary, participles can also be in the perfect or perfect progressive tense, indicating a time earlier than that of the main verb:

> <u>Having painted</u> himself into a corner, George climbed out the window.

> <u>Having been painting</u> for over two hours, Leah decided to take a break.

Participles in the present progressive and the perfect tenses can also be in the passive voice:

> The subject <u>being discussed</u> was the environment.

> <u>Having been warned</u>, she knew better than to accept the offer.

PROOFREADING TIP

EAL

Present Participles and Sentence Fragments

It is particularly important that you know a present participle when you write one. If you use a present participle and think it's functioning as a finite verb, you may well produce a fragment (see #12x):

frag: **The parking lot being paved.**

frag: **The meal being prepared for the picnic.**

21f Gerunds

When the *ing* form of a verb functions as a noun, it is called a gerund:

> <u>Designing</u> posters can be fun.

> André gave himself a good <u>talking</u> to.

> Min has a profound fear of <u>flying</u>.

> Careful preparation—<u>brainstorming</u>, <u>organizing</u>, and <u>outlining</u>—helps produce good essays.

The gerund *Designing* is the subject of the sentence, and it has *posters* as a direct object. The gerund *talking* is a direct object and is itself modified by the adjective *good*. The gerund *flying* is the object of the preposition *of*. In the final example, the three gerunds constitute an appositive or definition of the subject noun, *preparation* (see #12q).

 ## 21g Tense and Voice of Gerunds (see #17g and #17-l)

As with infinitives and participles, the *perfect* form of a gerund indicates a time earlier than that of the main verb:

> My <u>having answered</u> the phone myself may have secured the contract.

And a gerund can be in the passive voice:

> His <u>being praised</u> by the supervisor gave him a big lift.

Be aware, though, that using either the perfect or the passive gerund can produce awkward results:

> The misunderstanding resulted from <u>our not having received</u> the latest information.

> He was proud of <u>her being awarded</u> the gold star for excellence.

Rephrasing such examples to avoid the gerund will produce clearer sentences:

> The misunderstanding occurred because we didn't receive the latest information.

> He was proud of her for receiving the gold star of excellence.

21h Possessives with Gerunds

In formal usage, a noun or a personal pronoun preceding a gerund will usually be in the possessive case:

> **His** cooking left much to be desired.

> She approved of **Bob's** cleaning the house.

> Can you explain the **engine's** not starting?

If the gerund is the subject, as in the first example, the possessive is essential. Otherwise, if you are writing informally, and especially if you want to emphasize the noun or pronoun, you don't need to use the possessive:

> She approved of **Bob** cleaning the house.

> Can you explain the **engine** not starting?

Further, in order to avoid awkward-sounding constructions, you usually won't use a possessive form when the noun preceding a gerund is (a) abstract, (b) plural, (c) multiple, or (d) separated from the gerund by modifiers (other than adverbs like *not* or *always* when they sound almost like part of the verbal):

> **(a)** He couldn't bear the thought of **love striking** again.

> **(b)** The possibility of the **thieves returning** to their hideout was slim.

> **(c)** There is a good chance of **Alberto and Maria agreeing** to your proposal.

> **(d)** One might well wonder at a **man** with such expertise **claiming** to be ignorant.

PROOFREADING TIP

The Gerund Followed Immediately by Another Noun

A gerund followed immediately by another noun will sometimes sound awkward or ambiguous. In such cases, interpose *of* or *the* or some similar term to keep the gerund from sounding like a participle:

his building (of) boats	your organizing (of the) material
my practising (the) piano	his revealing (of, the, of the) sources

21i Verbals in Absolute Phrases

Infinitives and participles (but not gerunds) can function in **absolute phrases** (see #12r):

> **To say the least**, the day was memorable.

> **Strictly speaking**, their actions were not legal.

> **All things considered**, the meeting was a success.

22 Prepositions

Prepositions are structure words or function words (see #12-l); they do not change their form. A preposition is part of a prepositional phrase, and it usually precedes the rest of the phrase, which includes a noun or pronoun as the object of the preposition:

> **This is a book about writing.**

> **She sent an email to her brother.**

Make a question of the preposition and ask *what* or *whom*, and the answer will always be the object: *About* what? Writing. *To* whom? Her brother.

22a Functions of Prepositions and Prepositional Phrases

A preposition *links* its object to some other word in the sentence; the prepositional phrase then functions as either an *adjectival* or an *adverbial* modifier:

> **He laid the camera on the table.**

Here, *on* links *table* to the verb *laid*; the phrase *on the table* therefore functions as an adverb describing *where* the camera was laid.

> **It was a time for celebration.**

Here, *for* links *celebration* to the noun *time*; the phrase therefore functions as an adjective indicating *what kind of* time.

22b Placement of Prepositions

ONLINE
EXERCISES

Usually, like articles, prepositions signal that a noun or pronoun soon follows. But prepositions can also come at the ends of clauses or sentences—for example, in a question, for emphasis, or to avoid stiffness:

Which backpack do you want to look <u>at</u>?

I want to know what the story is really <u>about</u>.

They had several issues to contend <u>with</u>.

It isn't wrong to end a sentence or clause with a preposition, in spite of what many people have been taught; just don't do it so often that it calls attention to itself.

22c Common Prepositions

ONLINE
EXERCISES

Most prepositions indicate a spatial or temporal relation, or such things as purpose, concession, comparison, manner, and agency. Here is a list of common prepositions; note that several consist of more than one word:

about	beneath	including	over
above	beside	in front of	past
according to	besides	in order to	regarding
across	between	in place of	regardless of
across from	beyond	in relation to	round
after	but	inside	since
against	by	in spite of	such as
ahead of	by way of	into	through
along	concerning	like	throughout
alongside	considering	near	till
among	contrary to	next to	to
apart from	despite	notwithstanding	toward(s)
around	down	of	under
as	during	off	underneath
as for	except	on	unlike
at	except for	on account of	until
away from	excepting	onto	up
because of	for	on top of	upon
before	from	opposite	with
behind	in	out	within
below	in addition to	outside	without

A learner's dictionary will be extremely helpful in guiding you in the use of prepositions.

22d Two-Part Verbs; Verb Idioms

English has many two-part and even three-part verbs consisting of a simple verb in combination with another word or words—for example, *cool off, act up, blow up, find out, hold up, carry on, get on with, stick up for.* You may think of the added words as prepositions, adverbs, or some sort of "particle." Indeed, sometimes it is difficult to say whether a word like *down* in *sit down* is functioning as part of the verb or as an adverb describing how one can sit; but the *down* and *up* in "sit down to a good meal" and "sit up in your chair" seem more like parts of the verbs than, say, the preposition *at* in "He sat at his desk." Usually you can sense a difference in sound: in "He *took over* the operation" both parts are stressed when said aloud, whereas in "He *took* over three hours to get here" only the *took* is stressed; *over* functions separately. Often, too, the parts of a verb can be separated and still mean the same, whereas the verb and preposition or adverb cannot:

> The children were <u>won over</u> by the actor's exuberance.
> The actor's exuberance <u>won</u> the children <u>over</u>.
> **Compare:** He <u>won</u> over his nearest opponent by three points.

> The construction crew <u>blew up</u> the remains of the old factory.
> The construction crew <u>blew</u> the remains of the old factory <u>up</u>.
> **Compare:** The wind <u>blew</u> up the chimney.

Some two-part verbs cannot be separated—for example, *see to, look after, run across, sit up, turn in* (as in *go to sleep*). Some simple verbs can take two or more different words to form new verbs; for example:

> try out – try on
> think out – think up
> fill up – fill in – fill out
> fall out – fall in – fall off

175

Some verbs can use several different words to form idiomatic expressions, as you will discover by looking them up in a learner's dictionary:

> bring about – bring around – bring down – bring forth –
> bring forward – bring in – bring off – bring on – bring out –
> bring over – bring to – bring up

> give away – give back – give in – give off – give out – give over –
> give up – give way

> let alone – let down – let go – let loose – let off – let on – let up

> turn down – turn in – turn loose – turn off – turn on – turn out –
> turn over – turn to – turn up

See #61k.15 on the spelling of two-part verbs.

PROOFREADING TIP

Two-Part Verbs and Tone

By consciously using or avoiding two-part verbs, you can control the tone of your writing. In a strictly formal piece, you may want to avoid or limit your use of two-part verbs, as they may sound too colloquial. Instead, use more formal equivalents:

> buy up the shares   acquire the shares

> give back the gift   return the gift

You can find these equivalents in a good dictionary.

23 Conjunctions

Conjunctions are another kind of structure word or function word (see #12-l). As their name indicates, conjunctions are words that "join together." There are three kinds of conjunctions: *coordinating*, *correlative*, and *subordinating*.

23a Coordinating Conjunctions

There are only seven **coordinating conjunctions**, so they are easy to remember:

and   **but**   **for**   **nor**   **or**   **so**   **yet**

When you use a coordinating conjunction, choose the appropriate one. *And* indicates addition, *nor* indicates negative addition (equivalent to *also not*), *but* and *yet* indicate contrast or opposition, *or* indicates choice, *for* indicates cause or reason, and *so* indicates effect or result. (See also #41, on **faulty coordination**.)

Some coordinating conjunctions can also be other parts of speech: *yet* can be an adverb (It's not *yet* ten o'clock); *so* can be an adverb (It was *so* dark that . . .), an adjective (Is that *so*?), a demonstrative pronoun (I liked him, and I told him *so*), and an interjection (*So!*); *for* is also a common preposition (*for* a while, *for* me); and *but* can be a preposition, meaning "except" (all *but* two).

Coordinating conjunctions have three main functions, which are discussed below.

1. Joining Words, Phrases, and Subordinate Clauses

And, but, or, and *yet* join coordinate elements within sentences. The elements joined are usually of equal importance and of similar grammatical structure and function. When joined, they are sometimes called compounds of various kinds. Here are examples of how various kinds of sentence elements may be compounded:

I saw <u>Jean</u> and <u>Rohan</u>. (two direct objects)

<u>Jean</u> or <u>Rohan</u> saw me. (two subjects)

They <u>danced</u> and <u>sang</u>. (two verbs)

<u>Tired</u> but <u>determined</u>, the hiker plodded on. (two past participles)

The gnome was <u>short</u>, <u>fat</u>, and <u>melancholic</u>. (three predicate adjectives)

He drove <u>quickly</u> yet <u>carefully</u>. (two adverbs)

> **The bird flew <u>in the door</u> and <u>out the window</u>.** (two adverbial prepositional phrases)

> **The children <u>loved the rat</u> but <u>hated the hamster</u>.** (two verbs with direct objects)

> **People <u>who invest wisely</u> and <u>who spend carefully</u> often have boring lives.** (two adjectival clauses)

> **I travel <u>when I have the time</u> and <u>when I have the money</u>.** (two adverbial clauses)

> **The career coach told him <u>what he should wear</u> and <u>how he should speak</u>.** (two noun clauses)

Obviously the elements being joined won't always have identical structures, but don't disappoint readers' natural expectations that compound elements will be parallel. For example, it would be weaker to write the last example—*The career coach told him what he should wear and how he should speak*—with one direct object as a clause and the other as an infinitive phrase (see #40, on faulty parallelism):

> weak: **The career coach told him <u>what he should wear</u> and <u>how to speak</u>.**

When three or more elements are compounded, the conjunction usually appears only between the last two, though *and* and *or* can appear throughout for purposes of rhythm or emphasis:

> **There was a tug-of-war <u>and</u> a sack race <u>and</u> an egg race <u>and</u> a three-legged race <u>and</u> . . . well, there was just about any kind of game anyone could want at a picnic.**

And occasionally *and* can be omitted for emphasis:

> **There were flowers galore—fuchsias, snap dragons, jonquils, dahlias, azaleas, tulips, roses, lilacs, camellias—more kinds of flowers than I wanted to see on any one day.**

2. Joining Independent Clauses

All seven coordinating conjunctions can join independent clauses to make compound (or compound-complex) sentences (see #12z). The clauses will be grammatically equivalent, since they are independent; but they needn't be grammatically parallel or even of similar length, though they often are both, for parallelism is a strong stylistic force. Here are some examples:

> **The players fought, the umpires shouted, <u>and</u> the fans booed.**

> **The kestrel flew higher and higher, in ever-wider circles, <u>and</u> soon it was but a speck in the sky overhead.**

> **Jean saw me, <u>but</u> Rohan didn't.**

> **I won't do it, <u>nor</u> will she.** (With nor there must be some sort of negative in the first clause. Note that after nor the normal subject–verb order is reversed.)

PROOFREADING TIP

Using the Conjunction *so*

The conjunction *so* is informal; in formal writing, you can almost always indicate cause–effect relations with a *because-* or *since*-clause instead:

> **<u>Because</u> there was no way to avoid it, I decided to get as much out of the experience as I could.**

And so is generally more acceptable, but don't use it too often, as it is a weak transition:

> **We overslept, <u>and so</u> we missed the keynote address.**

---

3. Joining Sentences

In spite of what many of us have been taught, it isn't wrong to begin a sentence with *And* or *But*, or for that matter any of the other coordinating conjunctions. Be advised, however, that *For*, since it is so similar in meaning to *because*, often sounds strange at the start of a sentence, as if introducing a fragmentary subordinate clause (see #23c). But the rest, especially *And* and *But*, make good openers—as long as you don't overuse them. An opening *But* or *Yet* can nicely emphasize a contrast or other turn of thought (as in the preceding sentence). An opening *And* can also be emphatic:

> He told the employees of the company he was sorry. <u>And</u> he meant it.

Both *And* and *But* as sentence openers contribute to paragraph coherence (see #5d). And, especially in a narrative, a succession of opening *Ands* can impart a feeling of rapid pace, even breathless excitement.

For punctuation with coordinating conjunctions, see Part V, especially #43a, #44a, #54b, and #54f.

23b Correlative Conjunctions

EAL   **Correlative conjunctions** come in pairs. They *correlate* ("relate together") two parallel parts of a sentence. The following are the principal ones:

either . . . or	neither . . . nor
whether . . . or	both . . . and
not . . . but	not only . . . but also

Correlative conjunctions enable you to write sentences containing forcefully balanced elements, but don't overdo them. They are also more at home in formal than in informal writing. Some examples:

> <u>Either</u> Rodney <u>or</u> Elliott is going to drive.

> She accepted <u>neither</u> the first <u>nor</u> the second job offer.

> <u>Whether</u> by accident <u>or</u> by design, the number turned out to be exactly right.

> <u>Both</u> the administration <u>and</u> the student body are pleased with the new plan.

> She <u>not only</u> plays well <u>but also</u> sings well.

> <u>Not only</u> does she play well, <u>but</u> she <u>also</u> sings well.

Notice, in the last example, how *also* (or its equivalent) can be moved away from the *but*; also note how *does* is needed as an auxiliary because the clause is in the present tense. Except for these variations, make what follows one term exactly parallel to what follows the other: *the first* || *the second*; *by accident* || *by design*; *plays well* || *sings well*. (See also #40, on faulty parallelism.)

Further, with the *not only . . . but also* pair, you should usually make the *also* (or some equivalent) explicit. Its omission results in a feeling of incompleteness:

incomplete: **He was not only smart but charming.**

complete: **He was not only smart but also charming.**

complete: **He was not only smart but charming as well.**

To ensure that you use this correlative pairing effectively, keep in mind the following:

1. For clauses containing *compound verbs* (one or more auxiliary verbs attached to a main verb), place *not only* at the beginning of the clause and then place the first auxiliary verb *before* the subject. Then, place *but* before the subject of the second clause and *also* after the auxiliary verb.

   He has been a great star and he has served his fans well.
   Not only *has* he been a great star, *but* he has *also* served his fans well.

2. For sentences in the *simple present* or *simple past* tenses (other than those in which the main verb is *to be*), you must add the appropriate form of *do* before the subject of the *not only* clause when *not only* appears at the beginning of the clause.

   She looks rested and she looks happy.
   Not only *does* she look rested, *but* she *also* looks happy.

   She looked rested and she looked happy.
   Not only *did* she look rested, *but* she *also* looked happy.

   She is rested and she is happy.
   Not only *is* she rested, *but* she is *also* happy.

3. When *not only* appears inside the clause, you do not have to reverse the order of the auxiliary verb and subject, nor do you have to add *do*, *does*, or *did*.

> **She has worked hard at her job and at her hobbies.**
> **She has worked hard <u>not only</u> at her job <u>but also</u> at her hobbies.**

See #18c for *agreement* of verbs with subjects joined by some of the correlatives.

23c Subordinating Conjunctions

A **subordinating conjunction** introduces a *subordinate* (or *dependent*) clause and links it to the *independent* (or *main* or *principal*) clause to which it is grammatically related:

> **She writes <u>because</u> she has something to say.**

The subordinating conjunction *because* introduces the adverbial clause *because she has something to say* and links it to the independent clause whose verb it modifies. The *because*-clause is *subordinate* because it cannot stand by itself: by itself it would be a *fragment* (see #12x). Note that a subordinate clause can also come first:

> **<u>Because</u> she has something to say, she writes articles for magazines.**

Even though *Because* does not occur between the two unequal clauses, it still links them grammatically.

> **<u>That</u> Raj will win the prize is a foregone conclusion.**

Here, *That* introduces the noun clause *That Raj will win the prize*, which functions as the subject of the sentence. Note that whereas a coordinating conjunction is like a spot of glue between two structures and not a part of either, a subordinating conjunction is an integral part of its clause. In the following sentence, for example, the subordinating conjunction *whenever* is a part of the adverbial clause that modifies the imperative verb *Leave*:

> **Leave <u>whenever you feel tired</u>.**

Here is a list of the principal subordinating conjunctions:

after	if	that	where(ever)
although	if only	though	whereas
as	in case	till	whether
as though	lest	unless	which
because	once	until	while
before	rather than	what	who
even though	since	whatever	why
ever since	than	when(ever)	

There are also many terms consisting of two or more words ending in *as*, *if*, and *that* that serve as subordinating conjunctions, including *inasmuch as, insofar as, as long as, as soon as, as far as, as if, even if, only if, but that, except that, in that, in order that, now that,* and *provided that.*

Note: Some subordinating conjunctions can also function as adverbs, prepositions, and relative pronouns. But for now you can think of all these terms as *subordinators*, including the relative pronouns and relative adverbs (*who, which, that, when, where*) that introduce adjectival clauses (see #14d and #20a.2). If you understand their *subordinating* function, you will understand the syntax of complex and compound-complex sentences (see #12z) and will be able to avoid *fragments* (see #12x).

24   Interjections

An **interjection** is a word or group of words *interjected* or inserted into a sentence in order to express emotion. Strictly speaking, interjections have no grammatical function; they are simply thrust into sentences and play no part in their syntax, though sometimes they act like sentence modifiers. They are often used in dialogue and are not that common in academic writing.

A mild interjection is usually set off with commas. A strong interjection is sometimes set off with dashes and is often accompanied by an exclamation point.

It was, <u>well</u>, a bit of a disappointment.

But—<u>good heavens!</u>—what did you expect?

An interjection may also be a minor sentence by itself (see #12w):

Ouch! That hurt!

Ok. I guess that means that the lesson is over.

Thanks, John! Your advice on dressing a wound was helpful.

Basic Sentence Elements: Subject, Verb, Object, Complement

Consider again the bare bones of a sentence. The two essential elements are a *subject* and a *verb* (see #12a).

Subject

The subject is what is talked about. It is the word or phrase answering the question *Who?* or *What?* More precisely, it is the source of the action indicated by the verb, or the person or thing experiencing or possessing the state of being or the condition indicated by the verb and its complement:

> **Sarah drove the bulldozer.** (*Who* drove? Sarah. Sarah is the source of the action of driving.)

> **We are happy about the outcome.** (*Who* is happy? We are. We are experiencing the state of being happy.)

> **Recycling is vital.** (*What* is vital? Recycling. Recycling possesses the condition of being vital.)

The subject of a sentence will ordinarily be one of the following: a basic noun (see #13), a pronoun (see #14), a gerund or gerund phrase (see #21f), an infinitive or infinitive phrase (see #21a), or a noun clause (see #12-o):

> **British Columbia joined Confederation on 20 July 1871.** (noun)

> **He is a Manitoba historian.** (pronoun)

> **Staring can be an aggressive act.** (gerund)

> **Checking the website is part of our daily routine.** (gerund phrase)

> **To travel is to enjoy life.** (infinitive)

<u>**To order tofu is to make a healthy choice.**</u> (infinitive phrase)

<u>**Whoever signs the contract**</u> **is legally responsible.** (noun clause)

25b Finite Verb

The **finite verb** is the focal point of the clause or the sentence. It indicates both the nature and the time of the action (see #17):

The prime minister <u>will respond</u> during question period. (action: responding; time: the future)

Lewis Carroll <u>invented</u> the adventures of Alice for a child named Alice Liddell. (action: inventing; time: past)

Edmonton <u>has</u> numerous distinct neighbourhoods. (action: having, possessing; time: present)

Syntax <u>is</u> word order. (state of being: being something; time: present)

25c Direct Object

If a verb is *transitive* (see #17a), it will have a **direct object** to complete the pattern (see #12d). Like the subject, the direct object may be a noun, a pronoun, a gerund or gerund phrase, an infinitive or infinitive phrase, or a noun clause:

The price includes <u>admission</u>. (noun)

The increase in gasoline taxes worried <u>us</u>. (pronoun)

Our economy needs <u>farming</u>. (gerund)

He enjoys <u>writing reports</u>. (gerund phrase)

We wanted <u>to participate</u>. (infinitive)

You need <u>to define your terms</u>. (infinitive phrase)

The reporter revealed <u>that his source feared retaliation</u>. (noun clause)

Along with a direct object, there may also be an indirect object or an objective complement (see #12f, #12i, and #12j).

We gave <u>you</u> a blank cheque. (*you*: indirect object; *cheque*: direct object)

She judged the situation <u>untenable</u>. (*situation*: direct object; *untenable*: objective complement)

 ## Subjective Complement

Similarly, a *linking verb* (see #17a) typically requires a **subjective complement** to complete the pattern. This complement will usually be either a *predicate adjective* or a *predicate noun* (see #12g and #12h). A predicate noun may be a noun or a pronoun, or (especially after *be*) a gerund or gerund phrase, an infinitive or infinitive phrase, or a noun clause:

We are <u>friends</u>. (noun)

Was he the <u>one</u>? (pronoun)

His passion is <u>travelling</u>. (gerund)

Her hobby is <u>repairing bicycles</u>. (gerund phrase)

My first impulse was <u>to run</u>. (infinitive)

Our next challenge will be <u>to take action</u>. (infinitive phrase)

She remains <u>what she has long been</u>: a loyal friend. (noun clause)

A predicate adjective will ordinarily be a descriptive adjective, a participle, or an idiomatic prepositional phrase:

The other team's fans are <u>obnoxious</u>. (descriptive adjective)

The novel's plot is <u>intriguing</u>. (present participle)

They seem <u>dedicated</u>. (past participle)

The government is <u>out of ideas</u>. (prepositional phrase)

The linking verb *be* (and sometimes others) can also be followed by an adverbial word or phrase (I am *here*; he is *in his office*).

These elements—**subject**, **finite verb**, and **object** or **complement**— are the core elements of major sentences. They are closely linked in the ways indicated above, with the verb as the focal and uniting element. (For a discussion of the *order* in which these elements occur, see #12s–u.)

26   Modifiers

ONLINE EXERCISES

Modifiers add to the core grammatical elements. They limit or describe other elements so as to modify—that is, to change—a listener's or reader's idea of them. The two principal kinds of modifiers are *adjectives* (see #19) and *adverbs* (see #20). Also useful, but less frequent, are *appositives* (see #12q) and *absolute phrases* (see #12r and #21i). An adjectival or adverbial modifier may even be part of the core of a sentence. For example, an adjectival modifier is essential if it completes the predicate after a linking verb (Recycling is *vital*). An adverbial modifier is essential if it modifies an intransitive verb that would otherwise seem incomplete (Ziad lives *in a condominium*). But generally modifiers do their work by adding to— enriching—a central core of thought.

26a Adjectival Modifiers (see #19)

Adjectival modifiers modify nouns, pronouns, and phrases or clauses functioning as nouns. They commonly answer the questions *Which? What kind of? How many?* and *How much?* An adjectival modifier may be a single-word adjective, a series of adjectives, a participle or participial phrase, an infinitive or infinitive phrase, a prepositional phrase, or a relative clause:

> **Early settlers of western Canada encountered sudden floods, prolonged droughts, and early frosts.** (single words modifying nouns immediately following)

> **He is skeptical.** (predicate adjective modifying the pronoun *He*)

That the author opposes deregulation is <u>evident</u> in her first paragraph. (predicate adjective modifying the noun clause *That the author opposes deregulation*)

<u>Four ambitious young</u> students are competing for the prestigious internship. (series modifying *student*)

The <u>train</u> station is filled with commuters and tourists. (noun functioning as adjective, modifying *station*)

<u>Grinning</u>, she replied to his text message. (present participle modifying *she*)

<u>Brimming with confidence</u>, they began their performance. (present participial phrase modifying *they*)

They continued the climb toward the summit, <u>undaunted</u>. (past participle modifying *they*)

Lijuan applied for the position, <u>having been encouraged to do so by her adviser</u>. (participial phrase, perfect tense, passive voice, modifying *Lijuan*)

They prepared a meal <u>to remember</u>. (infinitive modifying *meal*)

A tendency <u>to blame others</u> is not an admirable trait. (infinitive phrase modifying *tendency*)

The report <u>on the evening news</u> described the restoration of the Halifax Citadel. (prepositional phrase modifying *report*)

The lacrosse team, <u>which was travelling to a tournament in Winnipeg</u>, filed slowly through airport security. (relative clause modifying *team*)

 ## 26b Adverbial Modifiers (see #20)

Adverbial modifiers modify verbs, adjectives, other adverbs, and whole clauses or sentences. They commonly answer the questions *How? When? Where? Why?* and *To what degree?* An adverbial modifier may be a single word, a series, an infinitive or infinitive phrase, a prepositional phrase, or an adverbial clause:

Mix the chemicals <u>thoroughly</u>. (single word modifying the verb *mix*)

As new parents, we are <u>completely</u> happy. (single word modifying the adjective *happy*)

They planned their future together <u>quite</u> enthusiastically. (single word modifying the adverb *enthusiastically*)

<u>Theoretically</u>, these same services could be accessed online. (single word modifying the rest of the sentence)

He loves her <u>truly</u>, <u>madly</u>, <u>deeply</u>. (series modifying the verb *loves*)

<u>To succeed</u>, you must work well with others. (infinitive modifying the verb must *work*)

She was lucky <u>to have been selected</u> for the exchange program. (infinitive phrase modifying the predicate adjective *lucky*)

Biomedical engineers work <u>in this lab</u>. (prepositional phrase modifying the verb *work*)

We disagreed <u>because we were taking different theoretical approaches to the text</u>. (clause modifying the verb *disagreed*)

The election results trickled in slowly <u>because the ballots were being counted by hand</u>. (clause modifying the adverb *slowly*, or the whole preceding clause, *The election results trickled in slowly.*)

Shut off your computer <u>when you leave on vacation</u>. (clause modifying the preceding independent clause)

26c Overlapping Modifiers

The preceding examples illustrate each kind of adjectival and adverbial modifier separately, in tidy isolation from the other kinds. And such sentences are not uncommon, for relative simplicity of sentence structure can be a stylistic strength. But many sentences are more complicated, largely because modifiers overlap in them. Modifiers occur as parts of other modifiers: single-word modifiers occur as parts of phrases and clauses, phrases occur as parts of other phrases and as parts of clauses, and subordinate clauses occur as parts of phrases and as parts of other clauses. Here are examples illustrating some of the possible structural variety. (You may want to check sections #12c–k to match these sentences and their clauses with the various patterns they include.)

Her theory is briefly restated in the closing paragraph.

briefly – adverb modifying *restated*
in the closing paragraph – adverbial prepositional phrase modifying *restated*
closing – participial adjective modifying *paragraph*

He purchased a few of the off-the-rack suits.

of the off-the-rack suits – adjectival prepositional phrase modifying *a few*
off-the-rack – hyphenated prepositional phrase, adjective modifying *suits*

Hoping to learn to perform brilliantly, the cast rehearsed until dawn.

Hoping to learn to perform brilliantly – participial phrase modifying *cast*
to learn to perform brilliantly – infinitive phrase, object of the participle *hoping*
to perform brilliantly – infinitive phrase, object of the infinitive *to learn*
brilliantly – adverb modifying infinitive *to perform*
until dawn – adverbial prepositional phrase modifying *rehearsed*

It was daunting to think of the consequences that might ensue.

to think of the consequences that might ensue – infinitive phrase, delayed subject of sentence
of the consequences – adverbial prepositional phrase modifying infinitive *to think*
that might ensue – relative clause modifying *consequences*
daunting – participle, predicate adjective modifying subject

With several generous donations, we purchased what the homeless shelter had needed since October: warm blankets to distribute in cold weather.

With several generous donations – adverbial prepositional phrase modifying *purchased*
several generous – adjective series modifying *donations*

what the homeless shelter had needed since October – noun clause, direct
    object of *purchased*
since October – adverbial prepositional phrase modifying *had needed*
warm blankets to distribute in cold weather – appositive phrase modifying
    the noun clause *what the homeless shelter had needed since October*
to distribute — adjectival infinitive modifying *blankets*
in cold weather – adverbial prepositional phrase modifying *distribute*

**He was a child who, being quite introverted in large groups of adults,
chose a quiet corner where he could read a book.**

who chose a quiet corner where he could read a book – relative clause modifying the
    predicate noun *child*
where he could read a book – adjectival clause modifying *corner*
being quite introverted in large groups of adults – participial phrase modifying the
    relative pronoun *who*
introverted – past participle, predicate adjective after being
quite – adverb modifying *introverted*
in large groups of adults – adverbial prepositional phrase modifying *introverted*
of adults – adjectival prepositional phrase modifying *groups*

These examples suggest the richness of structure that is possible, the
kind you undoubtedly create at times without even thinking about it.
But think about it. Understanding sentences in this way can help you to
develop greater variety in your writing.

 ## 26d Using Modifiers: A Sample Scenario

Suppose you were asked to write a short paper on your reading habits.
In getting your ideas together and taking notes, you might draft a bare-
bones sentence such as this:

Recently, I've been reading fiction.

It's a start. But you soon realize that it isn't exactly true to your thoughts.
It needs qualification. So you begin modifying its elements:

Recently, I've been reading <u>historical</u> fiction.

The adjective specifies the kind of fiction you've been reading—you're focused on novels and short stories written about the past. Then you add an adjectival prepositional phrase to further limit the word *fiction*:

> **Recently, I've been reading historical fiction <u>about the First World War</u>.**

Then you realize that while the fiction you've been reading has been primarily historical and about World War I, you haven't read it all; therefore you insert another adjective to further qualify the noun *fiction*:

> **Recently, I've been reading <u>Canadian</u> historical fiction about the First World War.**

Next you realize that *Canadian historical fiction* implies that you are familiar with all such fiction. But you quickly see a way to revise the sentence to convey your thoughts accurately; you put the adjective *much* in front of the verb:

> **Recently, I've been reading <u>much</u> Canadian historical fiction about the First World War.**

So far so good. But you're not entirely satisfied with the sentence; you suspect that a reader might want a little more information about your reference to Canadian fiction about the First World War. You could go on to explain in another sentence or two, but you'd like to get a little more substance into this sentence. Then you have this thought: you can help clarify your point and at the same time inject some rhythm by adding a participial phrase modifying *fiction*:

> **Recently, I've been reading much Canadian historical fiction <u>representing our longstanding ambivalence</u> about the First World War.**

You rather like it. But working at this one sentence has got you thinking. Before you leave it, you consider your reasons for reading such fiction. You decide that you're doing this reading because this fiction focuses on a major event of the twentieth century, and because it tells stories of a time when Canada is said to have earned its national independence but when it also experienced deep political divisions over conscription. You feel the words beginning to come, and you consider your options: you can put the explanation in a separate sentence; you can join it to your present sentence with a semicolon or a colon or a coordinating conjunction like *for*, creating a compound sentence; or you can integrate it more closely by making it a subordinate clause, turning the whole into a complex sentence. You decide on the third method, and you put the new material in a *because*-clause modifying the verb *have been reading*. And while you're thinking about it, you begin to feel that, given the way your sentence has developed, the word *reading* now sounds rather bland, weak because it doesn't quite reveal your seriousness. So you decide to change it to the more precise verb *studying*. Now your sentence is finished, at least for the time being:

> **Recently, I've been studying much Canadian historical fiction about the First World War, because this fiction focuses on a major event of the twentieth century and because it tells stories of a time when Canada is said to have earned its national independence but also to have experienced deep political divisions over conscription.**

By adding modifiers, you can enlarge the reader's knowledge of the material being presented, and you can improve the precision, clarity, and style of your sentence. Minimal or bare-bones sentences can themselves be effective and emphatic. But many of your sentences will be longer. And it is in elaborating and enriching your sentences with modifiers that you as author and stylist can exercise much of your control: you take charge of what your readers will learn and how they will learn it.

27-29 Sentence Length, Variety, and Emphasis

ONLINE EXERCISES

27 Sentence Length

How long should a sentence be to achieve its purpose? That depends. A sentence may, in rare cases, consist of one word, or it may go on for a hundred words or more. There are no strict guidelines to tell you how long to make your sentences. If you're curious, do some research to determine the average sentence length in several pieces of writing you have handy—for example, this handbook, a recent novel, a collection of essays, newspaper and magazine articles, email messages, or articles posted on your favourite website or blog. You'll probably find that the average is somewhere between 15 and 25 words per sentence, that longer sentences are more common in formal and specialized writing, and that shorter sentences are more at home in informal and popular writing, in email, and in narrative and dialogue. There are, then, some general guidelines, and you'll probably fit your own writing to them. But if you're far off what seems to be the average for the kind of writing you are doing, you may need to make some changes to adapt to the writing situation.

27a Short Sentences

If you receive feedback that you're writing too many short sentences, try

- building them up by elaborating their elements with modifiers, including various kinds of phrases and clauses (see #26d);
- combining some of them to form compound subjects, predicates, and objects or complements; and/or
- combining two or more of them—especially if they are simple sentences—into a compound, complex, or compound-complex sentence (see #12z).

27b Long Sentences

If you find yourself writing too many long sentences, check them for three possible problems:

1. You may be rambling or trying to pack too much into a single sentence, possibly destroying its unity (see #41) and certainly making it difficult to read. Try breaking it up into more unified or more easily manageable parts.
2. You may be using too many words to make your point. Try cutting out any deadwood (see #71).
3. You may have slipped into what is called "excessive subordination"—too many loosely related details obscuring the main idea, or

confusing strings of subordinate clauses modifying each other. Try removing some of the clutter, and try reducing clauses to phrases and phrases to single words.

28 Sentence Variety

To create emphasis (see #29) and avoid monotony, vary the lengths and kinds of your sentences. This is a process you should engage in when revising your draft to strengthen its style. Examine some pieces of prose that you particularly enjoy or that you find unusually clear and especially readable: you will likely discover that they contain both a pleasing mixture of short, medium, and long sentences and a similar variety of kinds and structures.

28a Variety of Lengths

A string of short sentences will sound choppy and fragmented; avoid the staccato effect by interweaving some longer ones. On the other hand, a succession of long sentences may make your ideas hard to follow; give your readers a break—and your prose some sparkle—by using a few short, emphatic sentences to change your pace occasionally. Even a string of medium-length sentences can bore readers into inattention. Impart some rhythm, some shape, to your paragraphs by varying sentence length. Especially consider using a short, emphatic sentence to open or close a paragraph, and occasionally an unusually long sentence to end a paragraph.

28b Variety of Kinds

A string of simple and compound sentences risks coming across to a reader as simplistic. In some narratives and in certain technical and business documents, successive simple and compound sentences may be appropriate for recounting a sequence of events, but when you're writing in other modes and especially in academic writing, let some of the complexity of your ideas be reflected in complex and compound-complex sentences. Keep in mind, however, that a string of complex and compound-complex sentences may become oppressive. Give your readers a breather now and then by employing a simple or short compound sentence.

 28c **Variety of Structures**

Try to avoid an unduly long string of sentences that use the same syntactical structure. For example, though the standard order of elements in declarative sentences is subject–verb–object or –complement, consider varying that order occasionally for emphasis (see #12s and #29). Use an occasional interrogative sentence (see #12t), whether a rhetorical question (a question that doesn't expect an answer) or a question that you proceed to answer as you develop a paragraph. An occasional expletive pattern or passive voice can be refreshing—if you can justify it on other grounds as well (see #12e, #12k, #17-l, and #29f).

In particular, try not to begin a string of sentences with the same kind of word or phrase or clause—unless you are purposely setting up a controlled succession of parallel structures for emphasis or coherence (see #5a). Imagine the effect of several sentences beginning with such words as *Similarly, Especially, Consequently, Nevertheless*. Whatever else the sentences contained, the sameness would be distracting. Or imagine a series of sentences all starting with a subject-noun, or with a present-participial phrase. To avoid such undesirable sameness, take advantage of the way modifiers of various kinds can be moved around in sentences (see #12q, #12r, #19d, #20d, and #29e).

29 Emphasis in Sentences

emph To communicate effectively, make sure your readers perceive the relative importance of your ideas the same way you do. Learn to control emphasis so that what you want emphasized is what gets emphasized.

You can emphasize whole sentences in several ways:

- Set a sentence off by itself, as a short paragraph. (Use this strategy judiciously.)
- Put an important sentence at the beginning or, even better, at the end of a paragraph.

- Put an important point in a short sentence among several long ones, or in a long sentence among several short ones.
- Shift the style or structure of a sentence to make it stand out from those around it (see #6).

In similar ways, you can emphasize important parts of individual sentences. The principal devices for achieving emphasis within sentences are position and word order, repetition, stylistic contrast, syntax, and punctuation.

Endings and Beginnings

The most emphatic position in a sentence is its ending; the second most emphatic position is its beginning. Consider these two sentences:

> **Our accommodations will comprise four rooms.**

> **Four rooms will make up our accommodations.**

Each sentence emphasizes both *our accommodations* and *four rooms,* but the first emphasizes *four rooms* a little more, whereas the second emphasizes *our accommodations* more. Further, the longer the sentence, the stronger the effect of emphasis by position. Consider the following:

> a. **The best teacher I've ever had was my high-school chemistry teacher, a brilliant woman in her early fifties.**
> b. **A brilliant woman in her early fifties, my high-school chemistry teacher was the best teacher I've ever had.**
> c. **My high-school chemistry teacher, a brilliant woman in her early fifties, was the best teacher I've ever had.**
> d. **The best teacher I've ever had was a brilliant woman in her early fifties who taught me chemistry in high school.**

Each sentence contains the same three ideas, but each distributes the emphasis differently. In each the last part is the most emphatic, the first part next, and the middle part least.

Note that in all four versions the part referring to "the best teacher I've ever had" comes either first or last, since the superlative *best* would sound unnatural in the unemphatic middle position—unless one acknowledged its inherent emphasis in some other way, for example by setting off the appositive with a pair of dashes (see #46):

> **My high-school chemistry teacher—the best teacher I've ever had— was a brilliant woman in her early fifties.**

 ## 29b Loose Sentences and Periodic Sentences

A *loose, cumulative,* or *"right-branching"* sentence makes its main point in an early independent clause and then adds modifying subordinate elements:

> **The concert began modestly, minus special effects and fanfare, with the performers sitting casually onstage and taking up their instruments to play their first song.**

Such sentences are common, for they are "loose" and comfortable, easygoing, natural. In contrast to the loose is the *periodic* (or *"left-branching"*) sentence, which wholly or partly delays its main point, the independent clause, until the end:

> **With the performers sitting casually onstage and taking up their instruments to play their first song, the concert began modestly, minus special effects and fanfare.**

Full periodic sentences are usually the result of careful thought and planning. However, they can sometimes sound contrived, less natural, and therefore should not be used without forethought. They can also be dramatic and emphatic, creating suspense as the reader waits for the meaning to fall into place. When you try for such suspense, don't separate subject and predicate too widely, as a writer did in this sentence:

> ineffective: **The abrupt change from one moment when the air is alive with laughing and shouting, to the next when the atmosphere resembles that of a morgue, is dramatic.**

Many sentences delay completion of the main clause only until somewhere in the middle rather than all the way to the end. To the degree that they do delay it, they are partly periodic.

29c The Importance of the Final Position

Because the end of a sentence is naturally so emphatic, readers expect something important there; it is best not to disappoint them by letting something incidental or merely qualifying fall at the end, for then the sentence itself will fall: its energy and momentum will be lost, its essential meaning distorted. For example:

> emph: **That was a much easier assignment, I think.**

The uncertain *I think* should go at the beginning or, even less emphatically, after *That* or *was*.

> emph: **Cramming for exams can be counterproductive, sometimes.**

The qualifying *sometimes* could go at the beginning, but it would be best after *can*, letting the emphasis fall where it belongs, on *cramming* and *counterproductive*.

29d Changing Word Order

Earlier sections point out certain standard patterns: for example, subject–verb–object or –complement (#12c–j); single-word adjectives preceding nouns—or, if predicate adjectives, following them (#19d); and so on. But variations are possible, and because these patterns are recognized as standard, any departures from them stand out (see #12s and #19d for examples). If the inverted order calls attention to itself at the expense of meaning, however, the attempt may backfire. In the following sentence, for example, the writer strained a little too hard for emphasis:

> **It is from imagination that have come all the world's great literature, music, architecture, and works of art.**

29e Movable Modifiers

Many modifiers other than single-word adjectives are movable, enabling you to shift them or other words to where you want them. Appositives, for instance, can sometimes be transposed (see #12q). And you can move participial phrases, if you do so carefully (see #19d). Absolute phrases (see #12r), since they function as sentence modifiers, can usually come at the beginning or the end—or, if syntax permits, in the middle.

But adverbial modifiers are the most movable of all (see #20d). As you compose and revise your drafts, consider the various possible placements of any adverbial modifiers you've used. Take advantage of their flexibility to exercise maximum control over the rhythms of your sentences and, most important, to get the emphases that will best serve your purposes. Some examples:

> Two patrol cars crept <u>slowly and quietly</u> into the parking lot.

Would the adverbs be more emphatic at the end? Try it:

> Two patrol cars crept into the parking lot <u>slowly and quietly</u>.

A little better, perhaps. Now try them at the beginning, and instead of *and*, use punctuation to emphasize the slowness:

> <u>Slowly, quietly</u>, two patrol cars crept into the parking lot.

29f Using the Expletive and the Passive Voice for Emphasis

Two of the basic sentence patterns, the *expletive* (#12k) and the *passive voice* (#12e, #17-l), can be weak and unemphatic in some contexts. Used strategically, however, they can enable you to achieve a desired emphasis. For example:

> Passive voice can be used to move a certain word or phrase to an emphatic place in a sentence.

Here, putting the verb in the passive voice (*can be used*) makes *Passive voice* the subject of the sentence and enables this important element to come at the beginning; otherwise, the sentence would have to begin less strongly (e.g., with *You can use passive voice*). And consider this next example, which makes strategic use of the expletive pattern:

> There are advantages to using the expletive pattern for a deliberate change of pace in your writing.

In this case, opening the sentence with *There* is preferable to opening with long and unwieldy alternatives.

Use expletives and passive voice when you need to delete or delay mention of the agent or otherwise shift the subject of a sentence.

29g Emphasis by Repetition

You may wish to repeat an important word or idea to emphasize it, to make it stay in your readers' minds. Unintentional repetition can be wordy and tedious (see #71b); but intentional, controlled repetition—used sparingly—can be very effective, especially in sentences with balanced or parallel structures:

> **If you have the courage to face adventure, the adventure can sometimes give you courage.**

> **If it's a challenge they seek, it's a challenge they'll find.**

29h Emphasis by Stylistic Contrast

A stylistically enhanced sentence—for example, a periodic sentence (#29b), a sentence with parallel or balanced structure (#40, #29g), or a richly metaphorical or allusive sentence (#65)—stands out beside plainer sentences. For that reason, such a sentence may be most effective at the end of a paragraph (see #4c). In the same way, a word or phrase that differs in style or tone from those that surround it may stand out (and note that such terms often gravitate toward that position of natural emphasis, the end of the sentence):

> **The chef—conservative as her behaviour sometimes appears—dazzles the kitchen staff with her gutsy culinary experiments.**

> **My grandmother may be almost ninety years old, but she approaches each day with a child's *joie de vivre*.**

Terms from other languages naturally stand out, but don't use them pretentiously, for some readers are unimpressed by them or even resent them; use one only after due thought, and preferably when there is no satisfactory English equivalent.

29i Emphasis by Syntax

Put your most important claims in independent clauses; put lesser claims in subordinate clauses and phrases. Sometimes you have more than one option, depending on what you want to emphasize:

Avoiding his eyes, she spoke hesitantly.

Speaking hesitantly, she avoided his eyes.

But more often the choice is determined by the content. Consider the way subordination affects emphasis in the following pairs of sentences:

original: **I strolled into the laboratory, when my attention was attracted by the pitter-pattering of a little white rat in a cage at the back.**

revised: **When I strolled into the laboratory, my attention was attracted by the pitter-pattering of a little white rat in a cage at the back.**

original: **Choosing my courses carefully, I tried to plan my academic schedule around my co-op work placement.**

revised: **Because I was trying to plan my academic schedule around my co-op work placement, I chose my courses carefully.**

original: **I had almost finished downloading the file when the power failed and I lost my connection to the network.**

revised: **When I had almost finished downloading the file, the power failed and I lost my connection to the network.**

See also #41 and #23c.

29j Emphasis by Punctuation

An exclamation point (!) denotes emphasis. But using an exclamation point is not the only way, and usually not the best way (especially in academic writing), to achieve emphasis with punctuation. Try making your sentences appropriately emphatic without resorting to this sometimes artificial device. Arrange your words so that commas and other marks fall where you want a pause for emphasis (see #29e). Use dashes, colons, and even parentheses judiciously to set off important ideas. Occasionally use a semicolon instead of a comma to get a more emphatic pause (but only in a series or between independent clauses). (For more on punctuation, see Part V.)

> **PROOFREADING TIP**
>
> **Avoiding Artificial Emphasis**
>
> As much as possible, avoid emphasizing your own words and sentences with such mechanical devices as underlining, italics, quotation marks, and capitalization. See #57-o and #59d.

30 Analyzing Sentences

ONLINE
EXERCISES

Practise analyzing your own and others' sentences. The better you understand how sentences work, the better able you will be to write effective and correct sentences.

You should be able to account for each word in a sentence: no essential element should be missing, nothing should be left over, and the grammatical relations among all the parts should be clear. If these conditions aren't met, the sentence in question is likely to be misleading or ambiguous. If words, phrases, and clauses fit the roles they are being asked to play, the sentence should work.

The first step in analyzing a sentence is to identify the main parts of its basic structure: the subject, the finite verb, and the object or complement, if any. (If the sentence is something other than a simple sentence, there will be more than one set of these essential parts.) Then determine the modifiers of these elements, and then the modifiers of modifiers.

30a The Chart Method

Here is a convenient arrangement for analyzing the structure of relatively uncomplicated sentences:

Satirists on Twitter gleefully mocked the political gaffe.

subject	finite verb	object or complement	adjectival modifier	adverbial modifier
Satirists	mocked	gaffe (direct object of verb *mocked*)	on Twitter (prepositional adj.; modifies *Satirists*)	gleefully
			the (modifies *gaffe*)	
			political (modifies *gaffe*)	

This most beautiful summer is now almost gone.

subject	finite verb	object or complement	adjectival modifier	adverbial modifier
summer	is (linking verb)	gone (predicate adj.)	This (demonstrative adj. modifying *summer*)	most (modifies adj. *beautiful*)
				now (modifies verb *is*
			beautiful (modifies *summer*)	almost (modifies *gone*)

The very befuddled Roger realized that learning Sanskrit was not easy.

subject	finite verb	object or complement	adjectival modifier	adverbial modifier	other
Roger	realized	that ... easy (noun clause as direct object)	The, befuddled (modify *Roger*)	very (modifies *befuddled*)	
learning	was (linking verb)	easy (predicate adj.) Sanskrit (obj. of gerund *learning*)		not (modifies *easy*)	that (sub. conj.)

In the last example, the items below the dotted line belong to the subordinate clause of this complex sentence.

30b The Vertical Method

For more complicated sentences, you may find a different method more convenient, for example one in which the sentence is written out vertically:

When the canoe trip ended, Philip finally realized that the end of his happy summer was almost upon him.

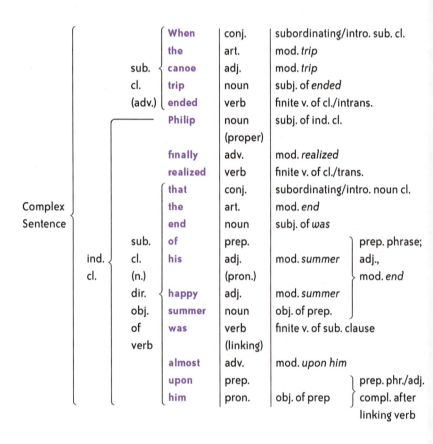

	When	conj.	subordinating/intro. sub. cl.	
	the	art.	mod. *trip*	
sub.	canoe	adj.	mod. *trip*	
cl.	trip	noun	subj. of *ended*	
(adv.)	ended	verb	finite v. of cl./intrans.	
	Philip	noun (proper)	subj. of ind. cl.	
	finally	adv.	mod. *realized*	
	realized	verb	finite v. of cl./trans.	
	that	conj.	subordinating/intro. noun cl.	
	the	art.	mod. *end*	
	end	noun	subj. of *was*	
sub.	of	prep.		prep. phrase;
cl.	his	adj. (pron.)	mod. *summer*	adj.,
(n.)				mod. *end*
dir.	happy	adj.	mod. *summer*	
obj.	summer	noun	obj. of prep.	
of	was	verb (linking)	finite v. of sub. clause	
verb	almost	adv.	mod. *upon him*	
	upon	prep.		prep. phr./adj.
	him	pron.	obj. of prep	compl. after linking verb

Complex Sentence / *ind. cl.*

As you can see, this method challenges you to account for the grammatical function of every word in the sentence.

31-42 Common Sentence Problems

In the remaining sections of Part IV we define some common problems that can affect the clarity of sentences, and we suggest ways to avoid or correct them.

The three sentence errors that can most impede clear communication in your writing are the *fragment*, the *comma splice*, and the *run-on sentence*. Edit closely for them.

31 Sentence Coherence

coh Although the word *coherence* usually refers to the connection between sentences and between paragraphs (see #3–5, #8b), the parts of a sentence must also cohere. Each sentence fault discussed in the next sections (#32–42) is capable of making a sentence incoherent. If a sentence lacks coherence, the fault probably lies in one or more of the following: faulty arrangement (*faulty word order, misplaced modifier*), unclear or missing or illogical connections and relations between parts (*faulty reference, lack of agreement, dangling modifier, faulty coordination, faulty logic, incongruous alignment*), or syntactic shift from one part to another (*mixed construction, shift in point of view, faulty parallelism*); or the weakness may be due to something that can be labelled only "unclear." Consult the following sections as necessary to ensure that your sentences are coherent within themselves.

32 Fragments

frag A **fragment** is a group of words that is not an acceptable sentence, either major or minor, but that is punctuated as if it were a sentence. The fragment is discussed along with the minor sentence, which it sometimes resembles: see #12w and #12x.

Comma Splices

cs A **comma splice** occurs when two independent clauses are joined with only a comma, rather than with a semicolon. Although the error usually stems from a misunderstanding of sentence structure, it is discussed under *punctuation*, since it requires attention to punctuation marks: see #54b.

Run-on (Fused) Sentences

run-on A **run-on sentence**, sometimes called a **fused sentence**, is in fact not
fs a single sentence but two sentences run together with neither a period to mark the end of the first nor a capital letter to mark the beginning of the second. An error most likely to occur when a writer is rushed, it can sometimes, like the comma splice, result from a problem in understanding how sentences work. And since a run-on sentence occurs with the same kind of sentence structure as the comma splice, and likely it requires attention to punctuation, we discuss it alongside the other error: see #54a.

Misplaced Modifiers

35a Movability and Poor Placement

mm As we point out in the introduction to Part III, part of the meaning in English sentences is conveyed by the position of words in relation

ONLINE EXERCISES

to each other. And though there are certain standard or conventional arrangements, a good deal of flexibility is possible (see #12s, #12t, #19d, #22b, and #26). Adverbial modifiers are especially movable (see #20d and #29e). Because of this flexibility, writers sometimes put a modifier where it conveys an unintended or ambiguous meaning, or where it is linked by juxtaposition to a word it can't logically modify. To say precisely what you mean, you have to be careful in placing your modifiers—especially adverbs. Note the changes in meaning that result from the different placement of the word *only* in the following sentences:

<u>Only</u> her son works in Fort McMurray. (No other member of her family works there.)

Her <u>only</u> son works in Fort McMurray. (She has no other sons.)

Her son <u>only</u> works in Fort McMurray. (He doesn't live in Fort McMurray, but commutes.)

Her son works <u>only</u> in Fort McMurray. (He works in no other place.)

The following sentence demonstrates how misplacement can produce absurdity:

mm: **While testifying before the Transport Committee, the minister denied allegations heatedly concerning inadequate passenger screening reported in a recent CBC documentary at Pearson Airport.**

The adverb *heatedly* belongs before *denied*, the verb it modifies. The adjectival phrase *reported in a recent CBC documentary* belongs after *allegations*, the noun it modifies. And the adverbial phrase *at Pearson Airport* belongs after the phrase *concerning inadequate passenger screening*.

Usually it is best to keep modifiers and the words they modify as close together as possible. Here is an example of an adjective out of place:

mm: **Love is a <u>difficult</u> emotion to express in words.**

clear: **Love is an emotion (that is) difficult to express in words.**

and an example of a misplaced relative clause:

mm: **Every year the Royal St. John's Regatta is held on Quidi Vidi Lake, which has been called "the world's largest garden party."**

Is it the lake that has been called "the world's largest garden party"? The writer likely meant something else:

> clear: **Every year the Royal St. John's Regatta, which has been called "the world's largest garden party," is held on Quidi Vidi Lake.**

35b Only, almost, etc.

Pay particular attention (as illustrated in the preceding section) to such adverbs as *only*, *almost*, *just*, *merely*, and *even*. In speech, we often place these words casually, but in writing we should put them where they clearly mean what we want them to:

> mm: **Hardy _only_ wrote novels as a sideline; his main interest was poetry.**
> clear: **Hardy wrote novels _only_ as a sideline; his main interest was poetry.**

> mm: **His mother built that shed by hand, and it _almost_ stood for thirty years.**
> clear: **His mother built that shed by hand, and it stood for _almost_ thirty years.**

35c Squinting Modifiers

squint A **squinting modifier** is a word or phrase put between two elements either of which it could modify. That is, the modifier "squints" so that a reader can't tell which way it is looking; the result is ambiguity:

> squint: **It was so warm _for a week_ we did hardly any skiing at all.**

Which clause does the adverbial phrase modify? It is ambiguous. A speaking voice could impart clarifying emphasis to such a sentence, but a writer must substitute words or structures for the missing vocal emphasis. Here, adding *that* removes the ambiguity:

> clear: **It was so warm that for a week we did hardly any skiing at all.**

> clear: **It was so warm for a week that we did hardly any skiing at all.**

Another example:

squint: **My sister advised me <u>now and then</u> to travel in the Rockies.**

This time, rearrangement is necessary:

clear: **My sister now and then advised me to travel in the Rockies.**

clear: **My sister advised me to travel now and then in the Rockies.**

36 Dangling Modifiers

dm Like a pronoun without an antecedent (see #15), a **dangling modifier** has no word in the rest of the sentence to attach to; instead it is left dangling, grammatically unattached, and so it often tries to attach itself, illogically, to some other word. Most dangling modifiers are *verbal phrases*; be watchful for them in editing drafts of your work.

36a Dangling Participial Phrases (see #21d)

dm: **<u>Strolling casually beside the lagoon</u>, my eyes fell upon two children chasing a pair of geese.**

Since the adjectival phrase wants to modify a noun, it tries to link with the subject of the adjacent clause, *eyes*. Eyes can scarcely be said to "stroll." To avoid the unintentionally humorous dangler, simply change the participial phrase to a subordinate clause:

revised: **<u>As I strolled casually beside the lagoon</u>, my eyes fell upon two children chasing a pair of geese.**

Or, if you want to keep the effect of the opening participial phrase, rework the clause so that its subject is the logical word to be modified:

revised: **Strolling casually beside the lagoon, <u>I</u> let my gaze fall upon two children chasing a pair of geese.**

Here is another example, one with no built-in absurdity:

> dm: **<u>Living in a small town</u>, there was a strong sense of community among us.**

To correct the dangling participle, you need to provide something for the phrase to modify, or revise the sentence in some other way:

> revised: **Living in a small town, <u>we</u> had a strong sense of community among us.**

> revised: **<u>Since we lived in a small town</u>, there was a strong sense of community among us.**

In the next example, passive voice causes the trouble (see #17-l):

> dm: **<u>Witnessing an increase in the significance of e-learning</u>, tablet computers are being introduced to many classrooms.**

> revised: **Witnessing an increase in the significance of e-learning, <u>educators</u> are introducing tablet computers to many classrooms.**

> revised: **<u>As educators witness an increase in the significance of e-learning</u>, tablet computers are being introduced to many classrooms.**

36b Dangling Gerund Phrases (see #21f)

When a gerund phrase is the object of a preposition, it can dangle much like a participial phrase:

> dm: **<u>After being informed of the correct procedure</u>, our attention was directed to the next steps.**

It isn't "our attention" that was "informed." The passive voice contributes to the confusion here.

> revised: **After informing us of the correct procedure, the instructor directed our attention to the next steps.**

36c Dangling Infinitive Phrases (see #21a)

> dm: **<u>To reach the other side of the lake</u>, a barge must be taken.**

Ineffective passive voice is the issue, depriving the infinitive phrase of a logical word to modify.

revised: **To reach the other side of the lake, <u>one</u> must take a barge.**

The next example is more complicated:

dm: **To make the instructor's lab demonstration successful, it requires the students' cooperation.**

Here, the infinitive phrase seems to be the antecedent of *it*. Dropping the *it* lets the phrase act as a noun; or the sentence can be revised in some other way:

revised: **To make the instructor's lab demonstration successful <u>will</u> require the students' cooperation.**

revised: **If the instructor's lab demonstration is to succeed, the students will have to cooperate.**

36d Dangling Elliptical Clauses

An **elliptical clause** is an adverbial clause abridged so that its subject and verb are only understood, or implied, rather than stated; the subject of the independent clause then automatically serves also as the implied subject of the elliptical clause. If the implied subject is different from the subject of the independent clause, the subordinate element will dangle, sometimes illogically.

dm: <u>**Once in disguise,**</u> **the hero's conflict emerges.**

It isn't "the hero's *conflict*" that is in disguise, but the *hero*. Either supply a logical subject and verb for the elliptical clause, or retain the elliptical clause and make the other subject logically agree with it:

revised: **Once <u>the hero</u> is in disguise, <u>his conflict</u> emerges.**

revised: **Once in disguise, <u>the hero</u> begins to reveal his conflict.**

Another example:

dm: <u>**When well marinated,**</u> **put the pieces of chicken on the barbecue.**

Here, the understood subject is *the pieces*, but the subject of the independent clause of this imperative sentence is an understood *you*. Give the elliptical clause a subject and verb:

> revised: **When the pieces of chicken are well marinated, put them on the barbecue.**

36e Dangling Prepositional Phrases and Appositives
(see #22 and #12q)

A prepositional phrase can also dangle. In this example, an indefinite *it* (see #16e) is the issue:

> dm: **Like a child in a toy shop, it is all she can bear not to touch everything.**

> revised: **Like a child in a toy shop, she can hardly bear not to touch everything.**

And so can an appositive prove to be problematic:

> dm: **A superb racing car, a Ferrari's engine is a masterpiece of engineering.**

The phrase seems to be in apposition with the noun *engine*, but it is illogical to equate an engine with an entire car (the possessive *Ferrari's* is adjectival). Revise it:

> revised: **A superb racing car, a Ferrari has an engine that is a masterpiece of engineering.**

37 Mixed Constructions

mix

Avoiding mixed constructions can be a particular challenge for anyone whose first language has a different sentence structure than English has. To begin a sentence with one construction and then inadvertently shift to another can create confusion.

> mix: **Eagle Creek is a small BC community is located near Wells Gray Provincial Park.**

The writer here sets up two clauses beginning with *is* but then omits a subject for the second occurrence of *is*. Either drop the first *is* and add commas around the resulting appositive phrase (*a small BC community*), or add *that* or *which* before the second *is*.

> mix: **Since my credit card payment was late, therefore I have to pay interest.**

Here, the writer begins with a subordinating *Since* but then uses *therefore* to introduce the second clause, which would be correct only if the first clause were independent. Fix this by dropping either the *Since* or the *therefore* (if you drop *Since*, change the comma to a semicolon to avoid a comma splice: see #54b).

38 Faulty Alignment

ONLINE EXERCISES

Poor **alignment** results when two or more elements in a sentence are illogically or incongruously aligned with each other. Such errors often take the form of a verb saying something illogical about its subject—an error sometimes called *faulty predication*; that is, what is predicated about the subject is an impossibility. For example:

> al, pred: **Many new inventions and techniques occurred during this period.**

An invention could, with some strain, be said to *occur*, but *techniques* do not occur. Revision is necessary; one possibility is to use an expletive and the passive voice:

> revised: **During this period there were many new inventions, and many new techniques were developed.**

In the next example the verb repeats the meaning of the subject:

al, pred: **The setting of the story takes place in Manitoba.**

revised: **The story takes place in Manitoba.**

better: **The story is set in Manitoba.**

Errors in predication often occur with a form of *be* and a complement:

al, pred: **The amount of gear to take along is the first step to consider when planning a long hike.**

But an *amount* cannot be a *step*; revision is needed:

revised: **The first step in planning a hike is to decide how much gear to take along.**

Note that this also removes the other illogicality: one does not consider a step; rather the considering, or deciding, is itself the step.

Other errors in alignment aren't errors in predication, but are similar to them in using words illogically:

al: **In her opening remarks, the speaker described the occurrences, environment, and hopes of her family.**

It is logical to speak of a *family* having *hopes* and an *environment*, but not *occurrences*; substitute *experiences*.

al: **Its fine texture was as smooth and hard as a waterworn rock.**

This, which illogically equates *texture* and *rock*, is also a form of incomplete comparison. Insert *that of* after *hard as*. (See also #42.)

al: **Professions such as a doctor, a lawyer, or an engineer require extensive post-secondary education.**

This sentence is illogical because *being* a doctor, a lawyer, or an engineer is not a *profession*. Change *professions* to *professionals*:

> revised: **Professionals such as doctors, lawyers, and engineers require extensive post-secondary education.**

Or recast the sentence completely:

> revised: **Professions such as medicine, law, or engineering require extensive post-secondary education.**

39 Shifts in Perspective: Inconsistent Point of View

EAL Be consistent in your point of view within a sentence and, except in *shift,* special cases, from one sentence to the next. Avoid illogical shifts in the *pv* *tense*, *mood*, and *voice* of verbs, and in the *person* and *number* of pronouns.

39a Shifts in Tense (see #17g)

Shifting from one verb tense to another without a clear reason for doing so can cause confusion.

> shift: **She read the article on the website and then she comments on it before logging off.**

This sentence begins in the past tense but shifts to the present. However, all of the events described in this sentence occurred at a particular time in the past. So, change *comments* to the past tense to coincide with *read*.

39b Shifts in Mood (see #17k)

> shift: **If it were Sunday and I was through with my work, I would go skiing with you.**

This sentence begins and ends in the subjunctive mood (*were, would go*), but *was* is indicative. Correct this by changing indicative *was* to subjunctive *were*.

> shift: **First <u>put</u> tab A in slot B; next <u>you will put</u> tab C in slot D.**

Omit *you will* to correct the shift from imperative to indicative.

39c Shifts in Voice (see #17-l)

In sentences containing two or more verbs, all verbs should be in the same voice.

> shift: **Readers should not ordinarily have to read instructions a second time before some sense <u>can be made</u> of the details.**

In this case, stay with active voice (and the same subject):

> revised: **Readers should not ordinarily have to read instructions a second time before <u>they can make</u> sense of the details.**

39d Shifts in Person of Pronoun (see #14a–b)

Shifts in person from words such as *one, a person, somebody*, or *someone* to the second-person *you*, while common in informal conversation, are likely to be questioned in print, and particularly in more formal academic writing. Edit to produce consistency in person.

> shift: **If <u>one</u> volunteers locally, <u>you</u> will make valuable connections to others in the community.**

> revised: **If <u>you</u> volunteer locally, <u>you</u> will make valuable connections to others in the community.**

> revised: **If <u>one</u> volunteers locally, <u>he or she</u> will make valuable connections to others in the community.**

While *you* is an ineffective replacement for *one*, it can be used effectively in the first revision suggested above. To avoid gender bias in references to one of unspecified gender, use *he or she* as in the second revision above.

39e **Shifts in Number of Pronoun** (see #14a)

> shift: **If the committee wants its recommendations followed, they should have written their report more carefully.**

The committee changed from a collective unit (*it*) to a collection of individuals (*they*, *their*); the committee should be either singular or plural throughout. See also #15e and #18f. (The errors in #39d and #39e could also be marked *agr*: see #15.)

40 Faulty Parallelism

fp,
//
Parallelism, the balanced and deliberate repetition of identical grammatical structures (words, phrases, clauses), can be a strong stylistic technique. Not only does it make for vigorous, balanced, and rhythmical sentences, but it can also help develop and tie together paragraphs (see #5a). Like any other device, parallelism can be overdone, but more commonly it is underused. Of course, if you're writing an especially serious piece, like a letter of condolence, you probably won't want to use lively devices like parallelism and metaphor (see #65). But in most writing, some parallel structure is appropriate. Build parallel elements into your sentences, and now and then try making two or three successive sentences parallel with each other. Here is a sentence from a paper on computer crime. Note how parallelism (along with alliteration) strengthens the first part, thereby helping to set up the second part:

> **Although one can distinguish the malicious from the mischievous or the harmless hacker from the more dangerous computer criminal, security officials take a dim view of anyone who romps through company files.**

Be careful as you experiment, for it is easy to set up a parallel structure and then lose track of it. Study the following examples of **faulty parallelism**. (See also #23a–b.)

40a **With Coordinate Elements**

Coordinate elements in a sentence should have the same grammatical form. If they don't, the sentence will lack parallelism and therefore be ineffective.

> fp: **Reading should be <u>engrossing</u>, <u>active</u>, and <u>a challenge</u>.**

The first two complements (*engrossing*, *active*) are predicate adjectives, the third (*a challenge*) a predicate noun. Change *a challenge* to the adjective *challenging* so that it will be parallel.

The coordinate parts of compound subjects, verbs, objects, and modifiers should be parallel in form.

> fp: **<u>Reducing debt</u>, <u>spending targets</u>, and <u>increasing revenue</u> can help the municipality improve its finances.**

This sentence can be corrected by making all three parts of the subject into gerunds:

> revised: **<u>Reducing debt</u>, <u>setting spending targets</u>, and <u>increasing revenue</u> can help the municipality improve its finances.**

Another example:

> fp: **He talks about his computer in terms <u>suggesting a deep affection for it</u> and <u>that also demonstrate a thorough knowledge of it</u>.**

Simply change the participial phrase (*suggesting . . .*) to a relative clause (*that suggest . . .*) so that it will be parallel with the second part.

Writers often produce faulty parallelism by omitting a second *that*:

> fp: **Marvin was convinced <u>that the argument was unsound</u> and <u>he could profitably spend some time analyzing it</u>.**

A second *that*, before *he*, corrects the error and clarifies the meaning, for this slip is not only a breakdown of parallelism but also an implied shift in point of view (see #39); it could be marked *shift* or *pv* as well as *fp*; it could also be marked *ambig*. The omission of a second *that* invites a reader to take *he could profitably spend some time analyzing it* as an independent clause (expressing the writer's own opinion about what Marvin should do) rather than a second subordinate clause expressing a part of Marvin's opinion, which is what the writer intended.

 ## 40b With Correlative Conjunctions (see #23b)

Check for parallel structure when using correlative conjunctions:

> fp: **Whether <u>for teaching a young child the alphabet</u> or <u>in finding the quickest route to the park</u>, cell phone apps are becoming an increasingly common part of everyday life.**

The constructions following *whether* and *or* should be parallel: change *in* to *for*.

The correlative pair *not only . . . but also* can be particularly troublesome:

> fp: **She not only <u>corrected my grammar</u> but also <u>my spelling</u>.**

The error can be corrected either by repeating the verb *corrected* (or using some other appropriate verb, such as *criticized* or *repaired*) after *but also*:

> revised: **She not only <u>corrected my grammar</u> but also <u>corrected my spelling</u>.**

or by moving *corrected* so that it occurs before *not only* rather than after it:

> revised: **She corrected not only <u>my grammar</u> but also <u>my spelling</u>.**

Either method makes what follows *not only* parallel to what follows *but also*. The second version is more economical. (See also #23b, on "not only . . . but also.")

40c In a Series

In any series of three or more parallel elements, make sure that little beginning words like prepositions, pronouns, and the *to* of infinitives precede either the first element alone or each of the elements. And don't omit needed articles:

> fp: **The new library is noted for <u>a large auditorium</u>, <u>state-of-the-art computer lab</u>, <u>an impressive collection of journals</u>, and <u>brilliant, hard-working staff</u>.**

In this example, the article *a* is missing before the second and fourth items and should be added to make the items parallel. Another way to fix this would be to remove the articles and insert the possessive pronoun *its* before the first item.

Another example:

> fp: **She urged her teammates <u>to obey the rules</u>, <u>to think positively</u>, and <u>ignore criticism</u>.**

Since *to* occurs in the first two phrases, it should lead off the third phrase as well—or else be omitted from the second one. If necessary, check your work by jotting down the items in such a series in a vertical list after the word that introduces them: any slips in parallelism should then be clearer to you.

> correction: **She urged her teammates   to obey the rules,**
> **to think positively,**
> **and   to ignore criticism.**

41 Faulty Coordination: Logic, Emphasis, and Unity

fc,
log,
emph,
u

If unrelated or unequal elements—usually clauses—are presented as coordinate, the result is **faulty coordination**.

ONLINE EXERCISES

> fc: **Watches are usually water-resistant <u>and</u> some have the ability to glow in the dark.**

There is no logical connection between the two clauses—other than that they both say something about watches. The ideas would be better expressed in separate sentences. Coordinating two such clauses produces a sentence that also lacks **unity**. Here is another example, from a description of a simple object; the lack of unity is even more glaring:

> fc: **One might find this kind of a jar in an antiques store <u>and</u> it can be used for anything from cotton balls to rings and things, or just to stand as a decoration.**

The suggestion about the antiques store should either be in a separate sentence or be subordinated.

Similarly, if two elements are joined by an inappropriate coordinating conjunction, the result is again faulty coordination—sometimes referred to as "loose" coordination. Here is an example of this more common weakness:

> fc: **Nationalism can affect the relations between nations by creating a distrustful atmosphere, <u>and</u> an ambassador's innocent remark can be turned into an insult by a suspicious listener.**

The *and* misrepresents the relation between the two clauses; the second is not an additional fact but rather an example or result of the fact stated in the first. It would be better either to join the two clauses with a semicolon or colon, or to change *and* to *in which*, and to drop the comma, thereby subordinating the second clause. (The first clause could be made subordinate by adding an opening *Because*, but this would distort **emphasis**, since the first clause is more important; see #29i). Here is another example, from a description of how a particular scene in *Hamlet* should be staged:

> fc: **In this scene Rosencrantz is the main speaker of the two courtiers; therefore he should stand closer to Hamlet.**

This sentence could be sharpened. The first clause would be better subordinated:

> revised: **<u>Because in this scene Rosencrantz is the main speaker of the two courtiers,</u> he should stand closer to Hamlet.**

The original *therefore* does express this relation, but the sentence was nonetheless a compound one, tacitly equating the two clauses. Emphasis and clarity are better served by letting the syntax acknowledge the logically subordinate nature of the first clause.

Sometimes faulty coordination produces a sentence that lacks not just clarity but also **logic** (log):

> fc, log: **Alliteration is a very effective poetic device when used sparingly <u>but</u> appropriately.**

The meaning expressed by *but* here is entirely illogical. *But* implies opposition, yet it is likely that a poet who uses alliteration sparingly would also use it appropriately. *And* would be a better coordinator here.

A particularly weak form of loose coordination overlaps with the overuse of *this* (see #16c):

> fc: **The poem's tone is light and cheery, <u>and this</u> is reinforced by the mainly one-syllable words and the regular rhythm and rhyme.**

If you ever find such an *and this* in your draft, try to revise it, for not only is the coordination weak, but the demonstrative *this* is weak as well, since it has no antecedent:

> revised: **The poem's light and cheery tone is reinforced by the mainly one-syllable words and the regular rhythm and rhyme.**

Another kind of faulty coordination links several short independent clauses with coordinating conjunctions, mostly *and*'s; the result is a loose string of seemingly unrelated parts. Such sentences tend to ramble on and on, emphasizing very little.

> fc, **The ferry rates were increased and the bigger commercial**
> rambling: **vehicles had to pay more to use the ferry service and so the cost of transporting goods rose and the consumers who bought those goods had to pay more for them but they had to pay higher fares on the ferries as well and naturally most people were unhappy about it.**

The information needed to make the point is here, but ineffective syntax leaves the reader floundering, trying to see the connections and the thoughts behind the whole utterance. The *but* seems to be used less for logic than for variety, and the vague *it* at the end effectively dissipates any emphasis the sentence might have had. A little tinkering sorts out the facts, shortens the sentence by almost half, reduces the five coordinating conjunctions to a pair of correlative conjunctions, reduces the six independent clauses to two independent and one subordinate, and achieves some emphasis at the end:

> revised: **Not only did the increased ferry rates cost travellers more, but, since the operators of commercial vehicles also had to pay more, the cost of transported goods rose as well, affecting all consumers.**

See also #29i and #27b.

42 Faulty Logic

log Clear and logical thinking is essential to clear and effective writing. For example, avoid sweeping statements: overgeneralization is one of the most common weaknesses in writing. Precise claims and statements of fact will make your writing clearer. Make sure that the evidence you use is sound and that the authorities you cite are credible, current, and reliable (see #73). Such matters are particularly important in argumentative writing. Weak reasoning will make the point you're trying to argue less convincing. You will want to avoid such logical missteps as begging the question, reasoning in a circle, jumping to conclusions, and leaning on false analogies, which can seriously decrease the effectiveness of an essay (see #10e–h).

There are many ways in which logic is important even in something so small as a sentence. The problems discussed in the preceding sections, from *Misplaced Modifiers* (#35) on, are in many instances problems in logic. Following are some examples of other ways in which sentences can be illogical. Unsound reasoning leads to sentences like this:

> log: **Wordsworth is perhaps the first English Romantic poet, for his major themes—nature and human life—are characteristic of the Romantic style of poetry.**

To begin with, the word *perhaps* is ineffective: either the writer is making a point of Wordsworth's primacy and there is no "perhaps" about it, or there is no point to be made and the whole clause is superfluous. Even more serious is the way evidence is given to substantiate the statement: if the mere presence in his poetry of themes common to Romanticism makes him first, then all Romantic poets are first. The writer probably meant something like "Wordsworth is the first English Romantic poet to develop the major themes of the Romantic movement." As for these "major themes," just how valid is the implication that "human life" is especially characteristic of Romantic writers? No amount of revision can repair this muddy thinking.

Even if writers know clearly what they want to say, they have to choose and use words thoughtfully:

> log: **The town is surrounded on one side by the ocean.**

If the town were indeed *surrounded* by the ocean, it would be an island. The correct word here is *bounded*. This error might equally well be designated an error in diction: see #69.

Faulty logic can also affect the way writers put sentences together:

> log: **Having a car with bad spark plugs or points or a dirty carburetor causes it to run poorly and to use too much gas.**

This sentence could just as easily be marked *ss* (sentence structure, or sentence sense). The intention is clear, but the verb, *causes*, has as its subject the gerund *having*; consequently the sentence says that the mere possession of the afflicted car is what causes it to run poorly—as if one could borrow a similar car and it would run well. A logical revision:

> revised: **Bad spark plugs or bad points or a dirty carburetor cause a car to run poorly and to use too much gas.**

Faulty comparisons are another cause of illogicality:

> log, comp: **French painting did not follow the wild and exciting forms of Baroque art as closely as most European countries.**

Again the meaning is apparent, but the syntax faulty; readers would be annoyed at having to revise the sentence themselves in order to understand it. The sentence says either that "European countries followed the wild and exciting forms of Baroque art" to some degree or that "French painting followed most European countries more closely than it followed the wild and exciting forms of Baroque art," neither of which makes sense. Simply completing the comparison straightens out the syntax and permits the intended meaning to come through unambiguously:

> revised: **French painting did not follow the wild and exciting forms of Baroque art as closely as did <u>that</u> of most European countries.**

Another kind of ambiguity appears in this sentence:

> log: **Numerous scientific societies were founded in every developed country.**

The intended meaning is probably that every developed country had at least one scientific society—but it could just as well mean that there were numerous such societies in each country.

Here's another kind of illogical sentence:

> log: **His lack of cynicism was visible in every paragraph of his essay.**

The meaning is clear, but a reader might find it odd to think of a lack being *visible*. Put it more logically:

> revised: **Every paragraph of his essay revealed his idealism.**

Make sure that nouns are inflected to agree logically with the context:

> log: **All the legislators appeared at the committee to express their view on health care reforms.**

Clearly the legislators expressed their *views*, not just one *view*.

Sometimes an extra word creeps in and weakens an otherwise logical sentence:

> log: **Alexander Graham Bell is known as the modern inventor of the telephone.**

The writer was probably thinking subconsciously of the telephone as a *modern* invention, and the word just popped into the sentence. Thinking critically, one sees that the word *modern* implies that there have been one or more earlier, perhaps even ancient, inventors of the telephone.

Finally, make sure your sentences actually say something worth saying. Here's one that doesn't:

> log: **The mood and theme play a very significant part in this poem.**

This could be called an "empty" sentence (the weak intensifier *very* suggests that the writer subconsciously felt the need to prop it up). It would be illogical for the theme of a poem to play other than a significant part in it.

WRITING TIP

Effective Workplace Writing

In today's competitive job market, the ability to prepare effective proposals, reports, memos, emails, and other forms of written communication is a highly valued skill. To get your message across successfully, you must not only understand your audience and your purpose in writing but also be able to construct sentences that are clear, concise, and free of the sorts of problems outlined in the preceding sections (#31–42). Moreover, you must be able to avoid common mistakes in grammar (see Part III), punctuation (see Part V), mechanics and spelling (see Part VI), and diction (see Part VII). Think of mistakes in these areas as static on the radio. Static can garble your message, making it difficult—and often frustrating—for your audience to understand what you are trying to say. The following tips should help you keep your workplace writing free of static:

1. Be specific, but don't provide more detail than your reader requires.
2. Make sure you are certain about the meaning of all words that you use. If you need help, consult a dictionary.
3. If you have difficulty composing complex and compound-complex sentences without errors, use mostly simple and compound sentences (see #12z).
4. Always proofread your work. Go slowly, and try to read your work from your reader's perspective. Look carefully for typos and errors you know you're prone to making.

Aim to produce clear, courteous, error-free writing in all workplace contexts. After all, even a short, quickly written email to a colleague may eventually find its way to your boss or even the head of your company. And if you consistently make errors in your writing, your coworkers and supervisors will question your professionalism and your commitment to doing a good job. Think of every piece of writing as an opportunity to make a good impression.

43 Internal Punctuation: The Comma ,

ONLINE EXERCISES

The **comma** is a light separator that makes the reader pause slightly. It is the most neutral and most used punctuation mark. Commas have three main functions:

1. Commas separate independent clauses joined by a coordinating conjunction (see #43a–b).
2. Commas separate items in a series (see #43c–d).
3. Commas set off parenthetical elements, such as introductory or concluding words, phrases, and clauses; nonrestrictive elements; and sentence interrupters (see #43e–g).

There are several other conventional uses of the comma:

1. A comma separates elements of an emphatic contrast:

   This is a practical lesson, not a theoretical one.

2. A comma indicates a pause where a word has been acceptably omitted:

   Ron is a conservative; Sally, a radical.

3. Commas set off a noun of address (see #13b):

   Thank you, Ava, for your wonderful speech.

4. Commas set off a verb of speaking before or after a quotation (see also #52a):

   Then Dora remarked, "That movie gave me nightmares."

   "I thought it was a comedy," said Alain laughingly.

5. A comma follows the salutation of informal letters (*Dear Gail,*) and the complimentary close of all letters (*Yours truly,*). (In formal letters, a colon is conventional after the salutation.)

6. Commas set off the year in dates when you use the month-day-year format:

> **She left on January 11, 2017, and was gone a month.**
> (Note the comma after the year.)

(But note that no comma is required for the day-month-year format: *11 January 2017*.)

7. Commas set off geographical names and addresses:

> **She left Fredericton, New Brunswick, and moved to Calgary, Alberta, in hopes of finding a better-paying job.**

> **The RCMP Heritage Centre is located at 5907 Dewdney Avenue, Regina, Saskatchewan, Canada.**

For some common errors with commas, see #54b–j.

43a The Comma with Independent Clauses Joined by a Coordinating Conjunction

Generally, use a comma between independent clauses joined by one of the coordinating conjunctions (*and, but, for, nor, or, so, yet*; see #23a.2):

> **I wanted to do something I had never done before, and dog sledding near Whitehorse sounded fun.**

> **Fiona knew she shouldn't tell Ivan what she really thought of his plan, yet she couldn't stop herself.**

> **Dorothy could go to Ottawa and visit the National Gallery, or she could go to Montreal and explore the Musée des Beaux-Arts.**

> **It was a serious speech, but Gordon included many jokes along the way, and the audience loved it.**

If the clauses are short, the comma may be omitted, especially if the clauses are parallel in structure:

> **Art is long and life is short.**

When two clauses have the same subject, a comma is less likely to be needed:

It was windy and it was wet.

When the subject is omitted from the second clause, a comma should not be used (see #54f):

It was windy and wet.

See also #54b for advice on avoiding *comma splices*.

PROOFREADING TIP

Using Commas Before *but*, *yet*, *for*, or *so*

Independent clauses joined by *but* and *yet*, which explicitly mark a contrast, will almost always need a comma, even if they are short or parallel, or have the same subject:

It was windy, yet it was warm.

And when you join two clauses with *for*, always put a comma in front of it to prevent its being misread as a preposition:

Amanda was eager to leave early, for the restaurant was sure to be crowded.

The conjunction *so* almost always needs a comma, but remember that *so* is considered informal (see the proofreading tip near the end of #23a.2).

 ## The Comma with Short Independent Clauses Not Joined by a Coordinating Conjunction

A comma can be used to join very short independent clauses that are not joined by a coordinating conjunction, especially if the clauses are also parallel in structure:

Lightning flashed, thunder roared.

He cooked, she ate, they fell in love.

But be careful: using a comma to join longer sentences can result in a comma splice (see #33 and #54b). When joining longer sentences not joined by a coordinating conjunction, it's best to use a semicolon instead of a comma (see #44a).

The Comma Between Items in a Series

Generally, use commas between words, phrases, or clauses in a series of three or more:

> **Robert Bateman, Emily Carr, and Mary Pratt are three Canadian painters.**

> **He speaks English, French, Spanish, and Hindi.**

> **Carmen explained that she had visited the art gallery, that she had walked in the park, and that eventually she had gone to a movie.**

The common practice of omitting the final comma (the "Oxford comma" or the "serial comma") can be misleading. That final pause gives sentences a better rhythm and avoids the kind of possible confusion apparent in sentences like these:

> **The manufacturers sent us shirts, wash-and-wear slacks and shoes.** (The shoes were wash-and-wear?)

> **They prided themselves on having a large and bright kitchen, a productive vegetable garden, a large recreation room with a huge fireplace and two fifty-foot cedar trees.** (The trees were in the recreation room?)

> **The Speech from the Throne discussed international trade, improvements in transportation, slowing down inflation and emergency-response measures.** (Do we want to slow down emergency-response measures?)

See also #44b.

The Comma Between Parallel Adjectives

Use commas between two or more adjectives preceding a noun if they are parallel, each modifying the noun itself; do not put commas between adjectives that are not parallel:

> **He is an intelligent, dedicated, ambitious student.**

She is a tall young woman.

She wore new black leather boots, a long red coat, and a scarf with blue, white, and grey stripes.

In the first sentence, each adjective modifies *student*. In the second, *tall* modifies *young woman*; it is a *young woman* who is *tall*, not a *woman* who is *tall* and *young*. In the third, *new* modifies *black leather boots*, *black* modifies *leather boots*, and *long* modifies *red coat*; *blue*, *white*, and *grey* all separately modify *stripes*.

PROOFREADING TIP

Deciding When to Separate Adjectives with a Comma

If you're having trouble telling whether or not a pair of adjectives is parallel, try inserting *and* between them. If it sounds logical there, the adjectives are probably parallel and should be separated by a comma. Another test is to change the order of the adjectives. If it sounds odd to say *a felt purple hat* instead of *a purple felt hat*, then the adjectives probably aren't parallel and no comma is required. Finally, remember that no comma is needed after a number (*three blind mice*) or after common adjectives for size or age (*tall young woman; long red coat; new brick house*). See also #19e and #54e.

 ## The Comma with Introductory or Concluding Words, Phrases, and Clauses

1. Introductory Words, Phrases, and Clauses

Generally, use a comma to set off an introductory word or phrase if you want to create a distinct pause, add emphasis or qualification, or prevent misreading:

Confidently, she raised her hand. (adverb)

However, some of the rules can be broken. (conjunctive adverb)

Puzzled, Kevin turned back to the beginning of the chapter. (participle)

The doors locked and bolted, they went to bed feeling secure. (absolute phrase)

To get the best results from your ice cream maker, you must follow the instruction manual carefully. (adverbial infinitive phrase)

Finding golf unexpectedly difficult, Mariam sought extra help.
(participial phrase)

After the sun had set, high above the mountains came the fighter jets.
(adverbial prepositional phrase; note that the comma prevents misreading)

The comma may occasionally be omitted if the introductory element is short and the meaning is clear without it:

In time Naieli will change her mind. (short adverbial prepositional phrase)

But note that introductory participles, participial phrases, and absolute phrases are always set off with commas. Introductory clauses are also always set off:

Since she was elected by a large majority, she felt that she had a strong mandate for her policies.

After I had selected all the items I wanted, I discovered that I had left my wallet at home.

> ### PROOFREADING TIP
>
> **Commas with Participles, Gerunds, and Infinitive Phrases**
>
> Don't mistake a gerund for a participle (see #21d and #21f). A gerund or gerund phrase functioning as the subject should not be followed by a comma (see #54c):
>
> participle: **Dancing in the street, we celebrated the arrival of summer.**
>
> gerund: **Dancing in the street is a wonderful release of energy.**
>
> Don't mistake a long infinitive phrase functioning as a subject noun for one functioning as an adverb (see #21a):
>
> noun: **To put together a meal for six without help is a remarkable feat.**
>
> adverb: **To put together a meal for six without help, you need to be very organized.**

2. Concluding Words, Phrases, and Clauses

In general, if you intend the concluding element to complete the sense of the main clause, don't set it off; if it merely provides additional information or comment, set it off. The presence or absence of punctuation tells your readers how you want the sentence to be read.

Adverbs and adverbial phrases that follow the main clause will almost always be restrictive (#43f) and therefore not set off with commas:

She raised her hand confidently.

You must follow the instruction manual carefully to get the best results from your ice cream maker.

Jean retired gracefully after many years as leader of the union.

Adverbial clauses may or may not need to be set off. If the subordinate clause is essential to the meaning of the sentence, it is in effect *restrictive* and should not be set off with a comma; if it is not essential but contains only additional information or comment, it is *nonrestrictive* and should be set off with a comma. Consider the following examples:

I went straight home when the party was over. (restrictive)

She did an excellent job on her second speech, although the first one was a disaster. (nonrestrictive)

In most cases, final clauses such as these will be necessary and won't require a comma. When in doubt, try omitting the clause to see if the sentence still says essentially what you want it to.

Closing participles and participial phrases almost always need to be set off. Read the sentence aloud; if you feel a distinct pause, use a comma:

Kevin turned back to the beginning of the chapter, puzzled.

Mariam sought extra help, finding golf unexpectedly difficult.

Higher prices result in increased wage demands, contributing to inflationary pressures.

Occasionally such a sentence will flow clearly and smoothly without a comma, especially if the modifier is essential to the meaning:

> **Shirin left the room feeling victorious.**

> **She sat there looking puzzled.**

If the closing participle modifies a predicate noun or a direct object, there usually should not be a comma:

> **He was a man lacking in courage.**

> **I left him feeling bewildered.** (He was bewildered.)

But if the participle in such a sentence modifies the subject, and if it could also conceivably modify the object, then a comma is necessary:

> **I left him, feeling bewildered.** (I was bewildered.)

Only the presence or absence of the comma tells a reader how to understand such a sentence.

Finally, as with introductory absolute phrases, concluding absolute phrases are always set off with commas:

> **Timmy marched on stage, a grin spreading across his face.**

In fact, absolute phrases are always set off with commas, no matter where they appear in a sentence.

43f The Comma with Nonrestrictive Elements

Words, phrases, and clauses are nonrestrictive when they are not essential to the principal meaning of a sentence. A nonrestrictive element should be set off from the rest of the sentence, usually with commas, though dashes and parentheses can also be used (see #46 and #47). A restrictive modifier is essential to the meaning and should not be set off:

> restrictive: **Anyone wanting a job at the firm should fill out an application.**

> nonrestrictive: **Kayla, wanting a job at the firm, filled out an application.**

In the second sentence, the participial phrase explains why Kayla filled out an application, but the sentence is clear without it: "Kayla filled out an application." But without the phrase the first sentence wouldn't make sense: "Anyone should fill out an application." Questions about restrictive and nonrestrictive elements most often arise with *relative clauses* and *appositives*.

1. Relative Clauses

Relative clauses modify a noun, a pronoun, or a noun phrase (see #14d). The information they provide may be either essential (in the case of a restrictive relative clause) or nonessential (in the case of a nonrestrictive relative clause) to the meaning of the sentence. Consider the following sentences:

> **She is a woman who likes to travel.**

> **Carol, who likes to travel, is going to Greece this summer.**

In the first sentence, the relative clause is essential and is not set off. In the second sentence, the relative clause is set off because it is merely additional—though explanatory—information: it is not essential to the identification of Carol, who has been explicitly named, nor is it essential to the meaning of the main clause.

Be careful not to set off a relative clause that should be restrictive:

correct: **Students who are hard-working should expect much from their education.**

incorrect: **Students, who are hard-working, should expect much from their education.**

Left unpunctuated, the relative clause is restrictive, making the sentence correctly apply only to students who are in fact hard-working. Set off as nonrestrictive, the relative clause applies to all students, which makes the sentence untrue.

A shift in punctuation won't always result in such an obvious error, but it will always have a significant impact on the meaning of the sentence. Compare these sentences:

> **The motorcycle, which I wanted to test drive, was not on the lot.**

> **The motorcycle which I wanted to test drive was not on the lot.**

With the clause set off as nonrestrictive, the reader must assume that the motorcycle has been clearly identified in an earlier sentence. Left unpunctuated, the clause identifies the motorcycle as the particular one the speaker wanted to test drive. (Note that many Canadian writers would use *which* in the nonrestrictive clause and *that* in the restrictive clause.)

> **PROOFREADING TIP**
>
> **Determining Whether a Clause Is Restrictive**
>
> If you can use the relative pronoun *that*, you know the clause is restrictive; *that* cannot begin a nonrestrictive clause:
>
> **The motorcycle that I wanted to test drive was not on the lot.**
>
> Further, if the relative pronoun can be omitted altogether (see #14d), the clause is restrictive, as with *that* in the preceding example and *whom* in the following:
>
> **The person [whom] I most admire is the one who works hard and plays hard.**

2. Appositives

Always set off a nonrestrictive appositive (see #12q):

Karl, <u>my accountant</u>, is very imaginative.

King Lear is a noble work of literature, <u>one that will live in human minds for all time</u>.

Virginia is going to bring her sister, <u>Vanessa</u>.

In the last example, the comma indicates that Virginia has only the one sister. Left unpunctuated, the appositive would be restrictive, meaning that Virginia has more than one sister and that the particular one she is going to bring is the one named Vanessa.

Don't mistake a restrictive appositive for a nonrestrictive one:

incorrect: **An interview with union leader, <u>Gabriel Simard</u>, will be broadcast live over the Internet.**

revised: **An interview with union leader Gabriel Simard will be broadcast live over the Internet**

revised: **An interview with <u>the</u> union leader, Gabriel Simard, will be broadcast live over the Internet.**

This error most often occurs when a proper name follows a defining or characterizing word or phrase. In the reverse order, such a phrase is set off as a nonrestrictive appositive:

The interview with Gabriel Simard, the union leader, will be broadcast live over the Internet.

See also #54i.

3. Because-Clauses and Phrases

Adverbial clauses or phrases beginning with *because* (or otherwise conveying that sense) can be a problem when they follow an explicit negative. When *because* follows a negative, punctuate the sentence so that it means what you want it to:

Mary didn't pass the exam, because she had stayed up all night studying for it: she was so groggy she couldn't even read the questions correctly. (She didn't pass.)

Mary didn't pass the exam because she had stayed up all night studying for it. Last-minute review may have helped, but her thorough grasp of the material would have enabled her to pass it without the cramming. (She would have passed anyway.)

Often you can avoid the possible awkwardness or ambiguity by simply rephrasing a sentence in which *because* follows a negative.

4. Modifiers with such as

Nonrestrictive modifiers beginning with *such as* should be set off with commas:

Johan played all kinds of sports, such as hockey, baseball, and lacrosse.

But be careful not to mistake a nonrestrictive *such as* modifier for a restrictive one. Consider the following example:

Antibiotics, <u>such as penicillin</u>, are ineffective against the disease.

Because the modifier *such as penicillin* is set off, the sentence implies that *all* antibiotics (of which penicillin is an example) are ineffective against the disease. If the commas were removed, the modifier would become restrictive, and the meaning would change: the sentence would imply that only those antibiotics that are like penicillin are ineffective, though other antibiotics might not be.

43g The Comma with Sentence Interrupters

Sentence interrupters are parenthetical words, phrases, and clauses that interrupt the syntax of a sentence. Set off light interrupters with a pair of commas:

> **You may, on the other hand, find it more convenient to take a web-based course.** (transitional prepositional phrase)

> **Please, Amanda, finish your homework.** (noun of address)

> **This document, the lawyer says, will complete the contract.** (explanatory clause)

> **Ms. Sun, beaming brightly, woke up to face the day.** (participial phrase)

> **It was, all things considered, a successful concert.** (absolute phrase)

> **Could you be persuaded to consider this money as, well, a loan?** (mild interjection)

> **Jet lag, it now occurs to me, may after all be responsible for our falling asleep at dinner.** (clause expressing afterthought)

For a stronger effect, dashes or parentheses may be used instead of commas to set off sentence interrupters. See #46 and #47.

> **PROOFREADING TIP**
>
> **Punctuation Marks That Occur in Pairs**
>
> Remember, punctuation marks that set off sentence interrupters come in pairs. If you put down an opening comma—or dash or parenthesis—you shouldn't omit the closing one. Reading aloud, perhaps with exaggerated pauses, can help you spot that a mark is missing.

44 Internal Punctuation: The Semicolon ;

ONLINE EXERCISES

The **semicolon** is a heavy separator, often almost equivalent to a period or "full stop." It forces a much longer pause than a comma does. Compared with the comma, it is used sparingly. Basically, semicolons have two functions: to join independent clauses not joined by a coordinating conjunction and to separate items in a list when commas are not strong enough.

44a The Semicolon Between Independent Clauses

Generally, use a semicolon between closely related independent clauses that are not joined by one of the coordinating conjunctions (*and, but, for, nor, or, so, yet*; see #23a.1):

> **Being a mere child, I didn't fully understand what I had witnessed; I just knew it was wrong.**

> **Leanna was exhausted and obviously not going to win; nevertheless, she persevered and finished the race.**

When independent clauses are joined by a coordinating conjunction, you would usually use a comma between them (see #43a), but a semicolon is appropriate when at least one of the clauses contains other punctuation:

> **Distracted as he was, the English professor, Herbert, the best cryptic crossword player in the district, easily won the contest; and no one who knew him—or even had only heard of him—was in the least surprised.**

Semicolons with Conjunctive Adverbs and Transitions

Be sure to use a semicolon and not just a comma between independent clauses that you join with a conjunctive adverb. Here is a list of most of the common conjunctive adverbs:

accordingly	anyway	consequently	finally
afterward	besides	conversely	furthermore
also	certainly	finally	hence

however	meanwhile	nonetheless	then
indeed	moreover	otherwise	thereafter
instead	namely	similarly	therefore
later	nevertheless	still	thus
likewise	next	subsequently	undoubtedly

The same caution applies to common transitional phrases such as these:

after this	if not	in the meantime
as a result	in addition	on the contrary
for example	in fact	on the other hand
for this reason	in short	that is

Conjunctive adverbs often have the *feel* of subordinating conjunctions (see #23c), but they are not true conjunctions. Think of them as adverbs doing a joining or "conjunctive" job:

Marie left her laundry in the dryer overnight; therefore, she had to iron most of her shirts.

Here, *therefore* works very much like *so*; nevertheless, *therefore* is a conjunctive adverb and requires the semicolon.

He felt well enough to go; however, his doctor ordered him to stay in bed.

Here, *however* works very much like *but*; nevertheless, *however* is a conjunctive adverb and requires the semicolon.

PROOFREADING TIP

The Comma Following *however*

Note that whereas other conjunctive adverbs will often, but not always, be followed by commas, *however* as a conjunctive adverb (unless it ends a sentence) is always followed by a comma. The comma prevents its being misread as a regular adverb meaning "in whatever way" or "to whatever degree," as in "However you go, just make sure you get there on time."

The Semicolon Between Items in a Series

Use a semicolon to separate items in a series if a comma would not be heavy enough; for example, if the series consists of phrases or clauses that are unusually long or contain internal commas of their own:

Saint John, New Brunswick; Victoria, British Columbia; and Kingston, Ontario, are all about the same size.

The presentation on life journeys examined three very different novels written by Canadian authors: Michael Ondaatje's *The Cat's Table*, which is set on an ocean liner headed for England; Jessica Grant's *Come, Thou Tortoise*, in which a woman travels back to her childhood home in Newfoundland; and David Bergen's *The Time in Between*, in which a man and his children travel to Vietnam to find answers.

See #54-l on how to avoid a common misuse of the semicolon.

 # 45 Internal Punctuation: The Colon :

Colons are commonly used to introduce lists, examples, and long or formal quotations (see #52b), but their possibilities in more everyday sentences are often overlooked. A colon is useful because it looks forward or anticipates: it gives readers a push toward the next part of the sentence. In the preceding sentence, for example, the colon sets up a sense of expectation about what is coming. It points out, even emphasizes, the relation between the two parts of the sentence (that is, the second part clarifies what the first part says). A semicolon in the same spot would bring readers to an abrupt halt, leaving it up to them to make the necessary connection between the two parts. Here are more examples:

> **He wanted only one thing from life: happiness.**

> **The simple sculpture evoked complex feelings: loss, isolation, yearning, and wonder.**

> **Let me add just this: anyone who expects to lose weight must be prepared to exercise.**

> **It was an unexpectedly lovely time of year: trees were in blossom, garden flowers bloomed all around, the sky was clear and bright, and the temperature was just right.**

Nevertheless, don't get carried away with this use of the colon: its effectiveness would wear off if it appeared more than once or twice a page.

Colons can also be used in a series, occasionally, for special emphasis. Colons add emphasis because they are unusual, but mainly their anticipatory nature produces a cumulative effect suitable when successive items in a series build to a climax:

> **He held on: he persevered: he fought back: and eventually he won out, regardless of the punishing obstacles.**

> **It blew: it rained: it hailed: it sleeted: it even snowed—it was a most unusual June even for Medicine Hat.**

See #54m on how to avoid a common misuse of the colon.

46 Internal Punctuation: The Dash —

ONLINE
EXERCISES

The **dash** is a popular punctuation mark, especially in email and other more informal communications. Hasty writers often use it as a substitute for a comma, or where a colon would be more emphatic. Use a dash only when you have a definite reason for doing so. Like the colon, the dash sets up expectations in a reader's mind. But whereas the colon sets up an expectation that what follows will somehow explain, summarize, define, or otherwise comment on what has gone before, a dash suggests that what follows will be somehow surprising, involving some sort of twist, or at least a contrary idea. Consider the following sentence:

The teacher praised my wit, my intelligence, my organization, and my research—and penalized the paper for its poor spelling and punctuation.

Here, the dash adds to the punch of what follows it. A comma there would deprive the sentence of much of its force; it would even sound odd, since the resulting matter-of-fact tone would not be in harmony with what the sentence was saying. Only a dash can convey the appropriate *tone* (see the introduction to Part VII). Another example:

It was a unique occasion—everyone at the meeting agreed on what should be done.

Here, the dash joins two independent clauses not joined by a coordinating conjunction. Note how the dash creates a longer pause, and therefore greater emphasis, than would a semicolon or a colon.

The dash is also handy in some long and involved sentences, for example after a long series before a summarizing clause:

Our longing for the past, our hopes for the future, and our neglect of the present moment—all these and more go to shape our everyday lives, often in ways unseen or little understood.

Even here, the emphatic quality of the dash serves the meaning, though its principal function in such a sentence is to mark the abrupt break.

A pair of dashes can be used to set off a nonrestrictive element or an interrupting clause:

My best friend—who is an award-winning chef—refused to make me dinner on my birthday.

What he wanted—and he wanted it very badly indeed—was the last piece of chocolate cake.

You could use commas in place of the dashes in these examples (see #43f), but the result would be weaker, for the content of the clause is clearly meant to be emphatic. A single dash used to set off a concluding summary or appositive results in a similar effect:

He wanted only one thing from life—everything.

Here, you could use a colon (see #45), but the dash is more emphatic.

Dashes are also useful to set off an interrupter consisting of a series with its own internal commas:

Sentence interrupters are parenthetical elements—words, phrases, or clauses—that interrupt the syntax of a sentence.

In this case, the sentence would be confusing if the interrupting element had been set off with commas.

Finally, dashes can be used in place of commas (or colons) to emphasize items in a series:

Rising taxes—rising insurance rates—rising gas costs—skyrocketing food prices: it is becoming more and more difficult to live decently and still keep within a budget.

Here, the omission of *and* before the final item, together with the repetition and parallel structure, heightens the stylistic effect by adding to the stridency; the dashes reinforce this effect.

As with colons, don't overuse dashes. They are even stronger marks, but they lose effectiveness if used often.

PROOFREADING TIP

Ending a Sentence with a Dash or an Ellipsis

Generally, in formal writing, it is inappropriate to end a sentence with a dash or an ellipsis unless the sentence appears within a quotation (see #53). In less formal or creative-writing contexts, a dash or an ellipsis may be used at the end of a sentence, especially in dialogue or at the end of a paragraph or a chapter in order to indicate a pause, a fading away, or an interruption, or to create mild suspense.

47 Parentheses ( )

ONLINE
EXERCISES

Parentheses have three principal functions in non-technical writing: (1) to set off certain kinds of nonrestrictive elements and sentence interrupters (see #43f–g), (2) to enclose cross-reference information within a sentence, as we just did, and (3) to enclose numerals or letters setting up a list or series, as we do in this sentence. Note that if a complete sentence is enclosed in parentheses within another sentence (here is an example of such an insertion), it needs neither an opening capital letter nor a closing period. Note also that if a comma or other mark is called for by the sentence (as in the preceding sentence, and in this one), it comes *after* the closing parenthesis. Exclamation points and question marks go inside the closing parenthesis only if they are a part of what is enclosed. (When an entire sentence or more is enclosed, the terminal mark of course comes inside the closing parenthesis—as does this period.)

Whereas dashes draw attention to a nonrestrictive or interrupting element (see #46), parentheses de-emphasize such an element; often interrupters that could be emphatic can be played down in order to emphasize the other parts of a sentence:

> I don't think that Nancy (who has won several prizes for her writing) understands how to use a comma.

> Speculation (I mean this in its pejorative sense) is not a safe foundation for a business enterprise.

> Some extreme sports (hang-gliding for example) involve unusually high insurance claims.

In some cases, by de-emphasizing something striking or unexpected, parentheses can create an ironic tone.

48 Brackets [ ]

Brackets (often referred to as "square brackets," since some people use the term *brackets* also to refer to parentheses) are used primarily to enclose something inserted in a direct quotation. For example, a clarifying fact or a change in tense (to make the quoted material fit the syntax of your sentence) should be enclosed in brackets:

> **The author states that "the following year [2000] marked a turning point in [his] life."**

> **One of my friends wrote me that her "feelings about the subject [were] similar to" mine.**

If you want to indicate that an error in the quotation occurs in the original, use the word *sic* (Latin for *thus*) in brackets:

> **One of my friends wrote me: "My feelings about the subject are similiar [*sic*] to yours."**

But keep such "editorial" changes to a minimum. See also #78f.

Brackets are also used when you have to put parentheses inside parentheses—as in a footnote or a bibliographical entry.

49 End Punctuation: The Period .

ONLINE
EXERCISES

The **period** is the most common terminal punctuation; it ends the vast majority of sentences. Use it to indicate the end of statements and neutral commands:

> **Some Canadians celebrate New Year's Day by taking a "polar bear" swim in ice-cold bodies of water.**

> **Don't believe everything you read on the Internet.**

Periods are also used after most abbreviations:

abbr.	Mr.	Ms.	Dr.	Jr.
Ph.D.	B.A.	St.	Mt.	etc.

Generally, use a period in abbreviated place names:

B.C.	P.E.I.	Nfld.	N.Y.	Mass.

But note that two-letter postal abbreviations do not require periods:

BC	PE	NL	NY	MA

Periods are not used after metric and other symbols (unless these symbols occur at the end of a sentence):

km	cm	kg	mc^2	ml
kJ	C	Hz	Au	Zr

Periods are often omitted with initials (often called "initialisms"), especially of groups or organizations, and especially if the initials are acronyms—that is, an initialism pronounced as a word (AIDS, NATO, UNICEF):

EU	UN	WHO	RCMP	RAF
CBC	TV	APA	MLA	MP

When in doubt, consult a good dictionary.

PROOFREADING TIP

Abbreviations and Periods

(1) Although *Ms.* is not a true abbreviation, it is usually followed by a period.

(2) Some Canadian writers and publishers follow the British convention of omitting the period after abbreviations that include the first and last letter of the abbreviated word (sometimes called "suspensions"): Mr, Mrs, Dr, Jr, St, etc.

(3) If an abbreviation falls at the end of a sentence, as it does in the previous sentence, the period following the abbreviation serves as the sentence's period.

---

50 | End Punctuation: The Question Mark ?

ONLINE EXERCISES

Use a **question mark** at the end of direct questions:

Are you leaving so early?

Is that what you're wearing to the interview?

Do not use a question mark at the end of an indirect question: see #54k.

Note that a question mark is necessary after questions that aren't phrased in the usual interrogative way (as might occur if you were writing dialogue):

You're leaving so early?

That's what you're wearing to the interview?

And note that a question appearing as a sentence interrupter still needs a question mark at its end:

I went back to the beginning—what else could I do?—and tried to get it right the second time.

The man in the scuba outfit (what was his name again?) took a rear seat.

Since such interrupters are necessarily abrupt, dashes or parentheses are the appropriate marks to set them off.

See also #12t.

51 | End Punctuation: The Exclamation Point !

Use an **exclamation point** after an emphatic statement or after an expression of emphatic surprise, emphatic query, or strong emotion:

He came in first, yet it was only his second time in professional competition!

You don't say so!

Not again!

Occasionally an exclamation point may be doubled or tripled for emphasis. It may even follow a question mark, to emphasize the writer's or speaker's disbelief:

She said what?!

You bought what?! A giraffe?! What were you thinking?!

This device should not be used in formal and academic writing.

52 Quotation Marks " "

ONLINE EXERCISES

Quotation marks have two main functions: to indicate dialogue or direct speech (such as you might find in a story, novel, or non-fiction narrative) and to indicate verbatim quotation from a published work or other source (as in a research paper). For the use of quotation marks around titles, see #58b–c.

52a Direct Speech

Enclose all direct speech in quotation marks:

> **Adriana fumbled around in the dark and asked, "Now where are the matches?"**

Note that when a quotation ends a sentence, its own terminal punctuation serves as the terminal punctuation of the sentence. Note also that a comma usually follows the verb of speaking that precedes the quotation. With short or emphatic quotations, commas often aren't necessary:

> **Someone shouted "Fire!" and we all headed for the exits.**

On the other hand, if the quotation is particularly long or if the context is formal, a colon will probably be more appropriate than a comma:

> **When the movie was over, Jayden turned to his companion and said: "We have wasted ninety minutes of our lives. The movie lacked an intelligent plot, sympathetic characters, and an interesting setting. Even the soundtrack was pathetic."**

If the introductory element is itself an independent clause, then a colon or period must be used:

> **Jayden turned to him and spoke: "What a waste of time."**

Spoke, unlike *said*, is here an intransitive verb.

If a verb of speaking or a subject–verb combination follows a quotation, it is usually set off by a comma placed inside the closing quotation mark:

> **"You should find a sturdier ladder," he suggested.**

But if the quotation ends with a question mark or an exclamation point, no other punctuation is added:

> **"Where would I get another ladder at this time of night?" she asked.**

If you work a quotation into your own syntax, don't use even a comma to introduce it; for example, when the word *that* follows a verb of speaking:

> **It is often said that "sticks and stones may break my bones, but words will never hurt me"—a singularly inaccurate notion.**

If the clause containing the verb of speaking interrupts the quotation, it should be preceded by a comma and followed by whatever mark is called for by the syntax and the sense. For example,

> **"Since it's such a long drive," he said, "we'd better get an early start."**

> **"It's a long drive," he argued; "therefore I think we should start early."**

> **"It's a very long way," he insisted. "We should start as early as possible."**

In written dialogue, it is conventional to begin a new paragraph each time the speaker changes:

> I remember hearing my mother say to my absentminded father, "Henry, why is the newspaper in the fridge?"
>
> "Oh, yes," he replied. "The fish is wrapped in it."
>
> She examined it. "Well, there may have been a fish in it once, but there is no fish in it now."

 ## Direct Quotation from a Source

Enclose in quotation marks any direct quotation from another source that you run into your own text:

> According to Margaret Atwood in *Negotiating with the Dead*, "writing has to do with darkness, and a desire or perhaps a compulsion to enter it, and, with luck, to illuminate it, and to bring something back out to the light."

Even when the passage you quote is incomplete, the words that you take from the other source should be enclosed in quotation marks:

> According to Margaret Atwood in *Negotiating with the Dead*, "writing has to do with darkness" and the desire to "illuminate" that darkness.

Block Quotations

Quotations of no more than four lines are normally run into the text and enclosed in quotation marks. Quotations of more than four lines should be treated as "block quotations": they should begin on a new line, and the "block" should be indented one centimetre (approximately ten spaces).

> In *A Short History of Progress*, Ronald Wright compares contemporary civilization to a speeding ship:
>
> > Our civilization, which subsumes most of its predecessors, is a great ship steaming at speed into the future. It travels faster, further, and more laden than any before. We may not be able to foresee every reef and hazard, but by reading her compass bearing and headway, by understanding her design, her safety record, and the abilities of her crew, we can, I think, plot a wise course between the narrows and bergs looking ahead.

Do not place quotation marks around a block quotation, but do reproduce any quotation marks that appear in the original:

> **Budgets can be important. As Dickens has Mr. Micawber say in David Copperfield,**
>
> > **"Annual income twenty pounds, annual expenditure nineteen nineteen six, result happiness. Annual income twenty pounds, annual expenditure twenty pounds ought and six, result misery."**

If you are quoting a passage of multiple paragraphs that are in quotation marks in the original, include the quotation marks at the beginning of each paragraph, but at the end of only the last one.

Poetry

A quotation of one, two, or three lines of poetry is generally run into your text. When you run in more than one line of poetry, indicate the line breaks with a slash mark or virgule, with a space on each side:

> **Dante's spiritual journey begins in the woods: "Midway this way of life, we're bound upon / I woke to find myself in a dark wood / Where the right road was wholly lost and gone."**

Set off quotations of four or more lines of poetry in the same way you would set off a block quotation. If you want to give special emphasis to shorter quotations of two or three lines, you may set them off as well.

52c Quotation Within Quotation

Put single quotation marks around a quotation that occurs within another quotation; this is the only standard use for single quotation marks:

> **In Joseph Conrad's *Heart of Darkness*, the drama begins when the principal narrator first speaks: " 'And this also,' said Marlow suddenly, 'has been one of the dark places of the earth.' "**

52d Words Used in a Special Sense

Put quotation marks around words used in a special sense or words for which you wish to indicate some qualification:

> **What she calls a "ramble" I would call a thirty-kilometre hike.**

> **He had been up in the woods so long he was "bushed," as some Canadians might put it.**

Note that some writers prefer to italicize words referred to as words (see #59c).

PROOFREADING TIP

Overuse of Quotation Marks to Call Attention to Words

Don't put quotation marks around slang terms, clichés, and the like. If a word or phrase is so weak or inappropriate that you have to apologize for it, you shouldn't be using it in the first place. Even if a slang term is appropriate, putting quotation marks around it implicitly insults readers by presuming that they won't recognize slang when they see it. And avoid using quotation marks for emphasis; they don't work that way.

 ## Other Marks with Quotation Marks

Put periods and commas inside closing quotation marks; put semi-colons and colons outside them:

> **"Knowing how to write well," he said, "can be a source of great pleasure"; and then he added that it had "one other important quality": he identified it simply as "hard work."**

We recommend this standard North American practice. (In British usage, periods and commas are put outside quotation marks unless they are part of what is being quoted, and single rather than double quotation marks are conventional.)

Question marks and exclamation points go either outside or inside, de-pending on whether they apply to the quotation or to the whole sentence:

> **"What smells so good?" she asked.**

> **Who said, "Change is inevitable except from a pop machine"?**

53 Ellipses for Omissions . . .

An **ellipsis** indicates omission or, in informal writing, trailing off. In formal writing, use it only when you decide to omit one or more words from the middle of a quoted passage. For example, if you wanted to quote only part of the passage from Wright quoted earlier (#52b), you might do it like this:

> Ronald Wright describes contemporary civilization through a metaphor: "Our civilization . . . is a great ship steaming at speed into the future."

When the ellipsis is preceded by a complete sentence, include the period (or other terminal punctuation) of the original before the ellipsis points. Similarly, if when you omit something from the end of a sentence what remains is grammatically complete, a period (or question mark or exclamation point, if either of these is more appropriate) goes before the ellipsis. In either case, the terminal punctuation marking the end of the sentence is closed up:

> Our civilization, which subsumes most of its predecessors, is a great ship steaming at speed into the future. . . . We may not be able to foresee every reef and hazard, but . . . we can, I think, plot a wise course. . . .

Other punctuation may also be included before or after the ellipsis if it makes the quoted material clearer:

> [B]y reading her compass bearing and headway, . . . we can, I think, plot a wise course between the narrows and bergs looking ahead.

Three periods can also indicate the omission of one or more entire sentences, or even whole paragraphs. Again, if the sentence preceding the omitted material is grammatically complete, it should end with a period preceding the ellipsis.

An ellipsis should also be used to indicate that material from a quoted line of poetry has been omitted. When quoting four or more lines of poetry, use a row of spaced dots to indicate that one or more entire lines have been omitted:

> **E.J. Pratt's epic "Towards the Last Spike" begins:**
>
> **It was the same world then as now—the same,**
> **Except for little differences of speed**
> **And power, and means to treat myopia.**
> **. . . . .**
> **The same, but for new particles of speech. . . .**

Note that some instructors may ask that all ellipses added to quotations be enclosed in square brackets. Check with the reader of your work for his or her preference.

> **PROOFREADING TIP**
>
> **Ineffective Omission of Material from a Quotation**
>
> Don't omit material from a quotation in such a way that you distort what the author is saying or destroy the integrity of the syntax. Similarly, don't quote unfairly "out of context"; for example, if an author qualifies a statement in some way, don't quote the statement as if it were unqualified.

54 Avoiding Common Errors in Punctuation

54a Run-on (Fused) Sentences

Failure to put any punctuation between independent clauses where there is also no coordinating conjunction results in a **run-on** or **fused** sentence:

run-on: **Philosophers' views did not always meet with the approval of the authorities therefore there was constant conflict between writers and the church or state.**

A semicolon after *authorities* corrects this serious error. See #34.

> **Philosophers' views did not always meet with the approval of the authorities; therefore, there was constant conflict between writers and the church or state.**

 ## Comma Splice

Using only a comma between independent clauses not joined with a coordinating conjunction results in a comma splice:

> cs: **The actual prize is not important, it is the honour connected with it that matters.**

> cs: **He desperately wanted to eat, however, he was too weak to get out of bed.**

> cs: **Adverbs can usually move around in a sentence, conjunctions are not as flexible.**

This error can be corrected by adding a semicolon in place of the comma, to signal that an independent clause comes next.

> **The actual prize is not important; it is the honour connected with it that matters.**

> **He desperately wanted to eat; however, he was too weak to get out of bed.**

Inserting a coordinating conjunction after the comma can also be effective:

> **Adverbs can usually move around in a sentence, but conjunctions are not as flexible.**

But note that you can make an exception in the case of short independent clauses (see #43b).

 ## Unwanted Comma Between Subject and Verb

Generally, do not put a comma between a subject and its verb unless some intervening element calls for punctuation:

no p: **His enthusiasm for the project and his desire to be of help, led him to add his name to the list of volunteers.**

Don't be misled by the length of a compound subject. The comma after *help* in the last example is just as wrong as the comma in the following sentence:

no p: **Kiera, addressed the class.**

But if some intervening element, for example an appositive or a participial phrase, requires setting off, use a *pair* of punctuation marks (see #43f–g):

His enthusiasm for the project and his desire to be of help, both strongly felt, led him to add his name to the list of volunteers.

Kiera—the first presenter—addressed the class.

Unwanted Comma Between Verb and Object or Complement

Do not put a comma between a verb and its object or complement unless some intervening element calls for punctuation. Especially, don't mistakenly assume that a clause opening with *that* needs a comma before it:

no p: **Hafiz realized, that he could no longer keep his eyes open.**

The noun clause beginning with *that* is the direct object of the verb *realized* and should not be separated from it. Only if an interrupter requires setting off should there be any punctuation:

Hafiz realized, as he tried once again to read the paragraph, that he could no longer keep his eyes open.

Another example:

no p: **Ottawa's principal claim to fame is, that it has the world's longest skating rink.**

Here, the comma intrudes between the linking verb *is* and its complement, the predicate noun consisting of a *that*-clause.

Unwanted Comma After Last Adjective of a Series

Do not put a comma between the last adjective of a series and the noun it modifies:

> p: **How could anyone fail to be impressed by such an intelligent, outspoken, resourceful, fellow as Jonathan is?**

The comma after *resourceful* is wrong, though it may briefly feel right because a certain rhythm has been established and because there is no *and* before the last of the three adjectives.

Unwanted Comma Between Coordinated Words and Phrases

Generally, don't put a comma between words and phrases joined by a coordinating conjunction; use a comma only when the coordinate elements are clauses (see #43a–b):

> no p: **The dog and cat circled each other warily, and then went off in opposite directions.**

> no p: **I was a long way from home, and didn't know how to get there.**

> no p: **She was not only intelligent, but also very kind.**

The commas in these three sentences are all unnecessary. Sometimes a writer uses such a comma for a mild emphasis, but if you want an emphatic pause a dash will probably work better:

> **The dog and cat circled each other warily—and then went off in opposite directions.**

Or the sentence can be slightly revised in order to gain the emphasis:

> **She was not only intelligent; she was also very kind.**

> **I was a long way from home, and I had no idea how to get there.**

Commas with Emphatic Repetition

If the two elements joined by a conjunction constitute an emphatic repetition, a comma is sometimes optional:

I wanted not only to win, but to win overwhelmingly.

This sentence would be equally correct and effective without the comma. But in the following sentence the comma is necessary:

It was an object of beauty, and of beauty most spectacular.

 ## Unwanted Comma with Short Introductory or Parenthetical Element

Generally, do not set off introductory elements or interrupters that are very short, not really parenthetical, or so slightly parenthetical that you feel no pause when reading them:

no p: **Perhaps, she was trying to tell us something.**

no p: **But, it was not a case of mistaken identity.**

no p: **Therefore, he put on his mukluks.**

no p: **We asked if we could try it out, for a week, to see if we really liked it.**

When the pause is strong, however, be sure to set the element off:

It was only then, after the very formal dinner, that we were all able to relax.

Often such commas are optional, depending on the pattern of intonation the writer wants:

In Canada(,) the change of the seasons is sharply evident.

In Canada(,) as elsewhere, money talks.

Last year(,) we went to Quebec City.

As she walked(,) she thought of her childhood in Cabbagetown.

Sometimes such a comma is necessary to prevent misreading:

incorrect: **After eating the cat Irene gave me jumped out the window.**

revised: **After eating, the cat Irene gave me jumped out the window.**

See also #43e.

54i Unwanted Comma with Restrictive Appositive

Don't incorrectly set off proper nouns and titles of literary works as nonrestrictive appositives (see #43f.2). For instance, it's "Mordecai Richler's novel *Barney's Version*," not "Mordecai Richler's novel, *Barney's Version*." Richler, after all, wrote more than one novel.

p: **In her poem, "Daddy," Sylvia Plath explores her complicated relationship with her father.**

p: **The home port of the Canadian Coast Guard icebreaker, the *Terry Fox*, is St. John's, Newfoundland.**

The punctuation makes it sound as though Plath wrote only this one poem and that the *Terry Fox* is the only icebreaker in the Canadian Coast Guard's fleet. The titles are restrictive: if they were removed, the sentences would not be clear. If the context is clear, the explanatory words often aren't needed at all:

In "Daddy" Plath explores . . .

The home port of the *Terry Fox* is . . .

If Sylvia Plath had in fact written only one poem, or if the Canadian Coast Guard had only one icebreaker, it would be correct to set off the title. Similarly, it would be correct to set off a title after referring to an author's "first novel" or the like, since an author, regardless of how many novels she or he has written, can have only one *first* novel.

Unwanted Comma with Indirect Quotation

Do not set off indirect quotations as if they were direct quotations:

> no p: **The author says, that civilization as we have come to know it is in jeopardy.**

In an indirect quotation, what was said is being reported, not quoted.

Unwanted Question Mark After Indirect Question

Don't put a question mark at the end of indirect questions—questions that are only being reported, not asked directly:

> p: **I asked what we were doing here?**

> p: **What he asked himself then was how he was going to explain it to the shareholders?**

Each of these sentences should end with a period rather than a question mark.

Unwanted Semicolon with Subordinate Element

Do not put a semicolon in front of a mere phrase or subordinate clause. Use a semicolon only where you could, if you chose to, put a period instead:

> p: **They cancelled the meeting; being disappointed at the low turnout.**

> p: **Only about a dozen people showed up; partly because there had been too little publicity and no free muffins.**

Those semicolons should be commas. Periods in those spots would turn what follows them into fragments (see #12x); in effect, so do semicolons. If you find yourself trying to avoid comma splices and overshooting in this way, devote some further study to the comma splice (#33 and #54b) and to learning how to recognize an independent clause (see #12m–n and p).

Similarly, don't put a semicolon between a subordinate clause and an independent clause:

> p: **After the show, when they got home, tired and with their eardrums ringing; Sheila said she was never going to another musical again.**

> revised: **After the show, when they got home, tired and with their eardrums ringing, Sheila said she was never going to another musical again.**

 ## 54m Unwanted Colon After Incomplete Construction

Do not use a colon after an incomplete construction; a colon is appropriate only after an independent clause:

> p: **She preferred comfort foods such as: potatoes, bread, and pasta.**

The prepositional *such as* needs an object to be complete. Had the phrase been extended to "She preferred such comfort foods as these" or "She preferred comfort foods such as the following," it would have been complete, an independent clause, and a colon would have been correct. Here is another example of this common error:

> p: **His favourite pastimes are: swimming, hiking, and collecting rocks.**

Since the linking verb *are* is incomplete without a complement, the colon is incorrect.

 ## 54n Unwanted Double Punctuation: Comma or Semicolon with a Dash

Avoid putting a comma or a semicolon together with a dash. Use whichever mark is appropriate.

55 Formatting an Essay

In most cases, you will be required to prepare your essay using word-processing software. Make sure to save your work frequently, and always create backup files. As you format your essay, keep in mind that your aim is to produce a document with a professional appearance. Unless directed otherwise, follow these conventions:

1. Use a plain, readable typeface (12-point Times New Roman or 10-point Arial).

2. Double-space your essay throughout and leave margins of about 1 inch (2.5 cm) on all four sides of the page. Set the margins as either fully justified or justified flush left with a ragged (i.e., unjustified) right-hand margin.

3. Label all pages after a title page in the top right-hand corner. Include your surname before the page number, as a precaution against misplaced pages. Most word-processing software will enable you to generate these "headers" automatically. Page numbers should be set as Arabic numerals, without periods, dashes, slashes, circles, or other decorations.

4. On the first page of a long essay or research paper, begin about 1 inch (2.5 cm) from the top, at the left margin, and on separate double-spaced lines put your name, your instructor's name, the course number, and the date of submission; then double-space again and put the title, centred. If you wish or are instructed to use a separate title page, centre the title about 1 inch (2.5 cm) from the top of the first page following the title page. (See #79 for illustrations.)

5. Set the title in standard font size and in upper- and lowercase roman letters, making sure to capitalize the title correctly (see #57m). Do not put the whole title in capital letters or in boldface type, and do not underline it or put a period after it. Do not put your title in quotation marks (unless it is in fact a quotation); if it includes the title of a poem, story, book, etc., or a ship's name, use italics or quotation

marks appropriately (see #58 and #59). Do not use the title of a published work by itself as your own title. Here are two examples of effective titles:

Of Pigoons and Wolvogs: Wildlife in *Oryx and Crake* and *The Year of the Flood*

The Structure of Dennis Lee's "Civil Elegies"

6. Indent the first line of each paragraph one tab length (approximately 5 spaces). Do not leave extra space between paragraphs. Indent long block quotations two tab lengths (approximately 10 spaces). Do not leave any additional space before or after a double-spaced block quotation.

7. Leave only one space after any terminal punctuation, and remember to leave spaces before and after each of the three dots of an ellipsis (see #53). Use two hyphens, with no space before or after either one, to make a dash; most word-processing software will automatically convert two hyphens to a dash.

8. Never begin a line with a comma, semicolon, period, question mark, exclamation point, or hyphen. On rare occasions, a dash or the dots of an ellipsis may have to come at the beginning of a line, but if possible place them at the end of the preceding line.

9. Generally, do not divide words at the end of a line. The word-wrap feature of your word-processing software should automatically move a word that might otherwise be divided to the beginning of the next line. If, for some reason, you do need to divide a word, make sure you do so between syllables. (If you are uncertain, check your dictionary for a word's syllabication.)

10. Print your document on plain white recycled paper of good quality, 8.5 by 11 inches (or 21 by 28 cm) in size. Use only one side of each page. Make sure there is plenty of ink or toner in your printer's cartridge before you press "print."

11. If after proofreading your hard copy you decide that you have to make changes, call up the file, make the appropriate emendations, save the changes, and reprint the page or pages you have revised.

12. Staple the pages of your essay together. Unless requested by your instructor, do not submit your essay in a folder.

If you are preparing a handwritten document, as may be the case for an in-class essay or an examination, use a format similar to what you would create using software. Write on every other line, using blue or black ink, and write as legibly as possible. Use lined paper with clean edges. To change or delete a word or short phrase, draw a single horizontal line through it and write the new word or phrase, if any, above it. If you wish to insert a word or short phrase, place a caret (^) *below* the line at the point of insertion, and write the addition *above* the line. If you wish to start a new paragraph where you haven't indented, put the symbol ¶ in the left margin and insert a caret where you want the paragraph to begin. If you wish to cancel a paragraph indention, write "No ¶" in the left margin.

PROOFREADING TIP

Breaking a Web Address at the End of a Line

If a web address (also known as a *URL*, or *uniform resource locator*) needs to be spread over two lines, you may need to manually insert a break so that the division does not interrupt an important component of the address. When this is the case, the break should appear after one of the slashes in the web address.

Scott Messenger's article "Predicting the Storm: How Computers Are Replacing Humans to Forecast the Weather" is available online at http://www.canadiangeographic.ca/magazine/jf12/computers_predict_weather.asp.

Do not introduce a hyphen to indicate the break, for it may appear as though the hyphen is part of the address.

---

56 Abbreviations

abbr Abbreviations are expected in technical and scientific writing, legal writing, business writing, memos, reports, reference works, bibliographies and works cited lists, footnotes, tables, and charts, and sometimes in journalism. The following relatively few kinds are in common use.

56a **Titles Before Proper Names**

The following abbreviations (along with *Ms.*, which is not a true abbreviation) can be used with or without initials or given names:

Mr.	(Mr. Eng, Mr. Marc Ramsay)
Mrs.	(Mrs. L.W. Smith, Mrs. Tazim Khan)
M.	(M. Joubert; M. Stéphane Dion)
Mme.	(Mme. Girard; Mme. Nathalie Gagnon)
Mlle.	(Mlle. Stephanie Sevigny; Mlle. R. Pelletier)
Dr.	(Dr. Paula Grewal; Dr. P. Francis Fairchild)
St.	(St. Beatrice; St. Francis Xavier)

In informal writing, abbreviations of professional or honorific titles can also be used, but only before proper names with initials or given names:

Prof. Hana Jamalali (*but* Professor Jamalali)

Sen. H.C. Tsui (*but* Senator Tsui)

Gov. Gen. David Johnston (*but* Governor General Johnston)

the Rev. Lois Wilson (*more formally*, the Reverend Lois Wilson)

the Hon. Brad Wall (*more formally*, the Honourable Brad Wall, the Honourable Mr. Wall)

In formal writing, always spell out these and similar titles.

56b **Titles and Degrees After Proper Names**

David Adams, M.D. (*but not* Dr. David Adams, M.D.)

Claire T. McFadden, D.D.S.

Martin Luther King, Jr.

Eva-Marie Kröller, Ph.D., F.R.S.C.

Academic degrees not following a name may also be abbreviated:

Shirley is working toward her B.A.

Amir is working on his M.A. thesis.

Standard Words Used with Dates and Numerals

720 B.C.E. (or **720 B.C.**, or **720 B.P.**)

231 C.E. (or **A.D. 231**), **the second century C.E.** (or **the second century A.D.**)

7 a.m. (or **7 A.M.**), **8:30 p.m.** (or **8:30 P.M.**)

no. 17 (or **No. 17**)

 ## Agencies and Organizations Known by Their Initials

Capitalize names of agencies and organizations commonly known by their initials (see also #49):

RCMP   **CAW**   **CBC**   **WHO**   **NATO**   **UNICEF**

 ## Scientific and Technical Terms Known by Their Initials

Some scientific, technical, or other terms (usually of considerable length) are commonly known by their initials (see also #49):

LED   **URL**   **DDT**   **DNA**   **WMD**   **FM**

SARS   **ISBN**   **HTML**   **MP**   **GST**   **ISP**

 ## Latin Expressions Commonly Used in English

i.e. (that is)   **etc.** (and so forth)

e.g. (for example)   **vs.** (versus)

cf. (compare)   **et al.** (and others)

Note that in formal writing, it is better to spell out the English equivalent.

PROOFREADING TIP

Using Latin Expressions and Abbreviations

(a) If you use *e.g.*, use it only to introduce an example or a list of examples; following the example or list, write out *for example*:

> **Deciduous trees—e.g., oaks, maples, and birches—lose their leaves in the fall.**
>
> **Deciduous trees—oaks, maples, and birches, for example—lose their leaves in the fall.**

Note also that if you introduce a list with *e.g.* or *for example* or even *such as*, it is illogical to follow it with *etc.* or *and so forth*.

(b) Generally, use a comma after *i.e.* or *e.g.*, just as you would if you wrote out *that is* or *for example*.

(c) The abbreviation *cf.* stands for Latin *confer*, meaning "compare." Do not use it to mean "see"; for that, the Latin *vide* (*v.*) would be correct.

(d) Use *etc.* sparingly. Use it only when there are at least several more items to follow and when they are reasonably obvious:

> **Learning the Greek alphabet—alpha, beta, gamma, delta, etc.—isn't really difficult.**
>
> incorrect: **He considered several possible occupations: accounting, teaching, nursing, etc.**

In the last example, a reader can have no idea of what the other possible occupations might be. Further, don't write *and etc.*: *and* is redundant, since *etc.* (*et cetera*) means "and so forth."

56g Terms in Official Titles

Capitalize terms used in official titles being copied exactly:

Johnson Bros., Ltd.   **Ibbetson & Co.**

Smith & Sons, Inc.   *Quill & Quire*

PROOFREADING TIP

Limiting the Use of the Ampersand (&)

Don't use the ampersand (&) as a substitute for *and*; use it only when presenting the title of a company or a publication exactly, as in #56g.

57 Capitalization

cap,
uc
Generally, capitalize proper nouns, abbreviations of proper nouns, and words derived from proper nouns, as follows:

Names and Nicknames

Capitalize names and nicknames of real and fictional people and individual animals:

Frederick Banting   **Marilyn Monroe**   **Maurice "Rocket" Richard**
Clarissa Dalloway   **Rumpelstiltskin**   **Lassie**

Professional and Honorific Titles

Capitalize professional and honorific titles when they directly precede and thus are parts of names:

Professor Tamara Jones (*but* Tamara Jones, professor at Mount Allison)

Captain Janna Ting (*but* Janna Ting is a captain in the police force.)

Rabbi Samuel Singer (*but* Mr. Singer was rabbi of our synagogue.)

Capitalizing Titles After Names

Normally titles that follow names aren't capitalized unless they have become part of the name:

> **Justin Trudeau, prime minister of Canada**
> **Beverley McLachlin, chief justice of the Supreme Court**
> **Claude Carignan, the senator**

> *but*

> **Catherine the Great**
> **Smokey the Bear**

Some titles of particular distinction are customarily capitalized even if the person isn't named:

> **The Queen vacationed in Scotland.**

> **On Easter Sunday, the Pope will address the crowd gathered in St. Peter's Square.**

> **The university was honoured with a visit by the Dalai Lama.**

Opinion is divided on the question of whether "prime minister" and "president" are titles in the same category of distinction as "the Queen," "the Pope," and "the Dalai Lama." Some writers and news outlets make it a policy always to capitalize these titles. In your own writing, you should aim for consistency in whatever practices you adopt.

> **The Prime Minister met with the President in Paris.**

> *or*

> **The prime minister met with the president in Paris.**

57c Words Designating Family Relationships

Capitalize words designating family relationships when they are used as parts of proper names and also when they are used in place of proper names, except following a possessive:

> **Uncle Peter** (*but* I have an uncle named Peter.)

> **There's my uncle, Peter.** (*but* There's my Uncle Peter.)

I told Father about it. (*but* I told my father about it.)

I have always respected Grandmother. (*but* Diana's grandmother is a splendid woman.)

 ## 57d Place Names

Capitalize place names—including common nouns (*river*, *street*, *park*, etc.) when they are parts of proper nouns (see #13):

North America	Canada	Alberta	Moose Jaw
Yonge Street	Vancouver Island	Hudson Bay	Niagara Falls
Lake Ladoga	Active Pass	Mount Etna	the Miramichi River
the Suez Canal	the Gobi Desert	the Amazon	the Rockies

> **PROOFREADING TIP**
>
> **Capitalizing *North*, *South*, *East*, and *West***
>
> As a rule, don't capitalize *north*, *south*, *east*, and *west* unless they are part of specific place names (North Battleford, West Vancouver, the South Shore) or designate specific geographical areas (the frozen North, the East Coast, the Deep South, the Northwest, the Wild West, the Far East).
>
> Since writers in Canada usually capitalize *East*, *West*, and *North* (and sometimes *South*) to refer to parts of the country (the peoples of the North, the settlement of the West), it makes sense to capitalize *Eastern*, *Western*, *Northern*, and *Southern* when they refer to ideas attached to parts of the country (Northern peoples, Western settlement). Otherwise, except for cases when they appear as parts of specific place names (the Eastern Townships), these adjectives should not be capitalized. This practice applies to cases such as *northern Canada*, *eastern Canada*, and *western Canada*, which are not specific place names but descriptions of geographic regions.

 ## 57e Months, Days, and Holidays

Capitalize the names of months, days of the week, holidays, holy days, and festivals:

January	Monday	Canada Day	Remembrance Day
Christmas	Hanukkah	Ramadan	Diwali

Do not capitalize the names of seasons: spring, summer, autumn, fall, winter.

57f Religious Names

Capitalize names of deities and other religious names and terms:

Allah	Apollo	God	the Holy Ghost
Jupiter	the Prophet	the Virgin Mary	Vishnu
the Bible	the Talmud	the Torah	the Qur'an
Buddhism	Hinduism	Islam	Taoism

Note: Some people capitalize pronouns referring to a deity; others prefer not to. Either practice is acceptable as long as you are consistent. Also note that you do not italicize the proper names of religious texts unless you are referring to a specific edition, such as *The New Jerusalem Bible*.

57g Names of Nationalities and Organizations

Capitalize names of nationalities and other groups and organizations and of their members:

Canadian, Irish, Scandinavian, South American, Iraqi, Somali, Nova Scotian, Texan

New Democrats, the New Democratic Party

Bloquistes, the Bloc Québécois, the Bloc

Roman Catholics, the Roman Catholic Church

Teamsters

the Vancouver Canucks, the Toronto Blue Jays

57h Names of Institutions, Sections of Government, Historical Events, and Buildings

Capitalize names of institutions; sections of government; historical events, periods, and documents; and specific buildings:

McGill University, The Hospital for Sick Children

the Ministry of Health, Parliament, the Senate, the Cabinet, the Opposition the French Revolution, the Great War, World War I, the Gulf War, the Cretaceous Period, the Renaissance, the Magna Carta, the Treaty of Versailles, the Charter of Rights and Freedoms, the Ming Dynasty

Canada Place, the CN Tower, Westminster Abbey

57i Academic Courses and Languages

Capitalize specific academic courses, but not the subjects themselves, except for languages:

Philosophy 101, Fine Arts 300, Mathematics 204, English 112, Food Writing, Humanities 101

an English course, a major in French (*but* a history course, an economics major, a degree in psychology)

57j Derivatives of Proper Nouns

Capitalize derivatives of proper nouns:

French Canadian, Haligonian, Celtic, Québécois, Ethiopian, Kuwaiti

Confucianism, Christian

Shakespearean, Keynesian, Edwardian, Miltonic

57k Abbreviations of Proper Nouns

Capitalize abbreviations of proper nouns:

PMO   TVA   CUPE   CUSO   P.E.I   B.C.   the BNA Act

Note that abbreviations of agencies and organizations commonly known by their initials do not need periods (see #56d), but that non-postal abbreviations of geographical entities such as provinces usually do. See also #49.

57-l *I* and *O*

Capitalize the pronoun *I* and the vocative interjection *O*:

O my people, what have I done unto thee? (Micah 6:3)

Do not capitalize the interjection *oh* unless it begins a sentence.

Titles of Written and Other Works

In the titles and subtitles of written and other works, use a capital letter to begin the first word, the last word, and all other important words; leave uncapitalized only articles (*a*, *an*, *the*) and any conjunctions and prepositions less than five letters long (unless one of these is the first or last word):

> *Roughing It in the Bush*   "The Metamorphosis"
> *A Dangerous Method*   "O Canada"
> *Beyond Remembering: The Collected Poems of Al Purdy*

But there can be exceptions; for example, the conjunctions *Nor* and *So* are usually capitalized, the relative pronoun *that* is sometimes not capitalized (*All's Well that Ends Well*), and in Ralph Ellison's "Tell It Like It Is, Baby" the preposition-cum-conjunction *Like* demands capitalization.

If a title includes a hyphenated word, capitalize the part after the hyphen only if it is a noun or an adjective or is otherwise an important word:

> *Half-Blood Blues*
> *The Scorched-Wood People*
> *Murder Among the Well-to-do*

(See #58 for more on titles.)

First Words

Capitalize the first word of a major or minor sentence—of anything, that is, that concludes with terminal punctuation:

> Bebe turned pale when her instructor asked her to answer the question. (Math was not her strongest subject.)

> "I can't remember," she blurted out. "One? Seven? Fifty? Help!"

Capitalize the first word of a quotation that is intended as a sentence or that is capitalized in the source, but not fragments from other than the beginning of such a sentence:

> When he said "Let me take the wheel for a while," I shuddered at the memory of what had happened the last time I had let him "take the wheel."

If something interrupts a single quoted sentence, do not begin the second part of the sentence with a capital:

> "It was all I could do," she said, "to keep from laughing out loud."

An incorporated sentence following a colon may be capitalized if it seems to stand as a separate statement—for example, if it is itself long or requires emphasis—but the current trend is away from capitalization:

> There was one thing, she said, which we must never forget: No one has the right to the kind of happiness that deprives someone else of deserved happiness.

> It was a splendid night: the sky was clear except for a few picturesque clouds, the moon was full, and even a few stars shone through. (The first *the* could be capitalized if the writer wanted particular emphasis on the details.)

> It was no time for petty quarrels: everything depended on unanimity.

With Personification and for Emphasis

Although it is risky and should not be done often, writers who have good control of tone can occasionally capitalize a personified abstraction or a word or phrase to which they want to impart a special importance of some kind:

> In his quest to succeed, Greed and Power came to dominate his every waking thought.

Sometimes the slight emphasis of capitalization can be used for a humorous or ironic effect:

> He insisted on driving His Beautiful Car: everyone else preferred to walk the two blocks without benefit of jerks and jolts and carbon monoxide fumes.

And occasionally, but rarely, you can capitalize whole words and phrases or even sentences for a special sort of graphic emphasis:

> **When we reached the excavation site, however, we were confronted by a sign warning us in no uncertain terms to KEEP OUT— TRESPASSERS WILL BE PROSECUTED.**

58 Titles (see also #57m)

58a Italics for Whole or Major Works

title Use italics (see #59) for titles of written works published as units, such as books, magazines, journals, newspapers, and plays; for films and television programs; for entire websites; for paintings and sculptures; and for musical compositions (other than single songs), such as operas and ballets:

> *Paradise Lost* is Milton's greatest work.
>
> *The New Yorker* is a weekly magazine.
>
> The scholarly journal *Canadian Literature* is published quarterly.
>
> I prefer *The Globe and Mail* to the *National Post*.
>
> *The Passionate Eye* is a CBC program featuring the best in current documentaries.
>
> *Urban Dictionary* is an evolving website that informally chronicles regional slang terms not found in most dictionaries.
>
> Picasso's *Guernica* is a disturbing representation of the Spanish Civil War.
>
> One tires of hearing Ravel's *Boléro* played so often.

Note that instrumental compositions may be known by name or by technical detail, or both. A title name is italicized (Beethoven's *Pastoral Symphony*); technical identification is usually not (Beethoven's Sixth Symphony, or Symphony no. 6, op. 68, in F major).

58b Quotation Marks for Short Works and Parts of Longer Works

Put quotation marks around the titles of short works and of parts of longer works, such as short stories, articles, essays, short poems, chapters of books, songs, individual episodes of television programs, and sections of websites:

> "A Wilderness Station" is a story by Alice Munro that begins in Ontario in the 1850s.

> Leonard Cohen's "Joan of Arc" and "Democracy" are songs featured in this documentary about the music of Canada.

> Of the ten episodes in the CBC documentary *Hockey: A People's History*, I enjoyed the first one, "A Simple Game," the best.

> "The History of English," posted on the website *Oxford Dictionaries,* provides a very brief overview of historical influences on the English language.

58c Titles Within Titles

If an essay title includes a book title, the book title is italicized:

> "Things Botanical in *The Lost Garden* and *A Student of Weather*"

If a book title includes something requiring quotation marks, retain the quotation marks and italicize the whole thing:

> *From Fiction to Film: James Joyce's "The Dead"*

If a book title includes something that itself would be italicized, such as the name of a ship or the title of another book, either put the secondary item in quotation marks or leave it in roman type (i.e., not italicized):

> *The Cruise of the "Nona"*

> *D.H. Lawrence and* Sons and Lovers: *Sources and Criticism*

> **PROOFREADING TIP**
>
> **Treatment of *the* as Part of a Title**
>
> Double-check the role of the definite article, *the*, in titles you cite. Italicize and capitalize *the* only when it is actually part of the title:
>
> *The Stone Angel*   *The Canadian Encyclopedia*
> the *Life of Pi*   the *Partisan Review*
>
> Refer to a newspaper or a magazine the way it refers to itself on its front page or in its masthead:
>
> *The Vancouver Sun*   *The Globe and Mail*
> the *Calgary Herald*   the *Victoria Times Colonist*
> *The New Yorker*   the *Literary Review of Canada*

59 Italics

ital **Italics** are a special kind of slanting type that contrasts with the surrounding type to draw attention to a word or phrase, such as a title (see #58a). In handwritten work, such as an exam, represent italic type by underlining.

59a Names of Ships, Trains, and Planes

Italicize names of individual ships, trains, planes, and other vehicles:

the *Golden Hind*   *Spirit of St. Louis*
the *Bonaventure*   the *Discovery*

59b Non-English Words and Phrases

Italicize non-English words and phrases that are not yet sufficiently common to be entirely at home in English. English contains many terms that have come from other languages but that are no longer thought of as non-English and are therefore not italicized; for example:

arroyo	bamboo	chutzpah	cliché
eureka	façade	genre	in vitro
moccasin	prairie	spaghetti	sushi

But English also makes use of many terms still felt by many writers to be sufficiently non-English to need italicizing; for example:

chez	*caveat emptor*	*coup d'état*	*Bildungsroman*
joie de vivre	*jihad*	*raison d'être*	*savoir faire*

59c Words Referred to as Words

Italicize words, letters, numerals, and the like when you refer to them as such:

The word *helicopter* is formed from Greek roots.

There are two *r*'s in *embarrass*.

The number *13* is considered unlucky by many people.

Don't use *&* as a substitute for *and*.

See also #52d. For the matter of apostrophes for plurals of such elements, see #61-l.8.

59d For Emphasis

On rare occasions, italicize words or phrases—or even whole sentences—that you want to emphasize, for example, as they might be stressed if spoken aloud:

One thing he was now sure of: *that* was a bad idea.

Remember, *it is very dangerous to mix bleach and vinegar*, especially when you are working in a small space.

Like other typographical devices for achieving emphasis (boldface, capitalization, underlining), this method is worth avoiding, or at least minimizing, in academic and other writing.

60 Numerals

num Numerals are appropriate in technical and scientific writing, and newspapers sometimes use them to save space. But in ordinary writing certain conventions limit their use. Use numerals for the following purposes:

60a Time of Day

Use numerals for the time of day with *a.m.* or *p.m.* and *midnight* or *noon*, or when minutes are included:

3 p.m. (*but* three o'clock, three in the afternoon)

12 noon, 12 midnight (these are often better than the equivalents, *12 p.m.* and *12 a.m.*, which may not be understood)

4:15, 4:30 (*but* a quarter past four; half past four)

60b Dates

Use numerals for dates:

March 31, 2017, or **31 March 2017**

The year is almost always represented by numerals, and centuries are written out:

Wasn't 2000 the last year of the twentieth century, not the first year of the twentieth-first century?

See also #61-l.8.

PROOFREADING TIP

Adding Suffixes to Numerals in Dates

The suffixes *st*, *nd*, *rd*, and *th* go with numerals in dates only if the year is not given; or the number may be written out:

July 1, 1867	**July 1st**
the first of July	**July first**

60c Addresses

Use numerals for addresses:

2132 Fourth Avenue   **4771 128th Street**
P.O. Box 91   **Apartment 8**

60d Technical and Mathematical Numbers

Use numerals for technical and mathematical numbers, such as percentages and decimals:

31 per cent   **31%**
37 degrees Celsius   **37°C**
2.54 centimetres   **2.54 cm**

60e Parts of a Written Work

Use numerals for page numbers, chapters, and other divisions of a written work, especially in documentation (see #79):

page 27, p. 27, pp. 33–38   **line 13, lines 3 and 5, ll. 7–9**

Chapter 4, Ch. 4, chapter IV   **Section 3, section III**

Part 2, part II   **2 Samuel 22: 3, II Samuel 19: 1**

Book IX, canto 120 (IX, 120)   **Act 4, Scene 2; act IV, scene ii**

60f Numbers of More Than Two Words

Generally, spell out numbers that can be expressed in one or two words; use numerals for numbers that would take more than two words:

four; thirty; eighty-three; two hundred; seven thousand; 115; 385; 2120

one-third; one-half; five thirty-seconds

three dollars; five hundred dollars; $3.48; $517

If you are writing about more than one number, say for purposes of comparison or when giving statistics, numerals are usually preferable:

> **Enrolment dropped from 250 two years ago, to 200 last year, to only 90 this year.**

Don't mix numerals and words in such a context. On the other hand, if in your writing you refer alternately to two sets of figures, it may be better to use numerals for one and words for the other:

> **We're building a 60-foot border; we can use either five 12-foot timbers or six 10-foot timbers.**

Commas with Numerals

Commas have long been conventional to separate groups of three figures in long numbers:

> **3,172,450**   **17,920**

In the metric system, however, along with the rest of the SI (Système International, or International System of Units), groups of three digits on either side of a decimal point are separated by spaces; with four-digit numbers a space is optional:

> **7723**   or   **7 723**
>
> **3 172 450**
>
> **3.1416**   or   **3.141 6** (but 3.141 59)

Note that dollar figures are always separated with commas:

> **$3,500 £27,998.06**   **¥30,000**

Also note that street addresses are usually not separated by commas or spaces:

> **18885 Bay Mills Avenue**

61 Spelling Rules and Common Causes of Error

sp Some writers have little trouble with spelling; others have a lot—or is that "alot"? The good news is that good spelling comes with practice; taking the time to look up a word now will help you remember its proper spelling the next time you need to use it. And learning how to spell words properly will benefit you not only in your college or university classes but also in your future career. Accurate spelling signals professionalism, care for your work, and attention to detail—all qualities that employers value highly.

English spelling isn't as bizarre as some people think, but there are oddities. Sometimes the same sound can be spelled in several ways (fine, offer, phone, cough; or so, soap, sow, sew, beau, dough), or a single element can be pronounced in several ways (cough, tough, dough, through, bough, fought). When such inconsistencies occur in longer and less familiar words, sometimes only a dictionary can help us.

In Canada, we contend with the influence of British and American spelling. Broadly speaking, Canadian conventions—whether of spelling, punctuation, usage, or pronunciation—are closer to American than to British. Most Canadians write *centre* and *theatre* rather than *center* and *theater*, but we write *curb* rather than *kerb*, and *aluminum* rather than *aluminium*. Endings in *our* (colour, honour, labour, etc.) exist alongside those in *or*, although many Canadians prefer the former. Similarly, endings in *ise* exist alongside endings in *ize* (e.g., organise/organize), although the latter is clearly preferred. We have the useful alternatives *cheque* (bank), *racquet* (tennis), and *storey* (floor); Americans have only *check*, *racket*, and *story* for both meanings. But *draught* is losing ground to *draft*, and *program* and *judgment* are rapidly replacing *programme* and *judgement*.

Where alternatives exist, either is correct. But be consistent. If you choose *analyze*, write *paralyze* and *modernize*; if you choose *centre*, write *lustre* and *fibre*; if you spell *honour*, then write *humour*, *colour*, and *labour*. And if you choose the *our* endings, watch out for the trap: when you add the suffixes *ous*, *ious*, *ate* or *ation*, and *ize* (or *ise*), you must drop the *u* and write *humorous*, *coloration*, *vaporize*, and *laborious*, and there is no *u* in *honorary*.

Many spelling errors can be prevented only with the help of a good dictionary. Many others, however, fall into clear categories. Familiarizing yourself with the main rules and the main sources of confusion will help you avoid these errors.

61a *ie* or *ei*

The old jingle should help: use *i* before *e* except after *c*, or when sounded like *a* as in *neighbour* and *weigh*.

> *ie*: **achieve, believe, chief, field, piece, shriek**
> *ei* after *c*: **ceiling, conceive, deceive, perceive, receive**
> *ei* when sounded like *a*: **eight, neighbour, sleigh, veil, weigh**

However, there are a number of common exceptions to this "rule," including the following:

ancient	**caffeine**	**counterfeit**	**deficient**
either	**efficient**	**foreign**	**forfeit**
glacier	**height**	**heir**	**leisure**
neither	**their**	**science**	**society**
seize	**sovereign**	**weird**	**species**

When in doubt, consult your dictionary.

Prefixes and Suffixes

The more you know about how words are put together, the less trouble you will have spelling them. Many of the words that give writers difficulty are those with **prefixes** and **suffixes**. Understanding how these elements operate will help you avoid errors.

61b Prefixes

A prefix is one or more syllables added to the beginning of a root word to form a new word. Many common spelling mistakes could be avoided by recognizing that a word consists of a prefix joined to a root word. For example, *pre* is from a Latin word meaning "before"; *fix* is a root, meaning "fasten" or "place": the new word, *prefix*, is then literally something fastened before. *Prefix* is not a difficult word for most writers to spell, but recognizing its prefix and root will ensure that it is spelled correctly.

One mistake writers often make is omitting the last letter of a prefix when it is the same as the first letter of the root. When a prefix ends with the same letter that the root begins with, the result is a double letter; don't omit one of them:

> **ad + dress = address**　　**mis + spell = misspell**
> **com + motion = commotion**　　**un + necessary = unnecessary**

(Similarly, don't omit one of the doubled letters in compounds such as *beachhead*, *bookkeeping*, and *roommate*.)

In some cases the first letter of a root has "pulled" the last letter of a prefix over. In other words, the first letter of the root is doubled to replace the last letter of a prefix in order to make the resulting word less difficult to pronounce. Writers unaware of the prefix sometimes forget to double the consonant. The Latin prefix *ad*, meaning "to, toward, near," is commonly affected this way. For example, it became *af* in front of *facere* (a Latin verb meaning "to do"); hence our word *affect* has two *f*'s. Here are some other examples:

ad	>	**ac**	in	**access, accept, accommodate**
		al	in	**alliance, allusion**
		an	in	**annul, annihilate**
		ap	in	**apprehend, apparatus, application**
com	>	**col**	in	**collide, colloquial, collusion**
		con	in	**connect, connote**
		cor	in	**correct, correspond**
ob	>	**op**	in	**oppose, oppress**
sub	>	**suc**	in	**success, succumb**
		sup	in	**suppress, supply, support**

Note the structure of the frequently misspelled *accommodate:* both *ac* and *com* are prefixes, so the word must have both a double *cc* and a double *mm*. It may help to think of the meaning of the word: *to make room for.* Be sure to *make room for* the double *cc* and the double *mm*.

Errors can also be prevented by correctly identifying a word's prefix. A writer who knows that the prefix of *arouse* is *a* and not *ar* will not be tempted to spell the word with a double *rr*. Knowing that the prefix of *apology* is *apo*, not *ap*, will curb the temptation to spell the word with a double *pp*. Familiarize yourself with prefixes. The following are some of the more common prefixes, along with their meanings:

a	**not, without (*amoral*); onward, away, from (*arise, awake*); to, at, into a particular state (*agree*); utterly (*abash*)**
	▶ VARIANT **an** **before a vowel (*anaemia*)**
ab	**off, away, from (*abduct, abnormal, abuse*)**
	▶ VARIANT **abs** **before *c, t* (*abscess, abstain*)**
ad	**denoting motion towards (*advance*), change into (*adapt*), or addition (*adjunct*)**
	▶ VARIANTS **ac** **before *c, k, q* (*accept, accede; acknowledge; acquire*)**
	af **before *f* (*affirm*)**
	ag **before *g* (*aggravate*)**
	al **before *l* (*allocate*)**
	an **before *n* (*annotate*)**
	ap **before *p* (*apprehend*)**
	ar **before *r* (*arrive*)**
	as **before *s* (*assemble*)**
	at **before *t* (*attend*)**
ante	**before (*antecedent*)**
anti	**opposed to, against (*anti-hero, antibacterial*)**
bi	**two, twice (*bicoloured, biennial*)**
	▶ VARIANT **bin** **before a vowel (*binoculars*)**
by	**subordinate, secondary (*by-election, by-product*)**

com	with, together (*combine, command*)		
	▶ VARIANTS	**col**	before *l* (*collocate, collude*)
		con	before *c, d, f, g, j, n, q, s, t, v*, and sometimes before vowels (*concord, condescend, confide*)
		cor	before *r* (*correct*)

de down, away from (*descend, de-ice*); completely (*denude*)

di twice, two (*dichromatic, dilemma*)

dis not (*disadvantage*); denoting reversal (*disappear*), removal (*dismember*), or separation (*disjoin, dispel, dissect*)
 ▶ VARIANT **dif** before *f* (*diffuse*)

dys bad, difficult (*dysfunctional*)

e electronic (*email, ezine*)

en in, into (*ensnare, engulf, encrust, energy*); used in verbs ending in *en* (*enliven*)
 ▶ VARIANT **em** before *b, p* (*embed, embolden*)

epi upon, above (*epidemic, epicentre*); in addition (*epilogue*)

ex out (*exclude; exodus*); upward (*extol*); thoroughly (*excruciate*); into the state of (*exasperate*)
 ▶ VARIANT **e** (*elect, emit*)

ef before *f* (*efface*)

for denoting prohibition (*forbid*), neglect (*forget*), or abstention (*forbear, forgo*)

fore in front, beforehand (*forebear, foreshadow, forecourt*)

hyper over, beyond, excessively (*hypersensitive*); relating to hypertext (*hyperlink*)

hypo under, below normal (*hypotension*)

in	not, without (*infertile*); in, towards (*influx*, *inbounds*)
	▶ VARIANTS il before *l* (*illegal*, *illegible*)
	im before *b*, *m*, *p* (*immature*, *imbibe*)
	ir before *r* (*irrelevant*, *irradiate*)

inter	between, among (*interactive*)

intra	on the inside (*intravenous*, *intramural*)

intro	in, inwards (*introvert*)

mis	wrongly, badly (*misapply*, *mismanage*); expressing negativity (*misadventure*, *mischief*)

multi	more than one, many (*multicoloured*, *multiple*)

ob	blocking, opposing, against (*obstacle*, *object*); to, towards (*oblige*)
	▶ VARIANTS oc before *c* (*occasion*)
	of before *f* (*offend*)
	op before *p* (*oppose*)

para	beyond or distinct from but analogous to (*paranormal*, *paramilitary*); protecting from (*parachute*)
	▶ VARIANT par before a vowel (*parody*)

per	through, all over, completely (*pervade*, *perforate*, *perfect*)

peri	around, about (*perimeter*)

pre	before (*precaution*, *precede*)

pro	supporting (*pro-industry*); forwards or away (*proceed*); before (*proactive*)
	▶ VARIANT pur (*pursue*)

re	once more, afresh (*reactivate*, *restore*, *revert*); mutually (*resemble*); in opposition (*repel*); behind, back (*remain*, *recluse*)

se	apart, without (*separate*, *secure*)

sub	denoting subsequent or secondary action (*subdivision*); lower, less, below (*subalpine*, *subculture*)		
	▶ VARIANTS	suc	before *c* (*succeed*)
		suf	before *f* (*suffix*)
		sug	before *g* (*suggest*)
		sup	before *p* (*support*)

syn	united, acting together (*synchronize*)	
	▶ VARIANT	sym	before *b*, *m*, *p* (*symbiosis*, *symmetry*)

uni	one (*unicorn*, *unicycle*)

 ## 61c Suffixes

A suffix is one or more syllables added to the end of a root word to form a new word, often changing its part of speech. For example:

appear (v.) + **ance** = **appearance** (n.)
content (adj.) + **ment** = **contentment** (n.)
occasion (n.) + **al** = **occasional** (adj.)
occasional (adj.) + **ly** = **occasionally** (adv.)

Suffixes, like prefixes, can give writers difficulty. The following are some of the most common suffixes that consistently confuse even good spellers. Pay particular attention to pairs or groups of suffixes that are often confused.

able, ably, ability; *ible, ibly, ibility*

It should be helpful to remember that many more words end in *able* than in *ible*; yet it is the *ible* endings that cause the most trouble:

–able		*–ible*	
advisable	inevitable	audible	inexpressible
comparable	laudable	contemptible	irresistible
debatable	noticeable	deductible	negligible
desirable	quotable	eligible	plausible
immeasurable	respectable	flexible	responsible
indubitable	veritable	incredible	visible

ent, ently, ence, ency; ant, antly, ance, ancy

-en-		*-an-*	
apparent	independent	appearance	flamboyant
coherent	permanent	blatant	irrelevant
consistent	persistence	brilliant	maintenance
excellent	resilient	concomitant	resistance
existence	tendency	extravagant	warrant

tial, tian; cial, cian

-tia-		*-cia-*	
confidential	influential	beneficial	mathematician
dietitian	martial	crucial	mortician
existential	spatial	commercial	physician

ce; se

-ce		*-se*	
choice	fence	course	expense
defence	presence	dense	phrase
evidence	voice	dispense	sparse

PROOFREADING TIP

practice, practise; licence, license

Canadian writers tend to follow the British practice of using the *-ce* forms *practice* and *licence* as nouns and the *-se* forms *practise* and *license* as verbs:

> We will <u>practise</u> our fielding at today's slo-pitch <u>practice</u>.

> Are you <u>licensed</u> to drive?
> Yes, I've had my driver's <u>licence</u> since I was sixteen.

American writers tend to favour the *-ce* spelling of *practice* and the *-se* spelling of *license* regardless of whether each is being used as a noun or a verb.

Note also that Canadian as well as British writers generally prefer the *-ce* spelling for *offence* and *defence*, while American writers tend to use the *-se* spellings of these words

ative; *itive*

-ative		*-itive*	
affirmative	informative	additive	positive
comparative	negative	competitive	repetitive
imaginative	restorative	genitive	sensitive

ly

When *ly* is added to an adjective already ending in a single *l*, that final *l* is retained, resulting in an adverb ending in *lly*: *accidentally, coolly, incidentally, mentally, naturally, politically.* (If you pronounce such words carefully you will be less likely to misspell them.) If the root ends in a double ll, one *l* is dropped: *full + ly = fully, chill + ly = chilly, droll + ly = drolly.*

PROOFREADING TIP

The Suffix *ally*

Many adjectives ending in *ic* have alternative forms ending in *ical*. But even if they don't, nearly all add *ally*, not just *ly*, to become adverbs—as do nouns like *music* and *stoic*. Again, careful pronunciation will help you avoid error:

alphabetic, alphabetical, alphabetically
basic, basically
cyclic, cyclical, cyclically

drastic, drastically
scientific, scientifically
symbolic, symbolical, symbolically

An exception: *publicly.*

---

ness

Remember, if you add *ness* to a word ending in *n*, the result is a double *nn*: *barrenness, openness, stubbornness.*

ful

Remember that the correct suffix is *ful*, not *full*: *spoonful, cupful, shovelful, bucketful, roomful, successful.*

cede, ceed, or *sede*

The *sede* ending occurs only in *supersede*. The *ceed* ending occurs only in *exceed, proceed,* and *succeed*. All other words ending in this sound use *cede*: *accede, concede, intercede, precede, recede,* secede.

Final *e* Before a Suffix

When a suffix is added to a root word that ends in a silent *e*, certain rules generally apply. If the suffix begins with a *vowel (a, e, i, o, u)*, the *e* is usually dropped:

desire + able = desirable
sphere + ical = spherical
come + ing = coming
continue + ous = continuous

forgive + able = forgivable
rogue + ish = roguish
allure + ing = alluring
sense + ual = sensual

(Note that *dyeing* retains the *e* to distinguish it from *dying*.)

If a word ends with two *e*'s, both are pronounced and therefore not dropped:

agree + able = agreeable   flee + ing = fleeing

If the suffix begins with *a* or *o*, most words ending in *ce* or *ge* retain the *e* in order to preserve the soft sound of the *c* (like *s* rather than *k*) or the *g* (like *j* rather than hard as in gum):

notice + able = noticeable   outrage + ous = outrageous

Similarly, words like *picnic*, *frolic*, and *traffic* require an added *k* to preserve the hard sound before suffixes beginning with *e* or *i*: *picnicked*, *picnicking*; *frolicked*, *frolicking*; *trafficked*, *trafficking*. (An exception to this rule is *arc*: *arced*, *arcing*.) When the suffix does not begin with *e* or *i*, these words do not add a *k*: *tactical*, *frolicsome*.

If the suffix begins with a *consonant*, the silent e of the root word is usually not dropped:

awe + some = awesome   effective + ness = effectiveness
definite + ly = definitely   mere + ly = merely

(But note a common exception: *awe + ful = awful*.)

And there is a subgroup of words whose final *e*'s are sometimes wrongly omitted. The *e*, though silent, is essential to keep the sound of the preceding vowel long:

completely	extremely	hopelessness	livelihood
loneliness	remoteness	severely	tasteless

But such an e is sometimes dropped when no consonant intervenes between it and the long vowel:

due + ly = duly   **true + ly = truly**   **argue + ment = argument**

61e Final *y* After a Consonant and Before a Suffix

When the suffix begins with i, keep the y:

baby + ish = babyish   **carry + ing = carrying**
try + ing = trying   **worry + ing = worrying**

(Note: Words ending in *ie* change to *y* before adding *ing*: *die + ing = dying*; *lie + ing = lying*.)

When the suffix begins with something other than *i*, change *y* to *i*:

happy + er = happier   **duty + ful = dutiful**
happy + ness = happiness   **silly + est = silliest**
harmony + ous = harmonious   **angry + ly = angrily**

Some exceptions: *shyly, shyness; slyer, slyly; flyer* (though *flier* is sometimes used); *dryer* (as a noun—for the comparative adjective use *drier*).

61f Doubling of a Final Consonant Before a Suffix

When adding a suffix, *double* the final consonant of the root if all three of the following apply:

(a) that consonant is preceded by a single vowel,
(b) the root is a one-syllable word or a word accented on its last syllable, and
(c) the suffix begins with a vowel.

One-syllable words:

bar + ed = barred   **bar + ing = barring**
fit + ed = fitted   **fit + ing = fitting**   **fit + er = fitter**
hot + er = hotter   **hot + est = hottest**

Words accented on last syllable:

allot + ed = allotted   allot + ing = allotting
commit + ed = committed   commit + ing = committing
occur + ed = occurred   occur + ing = occurring   occur + ence =
                                                       occurrence

But when the addition of the suffix shifts the accent of the root word away from the last syllable, do not double the final consonant:

infer + ed = inferred   infer + ing = inferring   BUT inference
prefer + ed = preferred   prefer + ing = preferring   BUT preference
refer + ed = referred   refer + ing = referring   BUT reference

Do not double the final consonant if it is preceded by a single consonant (*sharp + er = sharper*) or if the final consonant is preceded by two vowels (*fail + ed = failed, stoop + ing = stooping*) or if the root word is more than one syllable and not accented on its last syllable (*parallel + ing = paralleling*) or if the suffix begins with a consonant (*commit + ment = commitment*).

> **PROOFREADING TIP**
>
> **Doubling the Final *l* Before a Suffix**
>
> Unlike *parallel*, other words often double a final *l*, even when they are of two or more syllables and not accented on the final syllable; for example, *labelled* or *labeled*, *traveller* or *traveler*. Either form is correct, though the Canadian preference is for the doubled *l*.

 ## Changes in Spelling of Roots

Be careful with words whose roots change spelling, often because of a change in stress, when they are inflected for a different part of speech, for example:

clear, clarity   maintain, maintenance
curious, curiosity   prevail, prevalent
despair, desperate   pronounce, pronunciation
exclaim, exclamatory   repair, reparable
generous, generosity   repeat, repetition
inherit, heritage, BUT heredity, hereditary

61h Confusion with Other Words

Don't let false analogies and similarities of sound lead you astray.

a writer who thinks of a word like this:	may spell another word **wrong**, like this:	instead of **right**, like this:
air	~~ordinairy~~	**ordinary**
breeze	~~cheeze~~	**cheese**
comrade	~~comraderie~~	**camaraderie**
conform	~~conformation~~	**confirmation**
democracy	~~hypocracy~~	**hypocrisy**
desolate	~~desolute~~	**dissolute**
diet	~~diety~~	**deity**
exalt	~~exaltant~~	**exultant**
familiar	~~similiar~~	**similar**
ideal	~~idealic~~	**idyllic**
knowledge	~~priviledge~~	**privilege**
prize	~~surprize~~	**surprise**
religious	~~sacreligious~~	**sacrilegious**
restaurant	~~restauranteur~~	**restaurateur**
sink	~~zink~~	**zinc**
size	~~rize~~	**rise**
solid	~~solider~~	**soldier**
summer	~~grammer~~	**grammar**
young	~~amoung~~	**among**

61i Homophones and Other Words That Are Similar

1. Be careful to distinguish between homophones that are pronounced alike but spelled differently. Here are some that can be troublesome; consult a dictionary for any whose meanings you aren't sure of (and see #69):

aisle, isle	**by, buy, bye**
alter, altar	**capital, capitol**
assent, ascent	**compliment, complement**
bear, bare	**council, counsel**
birth, berth	**course, coarse**
board, bored	**desert, dessert**
boarder, border	**die, dye, dying, dyeing**
born, borne	**discreet, discrete**
break, brake	**forth, fourth**

hear, here
heard, herd
hole, whole
its, it's
lead, led
manner, manor
meat, meet
past, passed
patience, patients
piece, peace
plain, plane
pore, pour
practice, practise

pray, prey
presence, presents
principle, principal
rain, rein, reign
right, rite, write
road, rode, rowed
seas, sees, seize
sight, site, cite
stationary, stationery
there, their, they're
to, too, two
whose, who's
your, you're

2. There are also words that are not pronounced exactly alike but that are similar enough to be confused. Again, look up any whose meanings you aren't sure of:

accept, except
access, excess
adopt, adapt, adept
adverse, averse
advice, advise
affect, effect
afflicted, inflicted
allude, elude
angle, angel
appraise, apprise
assume, presume
bizarre, bazaar
breath, breathe
choose, chose
cloth, clothe
conscious, conscience
custom, costume
decent, descent, dissent
decimate, disseminate
device, devise
diary, dairy

emigrate, immigrate
eminent, imminent, immanent
enquire, inquire, acquire
ensure, insure, assure
envelop, envelope
evoke, invoke
illusion, allusion
incident, incidence, instant, instance
incredulous, incredible
ingenious, ingenuous
insight, incite
later, latter
loose, lose
moral, morale
quite, quiet
tack, tact
than, then
were, we're, where
whether, weather
while, wile

3. Be careful also to distinguish between such terms as the following, for although they sound the same, they function differently depending on whether they are spelled as one word or two:

already, all ready
altogether, all together
anybody, any body
anymore, any more
anyone, any one
anytime, any time
anyway, any way

awhile, a while
everybody, every body
everyday, every day
everyone, every one
maybe, may be
someday, some day
sometime, some time

PROOFREADING TIP

The Limitations of Spell-Checking

Your word-processing program's spell-check feature will help you catch spelling mistakes like "grammer" and "surprize," but it will not help you when you've used *principle* when you meant to use *principal*, *birth* instead of *berth*, *forth* instead of *fourth*, *to* or *two* instead of *too*, or *their* instead of *there* or *they're*. You will need to catch such slips in your own close checking of your documents.

61j One Word or Two?

Do not spell the following words as two or three separate or hyphenated words; each is one unhyphenated word:

alongside	lifetime	outshine	sunrise
background	nevertheless	setback	sunset
countryside	nonetheless	spotlight	throughout
easygoing	nowadays	straightforward	wrongdoing

The following, on the other hand, should always be spelled as two words:

a bit	at least	in order (to)
a few	close by	in spite (of)
after all	even though	no longer
all right (*alright* is informal)	every time	(on the) other hand
a lot	in between	(in) other words
as though	in fact	up to

61k Hyphenation

ONLINE
EXERCISES

To hyphenate or not to hyphenate? Since the conventions are constantly changing, make a habit of checking your dictionary for current usage. Here are the main points to remember:

1. Use hyphens in compound numbers from *twenty-one* to *ninety-nine*.
2. Use hyphens with fractions used as adjectives:

   A two-thirds majority is required to defeat the amendment.

   When a fraction is used as a noun, you may use a hyphen, though many writers do not:

   One quarter of the members abstained from voting.

3. Use hyphens with compounds indicating time, when these are written out: *seven-thirty, nine-fifteen.*
4. Use a hyphen between a pair of numbers indicating a range: *pages 73-78, June 20-26.* The hyphen is equivalent to the word *to.* If you introduce the range with *from,* write out the word *to: from June 20 to June 26.* If you use *between,* write out the word *and: between June 20 and June 26.*
5. Use hyphens with prefixes before proper nouns:

all-Canadian	**pan-Asian**	**post-Confederation**
pseudo-Modern	**pre-Babylonian**	**trans-Siberian**

But note that there are well-established exceptions; for example: *antichrist, postmodern, transatlantic, transpacific.*

6. Use hyphens with compounds beginning with the prefix *self*: *self-assured, self-confidence, self-deluded, self-esteem, self-made, self-pity*, etc. (The words *selfhood, selfish, selfless*, and *selfsame* are not hyphenated, since *self* is the root, not a prefix.) Hyphens are conventionally used with certain other prefixes: *all-important, ex-premier, quasi-religious*. Hyphens are conventionally used with most, but not all, compounds beginning with *vice* and *by*: *vice-chancellor, vice-consul, vice-president, vice-regent*, etc., BUT *viceregal, viceroy*; *by-election, by-product*, etc., BUT *bygone, bylaw, byroad, bystander, byword*. Check your dictionary.

7. Use a "suspension" hyphen after the first prefix when you use two prefixes with one root, even if the resulting word would not normally be hyphenated:

   You may either pre- or postdate the cheque.

8. Use hyphens with the suffixes *elect* and *designate*: *mayor-elect, ambassador-designate*.

9. Use hyphens with *great* and *in-law* in compounds designating family relationships: *mother-in-law, son-in-law, great-grandfather, great-aunt*.

10. Use hyphens to prevent a word's being mistaken for an entirely different word:

    He recounted what had happened after the ballots had been re-counted.

    If you're going to re-strain the juice, I'll restrain myself from drinking it now, seeds and all.

11. Use hyphens to prevent awkward or confusing combinations of letters and sounds; for example:

anti-intellectual	**doll-like**	**e-learning**
photo-offset	**re-echo**	**set-to**

12. Hyphens are sometimes necessary to prevent ambiguity:

    ambig: **The ad offered six week old kittens for sale.**
    clear: **The ad offered six week-old kittens for sale.**
    clear: **The ad offered six-week-old kittens for sale.**

13. Some nouns composed of two or more words are conventionally hyphenated; for example:

free-for-all	half-and-half	jack-o'-lantern	runner-up
merry-go-round	rabble-rouser	trade-in	two-timer

Again, if you're in doubt, consult a good dictionary.

14. When two or more words occur together in such a way that they act as a single adjective before a noun, they are usually hyphenated to prevent misreading:

a <u>well-dressed</u> man	<u>greenish-grey</u> eyes
a <u>once-in-a-lifetime</u> chance	a <u>three-day-old</u> strike

When they occur after a noun, misreading is unlikely and no hyphen is needed—for example: the man was well dressed; her eyes are greenish grey. But many compound modifiers are already listed as hyphenated words; for example, the *Canadian Oxford Dictionary* lists these, among others:

first-class	good-looking	habit-forming	open-minded
short-lived	tongue-tied	warm-blooded	wide-eyed

Such modifiers retain their hyphens even when they follow the nouns they modify.

> **PROOFREADING TIP**
>
> **Hyphens and Adverbs Ending in *ly***
>
> Since one cannot mistake the first part of a compound modifier when it is an adverb ending in *ly*, even in front of a noun, do not use a hyphen:
>
> He entered the <u>brightly lit</u> room.

15. Verbs, too, are sometimes hyphenated. A dictionary will list most of the ones you might want to use; for example:

double-click	pan-broil	pole-vault	re-educate
second-guess	sight-read	soft-pedal	two-time

But be aware that some two-part verbs can never be hyphenated. Resist the temptation to put a hyphen in two-part verbs that consist of a verb followed by a preposition (see #22d). Be particularly careful with those that are hyphenated when they serve as other parts of speech:

I was asked to set up the display. (*but* Many customers admired the set-up.)

Call up the next group of trainees. (*but* The rookie awaited a call-up to the big leagues.)

61-I Plurals

ONLINE EXERCISES

1. Regular Nouns

For most nouns, add *s* or *es* to the singular form to indicate plural number:

one building, two buildings	**one box, two boxes**
one class, two classes	**one wish, two wishes**

Note that the *es* ending is standard when a word ends in *s*, *x*, *ch*, *sh*, or *z*.

2. Nouns Ending in *o*

Some nouns ending in *o* preceded by a consonant form their plurals with *s*, while some use *es*. For some either form is correct—but use the one listed first in your dictionary. Here are a few examples:

altos	**echoes**	**cargoes** or **cargos**
pianos	**heroes**	**mottoes** or **mottos**
solos	**potatoes**	**zeros** or **zeroes**

If the final *o* is preceded by a vowel, usually only an *s* is added: *arpeggios,
cameos, ratios, cuckoos, embryos.*

3. Nouns Ending in *f* or *fe*

For some nouns ending in a single *f* or an *fe*, change the ending to *ve*
before adding *s*; for example:

knife, knives	life, lives	shelf, shelves
leaf, leaves	loaf, loaves	thief, thieves

But for some simply add *s*:

beliefs	gulfs	safes
griefs	proofs	still lifes

Some words ending in *f* have alternative plurals:

dwarfs *or* dwarves	scarves *or* scarfs
hoofs *or* hooves	wharves *or* wharfs

The well-known hockey team called the *Maple Leafs* is a special case, a
proper noun that doesn't follow the rules governing common nouns.

4. Nouns Ending in *y*

For nouns ending in *y* preceded by a vowel, add *s*:

bays	keys	toys	valleys

For nouns ending in *y* preceded by a consonant, change the *y* to *i* and
add *es*:

city, cities	cry, cries	kitty, kitties
country, countries	family, families	trophy, trophies

Exception: Most proper nouns ending in *y* simply add *s*:

There are two <u>Lilys</u> and three <u>Zacharys</u> in my daughter's class.

From 1949 to 1990 there were two <u>Germanys</u>.

But note that we refer to the Rocky Mountains as the *Rockies* and to the
Canary Islands as the *Canaries.*

5. Compounds

Generally, form the plurals of compounds simply by adding *s*:

lieutenant-governors   merry-go-rounds   second cousins
major generals   prizewinners   webmasters

But if the first part is a noun and the rest is not, or if the first part is the more important of two nouns, that one is made plural:

daughters-in-law   holes-in-one   mayors elect
governors general   jacks of all trades passersby

But there are exceptions, and usage is changing. Note for example *spoonfuls* (this is the form for all nouns ending in *ful*). And a few compounds conventionally pluralize both nouns, for example, *ups and downs*. And a few are the same in both singular and plural, for example, *crossroads*, *daddy-long-legs*, underpants.

6. Irregular Plurals

Some nouns are irregular in the way they form their plurals, but these are common and generally well known; for example:

child, children   tooth, teeth   foot, feet
mouse, mice   person, people   woman, women

Some plural forms are the same as the singular; for example:

one deer, two deer   one series, two series
one moose, two moose   one sheep, two sheep

7. Borrowed Words

The plurals of words borrowed from other languages (mostly Latin and Greek) can pose a problem. Words used formally or technically tend to retain their original plurals; words used more commonly tend to form their plurals according to English rules. Since many such words are in transition, you will probably encounter both plural forms. When in doubt, use the preferred form listed in your dictionary. Here are some examples of words that have tended to retain their original plurals:

alumna, alumnae
alumnus, alumni
analysis, analyses
bacterium, bacteria
basis, bases
crisis, crises
criterion, criteria
datum, data
hypothesis, hypotheses
kibbutz, kibbutzim
larva, larvae

madame, mesdames
medium, media (*mediums* for people who claim to communicate with spirits)
nucleus, nuclei
parenthesis, parentheses
phenomenon, phenomena
stimulus, stimuli
stratum, strata
synthesis, syntheses
thesis, theses

But note that it has become acceptable in informal and non-scientific contexts to treat *data* and *media* as if they were singular.

Here are some borrowed words that have both forms, the choice often depending on the formality or technicality of the context:

antenna, antennae (insects) *or* antennas (radios, etc.)
apparatus, apparatus *or* apparatuses
appendix, appendices *or* appendixes
beau, beaux *or* beaus
cactus, cacti *or* cactuses
château, châteaux *or* châteaus
curriculum, curricula *or* curriculums
focus, foci *or* focuses (focusses)
formula, formulae *or* formulas
index, indices *or* indexes
lacuna, lacunae *or* lacunas
matrix, matrices *or* matrixes
memorandum, memoranda *or* memorandums
referendum, referenda *or* referendums
stratum, strata *or* stratums
syllabus, syllabi *or* syllabuses
symposium, symposia *or* symposiums
terminus, termini *or* terminuses
ultimatum, ultimatums *or* ultimata

And here are a few that now tend to follow regular English patterns:

bureau, bureaus   **sanctum, sanctums**
campus, campuses   **stadium, stadiums**
genius, geniuses (*genii* for mythological creatures)

PROOFREADING TIP

Spelling Accented Words from Other Languages

If you use or quote words from other languages that have such diacritical marks as the cedilla (ˌ), the circumflex (ˆ), the tilde (˜), the umlaut (¨), or acute (´) or grave (`) accents, write them accurately. For example:

façade   **fête**   **cañon**   **Götterdämmerung**
passé   **à la mode**   **cliché**   **résumé**

See also #59b.

---

8. Numerals, Symbols, Letters, and Words Used as Words

An apostrophe and an *s* may be used to form the plural of numerals, symbols, letters, and words referred to as words:

the 1870's   **two ¶'s**
the three *R*'s   **two *and*'s**

Note that when a word, letter, or figure is italicized, the apostrophe and the *s* are not.

Many people prefer to form such plurals without the apostrophe: *1870*s, ¶s, *R*s, *and*s. But this practice can be confusing, especially with lowercase letters and words, which may be misread:

confusing: **How many *s*s are there in Nipissing?**

confusing: **Too many *this*s can spoil a good paragraph.**

In cases such as these, it is clearer and easier to use the apostrophe.

Apostrophes Misused with Regular Common and Proper Nouns

Beware of the "grocer's apostrophe," so called because of its frequent appearance on signs in store windows:

incorrect: **Banana's and tomato's are sold here.**

correct: **Bananas and tomatoes are sold here.**

In your own writing, you should never use an apostrophe to form plurals of regular common and proper nouns.

61m Apostrophes to Indicate Omissions

ONLINE EXERCISES

Use apostrophes to indicate omitted letters in contractions and omitted (though obvious) numerals:

aren't (are not)	**they're** (they are)
can't (cannot)	**won't** (will not)
doesn't (does not)	**wouldn't** (would not)
don't (do not)	**you're** (you are)
isn't (is not)	**back in '03**
it's (it is)	**the crash of '29**
she's (she is)	**the summer of '96**

If an apostrophe is already present to indicate a plural, you may omit the apostrophe that indicates omission: the *20's*, the *90's*.

61n Possessives

ONLINE EXERCISES

1. To form the possessive case of a singular or a plural noun that does not end in *s*, add an apostrophe and *s*:

Canada's capital	**Carter's pen**	**the girl's teacher**
the house's roof	**a day's work**	**yesterday's news**
the women's jobs	**deer's hide**	**children's books**

2. To form the possessive of compound nouns, use *'s* after the last noun:

the prime minister's speech   **Logan and Mateo's party**

If the nouns don't actually form a compound, each will need the *'s*:

Logan's and Mateo's plans for the party were markedly different.

3. You may correctly add an apostrophe and an *s* to form the possessive of singular nouns ending in *s* or an *s*-sound:

a platypus's bill   **the class's achievement**
an index's usefulness   **Keats's poems**

However, some writers prefer to add only an apostrophe if the pronunciation of an extra syllable would sound awkward:

Achilles' heel   **Moses' sons**
for convenience' sake   **Bill Gates' Foundation**

But the *'s* is usually acceptable: *Achilles's heel*; *for convenience's sake*; *Moses's sons*; *Bill Gates's Foundation*. In any event, one can usually avoid possible awkwardness by showing possession with an *of*-phrase instead of *'s* (see number 5, below):

for the sake of convenience   **the bill of a platypus**
the sons of Moses   **the poems of Keats**

4. To indicate the possessive case of plural nouns ending in *s*, add only an apostrophe:

the cannons' roar   **the girls' sweaters**
the Joneses' garden   **the Chans' cottage**

PROOFREADING TIP

Forming/Spelling Possessive Pronouns

Do not use apostrophes in possessive pronouns:

hers (NOT her's)   **its** (NOT it's)
ours (NOT our's)   **theirs** (NOT their's)
yours (NOT your's)   **whose** (NOT who's)

(See also #14a.)

---

5. Possessive with *'s* or with *of*: Especially in formal writing, the *'s* form is more common with the names of living creatures, the *of* form with the names of inanimate things:

the cat's tail	**the leg of the chair**
the girl's laptop	**the contents of the report**
Sheldon's home town	**the surface of the desk**

But both are acceptable with either category. The *'s* form, for example, is common with nouns that refer to things thought of as made up of people or animals or as extensions of them:

the team's strategy	**the committee's decision**
the company's representative	**the government's policy**
the city's bylaws	**Canada's climate**
the factory's output	**the heart's affections**

or things that are "animate" in the sense that they are part of nature:

the dawn's light	**the wind's velocity**
the comet's tail	**the sea's surface**
the tree's roots	**the sky's colour**

or periods of time:

today's paper	**a day's work**
a month's wages	**winter's storms**

Even beyond such uses the *'s* is not uncommon; sometimes there is a sense of personification, but not always:

at death's door	**freedom's light**
time's fool	**the razor's edge**

For the sake of emphasis or rhythm you will occasionally want to use an *of*-phrase where *'s* would be normal—for example, *the jury's verdict* lacks the punch of *the verdict of the jury.* You can also use an *of*-phrase to avoid awkward pronunciations (see above: those who don't like the sound of *Dickens's novels*, for example, can refer to *the novels of Dickens*) and unwieldy or ambiguous constructions (*the opinion of the minister of finance* is clearer than *the minister of finance's opinion*). Further, whether you use *'s* or just s to form the plural of letters and figures, it is probably best, in order to avoid ambiguity, to form possessives of abbreviations with *of* rather than with apostrophes: *the opinion of the MP, the opinion of the MP's, the opinion of the MPs.*

6. Double possessives: There is nothing wrong with double possessives, which show possession with both an *of*-phrase and a possessive inflection. They are standard with possessive pronouns and can be used similarly with common and proper nouns:

> **a favourite of mine**   **a friend of the family** or **of the family's**
>
> **a friend of hers**   **a contemporary of Shakespeare** or **of Shakespeare's**

And a sentence like "*The story was based on an idea of Marshall McLuhan*" is at least potentially ambiguous, whereas "*The story was based on an idea of Marshall McLuhan's*" is clear. But if you feel that this sort of construction is unpleasant to the ear, you can usually manage to revise it to something like "*on one of Marshall McLuhan's ideas.*" And avoid such double possessives with a *that*-construction: "*His hat was just like that of Arthur's.*"

62 Spelling List

In addition to the words listed and discussed in the preceding pages, other words often cause spelling problems. Following is a list of frequently misspelled words. If you are at all weak in spelling, test yourself on these words, as well as on those discussed earlier. You should also keep your own spelling list, using the notes pages at the back of this book: whenever you misspell a word, add it to your list, and try to decide which rule the error violates. If a word continues to give you trouble, try taking a mental "photo" of it by concentrating on how it looks on the page.

absence	acknowledgement	affidavit
absorption	acquaintance	aforementioned
academic	acquire	aging
accelerate	additional	allege
accessible	advertise	alternately
accidentally	adviser (*or* advisor)	always
acclaim	aesthetic (*or* esthetic)	amateur
accumulate	affection	amour

amphitheatre
analogy
analyze (or analyse)
anonymous
anticipated
apartment
appall (or appal)
approach
approximately
architect
architectural
arctic
arithmetic
article
athlete
atmosphere
audience
authoritative
automatically
auxiliary
axe (or ax)
background
beggar
beneficent
benefit
biathlon
botany
bullet
buoyant
bureau
burglar
buried
cafeteria
calendar
camaraderie
candidate
cannibal
captain
careful
carnival

cartilage
catalogue
category
celebration
cemetery
chagrin
challenge
champion
changeable
chocolate
cinnamon
clamour (or clamor)
clothed
coincide
colossal
committee
complexion
comprise
comrade
concomitant
conference
congratulate
conqueror
conscious
consensus
conservative
consider
consumer
continuing
control
controlled
controversial
convenience
convenient
court
courteous
create
criticism
criticize (or criticise)
curiosity

cylinder
decorative
decrepit
defence (or defense)
defensive
definitely
delusion
describe
desperate
deteriorating
detrimental
devastation
develop
dialogue
diameter
dilapidated
dilemma
diminution
dining
diphtheria
disappoint
disgruntled
disgust
disillusioned
dispatch
dissatisfied
dissipate
divide
doctor
drunkenness
eclectic
ecstasy
efficient
elaborate
elegiac
eligible
emancipation
embarrassment
emphasize (or
    emphasise)

emperor
employee
emulate
encompass
encyclopedia
endeavour (or
  endeavor)
enforced
engraver
enterprise
environment
epilogue
epitomize
equip
equipment
equipped
erupt
escape
especially
etcetera
euphonious
evident
exaggerate
exalt
examining
excel
excerpt
exercise
exhausted
exhilarating
exorbitant
exuberant
facilities
fallacy
fascination
feasible
February
fervour (or fervor)
film
filter

flippant
flourish
flyer (or flier)
focuses (or focusses)
foliage
foreign
foresee
forty
fulfill
fundamentally
furor
further
gaiety
gauge
genealogy
gleam
goddess
gorgeous
government
governor
grammar
gravitation
grey (or gray)
grievous
guarantee
guard
harass
harmonious
height
heinous
hereditary
heroin
heroine
hesitancy
hindrance
homogeneous
horseshoe
household
humorous
hurriedly

hygienist
hypocrisy
hypocrite
illegal
illegitimate
illiterate
imagery
imagination
imitate
immediate
immersing
impious
implementation
importance
imposter
improvise
inadequacy
inappropriate
incidentally
incompatible
indefinite
industrialization
inevitable
influence
initiative
injuries
innocent
inoculate
inquire (or
  enquire)
institution
insurgence
integrated
interpretation
interrupt
intimacy
intimate
intriguing
inviting
irrelevant

itinerary
jealousy
jeweller (*or* jeweler)
jewellery (*or* jewelry)
judgment (*or*
    judgement)
knowledge
knowledgeable
laboratory
larynx
leeches
liaison
library
licence (*or*
    license) (n.)
license (*or*
    licence) (v.)
lieutenant
lightning
likelihood
limpidly
lineage
liquefy
liqueur
liquor
lustrous
luxury
magnificent
mammoth
manoeuvre (*or*
    maneuver)
manual
manufactured
marriage
marshal
mathematics
mattress
meant
medieval
melancholy

menace
metaphor
millimetre
mineralogy
miniature
minuscule
mischievous
misspelling
molester
monologue
monotonous
mould (*or* mold)
moustache (*or*
    mustache)
museum
naive, naïveté
necessary
negative
ninety
nostrils
nosy (*or* nosey)
nuclear
numerous
obstacle
occasion
occurred
occurrence
offence (*or* offense)
omniscient
oneself
operator
optimism
opulent
original
ostracize (*or*
    ostracise)
paralleled (*or*
    parallelled)
paralyze (*or* paralyse)
paraphernalia

parliament
particular
partner
peculiar
peddler
peninsula
perfectible
permanently
perseverance
personality
personify
personnel
persuade
pharaoh
phenomenon
philosophical
phony (*or* phoney)
plagiarism
playwright
plough (*or* plow)
poem
politician
pollution
porous
portraying
positioning
possession
practicality
practice (n.)
practise (v.)
predecessors
predilection
prejudice
prestige
pretense (*or*
    pretence)
prevalent
primitive
procedure
professor

proletariat
prominent
pronunciation
proscenium
psychiatry
psychology
pursue
putrefy
puzzled
quandary
quantity
quatrain
quizzically
rarefied
reality
recognize
recommend
reflection
registration
remembrance
reminisce
repel
repetition
repetitive
reservoir
restaurant
rhythm
ridiculous
sacrifice
sacrilegious
safety
scandal
sentence
separate
sheik
shepherd
sheriff
shining
shiny

significant
signifies
similar
simile
simultaneous
sincerity
siphon (or syphon)
skeptic (or sceptic)
skiing
skilful (or skillful)
smoulder (or
    smolder)
solely
soliloquy
species
spectators
speech
sponsor
storey (or story)
    (floor)
straddle
strategy
strength
stretched
styrofoam
subconsciously
subsequent
subsidiary
subtly
suffocate
superintendent
surprise
susceptible
suspense
symbolic
symbolize (or
    symbolise)
symmetry
synonymous

syrup
tariff
temperament
temperature
temporarily
territory
theory
therein
threshold
tragedy
trailed
tranquility (or
    tranquillity)
transferred
triathlon
troubadour
tyranny
ultimatum
unavailing
undoubtedly
unmistakable
until
usefulness
vehicle
vengeance
veterinarian
village
villain
visible
vulnerable
weary
whisky (or whiskey)
wilful (or willful)
wintry
wistfulness
withdrawal
wondrous
writing
written

PROOFREADING TIP

Pronunciation and Spelling

Many common misspellings can be prevented by careful pronunciation. As you proofread your work, sound words to yourself—exaggeratedly if necessary—even at the expense of temporarily slowing your reading speed.

Be particularly careful not to omit the *d* or *ed* from such words as *used* and *supposed*, *old-fashioned* and *prejudiced*, which are often pronounced without the *d* sound. And be careful not to omit whole syllables that are near duplications in sound. Here are some examples of words that are frequently "telescoped," or pronounced without key sounds:

right	*wrong*	*right*	*wrong*
convenience	convience	institution	instution
criticize	critize	politician	polition
examining	examing	remembrance	rembrance
inappropriate	inappriate	repetition	repition

About Dictionaries

The first suggestion is the simplest one: when you think "diction," think "dictionary." Make sure you have access to a good dictionary, and use it to full advantage. Become familiar with it: find out how it works, and discover the variety of information it offers. A good dictionary doesn't merely give you the spelling, pronunciation, and meaning of words; it also offers advice on such matters as usage and idioms to help you decide on the best word for a particular context; it lists irregularities in the principal parts of verbs, in the inflection of adjectives and adverbs, and in the formation of plurals; it supplies etymologies (or word histories); it tells you if a word or phrase is considered formal, informal, slang, or archaic. And it usually has an interesting and useful introductory essay and relevant appendices.

63a Kinds of Dictionaries

Dictionaries range in scope and function from multi-volume works offering detailed word histories to tiny word books designed to fit in your pocket for quick reference. Most of the information you will require as a student will be contained in one of three kinds of dictionary: an unabridged dictionary, an abridged dictionary, or a learner's dictionary for students of English as an additional language.

1. Unabridged Dictionaries

Unabridged dictionaries offer the most comprehensive view of English, both as it is used today and as it was used in the past. The *Oxford English Dictionary*, the most famous of unabridged dictionaries, is based on historical principles, which means that it presents definitions for each word, accompanied by historical quotations, in the order of their first recorded use. The *OED* is most useful when you want to see how the meaning of a word has changed over time. For example, a look at the *OED*'s entry for *silly* will enable you to trace the word to its Old English roots, when it meant "fortunate; blessed by God," to Middle English, when it meant "deserving of compassion," to the sixteenth century, when it came to be used to mean "showing a lack of judgment or common sense." Most libraries subscribe to the *OED Online* (http://www.oed.com/), which is updated quarterly and offers a convenient way to search for the information you might need.

Not all unabridged dictionaries are based on historical principles. Two excellent resources that focus on current English are the online dictionary sites *Oxford Dictionaries* (http://www.oxforddictionaries.com) and *Merriam-Webster Unabridged* (http://unabridged.merriam-webster.com; available by subscription). Both sites are comprehensive and updated regularly. Although somewhat out of date, *Webster's Third New International Dictionary of the English Language* (1993) and *Random House Webster's Unabridged Dictionary* (2nd ed., 2005) are good single-volume unabridged print dictionaries.

2. Abridged Dictionaries

Although some questions will demand a check online or a trip to the library to consult an unabridged dictionary, an abridged dictionary is the most useful for the everyday needs of most students. An abridged dictionary may be as large as the two-volume *Shorter Oxford English Dictionary* (6th ed., 2007) or as small as a mini-dictionary, but the most practical is a "college" or "desk" dictionary that includes words and senses in current use, along with some historical senses, pronunciations, illustrative examples, etymologies, usage notes, and "encyclopedic" entries that provide information on people and places.

In the past, Canadians had to choose from among British and American dictionaries. Today, there are some very good Canadian desk dictionaries, including the *Canadian Oxford Dictionary* (2nd ed., 2004), the *Collins Canadian English Dictionary and Thesaurus* (3rd ed., 2010), and the *Gage Canadian Dictionary* (rev. ed., 1997), which offer a more accurate reflection of the language as it is spoken, written, and used by Canadians.

EAL 3. Learner's Dictionaries

Learner's dictionaries are designed especially for people whose first language is not English, but the advice they offer on usage and grammar makes them helpful even to native speakers of English. Some learner's dictionaries use a limited defining vocabulary of a few thousand words likely to be understood, or at least recognized, by readers of English as an additional language. This reduces the chances that a definition will contain words the user will have to look up.

A good learner's dictionary features numerous notes and examples to illustrate the idiomatic use of words. It may also contain pages of information on such matters as understanding English grammar and spelling. Some excellent learner's dictionaries include the *Oxford ESL Dictionary* (2nd ed., 2012), the *Oxford Advanced Learner's Dictionary* (9th ed., 2015), the *Collins Cobuild Advanced Learner's Dictionary* (2014), and the *Longman Dictionary of Contemporary English* (6th ed., 2015).

 Features of Dictionaries

Most people who consult a dictionary are looking for one of two things: the meaning of a word or the spelling of a word. When assessing a dictionary, it is helpful to know how its editors made their decisions about meaning, spelling, and usage. Did they conduct extensive research? Did they examine a wide variety of sources to capture new words and usages? For words with variant spellings, how did they determine the preferred spelling? All of this sort of information can usually be found in the preface.

You will also want to make sure that the dictionary you're using is up to date and not just a recent reissue of an older work. When comparing dictionaries, have a list of newer words and see how many of them are included in each of the dictionaries you're considering. This should give you a good indication of whether or not a dictionary is up to date.

Beyond meaning and spelling, a dictionary entry includes several features that may be useful. Deciding how important each of the following is to you will help you decide which dictionary is most appropriate for your needs.

1. Word Breaks

Most good dictionaries indicate syllable breaks or word breaks in headwords by means of points (·), pipes (|), or other symbols. Knowing an unfamiliar word's syllabication can make it easier to pronounce. It can also help if, when writing an essay, you need to hyphenate a long word at the end of a line. Remember, though, that not all syllable breaks are good places to insert a hyphen; in some multisyllabic words there is no desirable place to insert a hyphen, and these words should not be broken at all (see also #61k).

2. Pronunciations

All dictionaries contain pronunciations, though some may not provide pronunciations for all words. A dictionary may transcribe a word's pronunciation using the International Phonetic Alphabet, or IPA, so that various sounds are represented by specific symbols that are usually displayed across the bottom of the page. Or a dictionary may "respell" the word using a combination of letters and diacritical marks to indicate long and short vowels.

	IPA	respelling
curtains	ˈkɜrtənz	kûr′tnz
eavestroughing	ˈiːvzˌtrɒfɪŋ	ēvz′trôfɪŋ

The IPA pronunciations, though they may appear at first confusing, produce the most accurate representations of a word's pronunciation. The respelling method is the easiest way to convey a reasonably accurate pronunciation without the user's having to learn a complicated set of symbols.

Note that many online and CD-ROM versions of dictionaries include recorded audio of a word's pronunciation.

3. Examples and Illustrations

Definitions for technical words can often be enhanced with illustrations. Not all dictionaries contain illustrations, and of those that do, some provide illustrations to accompany definitions that don't really require them. If you are considering the suitability of a dictionary with illustrations, make sure the illustrations really benefit the definitions they accompany, bearing in mind that illustrations often take space away from definitions.

In a similar way, a definition may be greatly enhanced by an example that shows the way a word is used in a sentence. This is an important feature of learner's dictionaries, which strive to show their users not just what words mean but how they should be used in speech.

4. Usage Information

Dictionaries are descriptive, not prescriptive. They record the language as it is actually used, not as some people think it should be used. As a result, a dictionary includes words or senses that may meet with the disapproval of some users. For example, most dictionaries include two nearly opposite definitions for the word *peruse*: "to read thoroughly or carefully" (the original sense), and "to read in a casual manner" (the more common sense). Many critics object to the second use, yet it would be inappropriate for a dictionary to exclude this sense, since it is the one most people have in mind when they use the word. A good dictionary will point out the usage issue in a brief note in the entry.

Most dictionaries also include register labels to indicate whether a word is formal, informal, slang, archaic, and so on.

5. Idioms and Phrasal Verbs

An idiom is an expression whose meaning is not easily deduced from the meanings of the words it comprises, for example *off the top of my head*, *out on a limb*, *be run off one's feet* (see #70). Idioms and phrasal, or two-part, verbs (see #22d) are often defined toward the end of a word's entry. Bear in mind that an idiom such as *off the top of my head* could be defined at the entry for *top* or at the entry for *head*.

6. Derivatives

A derivative is a word derived from another word, such as *quickness* or *quickly* from *quick.* It is common for dictionaries to "nest" undefined derivatives at the main entry for a word if the derivatives' meanings can be easily deduced. For example, a word like *logically* does not require a separate definition as long as *logical* is well defined; the reader can safely assume that *logically* means "in a logical manner." But the word *practically* should not be nested in the entry for *practical*, since it has a sense beyond "in a practical manner." Be aware that some smaller dictionaries, in order to save space, nest derivatives that should be defined separately; this is something you should keep in mind when evaluating the usefulness of a dictionary.

7. Etymologies

Knowing a word's etymology, its original form and meaning, can sometimes help you remember or get a clearer idea of its meaning. For example, knowing that the word *recalcitrant* comes from a Latin word meaning "kicking back," from *calx*, "heel," may help you remember that it means "stubborn, uncooperative." A word's etymology can be fascinating as well as helpful: *climax* comes from a Greek word for ladder, *vegetable* comes from a Latin verb meaning "to be healthy," *pyjamas* comes from a Persian word meaning "leg clothing." If you find this kind of information interesting, make sure your dictionary goes into detail in its etymologies.

8. Canadian Content

Because Canada has its own political, cultural, historical, and geographical realities, it has its own words to describe these realities. As a result of Canada's unique history and settlement patterns, Canadian English also includes certain borrowings (i.e., words borrowed from other languages) that do not appear in other varieties of English. Since dictionaries inevitably reflect the language and culture of the country in which they are edited, American and British dictionaries overlook some words, senses, spellings, and pronunciations unique to Canadian English. Good Canadian dictionaries, such as the *Canadian Oxford Dictionary* and the *Gage Canadian Dictionary*, which are not merely Canadian adaptations produced in other countries, offer a more accurate view of Canadian English than either American or British dictionaries do.

9. Encyclopedic Entries

Some abridged dictionaries include entries for important people, places, and events. These may be quite short, consisting of little more than a person's years of birth and death or a city's population, or they may provide more information about a person's life and work or a city's importance. If you are considering dictionaries with encyclopedic entries, pick a couple of people or places and see how various dictionaries treat them.

 ## Three Sample Dictionary Entries

The following three entries, from an abridged, a compact, and a learner's dictionary, illustrate some of the features just described. Dictionaries follow certain conventions, but each features a unique design. A final consideration when judging the suitability of a dictionary is how easy it is for you to navigate through it.

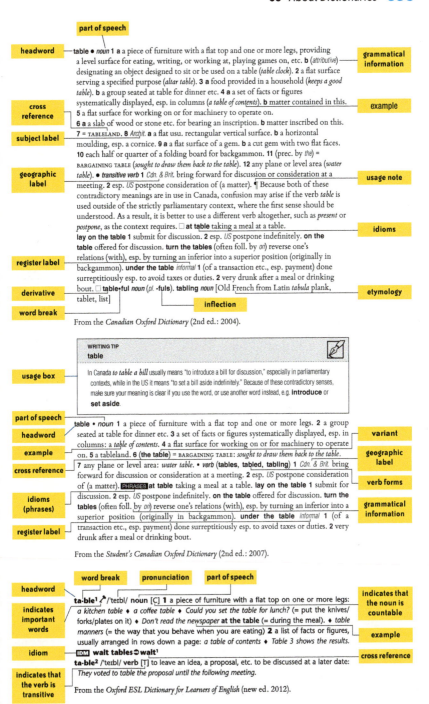

part of speech

headword — table ● *noun* **1 a** a piece of furniture with a flat top and one or more legs, providing a level surface for eating, writing, or working at, playing games on, etc. **b** (*attributive*) designating an object designed to sit or be used on a table (*table clock*). **2** a flat surface serving a specified purpose (*altar table*). **3 a** food provided in a household (*keeps a good table*). **b** a group seated at table for dinner etc. **4 a** a set of facts or figures systematically displayed, esp. in columns (*a table of contents*). **b** matter contained in this. **5** a flat surface for working on or for machinery to operate on. **6 a** a slab of wood or stone etc. for bearing an inscription. **b** matter inscribed on this. **7** = TABLELAND. **8** *Archit.* **a** a flat usu. rectangular vertical surface. **b** a horizontal moulding, esp. a cornice. **9 a** a flat surface of a gem. **b** a cut gem with two flat faces. **10** each half or quarter of a folding board for backgammon. **11** (prec. by *the*) = BARGAINING TABLE (*sought to draw them back to the table*). **12** any plane or level area (*water table*). ● *transitive verb* **1** *Cdn. & Brit.* bring forward for discussion or consideration at a meeting. **2** esp. *US* postpone consideration of (a matter). ¶ Because both of these contradictory meanings are in use in Canada, confusion may arise if the verb *table* is used outside of the strictly parliamentary context, where the first sense should be understood. As a result, it is better to use a different verb altogether, such as *present* or *postpone*, as the context requires. □ **at table** taking a meal at a table. **lay on the table 1** submit for discussion. **2** esp. *US* postpone indefinitely. **on the table** offered for discussion. **turn the tables** (often foll. by *on*) reverse one's relations (with), esp. by turning an inferior into a superior position (originally in backgammon). **under the table** *informal* **1** (of a transaction etc., esp. payment) done surreptitiously esp. to avoid taxes or duties. **2** very drunk after a meal or drinking bout. □ **table•ful** *noun* (*pl.* **-fuls**). **tabling** *noun* [Old French from Latin *tabula* plank, tablet, list]

From the *Canadian Oxford Dictionary* (2nd ed.: 2004).

WRITING TIP
table

In Canada *to table a bill* usually means "to introduce a bill for discussion," especially in parliamentary contexts, while in the US it means "to set a bill aside indefinitely." Because of these contradictory senses, make sure your meaning is clear if you use the word, or use another word instead, e.g. **introduce** or **set aside**.

table ● *noun* **1** a piece of furniture with a flat top and one or more legs. **2** a group seated at table for dinner etc. **3** a set of facts or figures systematically displayed, esp. in columns: *a table of contents*. **4** a flat surface for working on or for machinery to operate on. **5** a tableland. **6** (**the table**) = BARGAINING TABLE: *sought to draw them back to the table*. **7** any plane or level area: *water table*. ● *verb* (**tables, tabled, tabling**) **1** *Cdn. & Brit.* bring forward for discussion or consideration of (a matter). **2** esp. *US* postpone consideration of (a matter). PHRASES **at table** taking a meal at a table. **lay on the table 1** submit for discussion. **2** esp. *US* postpone indefinitely. **on the table** offered for discussion. **turn the tables** (often foll. by *on*) reverse one's relations (with), esp. by turning an inferior into a superior position (originally in backgammon). **under the table** *informal* **1** (of a transaction etc., esp. payment) done surreptitiously esp. to avoid taxes or duties. **2** very drunk after a meal or drinking bout.

From the *Student's Canadian Oxford Dictionary* (2nd ed.: 2007).

ta•ble¹ /'terbl/ *noun* [C] **1** a piece of furniture with a flat top on one or more legs: *a kitchen table* ♦ *a coffee table* ♦ *Could you set the table for lunch?* (= put the knives/forks/plates on it) ♦ *Don't read the newspaper at the table* (= during the meal). ♦ *table manners* (= the way that you behave when you are eating) **2** a list of facts or figures, usually arranged in rows down a page: *a table of contents* ♦ *Table 3 shows the results.*
IDM **wait tables** ⊃ **wait¹**
ta•ble² /'terbl/ *verb* [T] to leave an idea, a proposal, etc. to be discussed at a later date: *They voted to table the proposal until the following meeting.*

From the *Oxford ESL Dictionary for Learners of English* (new ed. 2012).

64 Level

lev In any piece of writing, use words that are appropriate to you, to your topic, and to the circumstances in which you are writing. Consider the *occasion*, the *purpose*, and the *audience*. Avoid words and phrases that call attention to themselves rather than to the meaning you want to convey. In writing a formal academic essay, adopt diction appropriate to the discipline and the audience. Avoid slang and colloquial or informal terms at one extreme, and pretentious language at the other. These principles also apply in other writing for your courses and the workplace, where it is usually preferable to adopt a straightforward, moderate style—a level of diction that both respects the intelligence of the reader and strives to communicate with the reader as effectively as possible. (See also #22d.)

64a Slang

ONLINE EXERCISES

Since **slang** is diction opposite to **formal diction**, it is seldom appropriate in a formal context. There is nothing inherently wrong with slang; it is a colourful part of the language and can help you express complicated ideas with clarity and force. But its very liveliness and vigour make it short-lived: some slang terms remain current for only a few weeks, some linger on for a few years, and new ones are constantly popping up to replace those going out of fashion. Some slang terms eventually become part of the standard written language, but most slang is so ephemeral that dictionaries cannot keep up with it.

Slang's lack of permanence makes it ineffective to use in the kind of writing you are likely doing for your courses. A word or phrase that is *hot* (or *cool*) when you write it may sound stale and dated soon after. Much slang is also limited to particular social groups, classes, or professions, and it is often regional as well. Hence terms that may be vivid to you and your friends may be unintelligible to an outsider. Or, given the nature of some slang words, a reader who finds them intelligible may also find them offensive.

If you are considering using slang in your writing, consult not only one or more good dictionaries but also members of your audience: trust your ear, your common sense, and your good taste.

64b Informal, Colloquial

inf,
colloq

ONLINE
EXERCISES

Even dictionaries can't agree on what constitutes slang versus **informal** or **colloquial** usage. Slang terms are in one sense simply extreme examples of the colloquial or informal. Yet even if they are not slang, words and phrases labelled inf or colloq in a dictionary do not ordinarily belong in formal writing. For example, unless you are aiming for a somewhat informal level, you should avoid such abbreviations as *esp., etc., no., orig.,* and *OK*; and you may wish to avoid contractions (*can't, don't,* etc.), though they are common in this book and in everyday speech.

Here are more examples of informal or colloquial usages that would be out of place in strictly formal writing:

informal or colloquial	acceptable equivalents
absolutely	very, thoroughly
a lot of, lots of, lots	much, many, a great deal of
anyplace, everyplace, noplace, someplace	anywhere, everywhere, nowhere, somewhere
around	approximately
awful	bad, ill, ugly, unpleasant, etc.
be sure and	be sure to
back of, in back of	behind
chance of + gerund (e.g., chance of getting)	chance + infinitive (chance to get)
expect (as in "I expect you want me here")	suppose, suspect, imagine
figure	think, believe, etc.
fix (verb)	prepare (food or drink); manipulate fraudulently (an election, a contract, a competition)

informal or colloquial	acceptable equivalents
fix (noun)	predicament
funny	odd, peculiar, strange, unusual
guess (as in "I guess that…")	believe, suppose, think
mean	cruel, evil, deceitful, etc.
most (as in "most everyone")	almost, nearly
nice	agreeable, attractive, pleasant, etc.
nowhere near	not nearly, not at all, not anywhere near
out loud	aloud
over with	ended, finished, done
photo	photograph
plan on + gerund (e.g., plan on going)	plan + infinitive (plan to go)
quite, quite a bit, quite a few, quite a lot	somewhat, rather, many, a large amount, much
real, really (as intensive adverb)	very, greatly
right away, right now	immediately, at once
shape (good, bad, etc.)	condition
show up	appear, arrive; prove better than, best
size up	judge, assess
sure and (as in "be sure and call")	sure to
terrible, terribly	unpleasant, uncomfortable; very, extremely
try and	try to
wait on	await, wait for

In addition, many words have been so abused in advertising, used for gushy and exaggerated effect, that they can now seldom be used with precision in formal writing. For example:

awesome   **fantastic**   **incredible**   **marvellous**
stupendous   **terrific**   **tremendous**

64c   "Fine Writing"

Unnecessarily formal or pretentious diction is called "fine writing"—here, an ironic term of disapproval. Efforts to impress with such writing almost always backfire. For example, imagine yourself trying to take seriously someone who wrote "It was felicitous that the canine in question was demonstrably more exuberant in emitting threatening sounds than in attempting to implement said threats by engaging in actual physical assault," instead of simply saying "Luckily, the dog's bark was worse than its bite." This is an exaggerated example, but it illustrates how important it is to be natural (within reason) and straightforward.

65 Figurative Language

fig **Figurative language** includes mostly "figures of speech," such as personification, synecdoche, metonymy, hyperbole, litotes, and even paradox, irony, and symbolism. Generally, however, the term *figurative language* refers to *metaphoric* language, whose most common devices are the **metaphor** and the **simile**. A simile is an explicit comparison that is usually marked by *like* or *as*:

> The river <u>is like</u> a snake winding across the prairie.

> The Internet <u>is like</u> a highway without speed limits.

A metaphor, on the other hand, is an implicit comparison; the items being compared are assumed to be identical:

> The river <u>is</u> a snake winding its way across the prairie.

> The Internet <u>is</u> a highway without speed limits.

Often a metaphor is condensed into a *verb*:

> The river <u>snakes</u> its way across the prairie.

an *adjective:*

> The <u>serpentine</u> river meanders across the prairie.

or an *adverb:*

> The river winds <u>snakily</u> across the prairie.

Figurative language is often an important element of good style. Writing that lacks this kind of language will be relatively dry, flat, and dull. But remember that a good metaphor doesn't merely enhance style: it also sharpens meaning. Use metaphors when they can convey meaning more effectively. For example, to say that "the hillside was covered with a profusion of colourful flowers" is clear enough; but if one writes instead that "the hillside was a tapestry of spring blossoms," the metaphor not only enriches the style but also provides readers with something *concrete* (see #66a), an *image* (that of the tapestry) that helps them visualize the scene.

Use figurative language. It can lend grace, charm, liveliness, and clarity to your writing. But be alert to its potential pitfalls: inappropriate, overextended, dead, and mixed metaphors.

65a Inappropriate Metaphors

If you force a metaphor into your writing just to embellish style, it will likely be inappropriate and call attention to itself rather than enhance the desired meaning. It will, to use a tired but still expressive simile, stick out like a sore thumb. For example, "the tide of emotion suddenly stopped" doesn't work, since tides don't start and stop; they ebb and flow. And a simile such as "he ran like an ostrich in heat" may confuse the reader with inappropriate associations.

65b Overextended Metaphors

Extended metaphors can be effective, but don't let yourself become so enamoured with a metaphor that you extend it too far, to the point where it takes control of what is being said:

> When she came out of the surf her hair looked like limp spaghetti. A sauce of seaweed and sand, looking like spinach and grated cheese, had been carelessly applied, the red flower fastened in her tresses looked like a wayward piece of tomato, and globs of mud clung like meatballs to the pasty pasta of her face. The fork of my attention hovered hesitatingly over this odd dish. Clearly I would need more than one glass of the red wine of remembered beauty and affection to wash it all down.

This may all be very clever, but after the first sentence—the spaghetti image itself being somewhat questionable—one quickly loses sight of the original descriptive intention and becomes mired in all the associated metaphors and similes; in short, a reader is likely to feel fed up, or in this case giddy, and turn to something less overdone.

65c Dead Metaphors

Guard against dead metaphors and clichés (see #71e). English contains many dead metaphors like the "*leg* of a table," "*branching* out," and "*flew* to the rescue," which are acceptable since we no longer think of them as metaphors. But many other metaphors, whether altogether dead or with little metaphoric force left, can be ineffective. Such overused phrases as *the ladder to success, making mountains out of molehills, nipped in the bud, flogging a dead horse*, and *time is running out* are usually muddying and soporific instead of enlivening and clarifying.

65d Mixed Metaphors

Edit out of your writing incongruously mixed metaphors. The person who wrote, of the Great Depression, that "what began as a zephyr soon blossomed into a giant" had lost control of metaphor. The following paragraph about Shakespeare's *Othello* was written by one who began with the good intention of using metaphors to describe the evil of Iago, but who became lost in a maze of contradictions and incongruities:

> Iago has spun his web, and like a spider he waits. His beautiful web of silk is so fragile and yet it captures the souls of its victims by gently luring them into his womb. Unsuspecting are those unfortunate creatures who sense the poisonous venom oozing through their veins. It has a tranquil effect, for it numbs the mind with its magical potion. The victims are transformed into pawns as they satisfy the queen's appetite and so they serve their purpose.

Here, in contrast, is a paragraph that successfully uses a single extended metaphor to create its effect:

> I remember vividly my first days as a student teacher. They were the closest I have ever come to knowing what it must feel like to be part of a high-wire act. Walking into that high school classroom for the first time was like taking the first tentative steps onto the wire: the eyes of the audience were upon me, my knees were shaking, and I was struggling to keep my balance. But as that first morning went on

and as my students and I moved forward into the lesson, I felt the exhilaration of the high-wire performer as she finds her equilibrium and moves with confidence to the middle and then the end of that tightrope. The only thing missing was the cheering.

66 Concrete and Abstract Diction; Weak Generalizations

66a Concreteness and Specificity

ONLINE EXERCISES

Concrete words denote things that are tangible, capable of being apprehended by our physical senses (*children*, *skyscraper*, *flowers*). **Abstract** words denote intangibles, like ideas or qualities (*postmodernism*, *agriculture*, *nature*). Much of the writing you do is likely a blend of the abstract and the concrete. The more concrete your writing, the more readily your readers will grasp it, for the concreteness will provide images for their imaginations to respond to. If you write

Transportation is becoming a major problem in our city.

and leave it at that, readers will understand you. But if you write, or add,

In the downtown core of this city, far too many cars and far too few buses travel the streets.

you know that your readers will see exactly what you mean: in their minds they will see the traffic jams and the overloaded buses.

As your writing moves from generalizations to specifics, it will move from the abstract to the concrete. And the more specific your writing is, the clearer and more effective it will often be. *General* and *specific* are relative terms: a general word designates a *class* (e.g., *modes of transportation*); a less general or more specific word designates members of that class (*vehicles*, *ships*, *airplanes*); a still more specific word designates members of a still smaller class (*cars*, *trucks*, *bicycles*, *buses*); and so on, getting narrower and narrower, the classes and sub-classes getting smaller and smaller, until—if one wants or needs to go that far—one arrives at a single, unique item, a class of one (e.g., *the car sitting in your own parking spot, driveway, or garage*).

It is appropriate to write about "plant life," and then to narrow it, say, to "flowers"; and if you can write about "marigolds," "roses," "daffodils," and so on, you'll be more specific. Don't vaguely write "We experienced a warm day" when you could write more clearly "We stayed outdoors all afternoon in the 25-degree weather" or "We basked in the warm spring sunshine all afternoon."

The following passage makes sense, but its abstractness and generality prevent it from being more memorable or effective:

> **If one makes a purchase that a short time later proves to have been ill-advised due to the rapid deterioration of quality, then it is the opinion of this writer that one has every right to seek redress either by expressing one's displeasure to the individual who conducted the original transaction or, if it should prove necessary, by resorting to litigation.**

Writers sometimes assume that this kind of language is good because it sounds formal and sophisticated. But notice how much more vivid a revised version is:

> **If you buy a car on Thursday and the engine falls out of it on Saturday, I think you should complain to the dealer who sold it to you, and sue him if necessary to get back the good money you paid for what turned out to be a useless vehicle.**

Abstract and general terms are legitimate and often necessary, for one can scarcely present all ideas concretely, and the kind of concrete language illustrated in the above example is hardly appropriate to all situations. Try, though, to be as concrete and specific as your subject and the context will allow.

66b Weak Generalizations

gen A common weakness of student writing is an overdependence on unsupported generalizations. Consider: "Children today are reluctant readers." Few readers would or should accept such a general assertion, for the statement calls for considerably more illustration, evidence, and qualification. It evokes all kinds of questions: All children? Of all ages? In all countries? What are they reluctant to read? What is the connotation of "reluctant" here? Is such reluctance really something new?

Merely stating a generalization or assumption is not enough; to be clear and effective it must be illustrated and supported by specifics.

Here are two essays on the same topic. Read the first one through:

> Travel can be a very broadening experience for people who go with the intention of having their eyes opened, which may often occur by unpleasant means. Culture shock can be a very unpleasant and hurtful experience to people who keep their eyes and minds closed to different attitudes or opinions. This problem of culture shock is an example of why people should prepare for the unexpected and try to learn from difficult experiences, rather than keeping a closed mind which will cause them to come away with a grudge or hurt feelings.
>
> Besides causing negative attitudes, travel can also confirm the prejudices of people with narrow minds. For example, I once met a man from England who had travelled around the world visiting the last vestiges of the British Empire. He had even travelled to apartheid South Africa and still come away with his colonialist attitudes.
>
> Even if one goes to a country with an open mind, one may still come away with a superficial perception of that country. It takes time to get to know a country and understand its people. The time one spends in a country will thus greatly affect one's perception of that country.
>
> Time is also needed before travelling begins, for people to read and learn about the area they will be going to. This background will enable them to look for things they might otherwise never see, and they will appreciate more the things they do discover. For example, if one knows something about the architecture of a country before one visits it, one can plan one's trip to include visits to buildings of special interest.
>
> Thus an open, well-prepared mind will benefit from the experiences of travel, but otherwise travel is likely to have a very negative, narrowing effect on people's minds.

Now, without looking back at the essay, ask yourself what it said. You will probably have a vague sense of its thesis, and chances are you will remember something about a well-travelled but still narrow-minded traveller from England, and perhaps something about the advisability of knowing something in advance about foreign architecture—for those are the only two concrete items in the essay. (Think how much more vivid and therefore meaningful and memorable the point about architecture would have been had it included a reference to a specific landmark, such as the Leaning Tower of Pisa or the Taj Mahal or the Parthenon or St. Paul's Cathedral.)

Now read the second essay, noting as you read how much clearer its points are than the relatively unsupported generalizations of the first essay:

Travel can be broadening. The knowledge gained in the areas of historical background, cultural diversity, and the range of personalities encountered in foreign lands gives us a fuller outlook on ourselves, on Canada and Canadian issues, and on our position in the global context.

The impact of history upon visitors to other lands is immense indeed. One cannot help but feel somewhat small when looking across valley upon valley of white crosses in France, coming face to face with the magnitude of death taking place in the world wars of the last century. Before long, one realizes that many of the events that took place years ago have an effect upon the way in which we live today. In some areas, scars of the relatively recent past remain. The bits of rubble left from the once formidable Berlin Wall, for example, remind visitors that the way they live is not the same way others live, that, indeed, for decades millions lived grim and limited lives, never dreaming that in their lifetimes revolutionary changes would bring freedom, if not immediate comfort and prosperity.

This is not to say that there are not pleasant aspects of history as well. Sixteenth-century cobblestone lanes, usually less than ten feet wide, still remain in many old English villages, surrounded by Tudor cottages, complete with thatched roofs, oil lamps, and sculpted wrought-iron fences. Standing in such an environment and thinking about the writings of masters like Shakespeare brings out a much deeper and richer taste than merely reading about them in a classroom at home. And places like this remind us of how our ancestors lived, making it easier to understand the customs and ideas of the past.

In going through different foreign lands, one cannot ignore the great cultural diversity. This is well illustrated by contrasting fiestas in Spain and Oktoberfest in Munich with Canadian celebrations. Many countries, besides having different languages (and dialects of those languages), also have their own dress, holidays, and religious beliefs. This variety is often startling to the tourist, who often takes it for granted that what is standard for him or her is also the norm throughout much of the rest of the world.

Above all, the differences among people from other countries are what leave a visitor with the most lasting impression. From the street person in the slums of Casablanca, to the well-dressed gentleman walking briskly in the streets of Hanover, to the British executive sipping beer in "the local" on Hyde Street, there are myriad personalities in other lands. When we look at the world from this perspective, realizing that we are not all the same, we are better equipped to understand many of the problems throughout the globe.

The first essay is not without a message, for unsupported generalizations do have content, do say something. But the message of the second is clearer, more forceful; readers will better understand and remember what it said because their minds have something concrete and specific to hang on to.

67 Connotation and Denotation

Keep **connotation** in mind both to convey the meaning you intend and to avoid adding particular shades of meaning you do not intend. A word may **denote** (literally mean) what you want it to, yet **connote** (suggest) something you don't intend. For example, if you describe someone as "brash," your reader will understand the denotative meaning of "confident" but will also understand you to feel that this confidence is an unfavourable quality or condition. If you in fact approve of the condition (and the person), you'll use a word like "self-assured," for its connotation is favourable rather than unfavourable.

> **PROOFREADING TIP**
>
> **Using a Thesaurus**
>
> It is best not to use an online or printed thesaurus without using a standard dictionary in conjunction with it. Words listed together in such books are not necessarily identical in meaning; they can be subtly different not only in denotation but, especially, in connotation as well. A thesaurus is a vocabulary-building tool, but it should be used with care, for it can trap unwary writers into saying things they don't mean.

68 Euphemism

euph **Euphemisms** are substitutes for words whose meanings are felt to be unpleasant and therefore, in certain circumstances, undesirable. In social settings we tend to ask for the location not of the toilet, which is what we want, but of the restroom, the bathroom, the washroom, or the powder room.

But the euphemism is sometimes abused. Euphemisms used to gloss over some supposed unpleasantness may actually deceive. Innocent civilians killed in bombing raids are referred to as "collateral damage," and assassination squads are termed "special forces." What was once faced squarely as an economic depression is now, in an attempt to mitigate its negative implications, termed at worst a "recession," or an "economic downturn," or even a mere "growth cycle slowdown." Government officials who have patently lied admit only that they "misspoke" themselves.

Such euphemisms commonly imply a degree of dignity and virtue not justified by the facts. Calling genocide "ethnic cleansing" seriously distorts the meanings of both "ethnic" and "cleansing." Some euphemisms cloud or attempt to hide the facts in other ways. Workers are "laid off" or "declared redundant" or even "downsized" rather than "fired." A man who has died in a hospital is said to have "failed to fulfill his wellness potential" or undergone a "negative patient-care outcome." An escalation in warfare is described as a "troop surge"; a civil war is referred to as "factional unrest" or "an insurgency." Such usages are often misleading, and careful readers tend to distrust writers who use them. In your own writing, you should use them only when you have a strong reason for doing so.

Other euphemisms help people avoid the unpleasant reality of death, which is often called "passing away" or "loss"; the lifeless body, the cadaver or corpse, is deemed "the remains." Such usages may be acceptable, even desirable, in certain circumstances, since they may enable one to avoid aggravating the pain and grief of the bereaved. But in other circumstances, direct, more precise diction is preferable.

69 Wrong Word

ONLINE EXERCISES

ww Any error in diction is a "wrong word," but a particular kind of incorrect word choice is customarily marked **wrong word**. The use of *infer* where the correct word is *imply* is an example. Don't write *effect* when you mean *affect*. Don't write *ex-patriot* when you mean *expatriate*. (Such errors are also sometimes marked *spelling* or *usage*: see the lists of often-confused words in #61h and #61i; and see #72.) But other kinds of wrong word choices occur as well; here are a couple of examples:

ww: **She said her sister, <u>which</u> she earlier described as very beautiful, would be at the party.**

ww: **Several kilometres of beach on the west coast of Vancouver Island are <u>absent</u> of rocks.**

Whom, not *which*, is the correct pronoun for a person (see #14d). The wrong phrase came to the second writer's mind; *devoid of* was the one wanted (and see #70, on idiom).

70 Idiom

id

A particular kind of word choice has to do with **idiom**. An idiom is an expression peculiar to a given language, one that may not make logical or grammatical sense but that is understood because it is customary. Here are some peculiarly English turns of phrase: *to have a go at, to be down in the dumps, to be at loose ends.* You will notice that these idioms have a colloquial flavour about them and may even sound like clichés or euphemisms. But other similar idioms are a part of our everyday language and occur in formal writing as well; for example: to "do justice to" something, to "take after" someone, to "get along with" someone.

Most mistakes in idiom result from using a wrong preposition in combination with certain other words. For example, we get *in* or *into* a car, but *on* or *onto* a bus; one is usually angry *with* a person, but *at* a thing; one is *fond of* something or someone, but one has *a fondness for* something or someone. Here are some examples of errors in idiom:

> incorrect: **I agree about her analysis of the situation.**
> (*correct*: agree with)

> incorrect: **She took the liberty to introduce herself to the group.**
> (*correct*: liberty of introducing)

> incorrect: **He plans to get married with my youngest sister.**
> (*correct*: get married to)

Idiomatic expressions sometimes involve choosing between an infinitive and a prepositional gerund phrase. After some expressions either is acceptable; for example:

> **He is afraid to lose. He is afraid of losing.**

> **They are hesitant to attend. They are hesitant about attending.**

But some terms call for one or the other:

> **They propose <u>to go</u>. They are prepared <u>to go</u>.**

> **They insist <u>on going</u>. They are insistent <u>on going</u>.**

And sometimes when a word changes to a different part of speech, the kind of phrase that follows must also change:

> **It was <u>possible to complete</u> the project in three days. We agreed on the <u>possibility of completing</u> the project in three days.**

> **Our tennis coach <u>emphasized basic skills</u>. Our tennis coach <u>puts emphasis on basic skills</u>.**

But it isn't always predictable:

> **He <u>intended to go</u>. He spoke of his <u>intention to go</u>. He had every <u>intention of going</u>.**

And sometimes a *that*-clause is the only idiomatic possibility:

> **I asked them <u>to attend</u>. I recommended <u>that they attend</u>. I requested <u>that they attend</u>.**

See also **different from, different than**; **let, make**; **recommend**; and **very** in #72.

Idiom is a matter of usage. But a good learner's dictionary such as the *Oxford Advanced Learner's Dictionary (OALD)* can often help. For example, if you look up *adhere* in the *OALD*, you will find that it is to be used with *to*, so you would know not to write "adhere on" or "adhere with." Or, should you be wondering about using the word *oblivious*, your dictionary will inform you that it can be followed by either *of* or *to*.

Other references that help with idiom (and with other matters) are *Fowler's Modern English Usage*, the *Canadian Oxford Dictionary*, and the *Guide to Canadian English Usage*. Students for whom English is an additional language will benefit from using specialized learner's dictionaries, which offer a wealth of information about idiomatic uses of articles and prepositions and examples of idioms used in complete sentences (see #63a.3).

Wordiness, Jargon, and Associated Problems

w Avoid diction that decreases precision and clarity. Using too many words, or tired words, or fuzzy words weakens communication. We discuss and illustrate these weaknesses all in one section because they are related and sometimes overlapping. For example, phrases like "on the order of" and "on the part of" could be labelled *w*, *trite*, or *jarg*.

Even without such overlapping, there is a close relationship among the several groupings of weaknesses—if only because one bad habit frequently leads to, or is accompanied by, others. Considering them all together rather than separately should give you a better sense of the kinds of difficulties they may cause. No lists such as those that follow can be exhaustive, because new words and phrases are making their way into these categories every day. But once you understand the principles, you will get a feeling for the kinds of impediments to good communication such terms represent.

71a Wordiness

ONLINE
EXERCISES

Generally, the fewer words you use to make a point, the better. Useless words—often called *deadwood*—clutter up a sentence; they dissipate its force, cloud its meaning, blunt its effectiveness. The writer of the following sentence, for example, used many words where a few would have been better:

> w: **What a person should try to do when communicating by writing is to make sure the meaning of what he is trying to say is clear.**

Notice the gain in clarity and force when the sentence is revised:

> revised: **A writer should strive to be clear.**

Expletive Constructions

When used to excess, expletive constructions can be a source of weakness and wordiness (see #12k and #29f). There is nothing inherently wrong with them (there are many in this book—two already in this sentence), and they help us to form certain kinds of sentences the way we want to. Nevertheless, writers sometimes use them when a tighter and more direct form of expression would be preferable. If you can get rid of an expletive without creating awkwardness or losing desired emphasis, do so. Don't write

> w: **There are several reasons why it is important to revise carefully.**

when you can easily get rid of the excess caused by the *there are* and *it is* structure:

> revised: **Careful revision is important for several reasons.**
> revised: **For several reasons, careful revision is important.**

In many cases, use of the verb *to be* instead of a stronger verb weakens the sentence:

> w: **It is one of the rules in this dorm that you make your own bed.**
> revised: **One rule in this dorm requires you to make your own bed.**
> revised: **In this dorm you must make your own bed.**

Eliminating ineffective expletives from your writing may not save you a great number of words, but it will help strengthen your style.

71b Repetition

rep Repetition can be useful for coherence and emphasis (see #5b and #29g). But unnecessary repetition usually produces wordiness and often awkwardness as well. Consider this sentence:

ONLINE
EXERCISES

> rep: **Looking at the general appearance of the gardens, you can see that special consideration was given to the choice of plants for these gardens.**

The sentence is wordy in general, but one could begin pruning by cutting out the needless repetition of *gardens*. Another example:

rep: **She is able to make the decision to leave her job and to abide by her decision.**

It might be argued that the repetition of *decision* adds emphasis, but "make the decision" could be shortened to "decide," or the final "her decision" could be simply "it."

71c Redundancy

ONLINE EXERCISES

red Redundancy, another cause of wordiness, is repetition of an idea rather than a word. Something is redundant if it has already been expressed earlier in a sentence. In the preceding sentence, for example, the word *earlier* is redundant, since the idea of *earlier* is present in the word *already*: repeating it is illogical and wordy. (Double negatives are a kind of redundancy, and also illogical: *can't never, don't hardly.*) The construction, "In my opinion, I think . . . " is redundant. To speak of "cooperating together" is to unnecessarily repeat the same meaning. The person who wrote, in a letter to a prospective employer, that "an interview would be mutually helpful to both of us" might not make a good first impression. Here are some other frequently encountered phrases that are redundant because the idea of one word is present in the other as well:

absolutely essential	erode away
advance planning	general consensus
added bonus	mental attitude
basic fundamentals	more preferable
but nevertheless	necessary prerequisite
character trait	proceed ahead
climb up	protest against
close scrutiny	readily apparent
completely eliminate	past history
consensus of opinion	reduce down
continue on	refer back
enter into	revert back

One common kind of redundancy is called "doubling"—adding an unnecessary second word (usually an adjective) as if to make sure the meaning of the first is clear:

red: **The report was brief and concise.**

Either *brief* or *concise* alone would convey the meaning.

71d **Ready-Made Phrases**

"Prefabricated" or formulaic phrases that leap to our minds whole are almost always wordy. They are a kind of cliché (see #71e), and many also sound like jargon (see #71h). You can often edit them out of a draft altogether or at least use shorter equivalents:

a person who, one of those who
at that time, at that point in time (use *then*)
at the present time, at this time, at this point in time (use *now*)
at the same time (use *while*)
by and large
by means of (use *by*)
due to the fact that, because of the fact that, on account of the fact
    that, in view of the fact that, owing to the fact that (use *because*)
during the course of, in the course of (use *during*)
except for the fact that (use *except that*)
for the purpose of (use *for, to*)
for the reason that, for the simple reason that (use *because*)
in all likelihood, in all probability (use *probably*)
in a very real sense
in colour (as in "was blue in colour")
in fact, in point of fact
in height (use *high*)
in length (use *long*)
in nature
in number
in order to (use *to*)
in reality
in shape (as in "was triangular in shape")
in size
in spite of the fact that (use *although*)
in the case of
in the event that (use *if*)
in the form of
in the light of, in light of (use *considering*)
in the midst of (use *amid*)
in the near future, in the not too distant future (use *soon*)
in the neighbourhood of, in the vicinity of (use *about, near*)
in this day and age (use *now, today*)

manner, in a . . . manner
period of time (use *period, time*)
personal, personally
previous to, prior to (use *before*)
the fact that
up until, up till (use *until, till*)
use of, the use of, by the use of, through the use of
when all is said and done
with the exception of (use *except for*)
with the result that

And the prevalence of such ready-made phrases as *point of view* caused a student unthinkingly to tack *of view* onto *point* in the following sentence: "The carpenter made the point of view that careful measurement is essential." Two-part verbs (see #22d) sometimes trip up writers in the same way: *fill in* is correct for "*Fill in* this form," but not for "The pharmacist *filled in* the prescription."

 ## 71e Triteness, Clichés

trite,   Trite or hackneyed expressions, clichés, are another form of wordiness:
cliché   they are tired, worn out, all too familiar, and therefore contribute little to a sentence. Since they are, by definition, prefabricated phrases, they are another kind of deadwood that can be edited out of a draft. Many trite phrases are metaphors, once clever and fresh, but now so old and weary that the metaphorical sense is weak at best (see #65c); for some, the metaphor is completely dead, which explains errors such as "tow the line" (for "toe the line"), "the dye is cast" (for "the die is cast"), and "dead as a doorknob" (for "dead as a doornail"). "To all intents and purposes" now sometimes comes out "to all intensive purposes"; "by a hair's breadth" turns up as "by a hare's breath"; and so on. A writer aiming for "time immemorial" instead wrote "time in memoriam." Another referred to the passage of a lifetime as "from dawn to dust."

Some clichés are also redundant; that is, they express the same idea twice: *first and foremost, few and far between, over and above, each and every, one and only, to all intents and purposes, ways and means, various and sundry, part and parcel, in this day and age, in our world today,* and so on.

No list can be complete, but here are a few more examples to suggest the kinds of expressions to edit from your work:

a bolt from the blue
a far cry
a matter of course
all things being equal
as a last resort
as a matter of fact
as the crow flies
beat a hasty retreat
bored to tears
busy as a bee
by leaps and bounds
by no means
clear as crystal (or mud)
conspicuous by its absence
cool as a cucumber
corridors of power
doomed to disappointment
easier said than done
fast and furious
from dawn till dusk
gentle as a lamb
good as gold
if and when
in a manner of speaking
in one ear and out the other
in the long run
it goes without saying

it stands to reason
last but not least
lock, stock, and barrel
love at first sight
many and diverse
moment of truth
needless to say
nipped in the bud
no way, shape, or form
off the beaten path, track
on the right track
one and the same
par for the course
pride and joy
raining cats and dogs
rears its ugly head
rude awakening
sadder but wiser
seeing is believing
slowly but surely
strike while the iron is hot
strong as an ox
take one for the team
the wrong side of the tracks
think outside the box
what goes around comes around
when all is said and done

Edit for the almost automatic couplings that occur between some adjectives and nouns. A few examples:

acid test
ardent admirers
budding genius
bulging biceps
blushing bride
consummate artistry

devastating effect
drastic action
festive occasion
hearty breakfast
heated opposition
knee-jerk reaction

penetrating insight
proud possessor
sacred duty
severe stress
tangible proof
vital role

Several of this kind are redundant as well:

advance notice
advance warning
blazing inferno
cozy (little) nook
end result
final outcome
final result

foreseeable future
just desserts
perfectly clear
serious concern
serious crisis
terrible tragedy
total (complete) surprise

71f Overuse of Nouns

The overreliance on nouns is another source of deadwood. The focus of a sentence or clause is its main verb; the verb activates it, moves it, makes it go. Too many nouns piled on one verb can slow a sentence down, especially if the verb is *be* or some other verb with little or no action in it. Consider the following:

> **The opinion of the judge in this case is of great significance to the outcome of the investigation and its effects upon the behaviour of all the members of our society in the future.**

The verb in this sentence must struggle to move the great load of nouns and prepositional phrases along to some kind of finish. One could easily improve the sentence by reducing the proportion of nouns to verbs and making the verbs more vigorous:

> **The judge's decision will inevitably influence how people act.**

The piling up of *-tion* nouns can also weaken style and bury meaning:

> **The depredations of the conflagration resulted in the destruction of many habitations and also of the sanitation organization of the location; hence the necessity of the introduction of activation procedures in relation to the implementation of emergency preparations for the amelioration of the situation.**

This example is not so exaggerated as you might think. In any event, here is a simpler version of it:

> **Since the fire destroyed not only many houses but also the water-treatment plant for the town, emergency procedures had to be set up quickly.**

The verbs in this revised sentence have a third as much noun-baggage to carry as the original verb *resulted* had. There is nothing inherently wrong with nouns ending in *tion*; the damage is done when they come in clusters.

Checking on the Sound of Your Prose

Reading your work aloud can help you avoid other unpleasant patterns of sound and rhythm, such as excessive alliteration or too regular a metrical pattern:

> At the top of the tree sat a bird on a branch.

or jarring repetitions of sound:

> They put strict restrictions on lending, which constricted the flow of funds.

or accidental rhyme:

> At that time he was in his prime; the way he later let himself go was a crime.

71g Nouns Used as Adjectives

Another insidious trend is the unnecessary use of nouns as if they were adjectives. Many nouns function adjectivally, some even becoming so idiomatic as to form parts of compounds:

> school board, school book, schoolteacher
> bathing suit, bath towel, bathtub
> fire alarm, fire engine, firewood
> web browser, web designer, weblog
> heart attack, heart monitor, heart-smart
> business school, business card, businessperson

Such nouns-cum-adjectives are quite acceptable, but the practice can be carried too far. "Lounge chair" is clearly preferable to "chair for lounging," but just as clearly "medicine training" does not conform to the usages of English as well as "medical training" or "training in medicine," nor "poetry skills" as well as "poetic skills" or "skill in poetry." In these last two examples, since there is a standard adjectival form available, the simple nouns need not and should not be so used.

But increasingly in recent years, speakers and writers—especially those in government, business, and the media—have settled for, or even actively chosen, noun combinations that contribute heavily to the jargon cluttering the language, cumbersome phrases such as *learning facilitation*, *resource person*, *demonstration organizer*, *cash-flow position*, *opinion sampling*, or *consumer confidence number*. Newspapers report that "a weapons of mass destruction update is expected next month," where "an update on weapons of mass destruction" would be better. The piling up of several nouns, as in such phrases as "the labour force participation rate," "the Resource Management Personnel Training and Development Program," and "a city park recreation facility area" can confuse or alienate readers.

 ## 71h Jargon

jarg The word jargon, in a narrow sense, refers to terms peculiar to a specific discipline, such as psychology, chemistry, literary theory, or computer science, terms unlikely to be fully understood by an outsider. Here, we use it in a different sense, to refer to all the incoherent, unintelligible phraseology that clutters contemporary expression. The private languages of particular disciplines or special groups are quite legitimately used in writing for members of those communities. Much less legitimate is the confusing, incomprehensible language that so easily finds its way into the speech and writing of most of us.

The following list is a sampling of words and phrases that are virtually guaranteed to decrease the quality of expression, whether spoken or written. Some of the terms sound pretentious and technical, imported from specialized fields; others are fuzzy, imprecise, unnecessarily abstract; and still others are objectionable mainly because they are overused. If you are thinking of using these words or phrases in your writing, consider the context in which you are writing. Are you, for example, writing an academic essay in a particular discipline in which such language is appropriate? Are you addressing readers who will be familiar and comfortable with such language? Ask yourself whether another word or words would communicate your thoughts more effectively. If you don't come up with a more suitable alternative, then you are likely choosing well.

access (as a verb)
affirmative, negative
along the lines of, along that line, in the line of
angle
area
aspect
at that point in time (*then*)
at this point in time (*now*)
background (as a verb)
basis, on the basis of, on a . . . basis (see #72)
bottom line
case
concept, conception
concerning, concerned
connection, in connection with, in this (that) connection
considering, consideration, in consideration of
definitely
dialogue (especially as a verb)
escalate
eventuate
evidenced by
expertise
facet
factor
feedback
hopefully (see #72)
identify with
image
impact (especially as verb)
implemented, implementation
importantly
indicated to (for *told*)
infrastructure
input, output
in regard to, with regard to, regarding, as regards
in relation to
in respect to, with respect to, respecting
interface
in terms of (see #72)
in the final analysis
lifestyle
marginal

meaningful, meaningful dialogue
mega-
motivation
ongoing
on stream
parameters
personage
phase
picture, in the picture
profile, low profile
realm
relate to
relevant
replicate
scenario, worst-case scenario
sector
self-identity
situation
standpoint, vantage point, viewpoint
type, -type
viable
worthwhile

In addition, watch out for modifiers ending in *-wise* (see #72) and verbs ending in *-ize* (or *-ise*).

PROOFREADING TIP

Using Short Rather Than Long Word Forms

Writers addicted to wordiness and jargon will prefer long words to short ones, and pretentious-sounding words to relatively simple ones. Generally, choose the shorter and simpler form. For example, the shorter word in each of the following pairs is preferable:

analysis, analyzation
connote, connotate
courage, courageousness
disoriented, disorientated
existential, existentialistic

(re)orient, (re)orientate
preventive, preventative
remedy (v.), remediate
symbolic, symbolical
use (n. & v.), utilize, utilization

72 Usage: A Checklist of Troublesome Words and Phrases

us
EAL This section features words and phrases that have a history of being especially confusing or otherwise troublesome. Like any such list, this one is selective rather than exhaustive; we have tried to keep it short enough to be manageable. As with the list of frequently misspelled words, you should keep a list of your own for special study. You can often supplement the information and advice provided here by consulting a good dictionary—especially one that includes notes on usage. See also the index and at the end of this book the following lists and discussions: Confusion with Other Words (#61h), Homophones and Other Words That Are Similar (#61i), Slang (#64a), Informal, Colloquial (#64b), Wordiness (#71a), Triteness, Clichés (#71e), Overuse of Nouns (#71f), Nouns Used as Adjectives (#71g), and Jargon (#71h).

advice, advise

Advice is a noun, usually used in uncountable form. *Advise* is a verb that is usually transitive.

> **The travel agent gave me good <u>advice</u> on finding hotels in the area.**
> (noun)

> **She <u>advised</u> her sister to consider taking a computer science course.**
> (transitive verb in past-tense form; its direct object is *her sister*.)

affect, effect

Avoid the common confusion of these two words. *Affect* is a transitive verb meaning "to act upon" or "to influence"; *effect* is a noun meaning "result, consequence":

> **They tried to <u>affect</u> the outcome, but their efforts had no <u>effect</u>.**

(Note: *Effect* can also be a verb meaning "to bring about, to cause"; see your dictionary for two other meanings of *affect*, one a verb and one a noun.)

agree to, agree with, agree on

Use the correct preposition with *agree*. One agrees *to* a proposal or request, or agrees *to* do something; one agrees *with* someone about a question or opinion, and certain climates or foods agree *with* a person; one agrees *on* (or *about*) the terms or details of something settled after negotiation, or agrees *on* a course of action.

along the lines of (See **in terms of**.)

although, though

These conjunctions introduce adverbial phrases or clauses of concession. They mean the same at the beginning of a sentence, but the two words are not always interchangeable: in *even though* and *as though* one cannot substitute *although*, and *although* cannot serve as an adverb at the end of a sentence or clause. (See also **while**.)

among (See **between, among**.)

amount, number

Use *number* to refer to countable things (i.e., nouns with singular and plural forms), and use *amount* to refer to uncountable things (i.e., uncountable nouns; see #13a.1): a *number* of coins, an *amount* of change; a large *number* of factories, a large *amount* of industrialization. *Number* usually takes a singular verb after the definite article, and a plural verb after the indefinite article (see #18f).

> The number of students taking the workshop is encouraging.

> A number of students are planning to take the workshop.

(See also **less, fewer**.)

as

To avoid ambiguity, don't use *as* in such a way that it can mean either "while" or "because":

ambig: **As I added the brandy, the cherries jubilee caught fire.**

Because of such potential ambiguity, some writers have banished *as* in the sense of *because* from their vocabularies. (See also **like, as, as if, as though** and **so . . . as, as . . . as.**)

as . . . as (See **so . . . as, as . . . as.**)

as regards (See **in terms of.**)

as such

This phrase shouldn't be used as if it were equivalent to *thus* or *therefore*:

> us: **My uncle wants to be well liked. <u>As such</u>, he always gives expensive gifts.**

In this phrase, *as* is a preposition and *such* is a pronoun that requires a clear noun antecedent:

> **My uncle is a generous man. <u>As such</u>, he always gives me expensive gifts.**

as though (See **like, as, as if, as though.**)

as to

This is a stiff jargon phrase worth avoiding; substitution or rephrasing will usually improve expression:

> ineffective: **He made several recommendations <u>as to</u> the best method of proceeding.**

> better: **He made several recommendations with respect to the best method of proceeding.**

> still better: **He recommended several methods of proceeding.**

backward, backwards (See **toward, towards.**)

bad, badly (See **good, bad, badly, well.**)

basis, on the basis of, on a . . . basis

Basis is a perfectly good noun, but some prepositional phrases using it are worth avoiding when possible, for outside of technical contexts they usually amount to wordy jargon.

> **He made his decision <u>on the basis of</u> her performance in the last game.**

This can easily be improved:

> **He based his decision on her performance in the last game.**

The other phrase—*on a . . . basis*—is sometimes useful, but more often than not it can profitably be edited out: *on a daily basis* is usually jargon for *daily*; *on a voluntary basis*, for *voluntarily*; *on a political basis*, for *politically* or *for political reasons*; *We'll do this for a month on a trial basis* is jargon for *We'll try this for a month*; and so on.

because (See **reason . . . is because**; see also #43f.3.)

because of (See **due to**.)

beside, besides

Beside, a preposition, means "next to, in comparison with"; *besides* as an adverb means "in addition, also, too, as well"; as a preposition, *besides* means "in addition to, except for, other than":

> **She stood <u>beside</u> her car.**

> **She knew she would have to pay the cost of repairs and the towing charges <u>besides</u>.**

> **<u>Besides</u> the cost of repairs, she knew she would have to pay towing charges.**

between, among

Generally, use *between* when there are two persons or things, and *among* when there are more than two:

> **There is ill feeling <u>between</u> the two national leaders.**

> **They divided the cost equally <u>among</u> the three of them.**

On occasion *between* is appropriate for groups of three or more, for example if the emphasis is on the individual persons or groups as overlapping pairs:

> **It seems impossible to keep the peace <u>between</u> the nations of the world.**

can, may (could, might)

Opinion and usage are divided, but in formal contexts it is still advisable to use can (and its past-tense form *could*) to denote ability, and *may* (and its past-tense form *might*) to denote permission.

> **<u>May</u> I have your attention, please?**

> **She <u>can</u> play four different instruments.**

> **He knew that he <u>might</u> leave if he wished, but he <u>could</u> not make himself rise from his chair.**

But both *may* and *can* are commonly used to denote possibility: "Things *may* (*can*) turn out worse than you expect. Anything *can* (*may*) happen." And *can* is often used in the sense of permission, especially in informal contexts and with questions and negatives ("*Can* I go?" "No, you *cannot!*") or where the distinction between ability (or possibility) and permission is blurred ("Anyone with an invitation *can* get in"). (See also **may, might** and #17e.)

compare to, compare with

In formal contexts, use *compare to* to liken one thing to another, to express similarity:

> **He <u>compared</u> his thought process <u>to</u> an assembly line.**

and *compare with* to measure or evaluate one thing against another:

> **She <u>compared</u> the sports car <u>with</u> the SUV.**

complementary, complimentary

Complementary is the adjective describing something that adds to or completes something else. *Complimentary* is the adjective describing something free (*complimentary* tickets or passes) or comments intended to praise or flatter someone.

> **Complementary exercises reinforcing the principles covered in this module are available on the course website.** (the exercises will complete the module)

> **We are pleased to offer a complimentary appetizer with your meal.** (the appetizer is free)

> **Her comments on his new haircut were complimentary.** (she had positive things to say about his haircut)

complete (See **unique etc.**)

comprise, compose

Distinguish carefully between these words. Strictly, *comprise* means "consist of, contain, take in, include":

> **The municipal region comprises several cities and towns.**

Compose means "constitute, form, make up":

> **The seven cities and towns compose the municipal region.**

continual, continuous

These words are sometimes considered interchangeable, but *continual* more often refers to something that happens frequently or even regularly but with interruptions, and *continuous* to something that occurs constantly, without interruptions:

> **The speaker's voice went on in a continuous drone, in spite of the heckler's continual attempts to interrupt.**

could (See **can, may.**)

different from, different than, different to

In North American usage, both *from* and *than* are idiomatic after *different*. However, *different from* is more appropriate when what follows is a noun, a pronoun, or a noun phrase; *different than* is more appropriate when what follows is a clause:

> **Your accent is noticeably different from mine.**

> **She felt far different than she did yesterday.**

While common in British usage, *different to* is not widely accepted in Canada or the United States. To avoid the label "colloquial" or "informal," avoid using *different to* in your writing.

differ from, differ with

To *differ from* something or someone is to be unlike in some way; to *differ with* someone is to disagree, to quarrel:

> She <u>differed from</u> her boyfriend in that she was less prone than he to <u>differ with</u> everyone on every issue.

disinterested, uninterested

The adjective *disinterested* means "impartial, objective, free from personal bias"; *uninterested* means "not interested." In formal contexts retain the distinction between the two:

> It is necessary to find a judge who is <u>disinterested</u> in the case, for she will then try it fairly; we assume that she will not also be <u>uninterested</u> in it, for then she would be bored by it and not pay careful attention.

due to

Use *due to* only as a predicate adjective + preposition after a form of the verb *be:*

> The decrease in traffic was <u>due to</u> the holiday.

Avoid using it as a preposition to introduce an adverbial phrase, especially at the beginning of a sentence; use *because of* or *on account of* instead:

> <u>Because of</u> the holiday, traffic was light.

effect, affect (See **affect, effect**.)

either, neither

As indefinite pronouns or adjectives, these usually refer to one or the other of two things, not more than two; for three or more, use *any* or *any one* or *none*:

> <u>Either</u> of these two advisers can answer your questions.

> <u>Any one</u> of the four proposals is acceptable.

If *either* or *neither* is part of a correlative conjunction (see #23b), it can refer to more than two:

> **Either Howard, Kiu, or Carla will act as referee.**

empty (See **unique etc.**)

equal (See **unique etc.**)

especially, specially

Especially means "particularly, unusually"; *specially* means "specifically, for a certain or special purpose":

> **It's especially cold today; I'm going to wear my specially made jacket.**

-ess (See **man, woman, -ess, etc.**)

essential (See **unique etc.**)

farther, further

Use *farther* and *farthest* to refer to physical distance and *further* and *furthest* everywhere else, such as when referring to time and degree or when the meaning is something like "more" or "in addition":

> **To go any farther down the road is the furthest thing from my mind.**

> **Rather than delay any further, he started his deliveries, beginning with the location farthest from him.**

Further, only *further* can function as a sentence adverb, as in this sentence.

fatal (See **unique etc.**)

fatal, fatalistic (See **simple, simplistic.**)

feel(s)

Don't loosely use the word *feel* when what you really mean is *think* or *believe*. *Feel* is more appropriate to emotional or physical attitudes and responses, think and believe to those dependent on reasoning:

> **The defendant felt cheated by the decision; she believed that her case had not been judged impartially.**

fewer (See **less, fewer**.)

figuratively (See **literally, figuratively**.)

following

If you avoid using *following* as a preposition meaning simply "after," you'll avoid both the criticism of those who object to it as pretentious and the possibility of its being momentarily misread as a participle or a gerund:

> ambig: **Following the incident, she interviewed those involved to gain further details.**

forward, forwards (See **toward, towards**.)

from the standpoint (viewpoint) of (See **in terms of**.)

frontward, frontwards (See **toward, towards**.)

full (See **unique etc.**)

further (See **farther, further**.)

good, bad, badly, well

To avoid confusion and error with these words, remember that *good* and *bad* are adjectives, *badly* and *well* adverbs (except when *well* is an adjective meaning "healthy"). (See also #20b.2.)

> **The model looks good in that suit.** (He is attractive.)

> **That suit looks bad on you because it fits badly.**

> **Konrad acted badly.** (His performance as Hamlet was terrible.)

> **Samra looks well.** (She looks healthy, not sick.)

> **This wine travels well.** (It wasn't harmed by the long train journey.)

half a(n), a half

Both are correct; use whichever sounds smoother or more logical. But don't use *a half a(n)*; one article is enough.

hanged, hung

In formal writing, use the past-tense form *hanged* only when referring to a death by hanging. For all other uses of the verb *hang*, the correct past form is *hung*.

happen, occur

These verbs sometimes pose a problem for students with English as an additional language. Both verbs are intransitive and cannot take the passive-voice form in any tense.

> incorrect: **The revolution was happened in 1917.**

> correct: **The revolution happened in 1917.**

hopefully

In formal writing, use this adverb, meaning "full of hope," only to modify a verb or a verbal adjective:

> **"Will you lend me ten dollars?" I asked hopefully.**

> **Smiling hopefully, she began to untie the package.**

To avoid potential ambiguity, don't use it as a sentence adverb (in spite of its similarity to such acceptable sentence adverbs as *happily* and *fortunately*):

> us: **Hopefully, our friends will arrive tomorrow.**

> ambig: **Hopefully, many people will enter the contest.**

Instead use *I hope* or *we hope* or *one hopes*.

hung (See **hanged, hung**.)

imply (See **infer, imply**.)

impossible (See **unique etc.**)

in connection with (See **in terms of**.)

infer, imply

Use *imply* to mean "suggest, hint at, indicate indirectly" and *infer* to mean "conclude by reasoning, deduce." A listener or reader can *infer* from a statement something that its speaker or writer *implies* in it:

> **Her speech strongly <u>implied</u> that we could trust her.**

> **I <u>inferred</u> from her speech that she was trustworthy.**

infinite (See **unique etc**.)

in regard to (See **in terms of**.)

in relation to (See **in terms of**.)

in respect to (See **in terms of**.)

in terms of

This phrase is another example of contemporary clutter. Although it is common in speech, and though occasionally it is the precisely appropriate phrase, it is more often vague; worse, it is capable of leading to such inane utterances as this (by a mayor of a drought-stricken town): "We're very scarce in terms of water." If you can avoid it, especially in writing, do so; don't write sentences like this:

> w: **He tried to justify the price increase <u>in terms of</u>** [or *on the basis of*] **the company's increased operating costs.**

Instead use sentences such as this:

> **He tried to justify the increase in price by citing the company's increased operating costs.**

And note the further family resemblance of this phrase to others like *along the lines of, in connection with, in relation to, in (with) regard to, as regards, regarding, in (with) respect to*, and *from the standpoint (viewpoint) of. Perspective* and *approach* are two more words often used in a similar way. (See also #71d and #71h.)

irregardless

This is nonstandard, as your dictionary should tell you. The correct word is *regardless*.

is because (See **reason . . . is because**.)

is when, is where

Avoid these phrases in statements of definition, where adverbial clauses following linking verbs are considered ungrammatical:

us: **A double play is when two base runners are put out during one play.**

rev: **In a double play, two base runners are put out during one play.**

its, it's

Its—without the apostrophe—is the possessive form of *it*; *it's*—with the apostrophe—is the contracted form of *it is*, or occasionally of *it has* (as in "*It's* been a long day").

kind of, sort of

Used adverbially, as in "*kind of* tired" or "*sort of* strange," these terms are colloquial and should be avoided in formal writing. Do not follow either phrase with an article: "I had a bad *kind of an* afternoon"; more formally, say "I had a bad afternoon." (See also #15f.)

lack, lack of, lacking, lacking in

Lack in its various forms and parts of speech can sometimes pose problems for students with English as an additional language. Note the following standard usages:

This paper lacks a clear argument. (*lack* as a transitive verb)

A major weakness of his argument was its lack of evidence.
(*lack* as a noun followed by the preposition *of*)

Lacking confidence, she hired a web designer to do the work.
(*lacking* as a present participle followed by a direct object)

Lacking in experience, they had difficulty in job interviews. (*lacking* as a present participle in combination with the preposition *in*)

lay (See **lie, lay**.)

lend (See **loan, lend**.)

less, fewer

Use *fewer* to refer to things that are countable (i.e., nouns that have both singular and plural forms), and use *less* to refer to things that are measured rather than counted or that are considered as units (i.e., uncountable nouns; see #13a.1):

fewer dollars, fewer hours, fewer cars

less money, less time, less traffic

(See also **amount, number**.)

less, least; more, most (See #19b and #20c.)

let, make

The verbs *let* and make are parts of an idiom that causes problems, especially for those with English as an additional language. When *let* or *make* is followed by a direct object and an infinitive, the infinitive does not include the customary *to*:

id: **She let me to borrow her laptop.**
revised: **She let me borrow her laptop.**

id: **My parents made me to learn ballroom dancing.**
revised: **My parents made me learn ballroom dancing.**

lie, lay

Since *lay* is both the past tense of *lie* and the present tense of the verb *lay*, some writers habitually confuse these two verbs. If necessary, memorize their principal parts: *lie, lay, lain; lay, laid, laid*. The verb *lie* means "recline" or "be situated"; *lay* means "put" or "place." *Lie* is intransitive; *lay* is transitive:

I lie down now; I lay down yesterday; I have lain down several times today.

I lay the book on the desk now; I laid the book on the desk yesterday; I have laid the book on the desk every morning for a week.

like, as, as if, as though

Like is a preposition:

> **Roger is dressed exactly <u>like</u> Kazuhiro.**

But if a verb is placed after *Kazuhiro*, then what follows like becomes a full clause, forcing *like* to serve incorrectly as a conjunction; use the conjunction *as* when a clause follows:

> us: **Roger is dressed exactly <u>like</u> Kazuhiro is.**

> revised: **Roger is dressed exactly <u>as</u> Kazuhiro is.**

In similar constructions that express an imagined comparison or possibility, use *as if* or *as though* to introduce clauses:

> **It looks <u>like</u> rain.**

> **It looks <u>as if</u>** [or *as though*] **it will rain.**

literally, figuratively

Literally means "actually, really." *Figuratively* means "metaphorically, not literally." Do not use *literally* when the meaning is figurative:

> us: **My legs <u>literally</u> turned to jelly.** (i.e., *figuratively*)

loan, lend

Although some people restrict *loan* to being a noun, it is generally acceptable as a verb equivalent to *lend*—except in such figurative uses as "*lend* a hand."

make (See **let, make.**)

man, woman, -ess, etc.

Like the use of *he* as a generic pronoun (see #15d), the general or generic use of the word *man* causes difficulties. To avoid biased language, most writers now try to avoid the term *man* where it could include the meaning *woman* or *women*. If you're referring to a single individual, often simply substituting the term *person*, or in some contexts *human being*, will do.

If you're referring to the race, instead of *man* or *mankind*, use *human beings*, *humanity*, *people*, *humankind*, or *the human race*. Instead of *manmade*, use *synthetic* or *artificial*. Similarly, in compounds designating various occupations and positions, try to avoid the suffix *-man* by using gender-neutral terms such as *firefighter*, *police officer*, *letter carrier*, *spokesperson*, *chairperson* (or *chair*), *anchorperson* (or *anchor*), *businessperson*, or *salesperson*.

Another concern is the suffix *-ess*. Usefully gender-specific (and power-designating) terms like *princess* and *goddess* are firmly established, but there is seldom if ever any need to refer to an *authoress* or *poetess* when simply *author* or *poet* will serve; many now eschew *actress*, finding *actor* more suitable in almost all contexts. *Stewardess* has given way to *flight attendant*; and *waitress* and *waiter* have been replaced by *server*.

Further, don't thoughtlessly gender-stereotype occupations and other activities that are engaged in by both men and women; think about doctors, business executives, nurses, construction workers, cab drivers, fishing enthusiasts, and so on. And don't highlight gender (as in *female athlete*, *male nurse*) unless it adds necessary clarification or is otherwise relevant to the particular context: for example, if you are writing about the experiences of female athletes in a male-dominated sport. Finally, note that *male* and *female*, rather than *man* and *woman*, are the appropriate terms to use as modifiers when referring to gender:

> **The accident victim asked to be examined by a <u>female</u> doctor.**

> **She has been featured in a magazine story as the longest-serving <u>female</u> premier in Canada.**

may (See **can, may** and **may, might**)

may, might

Don't confuse your reader by using *may* where *might* is required:

(a) after another verb in the past tense:

> us: **She thought she <u>may</u> get a raise.** (use *might*)

In the present tense, either *may* or *might* would be possible:

> **She thinks she <u>may</u> get a raise.** (It's quite likely that she will.)

> **She thinks she <u>might</u> get a raise.** (It's less likely, but possible.)

(b) for something hypothetical rather than factual:

> us: **This imaginative software program <u>may</u> have helped Beethoven, but it wouldn't have changed the way Mozart composed.** (use *might*)

The word *may* makes it sound as if it is possible that the program *did* help Beethoven, which is of course absurd. (For other examples, see #17e.)

media (See #18h and #61-l.7.)

might (See **may, might** and **can, may**.)

more, most; less, least (See #19b and #20c.)

myself, herself, himself, etc. (See #14h.)

necessary (See **unique etc**.)

neither (See **either, neither**.)

number (See **amount, number**.)

occur (See **happen, occur**.)

of

Avoid incorrect use of *of* as a result of mispronunciation:

> ww: **We would <u>of</u> stayed for dinner if not for the weather.**
> (use *have*)

> ww: **The prime minister should <u>of</u> apologized for his remarks.**
> (use *have*)

Because of the way we sometimes speak, such verb phrases as "would have," "could have," "should have," and "might have" are mispronounced (*would've, could've, should've, might've*). Because of the way we hear these words, the *'ve* mistakenly becomes *of*.

off of

Including *of* after the prepositions *off*, *inside*, and *outside* is usually unnecessary:

> **She fell <u>off</u> the fence.** (Don't write *off of*.)

> **He awoke to find himself <u>inside</u> a large crate.** (Don't write *inside of*.)

on account of (See **due to**.)

outside, outside of (See **off of**.)

perfect (See **unique etc.**)

perspective (See **in terms of**.)

possible (See **unique etc.**)

presently

Presently can mean either "in a short while, soon" or "at present, currently, now"; as a result, its use can lead to ambiguity. Use the alternative terms (*soon*, *now*, etc.) and your meaning will be clear.

raise, rise

The verb *raise* is transitive, requiring an object: "I *raised* my hand; she *raises* alpacas." *Rise* is intransitive: "The temperature *rose* sharply; I *rise* each morning at dawn." If necessary, memorize their principal parts: *raise, raised, raised; rise, rose, risen.*

real, really (See **very**.)

reason . . . is because

Although this construction has long been common, especially in speech, many people object to it as redundant, since *because* often means "for the reason that." Omit either *reason* or *because*:

> **They left because they were bored.**

> **The reason they left is that they were bored.**

reason why

The *why* in this phrase is often redundant, as in "His comments were the reason *why* I showed up." Check to see if you need the *why*.

recommend

When this transitive verb appears in a clause with an indirect object, the indirect object must be expressed as a prepositional phrase with *to* or *for*, and it must follow the direct object:

> id: **She recommended <u>me</u> this restaurant.**

> id: **She recommended <u>to me</u> this restaurant.**

> revised: **She recommended this restaurant <u>to me</u>.**

A number of other verbs fit the same idiomatic pattern as *recommend*. Among the most common are *admit, contribute, dedicate, demonstrate, describe, distribute, explain, introduce, mention, propose, reveal, speak, state,* and *suggest.* Note, however, that with several of these verbs, the direct object may follow the prepositional phrase if it is itself a noun clause, in order to avoid confusion. For example, compare *He admitted to me that he had lied* to *He admitted that he had lied to me.*

regarding (See **in terms of**.)

rise, raise (See **raise, rise**.)

round (See **unique etc.**)

sensual, sensuous

Sensuous is traditionally used to refer broadly to intellectual or physical pleasure derived from the senses ("He writes *sensuous* poetry in response to the beauty of his surroundings"), while *sensual* usually refers to the gratification of physical—particularly sexual—appetites ("They temporarily escaped their everyday lives by means of a *sensual* love affair").

set, sit

Set (principal parts *set, set, set*) means "put, place, cause to sit"; it is transitive, requiring an object: "He *set* the vase on the table." *Sit* (principal parts *sit, sat, sat*) means "rest, occupy a seat, assume a sitting position"; it is intransitive: "The vase *sits* on the table." "May I *sit* in the chair?"— though it can be used transitively in expressions like "I sat myself down to listen." "She sat him down at the desk." (See also **lie, lay**.)

shall, will (should, would) (See #17e, #17g.3, and #17h.2.)

she or he, her or his, she/he, s/he (See #15d.)

simple, simplistic

Don't use *simplistic* when all you want is *simple*. *Simplistic* means "over-simplified, unrealistically simple":

> We admire the book for its <u>simple</u> instructions and straightforward advice.

> The author's assessment of the war's causes was narrow and <u>simplistic</u>.

Similarly, *fatalistic* does not mean the same as fatal.

since

Since can refer both to time ("*Since* April we haven't had any rain") and to cause ("*Since* she wouldn't tell him, he had to figure it out for himself"). Therefore, don't use *since* in a sentence where it could refer either to time or to cause:

> ambig: <u>Since</u> you went away, I've been sad and lonely.

sit, set (See **set, sit**.)

so, so that, therefore

As a conjunction, *so* is informal but acceptable (see #23a); just don't over-work it. To introduce clauses of purpose and to avoid possible ambiguity, you will often want to use *so that* or *therefore* instead:

> He sharpened the saw <u>so that</u> it would cut the boards properly.

so . . . as, as . . . as

Use *so . . . as* only with negative comparisons; use *as . . . as* with either positive or negative comparisons:

> **He was not <u>so</u> quick <u>as</u> he once was, but he was <u>as</u> strong <u>as</u> ever.**

sort of (See **kind of, sort of**.)

specially (See **especially, specially**.)

square (See **unique etc.**)

straight (See **unique etc.**)

sure, surely

Don't use *sure* as an adverb.

> **He <u>surely</u> was right about the weather.** (not sure)

therefore (See **so, so that, therefore**.)

these (those) kinds (sorts), this kind (sort) (See #15f.)

think (See **feel(s)**.)

though, although (See **although, though**.)

till, until, 'til

Till and *until* are both standard, and have the same meaning. *Until* is somewhat more formal and is usually preferable at the beginning of a sentence. The contraction *'til* is little used nowadays, except in informal contexts, such as personal letters.

too

Used as an intensifier, *too* is sometimes illogical; if an intensifier is necessary in such sentences as these, use *very:*

> ww: **She didn't care for the brown suit <u>too</u> much.**

> revised: **She didn't care for the brown suit <u>very</u> much.**

But often you can omit the intensifier as unnecessary:

She didn't care much for the brown suit.

(See also **very**.)

toward, towards

These are interchangeable, but in North American (as opposed to British) English, the preposition *toward* is usually preferred to *towards*, just as the adverbs *afterward*, *forward* (meaning *frontward*), and *backward* are preferred to their counterparts ending in *s*.

unique, absolute, necessary, essential, complete, perfect, fatal, equal, (im)possible, infinite, empty, full, straight, round, square, etc.

In writing, especially formal writing, treat these and other such adjectives as absolutes that cannot logically be compared or modified by such adverbs as *very* and *rather*. Since by definition something *unique* is the *only one of its kind* or *without equal*, clearly one thing cannot be "more unique" than another, or even "very unique"; in other words, *unique* is not a synonym for *unusual* or *rare*. Similar uses of other adjectives and absolutes (such as *round*, *square*, *full*, *empty*, and *straight*) should be avoided, although, colloquially, they are fairly common. And note that you can easily get around this semantic limitation by calling one thing, for example, "more nearly perfect" or "closer to round" than another, or by referring to something as "almost unique" or "nearly unique" (but you could simply call it "very rare" or "highly unusual").

until (See **till, until, 'til**.)

usage, use, utilize, utilization

The noun *usage* is appropriate when you mean customary or habitual use ("British usage"), or a particular verbal expression being characterized in a particular way ("an elegant usage"). Otherwise, the shorter noun *use* is preferable. As a verb, *use* should nearly always suffice; *utilize*, often pretentiously employed instead, should carry the specific meaning "put to use, make use of, turn to practical or profitable account." Similarly, the noun use will usually be more appropriate than *utilization*. Phrases like *use of*, *the use of*, by the use of, and *through the use of* tend toward jargon and are almost always wordy.

very

When revising, you may find that where you have used *very* you could just as well omit it. Often it is a vague or euphemistic substitute for a more precise adverb or adjective:

> I was <u>very</u> tired. (exhausted?)

> Her embarrassment was <u>very</u> obvious. (It was either obvious or it wasn't; drop *very*, or change it to something like *painfully*.)

The same goes for *really* and actually. Such weak intensifiers sometimes even detract from the force of the words they modify.

Note that before some past participles, it is idiomatic to use another word (e.g., *much*, *well*) along with very:

> Sharon is <u>very well</u> prepared for the role.

well (See **good, bad, badly, well**.)

when, where (See **is when, is where**.)

whereas (See **while**.)

while

As a subordinating conjunction, *while* is best restricted to meanings having to do with time:

> <u>While</u> Vijay mowed the lawn, Sam raked up the grass clippings.

When it means "although (though)" or "whereas," it can be imprecise, even ambiguous:

> <u>While</u> she mows the lawn, he cooks the meals. (Ambiguous; *whereas* would make the meaning clear.)

(See also **although, though**.)

will, shall (See #17g.3.)

-wise

Just as *-ize* (or *-ise*) has long been used to turn nouns and adjectives into verbs, *-wise* has long been used to turn them into adverbs, e.g., of manner or position: *clockwise, lengthwise, sidewise,* likewise. But this suffix, in its sense of "with reference to" (and equivalent phrases), is so overused in modern jargon (*moneywise,* personnel-wise, etc.) that it is now employed mainly as a source of humour ("And how are you otherwise-wise?"). Therefore, do not tack it onto nouns. It is acceptable in established words but not, or seldom, in new coinages. You can easily find a way to say what you mean without resorting to it:

not: **Grammarwise, Stephen is doing well.**

but: **Stephen is doing well with grammar.**

And avoid using cluttering phrases that begin with *in terms of* or *with respect to* in place of adverbs ending in *-wise*. (See **in terms of**.)

with regard to (See **in terms of**.)

with respect to (See **in terms of**.)

woman (See **man, woman, -ess, etc.**)

would, should (See #17e and #17h.2.)

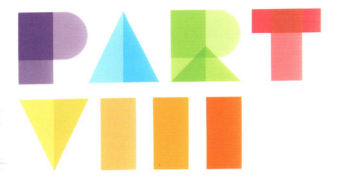

PART VIII

Research, Writing, and Documentation

Part VIII outlines the stages of writing a research essay and the deta[il] to keep in mind to do a good job. A research paper should follo[w] the principles governing any good essay. It should represent you [as] a thinker, and it should contribute your distinctive perspectives on [a] question of interest to you. Research essays also call upon writers [to] seek out the findings and the views of others who have investigated [a] topic and to give full credit to those sources.

The techniques outlined here are not the only possible ones, b[ut] they are tested ones. An instructor may ask you to follow a differe[nt] method—for example, to take notes or to compile your bibliograph[y] in a different way or to cross-reference material in a special way. A[s] you gain experience, you may yourself devise a method that wor[ks] best for you. No one method is inherently better than all others: th[e] important thing is to have a method.

73 Finding Resources

Before you begin searching for resources related to your topic, you may want to ask your instructor what types of resources she or he expects you to consult. For example, most instructors will require that you avoid using material that is published informally on the Internet; many will also recommend that you limit your use of reference works (encyclopedias, dictionaries, guidebooks, etc.), as they do not usually provide the level of analysis necessary for an academic essay.

Whatever your instructor's requirements, you will likely find yourself searching for resources through two primary avenues: libraries and the Internet.

73a Libraries

Most of the research you do for an academic research paper will involve finding and consulting library resources. Therefore, you will need to learn your way around your library and its website. If your library offers remote access to its electronic resources, you may be able to do much of your research from home, but there will likely still be times when you need to visit your library in person to find a specific resource. To access resources remotely, you will likely need to set up an account or provide proof of your status as a student. If you have any questions, you can always contact a librarian, either in-person or through the "ask a librarian" tool provided on most libraries' websites. Librarians can provide invaluable advice on navigating the many electronic and non-electronic resources available.

Once you have familiarized yourself with your library's access policies and requirements, you will be ready to perform your first search. If you are looking for a book, an audio or video recording, or any other form of media, your best option is to search your library's *catalogue*. If you are looking for specific *articles* in a periodical, your best option is to search your library's collection of *databases*.

A Catalogue Search

Library catalogues contain brief descriptions of all resources available through the library. Some listings may provide a link to the full text of the resource, but in other cases you will need to use the **call number** provided in the listing to find the resource on the library shelves.

Most catalogues allow you to perform a simple search or an advanced search. In a simple search, you can look for a resource by typing a specific title, an author's name, or keywords related to the topic into the catalogue's main search field. Simple searches work best when you already know the exact resource that you want to find. In contrast, advanced searches—in which you can specify keywords as well as additional information such as the format, language, year of publication, and even genre of the resource—work best when you have a more general idea of the *sort* of material you want to find.

A Database Search

Databases provide information on articles published in magazines, newspapers, and academic journals. In most cases, you should be searching for journal articles, as these resources are peer-reviewed and therefore the most credible sources of information for academic purposes.

Your library likely subscribes to many databases, each of which is tailored to a specific topic or discipline, so it is worthwhile to take some time to get to know the options your library offers for searching different databases. You can often find guidelines and advice for using databases on your library's website; if you have any additional questions, remember that you can always consult a librarian.

Once you have determined the sorts of databases you want to explore, you can begin by searching for a few keywords or phrases identifying your topic or subtopic. If your search turns up too many articles that are not directly related to your topic, you may need to use more specific keywords. When you do find an article of interest, you will likely be able to access it online; if it is not available online—for example, if it is an older article that has not yet been digitized—you may need to do a simple search to determine the call number and location of the print-based periodical on the library shelf.

73b The Internet

The Internet can provide you with easy access to a wide array of resources related to your topic. Some of these resources—such as government reports and articles in online journals—may offer you very reliable information. Others—such as independent websites and blogs—are far less reliable and may even contain inaccuracies. Because most of the information available on the Internet is largely unregulated, you need to evaluate carefully and critically the websites you locate in your research. The following suggestions will help you with this task:

1. Look for information on websites maintained by recognized researchers or scholars, or by public or private institutions. Anonymous and personal websites and sites such as *Wikipedia* are not considered authoritative sources for scholarly research.

2. Examine the credentials (the accomplishments and publications) of the identified author(s) of the website and consider these when weighing the research value of the site.

3. Consider the objectivity of information presented and the website's purpose. If information is hosted by an organization or business, take time to understand their goals or purpose. If a website's primary purpose is commercial or political, the information it provides may lack objectivity. Large numbers of advertisements or links to third-party websites often indicate that a website's main purpose may be commercial.

4. Check that the websites you plan to use are current—that is, recently updated—and that evidence and claims provided on the site are supported with detailed and accurate documentation. Check facts and figures and evaluate the sources cited by websites. Just as with printed material, the mere presence of documentation is not enough to lend credibility to online writing. Websites used for scholarly purposes should cite authoritative and trustworthy sources and not less-reliable materials such as blogs or personal websites.

5. Evaluate the general quality of the site. Avoid using websites whose links to other sites are broken, as they may not be well maintained or particularly reliable in their content. Similarly, grammatical errors and typos usually indicate unprofessional work that has not been checked for accuracy.

Of course, you can also use the Internet in conjunction with library resources. For example, your Internet searches might lead you to discover the titles of books or articles that you can then access through your library.

74 The Research Plan

As you get underway on a research project, you should begin by preparing a **research plan**, a strategy to focus your research and especially to budget the right amount of time to spend on the stages of the assignment. Draft this plan early—that is, no more than a day or two after you first receive the assignment—and then be prepared, if necessary, to revise it as circumstances change.

Your plan should consist first of a **researchable question**. This question should be of sufficient interest and importance to sustain you through the research and writing process. As you move on and gain more insight into the topic, be confident enough to modify the original question.

As important as determining the researchable question is establishing a **realistic timeline** for the stages of your project. Consider how your assignment will fit in with other projects and commitments you have. Then ask yourself how much time you will give to each of the following:

- your search for sources;
- your evaluation and reading of sources;
- your notetaking, summarizing, and synthesizing of sources;
- your organization and planning of the first draft;
- your writing and revising of second and subsequent drafts; and
- your editing and polishing of the final draft.

Try as much as possible to set a firm date for the end of your research and the beginning of your writing, and try to give yourself at least a week for the writing and polishing of the drafts of your assignment.

74a Academic Proposals

For some course assignments you may be required to prepare a formal **academic proposal** or research plan. Academic proposals are also a common requirement for major research projects and theses. While formal proposals follow many of the same steps as a research plan for your personal use, academic proposals differ because they generally require a greater amount of preliminary research—enough to ensure that your approach to the topic is novel and that what you're proposing is feasible.

A formal proposal will usually include a detailed rationale that explains why the project is worth pursuing and, if applicable, how it relates to the course material. It also will likely include some form of literature or research review that summarizes what has already been said about your topic and how your project will build on the existing research to say something new. Some proposal formats will also require you to discuss how you will accommodate potential shifts in your research and may require an outline of the essay or thesis itself (see #9f–j). The elements and level of detail required for a formal academic proposal can vary greatly and will depend on the discipline you are working in, so it is important to first check if an established format has already been set by your instructor, supervisor, or department.

A Preliminary Bibliography

Once you have decided on a researchable question, the first major step in gathering information is to compile a **preliminary bibliography**. As you consult various sources (e.g., periodical indexes, essay indexes, general and particular bibliographies, encyclopedias and dictionaries, your library's catalogues, and the Internet), make a list of books, articles, websites, and so on that may be useful. Then look in the appropriate part of your library's catalogue or databases to find out which books and articles are available through your library. Record the call numbers of non-electronic resources as well as the URLs (uniform resource locators) or DOIs (digital object identifiers) of electronic resources.

> **RESEARCH TIP**
>
> *Record the Date of Your Access to Internet Sources*
>
> When you make notes on a web-based source, record the date of your access. Certain documentation styles require you to include this information in your reference list or notes (see #79), and your instructor may ask you to add access dates to your references. The reason for this requirement? Materials posted online are often updated, so the date of your access will help to explain to a reader why the content of a source may have changed between the time you conducted your research and the time you submitted your paper.

74c A Working Bibliography

When you begin looking at the actual books, articles, websites, and other sources on your preliminary list, you should record the publication and retrieval information for each source. You can do this in one of two ways:

1. Create a file on your computer that is dedicated to your working bibliography.
2. Create a bibliography card for each source. (Standard index cards make good bibliography cards.)

Whichever method you use, order the entries alphabetically (by the first author's last name), and make sure that you keep the entries separate from one another. If you are working in a computer file, you may want to enclose each entry in a text box, to make sure that you do not accidentally reformat the document and merge separate entries. In addition, try to record the bibliographical information exactly as it will appear later in your bibliography (see #79a–d)—this will save you time later on in the process. Record this information accurately and completely: double-check spellings, dates, page numbers, and so on.

As you study and evaluate each resource to see how useful it looks, add comments about its likely value as a source. Such notes are especially important when you are compiling an annotated bibliography. For example, note whether the source is scholarly and credible, whether it is promising or appears to be of little or no use, whether it looks good for a particular part of your research paper, or whether only part of the source looks useful. Be as specific as possible, for a glance at such a note may later save you a repeat trip to the library or Internet search.

You may also want to include a label, called a slug (see #75c), with each entry, indicating what part of your subject the resource pertains to. You may want to make each slug correspond to your preliminary outline (see #75); this information too could save you time. For the same reason, you might note just how thorough your examination of the source was—if you just glanced at it, you may want to return to it, but if you found it so interesting that you read it carefully and even took notes, then you will know that you need not return to it later. In case you do want to return to a source, save yourself time by recording the call number of each non-electronic item as well as the URL or DOI of each electronic item.

RESEARCH TIP

Keep Your Notes and Cards

Do not delete any of your electronic notes or throw away any of your note cards, even if you think they will be useless, for at a later stage you may decide to use them after all. In fact, don't throw anything away: keep all your notes, jottings, scribblings, lists, and drafts, for they may prove useful later when you want to check back on something or, in the light of new discoveries, restore something you earlier discarded. You may even find that something you are unable to use in one essay turns out to be useful in another assignment.

Below is an example of the type of information you might include in a note. (The note goes with the sample MLA research paper appearing later in #79a.) Note the arrangement and completeness of the note: it begins with the slug; it provides full bibliographic information, organized in MLA style; it concisely comments on the usefulness of the resource; and it concludes with a link to the page from which the article was retrieved.

Imagination and Belief

Cole, Stewart. "Believing in Tigers: Anthropomorphism and Incredulity in Yann Martel's *Life of Pi*." *Studies in Canadian Literature*, vol. 29, no. 2, 2004, pp. 22–36.

- comments on the distinction between subjective and objective truth
- objects to comparison between believing in the story and believing in god
- bibliographical information may be useful

Accessed on October 12, 2016, at http://journals.hil.unb.ca/index.php/scl/article/view/12747/13691.

75 Taking Notes

Once you have compiled your working bibliography and begun consulting the items it lists, taking notes will become a priority for you. Initially, your notes will likely focus on brief descriptions of sources and of their relevance. As you become more engaged in reading and studying individual sources for their specific details, data, and arguments, your note-taking will accelerate as you prepare a working outline and write a first draft.

> ### RESEARCH TIP
>
> #### Taking Notes in Your Own Words
>
> When you are taking notes on an electronic source, do not cut material from the source and paste it directly into your own notes. Making notes in your own words will help you synthesize the essential points, and it will help to ensure that you do not mistake another writer's words for your own when you are writing your final work. Whether inadvertent or not, the inclusion of such material in finished essays without proper acknowledgement constitutes plagiarism and breaches academic integrity.

Your preliminary research should explore your subject, investigating and weighing its possibilities, and attempting to limit it (see #9b) as much as necessary to meet the demands of time and length attached to the project. At some point during this early stage, you should be able to construct a **preliminary outline or plan** (see #9f-j), which will, understandably, be subject to change as you go along. It may be only sketchy at first, but even a rough outline will help you decide what kinds of notes to take.

At first you may be uncertain about the usefulness or relevance of some of the material you come across. Be generous with yourself: take substantive notes. If you toss aside a source that doesn't look useful now, you may discover later that you need it after all. And be particularly thorough when assessing non-electronic library materials; it is better to spend a few minutes taking some precise notes than to spend an hour or two on a return trip to the library only to find that the source has been borrowed by someone else.

If you prefer to make notes on a computer, create a separate file for each subtopic within your paper. If you prefer the card method, create a new stack of cards, and make sure the new cards are easy to distinguish from your bibliography cards. For each new note, you will need to include at least two things:

1. the note itself and
2. the exact source.

If you are using cards, you will also need to include a label or slug indicating just what part of your subject the note pertains to.

75a The Note Itself

The following tips will help you prepare clear, reliable notes:

1. **Create a new entry or card for each note, and be as brief as possible.** If you're working in an electronic file, you can easily reorder short entries by cutting and pasting them into a new position as your essay evolves. Likewise, if you're using cards with only one short note, you can easily shuffle them around as you see fit at various stages. If your entry or card contains too much information, you won't be able to move it so easily.

2. **Distinguish carefully between direct quotation and paraphrase or summary** (see #78). Generally, quote only when you feel strongly that the author's own way of putting something will be especially effective in your essay. When you do quote directly, be careful: your quotation must accurately reproduce the original, including its punctuation, spelling, and even any peculiarities that you think might be incorrect (see item 9 below); do not "improve" what you are quoting. In fact, it is a good idea to double-check for absolute accuracy immediately after writing a note. And when you do quote directly, put quotation marks around the quotation so that you cannot possibly later mistake it for summary or paraphrase. This safeguard is particularly important when a note is part quotation and part summary or paraphrase: the quotation marks will help keep your work clear.

3. **Enclose your own ideas in square brackets.** If a note consists of a combination of (a) summary or paraphrase or quotation and (b) your own interjected thoughts or explanations or opinions, enclose your own ideas in square brackets. You might even want to write your initials or "MY IDEA" beside the notes that contain your ideas to remind yourself that the insights are your own. This will prevent you from later assuming that the ideas and opinions came from your source rather than from you.

4. **Use your own words.** As much as possible, express the material in your own words. The more you can assimilate and summarize information at the note-taking stage, the less interpreting you will

need to do later—and it will never be fresher in your mind than at the time when you are taking the note. If you don't assimilate the information then, you may well have to return to the source to find out why you quoted it in the first place. It is all too easy to forget, over a period of days, weeks, or even months, just what the point was. This is especially true if you are working on two or three different papers at once, as many students often are.

5. **Quote from the original source.** When you quote, or even paraphrase or summarize, do so from the original source if possible. Second-hand quotations may be not only inaccurate but also misleading. Seek out the most authoritative source—the original—whenever possible, rather than accept someone else's reading of it. Similarly, if more than one edition of a sourcebook exists, use the most authoritative or definitive one—usually the most recent.

6. **Distinguish between facts and opinions.** If you are quoting or paraphrasing a supposed authority on a subject, be careful not to let yourself be unduly swayed. Rather than note that "aspirin is good for heart and stroke patients," say that "Dr. Jones claims that aspirin is good for heart and stroke patients." Rather than write that "the province is running out of natural resources," say that "the premier believes, after reading the report given to her by the investigating committee, that the province is running out of natural resources." In research-based writing, the credibility of your own presentation depends on such matters of attribution.

7. **Be careful with the page numbers.** If a quotation runs over from one page to another in your source, be sure to indicate just where the page break occurs, for you may later decide to use only a part of the material, and you must know which page that part came from in order to provide accurate documentation. A simple method is to indicate the end of a page with one or two slashes (/ or //).

8. **Enclose explanatory material in square brackets.** Whenever you insert explanatory material into a direct quotation (e.g., if you add a noun or noun phrase to explain an ambiguous pronoun), use square brackets (see #48).

9. **Use [*sic*].** When there is something in a quotation that is obviously wrong—whether it is a factual mistake or a mistake in the writing, such as a spelling error—insert [*sic*] after it (see #48).

10. **Indicate ellipses.** Whenever you omit a word or words from a quotation, use three spaced periods to indicate the ellipsis (see #53).

75b The Source

For each note, clearly indicate the last name(s) of the author or authors, the relevant page number(s), and a shortened title of the work. Indeed, it is always a good idea to include the title, for later in your note-taking you may come across a second work by an author you are already using. If the note comes from more than one page, indicate the inclusive page numbers; the note itself will show where the page changes (see #75a.7). If you are using note cards, include the source information in the upper left-hand corner of each card.

75c The Slug

If you are using note cards, write a slug in the upper right-hand corner of each note card. The slug should consist of a word or brief phrase identifying the topic of the note, and if possible indicating just what part of your essay the note belongs in. Be as specific as possible: this slug will be helpful when it comes to organizing the cards before writing the essay. If you've prepared a good outline, a significant word or two from its main headings and subheadings with the corresponding numerals will be the logical choice to use as a slug.

RESEARCH TIP

Cross-Referencing Note Cards

If you are using note cards for a project that is long or unusually complex, you may want to devise some system for cross-referencing closely related note cards, or even ones you think might later prove to be closely related. One way to do this is to number the cards once you are through taking notes, and to make your cross-references to these numbers. Make sure that your cards are organized according to your outline, or that your outline has been changed to conform to the organization of your cards. Then, when the cards are all arranged, number them, say at top centre. Be sure to number your cards consecutively so that you can put them back into order should you drop or shuffle them.

75d Recording Your Own Ideas

In addition to taking notes from other sources, preserve your own ideas, insights, and flashes of inspiration as you go along. However fragmentary or tentative they may seem at first, they are likely to be valuable at a later stage. Even if you suddenly have so strong an idea about something that you feel sure you will remember it forever, write it down; otherwise there is a good chance you will forget it, for another strong idea may dislodge it a few minutes later. It is also a good idea to add your initials in place of the source information, so that you can easily identify the note as your own.

76 Writing the Essay

When your research is complete and you've arranged your notes in the desired order, you are ready to begin writing the essay. If your note-taking has been efficient—that is, if you have kept quotation to a minimum, assimilating and interpreting and evaluating as much as possible as you went along, and if you have made detailed notes about your own ideas—then the essay will be much easier to write as you arrange material logically and compose necessary transitions as you move from note to note and follow your outline. (Of course, the usual steps of revising and proofreading must follow the writing of the first draft, as described in Part I; see #9m–o and the appendix.)

As you compose your essay, remember to save files at frequent intervals. When you rework material, always retain a backup file containing the previous version of your work. For example, when you revise a first draft, make sure to retain a copy of the original draft, just in case you aren't happy with the way the revision turns out; then you can retrieve the original and try again. In addition to saving these files on your computer's hard drive, you should save backup copies on an external hard drive or a flash drive, in case you later encounter a computer virus, a power failure, or some other problem with your computer.

76a Keeping Track of Notes in Your Drafts

As you write your first draft, proceeding from note to note, include in your text the information that will eventually become part of your documentation. That is, at the end of each quotation, paraphrase, summary, statistic, graphic, or direct reference, enclose in parentheses the last name of the author, the date the work was published, and the relevant page number or numbers. When you prepare your final draft, you can reformat these parenthetical notes to be consistent with the citation style you are using for your references (see #79).

77 Acknowledging Sources

The purpose of documentation is fourfold:

1. It demonstrates that you, the writer, are a genuine researcher who has done the considerable work of investigating authorities and experts in the field(s) assumed in your researchable question.
2. It acknowledges your indebtedness to particular sources.
3. It lends weight to your statements and arguments by citing experts and authorities to support them, and also demonstrates the extent of your investigation of a topic.
4. It enables an interested reader to pursue the subject further by consulting cited sources, or possibly to evaluate a particular source or to check the accuracy of a reference or quotation, should it appear questionable.

77a "Common Knowledge"

It is not necessary to provide documentation for facts or ideas or quotations that are well known, or "common knowledge"—such as the fact that Shakespeare wrote *Hamlet*, or that Hamlet said "To be or not to be," or that Sir Isaac Newton formulated the law of gravity, or that the story of Adam and Eve appears in the book of Genesis in the Bible, or that the moon is not made of green cheese. But if you are at all uncertain whether or not something is "common knowledge," play it safe: it is far better to over-document and appear a little naive than to under-document and engage in the unethical practice of plagiarism.

If a piece of information appears in the same form in multiple sources, it qualifies as "common knowledge" and need not be documented. For example, such facts as the elevation of Mt. Logan, the current population of the world, or the date of the execution of Louis Riel can be found in dozens of reference books. But it can be risky for a student, or any non-professional, to trust to such a guideline when dealing with other kinds of material. For example, there may be dozens of articles, websites, and books referring to or attempting to explain something like a neutrino, or red shift, or black holes, or discoveries at the Olduvai Gorge, or Jungian readings of fairy tales, or the importance of the Human Genome Project, or deep structure in linguistic theory, or warnings about bioterrorism, or neoplatonic ideas in Renaissance poetry, or the nature and consequences of the great potato famine, or the origin of the name *Canada*; nevertheless, it is unlikely that a relatively non-expert writer will be sufficiently conversant with such material to recognize and accept it as "common knowledge." If something is new to you, and if you have not thoroughly explored the available literature on the subject, it is best to acknowledge a source. When in doubt, check with your instructor.

When the question of "common knowledge" arises, ask yourself: *common to whom?* Your readers will probably welcome the explicit documentation of something that they themselves do not realize is, to a few experts, "common knowledge." Besides, if at any point in your essay you give your readers cause to question your data, you will lose their confidence. So be scrupulous: document anything about which you have the least doubt.

78 Quotation, Paraphrase, Summary, and Plagiarism

ONLINE EXERCISES

A **quotation** from someone else's work must preserve the wording of the original source. A well-documented **paraphrase**, on the other hand, reproduces the content of the original, but in different words. Paraphrase is a useful technique because it enables writers to make use of source material while still using their own words and thus to avoid too much direct quotation. But a paraphrase, to be legitimate, should give clear credit *at its beginning* to the source and should not use significant words and phrases from an original without enclosing them in quotation marks. In other words, begin your paraphrase by identifying your source in an attribution (e.g., "Biographer John English suggests . . . " or "John English, Pierre Trudeau's biographer, argues . . ."). You must also provide the page number(s) for the material you have presented, as you would for a direct quotation. A paraphrase will usually be shorter than the original, but it need not be. A summary, however, is by definition a condensation, a boiled-down version in one's own words expressing the principal points of an original source. It is often the best evidence of a writer's effective synthesis of secondary source material.

Some writers make the serious mistake of thinking that only direct quotations need to be documented; on the contrary, it is important to know and remember that *paraphrase and summary must also be fully documented*. Failure to document a paraphrase or summary is a breach of academic integrity known as plagiarism, a form of intellectual dishonesty and theft for which there are serious academic penalties. To familiarize yourself with your institution's policies on academic integrity and on plagiarism, consult your institution's most recent academic calendar.

To illustrate the differences between legitimate and illegitimate use of source material, here is a paragraph, a direct quotation, from Rupert Brooke's *Letters from America*, followed by

a.   legitimate paraphrase,
b.   illegitimate paraphrase,
c.   combination paraphrase and quotation,
d.   summary, and
e.   a comment on plagiarism.

Such is Toronto. A brisk city of getting on for half a million inhabitants, the largest British city in Canada (in spite of the cheery Italian faces that pop up at you out of excavations in the street), liberally endowed with millionaires, not lacking its due share of destitution, misery, and slums. It is no mushroom city of the West, it has its history; but at the same time it has grown immensely of recent years. It is situated on the shores of a lovely lake; but you never see that, because the railways have occupied the entire lake front. So if, at evening, you try to find your way to the edge of the water, you are checked by a region of smoke, sheds, trucks, wharves, storehouses, "depôts,"

railway-lines, signals, and locomotives and trains that wander on the tracks up and down and across streets, pushing their way through the pedestrians, and tolling, as they go, in the American fashion, an immense melancholy bell, intent, apparently, on some private and incommunicable grief. Higher up are the business quarters, a few sky-scrapers in the American style without the modern American beauty, but one of which advertises itself as the highest in the British Empire; streets that seem less narrow than Montreal [*sic*], but not unrespectably wide; "the buildings are generally substantial and often handsome" (the too kindly Herr Baedeker). Beyond that the residential part, with quiet streets, gardens open to the road, shady verandahs, and homes, generally of wood, that are a deal more pleasant to see than the houses in a modern English town. (Brooke 80–81)

The parenthetical reference for this block quotation, which is given in MLA style (#79a), begins one space after the final punctuation mark. It includes the author's surname and the page numbers on which the original appeared. The complete bibliographical entry for Brooke's work would appear in the list of works cited as follows:

Brooke, Rupert. *Letters from America*. Sidgwick and Jackson, 1916.

(For more information about handling quotations, see #52.)

 ## 78a Legitimate Paraphrase

During his 1913 tour of the United States and Canada, Rupert Brooke sent back to England articles about his travels. In one of them, published in the 1916 book *Letters from America*, he describes Toronto as a large city, predominantly British, containing both wealth and poverty. He says that it is relatively old, compared to the upstart new cities farther west, but that nevertheless it has expanded a great deal in the last little while. He implies that its beautiful setting is spoiled for its citizens by the railways, which have taken over all the land near the lake, filling it with buildings and tracks and smell and noise. He also writes of the commercial part of the city, with its buildings which are tall (like American ones) but not very attractive (unlike American ones); one of them, he says, claims to be the tallest in the British Empire. (He pokes fun at Baedeker for being over-generous with his comments about the city's downtown architecture.) The streets he finds wider than those of Montreal, but not too wide. Finally, he compares Toronto's attractive residential areas favourably with those of English towns (80–81).

This is legitimate paraphrase. Even though it uses several individual words from the original (*British, railways, tracks, American, British Empire, streets, residential, English town[s]*), they are a small part of the whole; more important, they are common words that would be difficult to replace with reasonable substitutes without distorting the sense. And, even more important, they are used in a way that is natural to the paraphraser's own style and context. Paraphrase, however, does not consist in merely substituting one word for another, but rather in assimilating something and restating it in your own words and your own syntax.

Note that the writer has carefully kept Brooke's point of view apparent throughout by including him in each independent clause (a technique that also establishes good coherence): *Rupert Brooke, he describes, He says, He implies,* He also writes, *he says, He pokes fun, he finds, he compares.*

Also note that the writer has clearly shown where the paraphrase begins (in the second sentence of the paragraph) and ends (at the end of the paragraph, as indicated by the closing page range). In this case, the closing citation falls naturally at the end of the paragraph because the paraphrase ends where the paragraph ends. But if a paragraph that contains paraphrased material ends with a statement expressing the essay writer's own views, the closing citation must appear earlier in the paragraph, precisely where the paraphrase ends; for example:

> Visitors to Toronto have long lamented the destructive effect of industry and development on what might otherwise be a picturesque view of Lake Ontario. English poet Rupert Brooke, for example, in a letter published in his 1916 book *Letters from America*, expressed his disappointment in finding the city's beautiful waterfront spoiled for observers by the noise, smell, and general commotion of the railways (80). Today, parts of the waterfront have been transformed into parks and other recreational areas, but the nearby skyscrapers prevent most visitors from noticing that these areas even exist.

78b Illegitimate Paraphrase

An illegitimate paraphrase of Brooke's paragraph might begin like this:

> Brooke describes Toronto as a <u>brisk</u> kind of city with nearly <u>half a million inhabitants</u>, with some <u>Italian faces popping up</u> among the British, and with both <u>millionaires and slums</u>. He deplores the fact that the <u>lake front</u> on which <u>it is situated</u> has been <u>entirely occupied by the railways</u>, who have turned it into <u>a region of smoke</u>

<u>**and storehouses**</u> **and the like, and** <u>**trains that wander back and forth,**</u> <u>**ringing their huge bells**</u> **(80–81).**

The parenthetical reference at paragraph's end does not protect such a treatment from the charge of plagiarism, for too many of the words and phrases and too much of the syntax are Brooke's own. The words and phrases underlined are all "illegitimate": they still have the diction, syntax, and stylistic flavour of Brooke's original, and therefore they constitute plagiarism.

Had the writer put quotation marks around the underlined words, the passage would no longer be plagiarism—but it would still be illegitimate, or at least very poor, paraphrase, for if so substantial a part is to be left in Brooke's own words and syntax, the whole might as well have been quoted directly.

78c Paraphrase and Quotation Mixed

A writer who felt that a pure paraphrase was too flat and abstract, who felt that some of Brooke's more striking words and phrases should be retained, might choose to mix some direct quotation into a paraphrase:

> In *Letters from America*, Rupert Brooke characterizes Toronto as a "brisk," largely British city having the usual urban mixture of wealth and poverty. Unlike the "mushroom" cities farther west, he says, Toronto has a history, though he points out that much of its growth has been recent. He notes, somewhat cynically, that the people are cut off from the beauty of the lake by the railways and all their "smoke, sheds, trucks, wharves, storehouses, 'depôts,' railway-lines, signals, and locomotives and trains" going ding-ding all over the place (80–81).

This time the context is very much the writer's own, but some of the flavour of Brooke's original has been retained through the direct quotation of a couple of judiciously chosen words and the cumulative list quoted at the end. The writer is clearly in control of the material.

78d Summary

The purpose of a summary is to substantially reduce the original, conveying its essential meaning in a sentence or two. A summary of Brooke's passage might go something like this:

> **Rupert Brooke describes Toronto as large and mainly wealthy, aesthetically marred by the railway yards along the lake, with wide-enough streets and tall but (in spite of Baedeker's half-hearted approval) generally unprepossessing buildings, and a residential area more attractive than comparable English ones (80–81).**

In general, try to refer to an author by name in your text—and the first time by full name—when you are summarizing, paraphrasing, or quoting. If for some reason you do not want to bring the author's name into your text (e.g., if you were surveying a variety of opinions about Toronto and did not want to clutter your text with all their authors' names), then you would still need to make the source clear, according to whichever citation style you are using (#79).

 ## Maintaining Academic Integrity and Avoiding Plagiarism

Had one of the foregoing versions of the passage not mentioned Brooke, nor included quotation marks around words taken directly from the original, nor ended with documentation, it would have been plagiarism. A student doing research is part of a community of scholars (professors, investigators, instructors, other students, and researchers), all of whom are governed by the codes of academic honesty that define effective research and identify plagiarism—whether intentional or accidental—as a serious offence. Your college or university calendar will no doubt include a detailed definition of plagiarism and a statement of policy on the academic discipline (failing marks, suspension, a note on one's academic transcript) arising from a finding of plagiarism. You should review this information and discuss any questions or concerns with your instructors and academic advisers.

When you are working on a research project, keep in mind that you are ethically bound to give credit twice—*in the text* of the written document and *in the works-cited list*—to all sources of information you have used. All of the following kinds of material require acknowledgement:

- direct quotations—whether short or long;
- your summaries and paraphrases of sources;
- ideas, theories, and inspirations drawn from a source and expressed in your own words;

- statistical data compiled by institutions (e.g., think tanks and governmental or non-governmental organizations) and other researchers;
- original ideas and original findings drawn from course lectures and seminars;
- graphic materials (diagrams, charts, photographs, illustrations, slides, film and television clips, audio and video recordings, and so on; and
- materials drawn from authored or unauthored Internet sites.

Remember that giving credit for this kind of material does not diminish your own work: it enhances the credibility of your claims and demonstrates just how much genuine research you have done on your project. It shows you adding your voice and your views to those of the community of scholars and researchers of which you are a part.

One final note. It is possible to commit self-plagiarism. This happens when a writer submits the same work—in whole or in part—for two different courses or assignments. If you are working in the same subject or topic area for two different courses or assignments, it is essential to discuss the ethical issues involved with both instructors to whom the work will be submitted.

78f Integrating and Contextualizing Quotations

When you use direct quotations, you must integrate them into your writing as seamlessly as possible, and you must ensure that their meaning remains clear in their new context. One reliable way of integrating a quotation is to introduce it with a phrase or a clause that establishes its context or significance; for example:

As Rupert Brooks observes about Toronto in the early 1900's, "It is no mushroom city of the West, it has its history; but at the same time it has grown immensely of recent years" (80). (note that a comma is used after an introductory phrase)

Rupert Brooks observes that in the early 1900's, Toronto already had a significant history: "It is no mushroom city of the West, it has its history; but at the same time it has grown immensely of recent years" (80). (note that a colon is used after an introductory clause)

This approach works well when you want to quote a complete phrase or clause, and it is usually the best way to introduce a block quotation. (See #52b and #52c for more examples, including two that show how to treat block quotations). But overuse of this approach can quickly become tiresome.

A more subtle—and often more effective—way of integrating and contextualizing quotations is to work them into the syntax of your own sentences; for example:

> Writing in the early 1900's, Rupert Brooks described Toronto as being unlike the "mushroom" cities of western Canada because, even though it had "grown immensely of recent years," it also had a significant "history" (80).

When you take this approach, you may well have to alter the quoted material in one way or another to incorporate it smoothly. That is, you may have to change the grammar, syntax, or punctuation of a quotation to make it conform to your own grammar and syntax. The examples that follow demonstrate how you might do this in a variety of situations. (See also #48.) The examples use quotations taken from the following passage, which comes from Mary Shelley's *Frankenstein; or, The Modern Prometheus*:

> I am by birth a Genevese; and my family is one of the most distinguished of that republic. My ancestors had been for many years counsellors and syndics; and my father had filled several public situations with honour and reputation. He was respected by all who knew him for his integrity and indefatigable attention to public business. He passed his younger days perpetually occupied by the affairs of his country; a variety of circumstances had prevented his marrying early, nor was it until the decline of life that he became a husband and the father of a family.

(a)   altered for pronoun reference:

> Victor Frankenstein begins his story by stating that "[he is] by birth a Genevese; and [his] family is one of the most distinguished of that republic" (Shelley 31).

The first-person pronouns have been changed to third person in order to fit the third-person point of view in the sentence as a whole. The changed pronouns and the accompanying verb (*is* for *am*) appear in square brackets. (The opening *he is* could have been left outside the quotation, but the writer preferred to incorporate the parallelism within the quotation.)

(b)   altered for consistent verb tense:

> As we first encounter him in the description at the beginning of his son's narrative, Victor's father is a man "respected by all who [know] him for his integrity and indefatigable attention to public business" (Shelley 31).

The verb in square brackets has been changed from past to present tense to conform with the tense established by the *is* of the student's sentence.

(c)   altered for punctuation:

> The first words of Victor Frankenstein's narrative—"I am by birth a Genevese" (Shelley 31)—reveal a narrator preoccupied with himself, his birth, and his nationality.

The semicolon of the original has been dropped to avoid its clashing with the enclosing dashes of the student's own sentence.

(d)   selective quotation:

> The first paragraph of Victor's narrative focuses more on Victor's father than on any other member of the Frankenstein family. Victor takes pains to describe him as a man of "honour and reputation ... respected by all who [know] him for his integrity and indefatigable attention to public business" and "perpetually occupied by the affairs of his country" (Shelley 31). A first-time reader of the novel might well assume that Victor's narrative will be more a tribute to his father than an account of his own creation of a monster.

Here, the student writer has selected key words and phrases from the opening paragraph of Victor Frankenstein's narrative in order to make a point about the novel's focus. The ellipsis indicates that material has been omitted in the interests of the student's own sentence structure.

WRITING TIP

Integrating Quotations

If you're having trouble integrating quotations into your sentences, try asking yourself (1) what the original author was *doing* with the words in their original context and (2) what you want the quotation to *do* in your paper. For example, was the author *analyzing, arguing, challenging, defending, demonstrating,* or *suggesting* an important point? Or, do the words *clarify, emphasize, explain, illustrate, highlight,* or *support* a point that you are trying to make? Once you've answered these questions, select the most appropriate verb and use it to anchor the quotation to your discussion.

> As Darwin suggests, "nothing can be more improving to a young naturalist, than a journey in distant countries" (603).

> The researchers' finding that "involvement in team sports assists youth in developing self-esteem" (47) supports my assertion that playing sports promotes mental well-being.

Finding the right verb to contextualize a quotation will help you convey to the reader—and clarify to yourself—your reason for including the quoted material in your paper.

79 Documentation

To be effective, documentation must be complete, accurate, and clear. Completeness and accuracy depend on careful recording of necessary information as you do your research and take notes. Clarity depends on the way you present that information to your reader. You will be clear only if your audience can follow your method of documentation. Therefore, it is important that before you begin any research project, you investigate the method of documentation you need to use. There are four main methods:

1. the name–page method recommended by the Modern Language Association (MLA), which is in wide use in the humanities (see #79a);

2. the name–date method recommended by the American Psychological Association (APA), which is used in some of the social and other sciences (see #79b);

3. the note method recommended in *The Chicago Manual of Style*, which is in use in various disciplines (see #79c); and

4. the number method, which is used in some of the sciences (see #79d).

Which method you choose will depend on what discipline you are writing in and on the wishes of your audience.

Below, we cover the basics of the four main methods. As you read through the examples, note that in an actual paper, the text would be double-spaced rather than single-spaced.

79a The Name–Page Method (MLA Style)

The name–page method is detailed in the eighth edition of the *MLA Handbook* (2016). Using this method, you provide a short parenthetical reference in the text, and you list all sources in a list titled "Works Cited" at the end of your paper:

sample in-text citation	sample reference-list entry
The reaction in China to the end of World War I has been described by one historian as "popular rejoicing" (MacMillan 322).	MacMillan, Margaret. *Paris 1919: Six Months That Changed the World.* Random House, 2001.

The pages that follow illustrate examples of the most common patterns of MLA documentation. First we cover the basics of in-text citation; then we give examples of how to treat various types of publications in the list of works cited.

In-Text Citations

In-text citations generally consist of the author's last name followed by a page number that indicates where the quoted or paraphrased material appeared in the original source. These citations are usually placed at the

Author   Title   Publication information   Electronic source

end of a sentence (see example above). However, if a sentence is long and complicated, a citation may be placed earlier, immediately after the quotation or paraphrase itself. If you include the author's name in your text, you do not need to repeat it in the parenthetical citation:

> **The reaction in China to the end of World War I has been described by historian Margaret MacMillan as "popular rejoicing"—particularly among young people, who had "an uncritical admiration for Western democracy, Western liberal ideals, and Western learning" (322).**

Note that most of the following conventions apply to print as well as electronic sources.

A Work by One or Two Authors (or Editors)

Include the last names of up to two authors or editors and the page reference, with no intervening punctuation:

> **In the book's introduction, the writers note that "newcomers to the prairies were beset by a seemingly endless series of unforgiving challenges" (Calder and Wardhaugh 11).**

A Work by Three or More Authors (or Editors)

Include the last name of the first author or editor followed by "et al." (an abbreviation for Latin *et alii*, "and others") and the page reference:

> **Messenger et al. advise readers that effective research requires more effort than simply searching for resources on the Internet (383).**

A Work by a Government Agency or a Corporate Author

In place of the author's last name, use either the name of the group acting as the author or a shortened version of the title, whichever appears first in the list of works cited (see page 413):

> **Photos depicting life "at the front" often showed soldiers in the trenches performing domestic activities such as reading a newspaper, shaving, or sharing a meal (Canadian Field Comforts Commission 81–84).**

Author   Title   Publication information   Electronic source

A Work by an Anonymous Author

For an anonymously written article, use a short version of the title in place of the author's last name:

> **The most expensive white diamond ever bought at auction is "the 118.28-carat oval-cut gem that sold . . . for $30.6 million [USD] in 2013" (*"Colors"* 34).**

In this example, "Colors" is short for "The Colors of Money," the title of an unsigned magazine article. For more on how to shorten titles in in-text examples, see the discussion under the heading "Two or More Works by the Same Author (or Editor)," below.

A Literary Work Available in Many Editions

When citing literary prose works (e.g., novels, prose plays) that are available in many editions, include the page number for the edition you have consulted as well as any volume, chapter, section, or other division number(s) attached to the material:

> **Jane Austen presents readers of *Pride and Prejudice* with the heroine's father, the likable Mr. Bennet, an "odd . . . mixture of quick parts, sarcastic humour, reserve, and caprice" (32; vol. 1, ch. 1).**

> **In Chekhov's *The Cherry Orchard*, Trofimov says to Anya, "All Russia is our orchard" (122; act 2).**

For poems or verse plays available in many editions, omit the page number but include all necessary act, scene, part, line, or other division numbers(s), separated with periods:

> **In *As You Like It*, Silvius describes what it means to love:**
> **It is to be all made of fantasy,**
> **All made of passion, and all made of wishes,**
> **All adoration, duty, and observance,**
> **All humbleness, all patience and impatience,**
> **All purity, all trial, all obedience. (5.2.94–98)**

> **Milton's *Paradise Lost* begins by recalling the story "Of man's first disobedience, and the fruit / Of that forbidden tree, whose mortal taste / Brought death into the world, and all our woe" (1.1–3).**

Author   *Title*   **Publication information**   **Electronic source**

As the above examples illustrate, quotations of more than three lines of verse should be set as block quotations, while quotations of three or fewer lines can be run into your sentence. In the latter case, a slash with a space on either side indicates where a line break appears in the original.

If a poem has numbered lines but no other numbered divisions, give the line number(s) preceded by "line" (for one line) or "lines" (for multiple lines) the first time the poem is cited. In subsequent citations, give only the line number(s):

> **Robert Burns begins the poem by comparing his love to "a red, red rose / That's newly sprung in June" (lines 1–2) and to "the melodie / That's sweetly play'd in tune" (3–4).**

If a poem has no numbered divisions, provide page references; do not assign numbers to unnumbered lines.

MLA STYLE

Treatment of Number Ranges

When you give a number range (e.g., a range of page numbers) in MLA style, provide the first and second numbers in full for numbers up to 99 (e.g., 5–88, 97–99). For larger numbers, give the first number in full but only the last two digits of the second number, unless additional digits are required for clarity (e.g., 122–28 for a range from 122 to 128, but 385–460 for a range from 385 to 460).

A Work of Scripture

If you are citing a work of scripture, include an abbreviated title of the book, the chapter number, the verse number, and/or any other significant division number(s). Also include a shortened title of the edition you are using (or whatever element begins the text's entry in the list of works cited) the first time you reference the work:

> **In the biblical account of the Flood, Noah is presented as a dutiful servant of God, "a just man and perfect in his generations" (*Holy Bible*, Gen. 6.9). In contrast, the earth is said to be "filled with violence" and "corrupt" (Gen. 6.11–12).**

An Online Document with No Page Numbers

If you are citing an online document that has no numbered divisions, include only the author's last name in the parenthetical citation:

> **The National Ballet of Canada's recent production of *Swan Lake* was hailed as "a gorgeous, sumptuous feast for the eyes and ears" (Leung).**

However, if the document consists of numbered paragraphs or sections, include the paragraph or section number where you would normally include the page number, and add the abbreviation "par." (for "paragraph") or "sec." (for "section") before the number. Also add a comma to separate the author's name from the abbreviation: for example, "(Wallenstein, par. 3)."

A Message on a Social Media Site

For a message posted to Twitter, Facebook, Google+, or some other social media site, provide the last name, username, or group name (whichever is used in the author position in the list of works cited) of the person or organization that posted the message:

> **Anne Shirley has been described as "a brilliant role model for young women" (Fullerton).**

A Video or Sound Recording

Begin with the last name of the recording's primary creator or the title of the recording (whichever comes first in the list of works cited), then provide the time range (in hours, minutes, and seconds) for the content you are citing:

> **Stories from our nation's past can provide valuable inspiration for Canadian novelists; after all, "all of the elements of fiction and drama are embedded in Canadian history: struggle, loss, pain, survival, triumph, love" (Hill 00:00:11–21).**

A Personal Email or Letter

If you need to cite an email, a letter, or some other form of personal communication, provide the last name of the person who sent the message:

> **Professional email messages should include a clear, concise subject line (Smith).**

Author   Title   Publication information   Electronic source

Quotation at Second Hand

Try as often as possible to quote from primary sources. If you find it necessary to quote from a secondary source, try to supply the original source and/or context of the quotation in the surrounding text:

> **When US president Woodrow Wilson set out for the Paris Peace Conference in late 1918, he stated that he felt a "duty" to support American servicemen: "It is now my duty . . . to play my full part in making good what they gave their life's blood to obtain" (qtd. in MacMillan 3).**

More Than One Work in the Same Citation

If you need to cite multiple sources in a single parenthetical citation, use semicolons to separate the sources:

> **The First World War left Canadians shaken and grieving, but it also brought them together as never before through a growing sense of national identity (Morton 226; Gwyn xxi).**

In the list of works cited, include a separate entry for each work.

Two or More Works By the Same Author (or Editor)

If you cite multiple works by the same author, the in-text citations must include short versions of the works' titles in addition to the author's last name and the page number(s). In most cases, you can reduce a title to an initial noun or noun phrase (omit an opening *A*, *An*, or *The*). For example, the following sentences show how to cite quotations from Keith Oatley's books *The Passionate Muse: Exploring Emotion in Stories and Such Stuff as Dreams: The Psychology of Fiction*:

> **The most talented fiction writers devote "time and effort into exploring particular emotional issues" and learning "how to externalize" the expression of emotion (Oatley, Passionate Muse 187). When they are successful in their efforts, their fiction "enters the mind" and "prompts us towards emotions" (Oatley, Such Stuff 7).**

If the title already consists of only a noun or a noun phrase, do not shorten it. And if the title begins with something other than a noun or a noun phrase (e.g., a verb, a conjunction, or a preposition), use the first word of the title.

Author　　*Title*　　**Publication information**　　**Electronic source**

Two or More Works By Authors (or Editors) with the Same Last Name

If your list of works cited contains works by multiple authors or editors with the same last name, either provide the individuals' full names in the main text—for example, "As Margaret MacMillan has argued, . . . (119–20)"—or add their first initials to the parenthetical citation—for example, "(M. MacMillan 119–20)." If you are citing two or more works by authors or editors with the same last name and the same first initial(s), provide the authors' full names.

Works-Cited List

The list of works cited appears at the end of your essay and includes the full publication information for all works that you have referenced. It begins on a new page, with the title "Works Cited" centred at the top of the page. The first line of each entry begins at the left-hand margin, with second and subsequent lines indented. You can achieve this format by selecting the entries and setting your word-processing program's paragraph orientation to "hanging indent."

List entries in alphabetical order. For an entry that begins with a title, ignore any opening article (*A*, *An*, or *The*). When you have two or more works by the same author or editor, alphabetize them by title, and replace the author's or editor's name with three consecutive hyphens in all entries after the first:

Oatley, Keith. *Such Stuff as Dreams: The Psychology of Fiction.* Wiley-Blackwell, 2011.

---. *The Passionate Muse: Exploring Emotion in Stories.* Oxford UP, 2012.

A Book By One Author (or Editor)

MacMillan, Margaret. *Paris 1919: Six Months That Changed the World.* Random House, 2001.

A standard works-cited reference for a book includes

1. the author's name (surname, followed by a comma, and full first name, followed by a period);

Author   Title   Publication information   Electronic source

2. the full title of the book, italicized and followed by a period;
3. the name of the publisher, followed by a comma; and
4. the year of publication, followed by a period.

Note that you should omit initial articles (A, *An*, *The*) and words like *Books*, *Company*, *Inc.*, and *Ltd.* from publishers' names. Also note that "UP" is the standard abbreviation for "University Press."

A Book by Two Authors (or Editors)

For a book by two authors or editors, invert only the first name:

Calder, Alison, and Robert Wardhaugh, editors. *History, Literature, and the Writing of the Canadian Prairies.* U of Manitoba P, 2005.

Note that the description "editors" is necessary to clarify that Calder and Wardhaugh are not the authors of the book. For a book with one editor, use the description "editor."

A Book by Three or More Authors (or Editors)

When you have three or more authors or editors, list only the first followed by "et al.":

Messenger, William E., et al. *The Concise Canadian Writer's Handbook.* 3ed ed., Oxford UP, 2017.

A Book With a Translator or an Editor in Addition to the Author

If a book has an author as well as a translator or an editor, begin with the name of the author and add the name of the translator (preceded by "Translated by") or the editor (preceded by "Edited by") after the title:

Charcot, Jean-Martin. *Charcot in Morocco.* Translated by Toby Gelfand, U of Ottawa P, 2012.

A Work by a Government Agency or a Corporate Author

If a work lists a group as its author, provide the name of the group in the usual author position, omitting any initial *The*:

Canadian Field Comforts Commission. *With the First Canadian Contingent.* Hodder and Stoughton, 1915.

Author   *Title*   Publication information   Electronic source

However, if the group listed as the author is also listed as the publisher, begin with the title:

Career Decision-Making Patterns of Canadian Youth and Associated Post-secondary Educational Outcomes. Statistics Canada, 2015.

Finally, if you list a government agency in the author position, begin with the name of the country, province, territory, or state in which the agency operates; for example, "Canada, Environment Assessment Agency" or "Alberta, Health Services."

A Work by an Anonymous Author

For a work with no identified author, begin with the title:

Beowulf. Translated by Seamus Heaney, W. W. Norton, 2000.

An Book Accessed Online

If you access a book online, follow the standard guidelines for citing a book, but also include at the end the DOI or the URL that will direct the reader to the book. If the book was accessed through a website or a database, also include the name of the website or database:

Grant, Jeannette A. *Through Evangeline's Country.* J. Knight, 1894. Early Canadiana Online, eco.canadiana.ca/view/oocihm.06344/3?r=0&s=1.

MLA STYLE

Inclusion of DOIs and URLs

When you create an entry for a web-based source in your list of works cited, include the work's digital object identifier (DOI) whenever possible. If the source has not been assigned a DOI, include the URL that will direct readers to the web page you consulted. The DOI or URL is generally placed at the end of the entry. For a URL, omit an opening *http://* or *https://*. If you need to break either a DOI or a URL across two or more lines, do so immediately after a punctuation mark. Never add a hyphen.

Author **Title** **Publication information** **Electronic source**

A Multivolume Work

If the book is part of a multivolume work, include the volume number before the publisher's name:

Montgomery, Lucy Maud. *The Selected Journals of L. M. Montgomery.* Edited by Mary Rubio and Elizabeth Waterston, vol. 1, Oxford UP, 1985.

An Edition Other Than the First

Include the edition number after the title:

New, W. H. *A History of Canadian Literature.* 2nd ed., McGill–Queen's UP, 2003.

If the book has an editor or a translator in addition to an author, the edition number follows the name of the editor or translator.

A Republished Book

Including the original publication date for a book that has been republished is optional; however, if you choose to provide it, do so immediately after the title:

Austen, Jane. *Pride and Prejudice.* 1813. Oxford UP, 1970.

A Play (Prose or Verse)

Treat a play as you would treat a book:

Chekhov, Anton. *The Cherry Orchard.* Translated by Laurence Senelick, W. W. Norton, 2010.

A Short Poem

Provide the name of the poem (in quotation marks) as well as the title of the collection in which the poem appears (in italics):

Hall, Phil. "Becoming a Poet." *Killdeer*, Bookthug, 2011, pp. 17–32.

Author   *Title*   Publication information   Electronic source

A Long Poem with Divisions

Treat a long poem published as a complete work as you would treat a book:

Milton, John. *Paradise Lost.* Edited by William Kerrigan et al., Random House, 2007.

A Work of Scripture

Begin with the title of the edition you have used. If the edition is based on a specific version of the work, include this information after the title:

The Holy Bible. King James Version, Nelson, 1944.

A Chapter, Article, or Entry in an Edited Collection

Begin with the name of the person who wrote the chapter, article, or entry. Next, provided the title of the work (in quotation marks), the title of the collection in which it appears (in italics), and the name(s) of the editor(s) of the collection. Include the name of the publisher and the date, and end by providing the pages on which the work appears:

Cruikshank, Julie. "Oral History, Narrative Strategies, and Native American Historiography." *The Canadian Oral History Reader*, edited by Kristina R. Llewellyn et al., McGill–Queen's UP, 2015, pp. 180–97.

A Journal Article

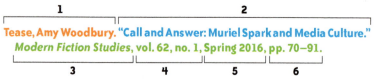

A standard works-cited entry for a journal article includes

1. the author's name, inverted and followed by a period;
2. the title of the article, followed by a period and enclosed in quotation marks;
3. the title of the journal, italicized and followed by a comma;

Author   Title   Publication information   Electronic source

4. the volume number, followed by a comma, and/or the issue number, followed by a comma;
5. the publication date (including the month or season of publication, as given on the cover of the publication) followed by a comma; and
6. the pages on which the article appears in the original, followed by a period.

Treat a journal article that you retrieved online in the same way, but omit page numbers if they do not appear in the online version, and include the DOI assigned to the article at the end. If the article has not been assigned a DOI, provide the URL that will lead your reader to the article. And if you accessed the article through an online database, provide the name of the database (in italics) immediately before the DOI or the URL:

Krotz, Sarah Wylie. "Place and Memory: Rethinking the Literary Map of Canada." *English Studies in Canada*, vol. 40, no. 2–3, June–September 2014, pp. 133–54. Project Muse, doi:10.1353/esc.2014.0012.

A Newspaper or Magazine Article

For an article in print, give the writer's name, the title of the article (in quotation marks), the name of the publication (in italics), the date of publication, and the page number(s):

Parkinson, David. "Carbon-Tax Revenue Isn't Dirty Money." *The Globe and Mail*, 7 Apr. 2016, B2.

In this example, "B2" indicates that the article appeared on page 2 of section B. If an article is spread across multiple pages that are nonconsecutive, list the first page followed by a plus sign—for example, T1+.

If you have accessed the article online, follow the article's title with the name of the website (in italics), the date of publication, and the URL:

Nurse, Donna Bailey. "The 'Indecently Curious' Carol Shields." *Maclean's*, 1 May 2016, www.macleans.ca/culture/books/the-indecently-curious-carol-shields/.

Author   *Title*   Publication information   Electronic source

A Thesis or a Dissertation

For a thesis or a dissertation retrieved from an online database, give the author's name, the title (in italics), the name of the institution acting as the publisher, the year of publication, the name of the database you used to access the work, and the URL:

Hackler, Neal. *Stuart Debauchery in Restoration Satire.* U of Ottawa, 2015. *Theses Canada*, www.collectionscanada.gc.ca/obj/thesescanada/vol2/ OOU/TC-OOU-32444.pdf.

For a print version of a published thesis or dissertation, omit the name of the database and the URL.

A Lecture or Other Address

List the speaker's name, the title of the lecture (in quotation marks), the name of the lecture series or forum and/or the name of the conference or event at which the lecture was given, the date on which the lecture was given, and the location:

Wright, Ronald. "The Gold Eaters." Vancouver Institute Lecture, 26 Sept. 2015, Woodward Instructional Resources Centre, Vancouver.

Omit the name of the city if it is included in the name of the venue.

A Work of Visual Art

For a work of visual art that you saw in person (e.g., in an art gallery), list the artist's name, the title of the work, the date the work was created, and the location:

Hughes, E. J. *Trees, Savary Island.* 1953, Museum of Fine Arts, Montreal.

Avoid repeating the name of the city if it is included in the name of the gallery or other institution.

A Music Recording

Begin with the name of the performer, the writer, or the composer who is most relevant to your discussion. Next, add the title of the work, the name of the recording company, and the date. For a song, include the title of the song (in quotation marks) and the title of the album on which it appears (in italics). If you retrieved the recording online, include the URL at the end:

Cohen, Leonard. "Born in Chains." *Popular Problems*, Columbia, 2014, www.myplaydirect.com/leonard-cohen/features/31693444.

A Motion Picture

If your paper discusses a particular artist or creator who worked on the motion picture, begin with that person's name followed by a brief description of his or her role. Also include the title of the work, the name of the main production company or distributor, and the year of release:

Baichwal, Jennifer, director. *Payback.* National Film Board of Canada, 2012.

If your paper discusses the motion picture more generally, begin with the title, and include the names of any relevant contributors along with a brief description of their roles. And if you accessed the motion picture online, also include the name of the video-hosting site and the URL:

A Drummer's Dream. Directed by John Walker, John Walker Productions, 2010. *Netflix*, www.netflix.com/ca/title/80084832.

A Television Program

Treat a television series as you would treat a motion picture. For an individual episode of a series, provide the name of the episode (in quotation marks) immediately before the name of the series. If you watched the episode when it originally aired, replace the name of the production company or the distributor with the name of the network that aired the show, and give the date of broadcast:

"Marked Twain." *Murdoch Mysteries*, directed by T. W. Peacocke, written by Peter Mitchell, performance by Yannick Bisson, season 9, episode 2, CBC, 12 Oct. 2015.

Author   *Title*   Publication information   Electronic source

A YouTube Video

For a video you watched on YouTube or a similar online video-sharing website, begin the entry as you would begin an entry for a motion picture (i.e., with either the title of the video or the name of a person who contributed to the creation of the video). Include the name of the video-sharing site, the name of the person or organization that posted the video, the date on which the video was posted, and the URL:

Hill, Lawrence, speaker. "Lawrence Hill—2015 History Award Recipient." *YouTube*, uploaded by Canada's History, 22 Sept. 2015, www.youtube. com/watch?v=ein3QNJMOQU.

If the video's description includes the date on which the events recorded in the video took place, you can add that date immediately after the video's title, followed by a period.

A Podcast

For an episode of a podcast, begin with either the title of the episode or the name of a significant contributor (whichever is most relevant to your discussion), as you would for a motion picture or a television show. Also include as many of the following details as you can find: the title of the podcast, the season number, the episode number, the producer (if different from a named contributor), the release date, and the URL:

"*The Outlander* by Gil Adamson." *Write Reads*, hosted by Kirt Callahan and Tania Gee, episode 36, 17 Feb. 2016, writereads.wordpress. com/2016/02/17/write-reads-36-the-outlander-by-gil-adamson/.

A Blog Post

Include the author's name, the title of the blog post (in quotation marks), the title of the blog (in italics), the date of the post, and the URL:

Laxer, Daniel. *"Drums, Bugles, and Bagpipes in the Seven Years' War." Borealia*, 22 Feb. 2016, earlycanadianhistory.ca/2016/02/22/drums-bugles-and-bagpipes-in-the-seven-years-war/.

If the blog has a publisher who is not the author, and that publisher's name is not contained in the title of the blog, you can include the publisher's name after the title of the blog, followed by a comma.

Author   *Title*   Publication information   Electronic source

A Tweet

For a tweet from an individual, provide the author's name, the full text of the tweet (in quotation marks, with spelling, punctuation, and capitalization that matches the original), the name of the site (*Twitter*), the date and time, and the URL:

Coupland, Doug. *"If you find yourself bcc'ing an email, you probably shouldn't be sending it at all." Twitter*, 21 Apr. 2016, 12:16 p.m., twitter.com/DougCoupland/status/723228986512302081.

If the author has not provided his or her real name, begin with the writer's screen name, including the @ symbol.

If the tweet was released by an organization, begin with the organization's full name:

Merriam-Webster. *"'Bumfuzzle' means 'to confuse; perplex; fluster.'" Twitter*, 29 Apr. 2016, 6:15 a.m., twitter.com/MerriamWebster/status/726037139931156484.

A Facebook Status Update

Treat a short Facebook status update as you would treat a tweet, but replace "*Twitter*" with "*Facebook*." If the exact time of the update is not available, omit that component:

Trudeau, Justin. "Canada will once again demonstrate real leadership on a number of United Nations priorities." *Facebook*, 16 Mar. 2016, www.facebook.com/JustinPJTrudeau/videos/10154133901320649/.

If the status update is longer—say, if it would take up more than two full lines in your list of works cited—include a brief description in place of the title:

Dalhousie University. Announcement of upcoming performance event "Different State of Mind." *Facebook*, 18 Feb. 2016, www.facebook.com/DalhousieUniversity/photos/a.113777601898.107830.7142486898/10153199944611899/?type=3&theater.

Author   *Title*   Publication information   Electronic source

A Google+ Post

Treat a Google+ post as you would treat a Twitter post or a Facebook status update, but replace "*Twitter*" or "*Facebook*" with "*Google+*":

L., Ronald. "Were women the first hunters using spears?" *Google+*, 17 Apr. 2015, plus.google.com/104078047498793487097.

Fullerton, Susannah. Comment on Anne Shirley being a positive role model for young women. *Google+*, 1 Dec. 2013, plus.google.com/ +susannahfullerton.

Material from a Website

For web-based material that does not fit into any of the categories described above, include as many of the following details as you can: the name of the author or creator of the material, the title of the material (enclose titles of web pages in quotation marks), the title of the website (in italics), the name of the website's publisher (if the publisher has not already been named in the title of the website or as the author or creator), the date the material was posted, and the URL:

Leung, Wayne. "Review: Swan Lake (the National Ballet of Canada)." *Mooney on Theatre*, Megan Mooney, 9 March 2014, www.mooneyontheatre. com/2014/03/09/review-swan-lake-the-national-ballet-of-canada/.

If the author or creator is not named, or if the author or creator is a group whose name is also the name of the website, begin with the title. And if the material is not dated, or if you think your reader would benefit from knowing when you accessed the material, you can add the date of your access at the end:

"Our History." *National Gallery of Canada*, 2006, www.gallery.ca/en/ about/history.php. Accessed 20 July 2016.

A Personal Email or Letter

Begin with the name of the person who wrote the email or the letter. For an email, provide the subject line (enclosed in quotation marks) as the title; for an untitled letter, provide a brief description of the material.

Author   *Title*   **Publication information**   **Electronic source**

Conclude with the name of the person who received the message (preceded by "Received by") and the date on which it was sent:

Smith, Henry. "Re: 5 Tips for Better Emails." Received by Chris Buonelli, 30 Nov. 2016.

Kurtz, Andrew. Personal letter about writing effective summaries. Received by Dani Norris, 6 Jan. 2017.

A Sample MLA Research Paper

The following sample research paper illustrates the principles of documentation described in the eighth edition of the *MLA Handbook*. It also illustrates the formatting conventions described online at the MLA Style Center (https://style.mla.org/formatting-papers/). Before you submit your paper, you should always ask your instructor if she or he has any additional requirements. For example, your instructor might want you to add a separate title page that lists the title of your paper, your name, your professor's name, the course code and section number of your class, and the date of submission.

If your instructor has not asked you to include a separate title page, list your name, your instructor's name, the course code, the course section number (if applicable), and the date at the top of the first page of your paper, aligned left. Add the title, centred, immediately before your first paragraph. Number all pages in the top right-hand corner, and include your last name before each page number (you can do this using your word-processor's automatic page-numbering feature). Double-space all lines of text, and indent the first line of all paragraphs, including the first. Set your margins to approximately 1 inch (2.5 cm) all around; in most cases, you can use the default settings of your word-processing program. Do not justify the right margin, and avoid breaking words at the ends of lines.

Begin your list of works cited on a new page at the end of your paper. Centre the title "Works Cited" at the top of the page. Each entry should be set with a hanging indent, so that the first line begins at the left-hand margin and the second and subsequent lines are indented. Arrange entries in alphabetical order, ignoring any initial article (*A*, *An*, or *The*) in entries that begin with a title.

Author   *Title*   Publication information   Electronic source

Badica   1

Gabby Badica

Professor Brown

English 390, Section 002

21 May 2015

"The Story with Animals Is the Better Story": The Co-Existence

of Human and Animal Intelligences in Martel's *Life of Pi*

The co-existence of human and animal intelligences lies at the

heart of the survivor's narrative presented in Yann Martel's *Life*

of Pi. From its very first mention, the account of Pi's 227 days of

endurance is argued to be "a story that will make you believe in God"

(Martel ix). Martel himself has described his novel as one that will

achieve this task, insisting on the significance of this central claim

(Wood). However, this crucial point becomes significantly more

complicated when the text presents two distinct narratives that explain

Pi's survival in severely diverging ways. While the first account,

characterized by meaningful interactions between human and animal

intelligences, presents a tale of endurance, intelligence, perseverance,

and controlled struggle, the second version, devoid of any animal

intelligences, is a dark account of cannibalism and human nature at

its most savage.

The stark contrast between the two explanations of Pi's survival

immediately makes those on the receiving end of the accounts

question not only which version they believe to be the truthful one, but also which one they prefer. When faced with the question of which of the accounts is "the better story" (Martel 352), even the novel's most fact-driven and logically oriented characters identify the version with animals as superior. However, is the first account better simply because it is a feel-good story rather than a tale illustrating how even the most religious and idealistic of men can be led to savagery in desperate and dire circumstances? This essay will explore the implications of the co-existence of human and animal intelligences in the first account of Pi's existence at sea; it will also explore the manner in which the connection that is formed between these two types of intelligences is crucial to religious belief and spirituality. While the second version of Pi's survival also holds significant value, especially when considered in conjunction with survivor-trauma theory, the first story is the one that allows for a holistic understanding of the role that religion plays in Pi's life both during and after his shipwreck. Essentially, the story with animals is the better story because it offers the reader insight into the human identity-formation process and highlights the important connection between animality and divinity.

The text highlights Pi's deep connection to animals and religion early in the narrative. As the son of "Mr. Santosh Patel, founder, owner, director" of the Pondicherry Zoo, Pi has "nothing but the fondest memories of growing up in a zoo" (15). He claims that he "lived the life of a prince," with an alarm clock of lions' roars and a breakfast that was "punctuated by the shrieks and cries of howler monkeys, hill mynahs and Moluccan cockatoos" (15). He anthropomorphizes the animals around him from an early age, recounting such daily routines as leaving for school "under the benevolent gaze not only of Mother but also of bright-eyed otters and burly American bison and stretching and yawning orang-utans" (15). Pi dismisses the frequent criticism that zoos strip animals of freedom through his claim that freedom in the wild, where "fear is high and the food low and where territory must constantly be defended and parasites forever endured" (17), is not something that would be in any way beneficial to animals. As James Mensch has highlighted, Pi describes zoos as artificial Gardens of Eden in which all animals are perfectly content (136).

Zoos are immediately paralleled with religion in this defence, as Pi states: "I know zoos are no longer in people's good graces. Religion faces the same problem. Certain illusions about freedom plague them both" (Martel 21). While Pi does not specifically state what the illusion about freedom that plagues religion is, it is evident that he does not feel constrained by religion at all. On the contrary, Pi has an inherent curiosity for learning about different religions; he becomes a practising Hindu, Christian, and Muslim all at once. Rather than choosing a single religion, he clings to his freedom to "love God" however he wants (74). Correspondingly, he asks his father both for a prayer rug and to be baptized. For Pi, embracing religion is a liberating experience. Indeed, along with his connection to animals, religion is one of the main pillars of Pi's identity formation from the early days of his childhood.

Badica 4

Pi's connection to animals undoubtedly informs his initial account of his time at sea. In the confined space of the lifeboat, the species boundary Pi observed in his childhood crumbles, and he recognizes a potent animality in himself. Previously a "puny, feeble, vegetarian life form" (203), Pi must now kill in order to survive. Over time, he "develop[s] an instinct, a feel, for what to do" (216). He asserts that he "descended to a level of savagery [he] never imagined possible" (238). As the days go by, his clothes rot away, and he is forced to live "stark naked except for the whistle that dangled from [his] neck by a string" (213). Yet perhaps the most potent moment that crumbles the species boundary is when Pi realizes, "with a pinching of the heart," that he had begun to eat "like an animal, that the noisy, frantic unchewing, wolfing-down of [his] was exactly the way Richard Parker ate" (250). This recognition of his animality becomes crucial to Pi's perspective and his identity.

Nevertheless, although the species boundary is certainly blurred, it is never fully crossed. One of the chief mechanisms that allow Pi to maintain a semblance of his humanity is his devotion to religion. Each day, he carefully says his prayers as part of the schedule that he creates for himself. Additionally, although many of the differences between Richard Parker and Pi collapse over the period of their co-existence in the lifeboat, their reactions to lightning during a thunderstorm illustrate that the species boundary is preserved (Mensch 138). While Pi is "dazed . . . but not afraid" and praises Allah, interpreting the storm as "an outbreak of divinity," Richard

Badica   5

Parker trembles and hides in fear (138). Thus, the crucial pillar that religion represents in Pi's identity never falters; as a result, it prevents the species boundary from completely collapsing. Ultimately, Pi's effort to understand Richard Parker, a feat that is necessary for his survival, leads Pi to gain a deeper understanding of his own identity. As Martel explains, it is in "understanding the other [that] you eventually understand yourself" (Sielke 20).

The relationship between animality and divinity is explored in a different manner when it comes to considerations of which of Pi's accounts is "the better story" (Martel 352). As Stratton argues, the two conflicting stories highlight the novel's "philosophical debate about the modern world's privileging of reason over imagination, science over religion, materialism over idealism, fact over fiction" (6). The two sides of the debate are embodied in the characters of Mr. Okamoto and Mr. Chiba, who initially have very different responses to Pi's story. For Mr. Okamoto, an individual who exemplifies the view of truth as an objective reality that can be uncovered and verified by the methods of science (Stratton 6), the story with animals is "incredible" (Martel 328), "too hard to believe" (329), and "very unlikely" (332) at first. Mr. Chiba, who represents Romanticism and its emphasis on spontaneity, subjectivity, imaginative creativity, and emotion (Stratton 7), immediately favours the animal version, exclaiming "What a story!" (Martel 345).

While Pi recognizes the importance of reason as a practical tool, asserting that "Reason is excellent for getting food, clothing and shelter" and for "keeping the tigers away," he also cautions: "be excessively reasonable and you risk throwing out the universe with the bathwater" (331). The debate comes to a climax when both Mr. Okamoto and Mr. Chiba answer Pi's question about "the better story":

> So tell me, . . . which story do you prefer? Which is the better
> story, the story with animals or the story without animals?
>
> Mr. Okamoto: "That's an interesting question. . . ."
>
> Mr. Chiba: "The story with animals."
>
> Mr. Okamoto: "Yes. The story with animals is the better story."
>
> Pi Patel: "Thank you. And so it goes with God." (352)

Mr. Okamoto's willingness to recognize the story with animals as the better one demonstrates a change in his own identity, one that Stratton identifies as a development of his imaginative capacity (8). Martel himself has stated that the mechanism of faith uses both imagination and reason (Sielke 25), the principal elements of the story with animals.

However, what is most crucial is the analogy that Pi introduces after having deconstructed the reason–imagination binary. The created link between the story with animals and religious belief illustrates that God's existence occupies the same status in relation to truth and reality as does Pi's experience of shipwreck. In this way, "God's existence is a better story than the one told by those who doubt or deny His being: atheists lack imagination and miss the better story" (Martel 6).

Stewart Cole takes issue with the comparison between believing in the story with animals and believing in God, arguing that it is "problematic in failing to recognize the difference between believing in a story—that is, acknowledging its aesthetic impact—and believing in God" (23). Cole also points out that to conflate these two types of belief is to obliterate the important epistemological distinction between subjective and objective truth, a distinction that he identifies as crucial to discussions of religion (24). However, what this view fails to take into account is that Martel's aim is to justify a belief in God's existence rather than to prove God's existence, and—as with the acceptance of the first of Pi's accounts as the better story—such faith might require a suspension of disbelief.

As Martel has argued, "religion operates in the same exact way a novel operates. . . . For a good novel to work, you have to suspend your disbelief. . . . Exactly the same thing happens with religion" (Steinmetz 18). Martel also asserts that religion works the same way as a novel does in that it makes its recipients suspend their disbelief so that factual truth becomes irrelevant (Sielke 24). He cautions that this does not mean that facts are ignored, but rather that "it's more how you interpret the facts and how much you value facts that affect the totality of your sense experience"; therefore, "to say that the book will make you believe in fiction . . . isn't very far from saying it'll make you believe in God" (24). He also emphasizes that it is acceptable to say that God is a fiction if you understand that "this doesn't necessarily mean that this fiction doesn't exist. It just exists

Badica 8

in a way that is only accessed through the imagination" (25). This view parallels the importance of imagination in Pi's first account of his survival narrative. In particular, "empathetic imagination" (25)—the ability to place oneself in another's shoes—is the crux of the story with animals; the co-existence of Pi's human intelligence with Richard Parker's animal intelligence allows Pi to examine and gain a deeper understanding of his own identity.

While the story with animals is the one that presents the enriching facet of the empathetic imagination, the second account and the implications of the first story being untrue have their own value. Several critics have interpreted Richard Parker as the outward manifestation of an internal split. As Robert Rogers notes, an individual suffering from internal conflict often grapples with contradictory impulses by "developing separate personality constellations" (109). Trauma theory explains that severe trauma explodes the cohesion of consciousness, and that "when a survivor creates a fully realized narrative that brings together the shattered knowledge of what happened and the emotions that were aroused by the meanings of the events, the survivor pieces back together the fragmentation of consciousness that trauma has caused" (Shay 188). Therefore, the second account suggests that the first account is Pi's attempt at recovery through the narration of experience and a coping mechanism in light of the trauma that he has suffered.

In a stark comparison to the first version, the story without animals portrays a view of life that is centred on greed, cruelty, corruption, and futility. God is notably left out of the picture, and human beings are completely alone and exiled from the comfort of religion. Thus, the second account demonstrates how even the most pacifist, devoted, and idealistic of men can be led to savagery in extenuating circumstances. While the story without animals contains its own intrinsic value, its lack of the co-existence of animal and human intelligences does not permit for either the fulfillment of the empathetic imagination (Sielke 25) or a connection between animality and divinity, two elements that remain crucial to Pi's identity.

While it is undeniable that, of Pi's two accounts, the story with animals is a feel-good tale of courage, endurance, and intelligence, and the story without animals is a horrifying description of human savagery and desperation, this difference appears only on the surface. The facet of the first account that is most significant and most illuminating is that the co-existence of human and animal intelligence is crucial to the process of identity formation and motivation for spiritual belief. Highlighting the link between animality and divinity, an empathetic imagination allows for the ignition of the "spark that brings to life a real story" (Martel vii), thereby representing the key to a holistic understanding not only of oneself, but of all subsequent social interactions that determine identity construction.

Works Cited

Cole, Stewart. "Believing in Tigers: Anthropomorphism and Incredulity in Yann Martel's *Life of Pi*." *Studies in Canadian Literature*, vol. 29, no. 2, 2004, pp. 22–36.

Martel, Yann. *Life of Pi*. Random House, 2001.

Mensch, James. "The Intertwining of Incommensurables: Yann Martel's *Life of Pi*." *Phenomenology and the Non-Human Animal: At the Limits of Experience*, edited by Corinne Painter and Christian Lotz, Springer, 2007, pp. 135–47.

Rogers, Robert. *A Psychoanalytic Study of the Double in Literature*. Wayne State UP, 1970.

Shay, Jonathan. *Achilles in Vietnam: Combat Trauma and the Undoing of Character*. Touchstone, 1994.

Sielke, Sabine. "'The Empathetic Imagination': An Interview with Yann Martel." *Canadian Literature*, no. 177, Summer 2003, pp. 12–32, canlit.ca/article/the-empathetic-imagination/.

Steinmetz, Andrew. "Pi: Summing Up Meaning from the Irrational: An Interview with Yann Martel." *Books in Canada*, vol. 31, no. 6, Sept. 2002, p. 18.

Stratton, Florence. "'Hollow at the Core': Deconstructing Yann Martel's *Life of Pi*." *Studies in Canadian Literature*, vol. 29, no. 2, 2004, pp. 5–21.

Wood, James. "Credulity." *London Review of Books*, vol. 24, no. 22, Nov. 2002, www.lrb.co.uk/v24/n22/james-wood/credulity.

79b The Name–Date Method (APA Style)

The name–date system is detailed in the sixth edition of the *Publication Manual of the American Psychological Association* (2010). Using this system, you provide a short parenthetical reference in the text, and you list all sources in a reference list at the end of your paper:

sample in-text citation	sample reference-list entry
Our understanding of national identity must allow for "the expression of diverse types of identities within the public space" (Winter, 2011, p. 3).	Winter, E. (2011). *Us, them, and others: Pluralism and national identity in diverse societies.* Toronto, ON: University of Toronto Press.

Here are some examples of name–date parenthetical references, followed by some examples of reference-list entries.

In-Text Citations

In-text citations generally begin with the author's last name followed by a comma and the date the source was published. If the reference is to a general argument or evidence presented by the entire work, list only the author's last name and the year of publication:

> **National identity is deeply connected to a sense that there is a boundary between those who belong to a nation and those who do not (Winter, 2011).**

But if you refer to a particular part of the source, or if you quote from it, supply the relevant page number or numbers, preceded by the abbreviation "p." (for a single page) or "pp." (for a page range):

> **As Elke Winter (2011) notes, "a pluralist 'national we' is bounded by opposition to a real or imagined 'Others' with a capital O" (p. 5).**

As the above example shows, you do not need to repeat the author's name in the parenthetical citation if you have provided his or her name elsewhere in the sentence.

Author *Title* *Publication information* *Electronic source*

A Work by One or Two Authors

For works by one or two authors, include the surname of each author every time you refer to the source:

> One study has found that progressive discipline in education "has the potential to enhance students' social and behaviour literacy" (Milne & Aurini, 2015, p. 51).

A Work by Three or More Authors

If the work has three, four, or five authors, list the surname of each author the first time you cite the work. In later citations to the same work, provide the surname of the first author followed by "et al.":

> Effective research requires more effort than simply searching for resources on the Internet (Messenger, de Bruyn, Brown, & Montagnes, 2017, p. 384). Wherever you conduct your research, make sure to avoid plagiarism by staying organized and taking notes on all sources you consult (Messenger et al., 2017, p. 384).

If the work has six or more authors, give the surname of the first author followed by "et al." each time you cite the work, including the first.

A Work by a Government Agency or a Corporate Author

If a work lists an agency or an organization as its author, provide the name of the agency or organization in the usual author position:

> Statistics Canada (2015) has found that for most young Canadians, "the process of identifying and narrowing career expectations lasts beyond adolescence and well into adulthood" (p. 4).

A Work by an Anonymous Author

For an article with no known author, include a short version of the title:

> The most expensive white diamond ever bought at auction is "the 118.28-carat oval-cut gem that sold . . . for $30.6 million [USD] in 2013" ("The Colors of Money," 2015, p. 34).

Author   *Title*   Publication information   Electronic source

A Work of Scripture

For a work of scripture, provide the name and number of the book and/
or section you are referencing, along with the standard name of the version or edition:

> **In the biblical account of the Flood, Noah is described as "a just man
> and perfect in his generations" (Gen. 6:9 King James Version).**

Note that you do not need to include a work of scripture in the reference
list if you have consulted a widely available version, such as the King
James Version of the Bible.

An Audio or Audiovisual Recording

For an audio or audiovisual recording such as a song, a motion picture, a television program, a podcast, or an online video, provide the
last name(s) of the contributor(s) or the name of the group listed at the
beginning of the corresponding reference-list entry (see pages 348–349)
and the date. If you are citing a direct quotation, also include the time at
which the quotation begins in the original source, as displayed in your
media player:

> **In a recent lecture, primatologist Jane Goodall offered the following
> inspirational words: "Each and every one of us makes a difference
> each and every day, and we have a choice what kind of difference
> we're going to make" (Concordia University, 2014, 53:28).**

An Online Document with No Page Numbers

If you need to cite a specific portion of an online document that does
not have page numbers, count the paragraphs following the title or a
heading and assign a number to the relevant paragraph:

> **Law professor Michael Geist argues that "the emergence of new voices
> and the innovative approaches at older ones point to the likelihood that
> journalism is neither dead nor dying" (Geist, 2016, para. 12).**

If you begin counting after a heading, include the first few words of the
heading after the year:

Author   *Title*   Publication information   Electronic source

The organization describes its guiding principle on its website: "CPAWS believes that by ensuring the health of the parts, we ensure the health of the whole" (Canadian Parks and Wilderness Society, n.d., "Our Vision," para. 1).

In this example, "n.d." indicates that no date of publication was provided.

An Entire Website

If you refer to an entire website, you can include the site's URL in the text:

World Wildlife Fund Canada provides a number of recent news reports on its website (http://www.wwf.ca).

In such a case, you do not need to list the source in the reference list.

A Message on a Social Media Site

If you need to cite a publicly available message posted to Twitter, Facebook, Google+, or some other social media site, provide the last name of the person who posted the message followed by the year:

The prime minister has promised that "Canada will once again demonstrate real leadership on a number of United Nations priorities" (Trudeau, 2016).

If the message was posted by an organization, provide the name of the organization followed by the year. And if it is a private message, treat it as you would treat an email (see below).

A Personal Email or Letter

For an email, a letter, or some other form of personal communication, provide the name of the author, the description "personal communication," and the full date on which the message was sent:

Henry Smith (personal communication, November 12, 2016) explained that his idea for the book came from a customer complaint.

Do not include a personal communication in the reference list.

Author   Title   Publication information   Electronic source

Quotation at Second Hand

If you must cite a quotation at second hand—for example, if you cannot find the original work that another author has cited—include the name of the original author and the title and date of publication for the original work (if known), and give a citation for the secondary source:

> **As Edward Said observed in *Culture and Imperialism* (1994): "No one today is purely *one* thing" (as cited in Winter, 2011, p. 213).**

Multiple Works by Different Authors

If you cite more than one work in a single parenthetical citation, order the entries alphabetically and separate them with a semicolon:

> **Several recent studies have looked at the ways in which Inuit peoples are adapting to the loss of sea ice in the Arctic (Meier et al., 2014; Pearce, Ford, Willox, & Smit, 2015).**

The first reference is to a journal article written by twelve authors; the second is to an article with four authors.

Multiple Works by the Same Author

If you cite two or more works by the same author, list the dates chronologically and separate them with commas (e.g., "Whitley, 2013, 2015, 2017"). When citing more than one work by the same author published in the same year, include lowercase letters to distinguish between the works:

> **Sport can be a useful tool for international development, but it must be used with care to avoid reinforcing social and political biases within a community (Darnell, 2010a, 2010b).**

Note that the letters must correspond to those assigned in the reference list (see below).

Reference List

The reference list appears at the end of your paper and includes the full publication information for all works that you have cited. It should begin on a new page, with the title "References" centred at the top. Each entry should be formatted with a hanging indent—that is, with the first line set flush left and the second and subsequent lines indented a few letter spaces, as shown below.

***

Author **Title** **Publication information** **Electronic source**

List entries in alphabetical order, according to the surname of the author, editor, or other creator whose name appears first. If no author or creator is named, alphabetize the entry by the first significant word in the title (ignore an initial *A*, *An*, or *The*). List works by the same author(s) or creator(s) chronologically, with the earliest article listed first. Arrange works by the same author or creator published in the same year alphabetically by title, and assign a letter to each entry, following the year:

Darnell, S. (2010a). Power, politics and "sport for development and peace": Investigating the utility of sport for international development. *Sociology of Sport Journal, 27*(1), 54–75.

Darnell, S. (2010b). Sport, race, and biopolitics: Encounters with difference in "sport for development and peace" internships. *Journal of Sport & Social Issues, 34*(4), 396–417.

Note that initials are used in place of authors' or creators' given names. Also note how the titles are capitalized. In most titles, including titles of journal articles and books, only proper nouns and the first word of a title or a subtitle are capitalized. However, in titles of periodicals (e.g., journals, magazines, and newspapers), all words except for prepositions (see #22), articles (see #19c), and conjunctions (see #23) are capitalized.

If a work has seven or fewer authors or creators, include each person's surname and initial(s). For a work with eight or more authors or creators, list the first six names followed by three ellipsis points and the final name (e.g., "Lam, G. F., Diaz, J. S., Castillo, G., Cooper, C., Reyes, H. N., Thorpe, J. R., . . . Li, B. F.").

APA STYLE

Treatment of Number Ranges

When you give a number range (e.g., a range of page numbers) in APA style, provide all numbers in full: 5–88, 108–122, 285–485.

A Print Book (Standard Reference)

1	2		3

Winter, E. (2011). Us, them, and others: Pluralism and national identity in diverse societies. Toronto, ON: University of Toronto Press.

	4	5

| Author | Title | Publication information | Electronic source |

A standard reference entry for a book includes

1. the author's name (surname, followed by a comma, and first initial or initials, followed by a period);
2. the year of publication, enclosed in parentheses and followed by a period (if the work does not list a date, write "n.d.");
3. the title of the book (italicized), followed by a period;
4. the city and province (or state) of publication, separated by a comma and followed by a colon; and
5. the name of the publisher, followed by a period.

In the publisher's name, omit unnecessary words such as *Inc.*, *Ltd.*, *Co.*, and *Publishers*, but retain the words *Books* and *Press*. If the publisher is located outside of Canada or the United States, include the full name of the country in place of the province or state abbreviation. And if the name of the province or state is included within the publisher's name, you can omit the abbreviation (e.g., "Calgary: University of Alberta Press")

An Electronic Book (Standard Reference)

If you have used an electronic version of a book that appears in print, add a description of the version (if applicable) in square brackets following the title, and include the book's DOI (digital object identifier; if available) or the URL of the site from which you retrieved the book:

Kastrup, H., & Mallow, J. V. (2016). *Student attitudes, student anxieties, and how to address them: A handbook for science teachers.* doi:10.1088/978-1-6817-4265-6

Todd, P. (2014). *Extreme mean: Ending cyberabuse at work, school, and home* [Adobe DRM version]. Retrieved from https://store.kobobooks.com

For a book that appears only online, include the retrieval information:

Stevens, K. (n.d.). *The dreamer and the beast.* Retrieved from http://www.onlineoriginals.com/showitem.asp?itemID=321

In this case, the abbreviation "n.d." signifies that no publication date was given for the book.

Author   *Title*   Publication information   Electronic source

APA STYLE

Citing Electronic Sources

When you cite an electronic source in APA style, include the work's digital object identifier (DOI) or, if there is no DOI assigned to the work, the uniform resource locator (URL) of the site where you found the work. For an electronic journal article with no DOI, include the URL for the journal's homepage. If you need to break a DOI or a URL across two or more lines, do so *before* a punctuation mark; do not add a hyphen. Note that you do not need to include the date you accessed the site.

A Work by a Government Agency or a Corporate Author

Begin with the name of the agency or organization listed as author. If the publication has been given an identifying number, include that number in parentheses after the title. If the publisher is the same as the author, use "Author" in place of the publisher's name:

Statistics Canada. (2015, January 27). *Career decision-making patterns of Canadian youth and associated postsecondary educational outcomes* (Catalogue No. 81-599-X-No.10). Ottawa, ON: Author.

If you accessed the document online, include the publication's URL in place of the publication information:

Statistics Canada. (2015, January 27). *Career decision-making patterns of Canadian youth and associated postsecondary educational outcomes* (Catalogue No. 81-599-X–No. 10). Retrieved from http://publications .gc.ca/collections/collection_2015/statcan/81-599-x/81-599-x2015010 -eng.pdf

A Work with an Editor in Place of an Author

If the work lists an editor in place of an author, add the abbreviation "Ed." after the editor's name:

Marcus, G. (Ed.). (2006). *The Norton Psychology Reader.* New York: W. W. Norton.

For multiple editors, use "Eds."

Author   *Title*   Publication information   Electronic source

A Work with No Identified Author

If no person or group is identified as the author or editor, use the title of the work in place of the author's name:

The Colors of Money. (2015, November 23). *Forbes*, 196(7), 34.

A Book in Translation

Add the name of the translator and the abbreviation "Trans." (enclosed in parentheses) after the title:

Piaget, J. (1952). *The Origins of Intelligence in Children* (M. Cook, Trans.). New York, NY: International Universities Press.

An Edition Other Than the First

For a second or subsequent edition, include the edition number after the title:

Gasher, M., Skinner, D., and Lorimer, R. (2016). *Mass communication in Canada* (8th ed.). Toronto, ON: Oxford University Press.

A Multivolume Work

For a work published in multiple volumes, include the number(s) of the volume or volumes you have referenced after the title:

Dutch, S. I. (Ed.). (2010). *Encyclopedia of global warming* (Vols. 1–3). Pasadena, CA: Salem Press.

If the volumes were published in different years, use the date range as the year of publication (e.g., "2010–2017"). If you have referenced only one volume and the volume number appears in the title, do not repeat the volume number in parentheses.

A Chapter or Article in an Edited Book

Begin with the name of the article's author, followed by the year of publication, the title of the article, the name of the book's editors, the title of the book (in italics), the pages on which the article appears (enclosed in parentheses), and the publisher's location and name:

Author   *Title*   Publication information   Electronic source

Macdonald, L., & Ruckert, A. (2014). Continental shift? Rethinking Canadian aid to the Americas. In S. Brown, M. den Heyer, & D. R. Black (Eds.), *Rethinking Canadian aid* (pp. 125–142). Ottawa, ON: University of Ottawa Press.

If the author is not listed—as might be the case in a reference book, for example—begin with the title of the article followed by the date.

A Journal Article

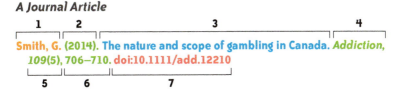

A standard reference-list entry for a journal article includes

1. the author's name (surname, followed by a comma, and first initial or initials, followed by a period);
2. the year of publication, enclosed in parentheses and followed by a period;
3. the title of the article, with only first words and proper nouns capitalized, followed by a period;
4. the title of the journal, italicized, with all words other than prepositions, articles, and conjunctions capitalized, followed by a comma;
5. the volume number, italicized (and, if applicable, the issue number, in parentheses and followed by a comma);
6. the pages on which the article appears, followed by a period; and
7. the digital object identifier (DOI).

Note that there is no space between a volume number and an issue number, there is no space after the colon that introduces the DOI, and there is no period after the DOI.

   If you have retrieved an article online but it has not been assigned a DOI, include the URL for the journal's homepage:

Milne, E., & Aurini, J. (2015). Schools, cultural mobility, and social reproduction: The case of progressive discipline. *Canadian Journal of Sociology, 40*(1), 51–74. Retrieved from http://ejournals.library .ualberta.ca/index.php/CJS/article/view/20891/18038

Author   *Title*   Publication information   Electronic source

If you have accessed an article online before it has been officially published, add "Advance online publication" and a period before the DOI or the "Retrieved from" statement. If you have referenced a printed article, provide the standard publication information:

Willoughby, B. J., & Belt, D. (2016). Marital orientation and relationship well-being among cohabiting couples. *Journal of Family Psychology, 30*(2), 181–192.

For an abstract, add "[Abstract]" immediately before the period at the end of the article's title.

A Magazine Article

Treat an article from a magazine as you would treat an article from a journal, but note that a magazine's publication date often includes the day and month of publication:

McLaren, L. (2016, January 11). Workers of the world, commute! *Maclean's, 129*(1), 32.

For a magazine article you accessed online, include the DOI; if no DOI has been assigned to the article, include the URL of the magazine's homepage:

Gatehouse, J. (2014, September 5). Why we need to clear our cluttered minds. *Maclean's.* Retrieved from http://www.macleans.ca

Here there is no volume or issue number because the magazine does not assign these numbers to the articles it publishes online.

A Newspaper Article

Treat a print newspaper article as you would treat an article from a print journal or magazine, but add "p." or "pp." before the page number or numbers:

Parkinson, D. (2016, April 7). Carbon-tax revenue isn't dirty money. *The Globe and Mail*, p. B2.

Author   *Title*   **Publication information**   **Electronic source**

For an online newspaper article, include the URL of the newspaper's homepage:

Plunkett, M. (2016, March 17). Millennials: The running generation. *The National Post*. Retrieved from http://www.nationalpost.com

An Editorial

Newspaper and magazine editorials are often not attributed to a particular writer or editor. When this is the case, begin with the title:

Why don't kids walk to school any more? [Editorial]. (2016, April 7). *The Globe and Mail*, p. A14.

A Thesis or a Dissertation from a Database

For a thesis or a dissertation, include the author's name, the date, the work's title, the description "Doctoral dissertation" or "Master's thesis" (in parentheses), and the retrieval information:

De Riggi, M. (2015). *Non-suicidal self-injury, online activity and emotional health among adolescents* (Master's thesis). Available from Theses Canada. (AMICUS No. 44230969)

If you accessed the document from a website rather than a database, include the website's URL (preceded by "Retrieved from") in place of the database information.

A Music Recording

Include the name of the writer or composer, the copyright year, the title of the song and/or album, the name of the performer (if different from the writer or composer), the medium (in square brackets), the music label's location and name, and the year of recording (if different from the copyright year):

Cohen, L. (1967). Sisters of mercy [Recorded by Serena Ryder]. On *If your memory serves you well* [CD]. Toronto, ON: EMI. (2006)

Author   *Title*   Publication information   Electronic source

A Motion Picture

List the producer and the director, the year of release, the title, the medium (in square brackets), the country of origin, and the studio's name:

Din, R. (Producer), & Baichwal, J. (Director). (2012). *Payback* [Motion picture]. Canada: National Film Board of Canada.

A Television Program

For a television program, include the names of the writer and the director, the year of release, the title, a description of the medium (in square brackets), and the location and name of the broadcasting network. If the program is an episode in a series, include the title of the episode, the name of the series' executive producer(s), and the title of the series:

Booth, A. (Writer), & Snow, R. (Director). (2016). The equalizer [Television series episode]. In R. Lang & K. Kähler (Executive producers), *The Nature of Things*. Toronto, ON: Canadian Broadcasting Corporation.

A YouTube Video

For a video from YouTube or a similar video-sharing website, provide the screen name of the person or organization that posted the video followed by the date on which the video was posted, the title of the video, the medium (in square brackets), and the URL:

Concordia University. (2014, June 10). *Jane Goodall at Concordia: Sowing the Seeds of Hope* [Video file]. Retrieved from https://www.youtube.com/watch?v=vibssrQKm60

If the real name of the person who posted the video differs from her or his screen name and is known, provide the person's real name first, followed by the screen name in square brackets:

Lynch, G. [garrett414]. (2013, July 28). *Marshall McLuhan—The global village* [Video file]. Retrieved from https://www.youtube.com/watch?v=AepP7dNp9YY

A Podcast

List the name of the producer, the date of release, the title of the podcast, the medium (in square brackets), and the URL of the podcast's homepage:

Jensen, K. (Producer). (2015, November 29). *Canadaland* [Audio podcast]. Retrieved from http://canadalandshow.com/podcast/

Author   *Title*   **Publication information**   **Electronic source**

A Blog Post

Provide the author's name, the date on which the content was posted, the title of the post, a description of the format (in square brackets), and the retrieval information:

Geist, M. (2016, February 12). Why journalism is not dying in the digital age [Web log post]. Retrieved from http://www.michaelgeist.ca/2016/02 /why-journalism-is-not-dying-in-the-digital-age/

If the author's real name is not given in connection with the blog post, begin with the author's screen name or the name of the organization for which the author has written the post. If you are citing a reader's comment on a blog post, use the description "Web log comment."

A Tweet

For a tweet from an individual, begin with the author's name followed by her or his screen name (in square brackets). Then provide the date on which the message was tweeted, the full text of the tweet (up to the first 40 words), a brief description of the format (in square brackets), and the retrieval information:

Garneau, M. [MarcGarneau]. (2016, January 25). Air turbulence can be unexpected and stronger than expected. My advice: keep your seat belt on all the time and you'll be fine [Tweet]. Retrieved from https://twitter .com/marcgarneau/status/691587167945031680

If the author has not provided his or her real name, begin with the screen name without brackets.

If the tweet was released by an organization, begin with the organization's full name followed by its screen name (in square brackets):

World Health Organization [WHO]. (2016, April 6). Worldwide 1 adult in 11 has #diabetes. And this number is growing fast [Tweet]. Retrieved from https://twitter.com/who/status/717749881390153728

A Facebook Status Update

For a Facebook status update from an individual, begin with the author's name; to help readers identify the right person among the more than one billion people who use Facebook, provide the author's full first name in square brackets following her or his first initial. Then provide the date on which the update was posted, the content of the message (up to the first 40 words), a brief description of the format (in square brackets), and the retrieval information:

Trudeau, J. [Justin]. (2016, March 16). Canada will once again demonstrate real leadership on a number of United Nations priorities [Facebook status update]. Retrieved from https://www.facebook.com/JustinPJTrudeau /videos/10154133901320649/

If the status update was released by an organization, use the organization's full name as the author name:

Dalhousie University. (2016, January 6). Dalhousie alumnus George Elliott Clarke (MA '89, LLD '99) named Canada's new parliamentary poet laureate [Facebook status update]. Retrieved from https://www.facebook.com /DalhousieUniversity/posts/10153127363126899?fref=nf

A Google+ Post

Treat a Google+ post as you would treat a Facebook status update, but use "Google+ post" as the description of the format:

Willer, P. [Patrick]. (2016, May 10). Rapport increases respect and understanding, which lead to trust and affinity, which leads to better collaboration. And that empowers our ability to execute our goals [Google+ post]. Retrieved from https://plus.google.com/+PatrickWiller /posts/VrBSBkcAHrZ

Material from a Website

For web-based material that does not fit into any of the categories described above, include the author, the date (or "n.d." if no date of publication is provided), the title, a short description of the format, and the retrieval information:

Canadian Parks and Wilderness Society. (n.d.). About [Online statement]. Retrieved from http://www.cpaws.org/about

---

Author   *Title*   Publication information   Electronic source

A Personal Email or Letter

Do not include in your reference list emails, letters, or other forms of personal communication that your reader would not be able to access. Rather, cite personal communications directly in the body of your essay; see page 436 for an example.

A Sample APA Research Paper

The research paper presented below was written and formatted according to the guidelines set out in the sixth edition of the *Publication Manual of the American Psychological Association*. Note that it begins with a title page. At the top of this page is a running header that displays the title of the paper (in full caps) on the left and the page number on the right. This header repeats on each page of the essay. In the upper half of the title page sit the title of the paper, the author's name, and the name of the author's university or college. These details appear on separate, double-spaced lines. If your professor asks you to include additional information such as the name and code of your course or the date of submission, add this information where she or he instructs you to do so.

If you are required to provide an abstract, do this on the first page following your title page. The heading "Abstract" should appear centred at the top of the page, and the abstract itself should provide a brief summary of your paper. In some cases, you may be required to add a list of keywords following the main paragraph of the abstract. If you aren't sure what to include in the abstract, ask your instructor.

Repeat your title on the first page of the essay itself, immediately before your first paragraph. Make sure to double-space your paper, and indent the first line of all paragraphs, including the first. Your margins should be approximately 1 inch (2.5 cm) all around; in most cases, you can use the default settings of your word-processing program. Do not justify the right margin, and avoid breaking words at the ends of lines.

Begin your reference list on a new page at the end of your paper. Centre the title "References" at the top of the page, and list the entries in alphabetical order. Each entry should be set with a hanging indent, so that the first line begins at the left-hand margin and the second and subsequent lines are indented.

The Power of Sociological Knowledge

Kasia Bulgarski

University of Toronto

The Power of Sociological Knowledge

Sociology offers valuable tools for deconstructing and analyzing the social constructs and ideologies embedded in our societal framework. The sociological perspective is useful in a variety of real-world contexts, as it seeks to interpret and understand human behaviour. It also has the potential to help restructure inequalities faced within society. Yet sociologists, particularly in their roles as makers and disseminators of sociological knowledge, must be careful to avoid losing their objectivity. This goal is crucial in the classroom, where students depend on instructors to put aside personal biases and create an environment that promotes critical engagement and independent thought. Sociological knowledge is most powerful when it is constructed and shared in open-minded, forward-thinking, socially aware manners.

People inevitably view the world through personal lenses. Often, these lenses are influenced by individual biases that can inhibit inclusive, solutions-oriented thinking. Such biases—whether they are overt or implicit—are particularly dangerous when they are revealed by educators within the classroom. Weber (1919/1946) argues that, while teachers will never entirely eliminate their personal opinions regarding a subject, imposing personal judgments on students is certainly not part of an educator's job (p. 146). Moreover, Weber continues, the potential for students to fully understand facts no longer exists when the teacher reveals bias while teaching. Indeed, the teacher's primary role should be to encourage students to be aware of facts that oppose their opinions (Weber, p. 147). Teachers should stimulate open discussion in the

THE POWER OF SOCIOLOGICAL KNOWLEDGE   3

classroom rather than obstructing such discussion with their personal judgments. Therefore, the teacher is not a leader (Weber, p. 150) but an enthusiast within a conversation about society.

Weber also examines religion as a force that fosters moral judgment regarding matters of society (p. 149). He argues that Christian moral fervor has blinded society for thousands of years and led to compromises and relative judgments. In a recent article on the debate over sharia law, Razack (2007) explores how academics might unknowingly reinforce the colour line and the secular–religious divide (p. 4). She discusses a presentation on honour killings that she attended in Europe (pp. 3–4). She notes that the keynote speaker began by presenting photographs taken at the funeral of a Kurdish woman who was killed by her father because he did not approve of her going to live with a non-Kurdish man. Razack was puzzled by the exploitation involved in showing the woman's dead body to an audience of over three hundred, mostly white, Western academics. Overall, the presentation misrepresented Muslims as barbaric and Westerners as civilized. As a result of the presenter's implicit bias, the audience became morally outraged instead of motivated to deconstruct the embedded social inequalities that had led to the woman's death in the first place.

Unfortunately, the prejudice that Razack experienced is not uncommon, and similar projections of bias can be found even in the field of sociology. Becker (2007) writes that sociologists frequently seek to understand the social structure by looking for problematic situations (p. 129). In doing so, they may take on the role of the storyteller,

THE POWER OF SOCIOLOGICAL KNOWLEDGE   4

which traditionally involves taking sides by introducing a hero and a villain. Users of this knowledge become captivated by the maker's report; they imagine that what they are hearing or reading is based on systematically gathered materials from the "real world" and, as a result, they fail to tackle the underlying issues (Becker, 2007, p. 144).

Moral judgments are sometimes apparent in the words researchers choose when they describe social phenomenon. Becker (2007) discusses the "labeling theory" of deviance, noting that many critics oppose the relativism associated with the term "deviant" (p. 145). He uses the example of murder and questions whether or not such an act would be classified as "very deviant." Significantly, labels such as "deviant" are applied not only in relation to community standards, but also in connection with scientific standards (Becker, p. 145). Thus, it is important to deconstruct the terms used within the field of sociology, as they can signify underlying biases.

Researchers, as makers of knowledge, must also avoid biasing their reports through the misrepresentation or fictionalization of facts. As Becker (2007) observes, "makers incorporate reasons for users to accept what they present as true" (p. 111). Thus, users must rely on makers to be accurate in the presentation of information. Becker uses journalists as an example of knowledge-makers who at times provide the public with accounts that are distorted through the subtraction or addition of factual information (p. 130). In such instances, the individual bias of the makers becomes insidious, and readers are unknowingly affected through this process (Becker, p. 133). Such misrepresentation may also happen implicitly within scholarly sources. Thus, academics must retain

THE POWER OF SOCIOLOGICAL KNOWLEDGE   5

the responsibility of providing the users of their knowledge with factual and accurate reports of the human condition.

Further, Becker (2007) notes that "representations are made in a world of cooperating users and makers" (p. 30). He writes that makers do most of the work, leaving users to interpret and theorize on the data. This relationship may be problematic: the freedom of interpretation allotted to users is somewhat of an illusion, as the makers have not left much room for interpretation (Becker, p. 30). Statistics, for example, have little value on their own; their significance must be *interpreted.* The researcher's method of coding data, finding variables, creating labels, and so on effectively tells users how to interpret the data. Thus, in order to give the user a full picture, researchers should provide users with accurate explanations of how they chose their variables, why they felt that the variables are important, and why they chose to leave out other possible variables.

Similarly, teachers of sociological research have the responsibility of forcing students to develop their critical-thinking skills. Vaughn (2005) explains that teaching critical thinking helps transform students from passive learners into active learners (p. xvii). The focus of critical thinking is the basis of a belief, not the question of whether something is worth believing. It is the systematic evaluation of statements, by means of rational standards (Vaughn, 2005, pp. 3–4). Critical thinking leads to understanding, knowledge, self-improvement, and, ultimately, empowerment. For students and researchers, empowerment comes from the ability to actively participate in the sociological examination of societal inequalities and ideologies.

As Lemert (2004) notes, reflecting on Michel Foucault's theory of knowledge as power, knowledge is empowering in that it breaks down the binary opposition between the ruler and the ruled (p. 466). In terms of the classroom experience, knowledge breaks down the barrier between the teacher and the student. Ideally, students can attain power by deliberating openly, from an informed perspective, amongst themselves and with the teacher.

In a recent interview, Stuart Hall has described the learning process as a journey (de Peuter, 2007, p. 117). In the beginning, the teacher is in an elevated position because he or she has been to a place that the learner has not yet experienced; over time, as the learner searches for and eventually finds the source of knowledge that the teacher possesses, the relationship becomes more equal (de Peuter, 2007, p. 117). Yet the burden of achieving this goal does not rest solely on the student. Educators must not only disseminate the knowledge they possess, but also recognize the cultural framework of the student and work to overcome the existence of social hierarchies embedded in the learning process; ultimately, they can do this by progressively equalizing the dialogue throughout the relationship with the learner (de Peuter, 2007, p. 118).

Neave (2000) explains that universities, in particular, have always been required to preserve, develop, and provide individuals with knowledge (p. xiii). The more society expects from the institutions of higher learning, the more complex the responsibility of academics becomes. Neave suggests that academics should analyze whether or not their research has improved the understanding of social inequalities (p. 67). Furthermore, educators should assess whether the students have been able to grasp the message that was initially sent out regarding the importance of societal matters at hand (Neave, 2000, p. 67). Thus, just as academics must focus on the needs of their students, they must also focus on the needs of society as a whole and aim to devise real-world solutions to social impediments.

A fairly recent development, service learning within post-secondary institutions has helped broaden experiences of students by means of hands-on work within the community. In their report on a service-learning initiative that took place in Queensland, Australia, Carrington and Saggers (2008) argue that community-based service learning promotes inclusive, socially aware education. Such courses, which foster work within the academic setting as well as in the real world, provide students with the ability to address the civic responsibility all sociologists face. With teachers, students, and community workers working together, students gain practical knowledge and experience; as a result, they are able to critically analyze their environment by working within it.

As researchers and educators, academics must use their interpretations and analyses to equip the world with sociological knowledge. Teachers have a duty to disseminate sociological knowledge both within and beyond their classrooms, and they must prepare their students to likewise disseminate this knowledge. In the absence of bias, sociology offers a way of looking at life as it is rather than as we wish it to be. It offers inquiring minds a deep, meaningful understanding of social structures, and it allows researchers to critically and productively engage with real-world social issues.

References

Becker, H. S. (2007). *Telling about society*. Chicago, IL: University of Chicago Press.

Carrington, S., & Saggers, B. (2008). Service-learning informing the development of an inclusive ethical framework for beginning teachers. *Teaching and Teacher Education, 24*(3), 795–806. doi:10.1016/j.tate.2007.09.006

de Peuter, G. (2007). Universities, intellectuals, and multitudes: An interview with Stuart Hall. In M. Coté, R. J. F. Day, & G. de Peuter (Eds.), *Utopian pedagogy: Radical experiments against neoliberal globalization* (pp. 108–128). Toronto, ON: University of Toronto Press.

Lemert, C. (2004). *Social theory: The multicultural and classical readings* (3rd ed.). Boulder, CO: Westview Press.

Neave, G. (2000). *The universities' responsibilities to society*. Paris, France: International Association of Universities.

Razack, S. (2007). The "sharia law debate" in Ontario: The modernity/premodernity distinction in legal efforts to protect women from culture. *Feminist Legal Studies, 15*, 3–32. doi:10.1007/s10691-006-9050-x

Vaughn, L. (2005). *The power of critical thinking*. New York, NY: Oxford University Press.

Weber, M. (1946). Science as a vocation. In H. H. Gerth & C. W. Mills (Eds. & Trans.), *Max Weber: Essays in sociology* (pp. 129–156). New York, NY: Oxford University Press. (Original work published 1919.)

The Note Method (Chicago Style)

The note method, which uses either footnotes or endnotes and a bibliography, appears in different forms. Here we discuss the version described in the sixteenth edition of *The Chicago Manual of Style*. (Note that *The Chicago Manual of Style* currently outlines two methods of documentation: the note method described below and an author–date method similar to the method described in #79b. If your instructor asks you to use "Chicago style" for documenting your sources, you should clarify which of the two methods you should use.)

Footnotes and Endnotes

Make sure to number notes sequentially in the text. Whenever possible, place a note number at the end of a sentence, after the period. If you need to place the number earlier in a sentence—as you would, for example, when only part of a sentence relates to a particular source—insert it *before* a dash or *after* any other punctuation mark.

If you are using endnotes, begin the notes on a new page, with the word *Notes* as the heading. The notes themselves—whether they are footnotes or endnotes—should be single-spaced and formatted with either a first-line indent or a hanging indent. Although the note numbers in the text are superscript, the note numbers preceding each endnote or footnote are not.

If you list all of your sources in your bibliography, you do not need to repeat all of the source information in the note. Rather, include only the surname(s) of the author(s), a shortened version of the title, and the appropriate page number(s):

1. Leduc, *A Canadian Climate*, 77–79.
2. Kilty, Felices-Luna, and Fabian, *Demarginalizing Voices*, 247–50.
3. Macdonald and Ruckert, "Continental Shift?," 129.
4. Stockwell et al., "Minimum Pricing," 913–14.

For works with three or fewer authors, list the surname of each author; for works with four or more authors, list the surname of the first author followed by *et al.* Note that this guideline applies to both shortened notes (illustrated above) and full notes (illustrated below).

Author   *Title*   **Publication information**   **Electronic source**

If you choose to include full citation information in your notes, do so only the first time you cite a particular source; for second and subsequent citations to the same source, use a shortened note. The following examples illustrate how to treat various types of works in full notes.

A Book (Standard Note)

Provide the name(s) of the author(s), the title (in italics), the city of publication, the publisher's name, the year of publication, and the page or pages on which the material you are referencing appears:

1. Timothy B. Leduc, *A Canadian Climate of Mind: Passages from Fur to Energy and Beyond* (Montreal: McGill-Queen's University Press, 2016), 77–79.

If you downloaded an electronic version of the book from a library or a bookseller, include a description of the file (e.g., "PDF e-book." or "Kindle edition.") at the end. If you used an online version of the book, include the digital object identifier (DOI) assigned to the book or, if the book has not been assigned a DOI, the URL that will direct your reader to the book.

CHICAGO STYLE

Treatment of Number Ranges

When you cite a range of numbers in Chicago style, provide the first and second numbers in full for ranges that begin with a number that is less than 100 (22–29; 87–110), 100 (100–112), or a multiple of 100 (200–212; 300–301). For ranges between 101 and 109, 201 and 209, 301 and 309, and so on, do not repeat the first two digits in the second half of the range (101–2; 705–9). For all other ranges, list the first number in full, the final two digits of the second half of the range, and any other numbers that are needed to show a change (120–25; 245–59; 298–304).

A Work by a Government Agency or a Corporate Author

2. Statistics Canada, *Career Decision-Making Patterns of Canadian Youth and Associated Postsecondary Educational Outcomes* (Ottawa: Statistics Canada, 2015), 2.

Author   *Title*   Publication information   Electronic source

A Book With an Editor in Place of an Author

3. Jennifer M. Kilty, Maritza Felices-Luna, and Sheryl C. Fabian, eds., *Demarginalizing Voices: Commitment, Emotion, and Action in Qualitative Research* (Vancouver: University of British Columbia Press, 2015), 247–50.

A Book With a Translator or an Editor in Addition to the Author

Use the abbreviation "trans." to denote a translator (or translators); use the abbreviation "ed." to denote an editor (or editors):

4. Jean-Martin Charcot, *Charcot in Morocco*, trans. Toby Gelfand (Ottawa: University of Ottawa Press, 2012), 118.

A Work with No Identified Author

For a work with no identified author, begin with the title:

5. "The Colors of Money," *Forbes*, November 23, 2015, 34.

An Edition Other Than the First

6. J. M. Bumsted and Michael C. Bumsted, *A History of the Canadian Peoples*, 5th ed. (Toronto: Oxford University Press, 2016), 204.

A Chapter or Article in an Edited Book

7. Laura Macdonald and Arne Ruckert, "Continental Shift? Rethinking Canadian Aid to the Americas," in *Rethinking Canadian Aid*, ed. Stephen Brown, Molly den Heyer, and David R. Black (Ottawa: University of Ottawa Press, 2014), 129.

A Journal Article (Print)

Provide the name(s) of the author(s), the title of the article (in quotation marks), the title of the journal (in italics), the volume and/or issue number(s), the year of publication, and the page number or numbers for the material you have referenced:

8. Monica Kidd, "Shadows, Slicksters, and Soothsayers: Physicians in Canadian Poetry," *Canadian Literature* 221 (2014): 42.

Author   *Title*   Publication information   Electronic source

A Journal Article (Electronic)

Treat an electronic journal article as you would treat a journal article in print, but include the digital object identifier (DOI) assigned to the article:

9. Tim Stockwell et al., "Does Minimum Pricing Reduce Alcohol Consumption? The Experience of a Canadian Province," *Addiction 107, no. 5 (2012): 913–14,* doi:10.1111/j.1360-0443.2011.03763.x.

If the article has not been assigned a DOI, include the full uniform resource locator (URL) that will direct the reader to the article:

10. Emily Milne and Janice Aurini, "Schools, Cultural Mobility, and Social Reproduction: The Case of Progressive Discipline," *Canadian Journal of Sociology 40, no. 1 (2015): 69–70,* https://ejournals.library .ualberta.ca/index.php/CJS/article/view/20891.

CHICAGO STYLE

Inclusion of DOIs and URLs

When you cite an electronic source in Chicago style, include a Digital Object Identifier (DOI) whenever possible. If the material has not been assigned a DOI, include the uniform resource locator (URL) for the page on which you found the material. The DOI or URL is generally placed at the end of the note. If you need to break either of these elements across two or more lines, do so *after* a colon or a double slash, *before or after* an equal sign or an ampersand, or *before* any other punctuation mark. Never add a hyphen.

A Magazine Article (Print and Electronic)

11. Leah McLaren, "Workers of the World, Commute!," *Maclean's,* January 11, 2016, 32.

Note that the publication date is not enclosed in parentheses. For an online magazine article, include the URL of the page where you accessed the article:

12. Chris Sorensen, "In Defence of Genetically Modified Food," *Maclean's,* March 13, 2016, http://www.macleans.ca/society/science /in-praise-of-genetically-modified-foods.

Author *Title* Publication information Electronic source

A Newspaper Article (Print and Electronic)

13. David Parkinson, "Carbon-Tax Revenue Isn't Dirty Money," *Globe and Mail*, April 7, 2016, B2.

14. Peter Kenter, "Canadian Credit Card Holders Looking to Cool Down Overheated Debt," *National Post*, March 23, 2016, http://news .nationalpost.com/life/canadian-credit-card-holders-looking-to-cool -down-overheated-debt.

Note that an initial *The* is omitted from the titles of newspapers, magazines, and journals.

A Thesis or a Dissertation

15. Melissa De Riggi, "Non-suicidal Self-Injury, Online Activity and Emotional Health Among Adolescents" (master's thesis, McGill University, 2015), 7, Theses Canada (AMICUS No. 44230969).

Note the inclusion of the database (Theses Canada) and the retrieval number following the page reference. If the work is a doctoral dissertation, replace "master's thesis" with "doctoral dissertation." If you retrieved the work from a website, include the website's URL in place of the database name and retrieval number.

A Music Recording

Begin with the name of the writer, the composer, or the performer who is most relevant to your discussion. Next, add the title of the work, the name of the recording company, the date of release, any number assigned to the piece, and the medium (e.g., "compact disc" or "audio file"). For a song, include the title of the song as well as the name of the album on which the song appears:

16. Leonard Cohen, "Born in Chains," on *Popular Problems*, Columbia, 2014, audio file.

A Motion Picture

Include the name of the writer or the director (choose the one most relevant to your discussion), the title of the video, the location and

---

Author   *Title*   Publication information   Electronic source

name of the production company, the date of release, and the medium (e.g., "DVD" or "video file").

17. Jennifer Baichwal, *Payback* (Montreal: National Film Board of Canada, 2012), DVD.

A YouTube Video

Include the name of the main creator of the content, the title of the video, the description "YouTube video," the length of the video, the screen name of the person or organization that posted the video, the date the video was posted, and the URL. If the video depicts a live lecture or performance, include a brief description of the live event after the length of the video:

18. Jane Goodall, "Jane Goodall at Concordia: Sowing the Seeds of Hope," YouTube video, 55:01, from a lecture given at Concordia University on March 28, 2014, posted by Concordia University, June 19, 2014, https://www.youtube.com/watch?v=vibssrQKm60.

If you can't determine the main content creator, begin with the title of the video.

A Podcast

Include the name of the main creator of the content, the title of the episode, the title of the podcast, the description "podcast audio," the length of the audio file, the date of release, and the URL:

19. Katie Jensen, "Vice," *Canadaland*, podcast audio, 30:57, November 29, 2015, http://canadalandshow.com/podcast/vice.

A Blog Post

Include the author's name, the title of the blog post, the title the blog, the description "blog" (in parentheses), the date on which the material was posted, and the URL.

20. Melany Hallam, "Volunteer Your Way into a Job," *Career Sense* (blog), April 4, 2016, https://careerlinkbc.wordpress.com/.

Author   *Title*   Publication information   Electronic source

A Tweet

Give the author's name followed by the description "Twitter post," the date on which the message was tweeted, the time of the tweet, and the URL:

   21. Marc Garneau, Twitter post, January 25, 2016, 3:43 a.m., https:// twitter.com/MarcGarneau.

A Facebook Status Update

Provide a brief description of the source, the date on which you accessed the material, and the URL:

   22. Justin Trudeau's Facebook page, accessed May 4, 2016, https:// www.facebook.com/JustinPJTrudeau/.

A Google+ Post

Use the same format as you would use for a Facebook status update, but change "Facebook page" to "Google+ page":

   23. Chris Hadfield's Google+ page, accessed September 17, 2016, https://plus.google.com/+ChrisHadfield.

A Web Page or a Work Available Only on the Internet

If you are citing material that is informally published only on a website, begin with the title of the web page (in quotation marks), and provide as much additional information as you can: the author, the site's sponsor (if different from the author), the publication date, and the page's URL. If no publication date is given, provide the date on which the content was last modified (preceded by "last modified"); if neither of these dates is available, give the date on which you accessed the site (preceded by "accessed"):

   24. "About," Canadian Parks and Wilderness Society, accessed March 31, 2016, http://www.cpaws.org/about.

A Personal Email or Letter

Provide the name of the person who wrote the message, a brief description, and the date on which the message was sent:

   25. Henry Smith, personal email message, November 20, 2016.

Author   *Title*   Publication information   Electronic source

More Than One Work Cited in a Single Note

If you need to include more than one work in a single note, separate the entries with semicolons, and list them in the order in which they apply in the text:

26. Lea Berrang-Ford, James Ford, and Jaclyn Patterson, "Are We Adapting to Climate Change?," *Global Environmental Change* 21 (2011): 33; Ford et al., "Climate Change and Hazards Associated with Ice Use in Northern Canada," *Arctic, Antarctic and Alpine Research* 40, no. 4 (2008): 649.

Treat short notes in a similar manner:

26. Berrang-Ford, Ford, and Patterson, "Are We Adapting," 33; Ford et al., "Climate Change and Hazards," 649.

Repeated References to the Same Source

If you are referring to the same source as you referred to in the previous note, use the abbreviation "Ibid." and the page number.

27. Ibid., 33.

Be careful to use "Ibid." only when you are referring to the exact same source you referred to in the previous note. This task can be challenging when you are writing, before you have set all of your notes in their final order. For this reason, you should retain the short or long version of the note until you have your final draft, at which point you can insert "Ibid." where appropriate.

Bibliography References

Unless you are instructed to do otherwise, list all of the sources you have used—including those you consulted but did not refer to directly—in a bibliography at the end of your paper. Bibliography entries contain essentially the same information as full notes contain, but they do not include page references for specific passages or quotations. However, unlike in notes, the first author's name is inverted in bibliography entries, and the punctuation is slightly different. List all entries in alphabetical order, according to the first letters in each entry. For works with ten or fewer authors, list the name of each author; for works with eleven or more authors, list the first seven followed by *et al.*

Author   *Title*   Publication information   Electronic source

A Book (Standard Entry)

Begin with the first author's name (inverted) followed by the title (in italics), the city of publication, the publisher's name, and the year of publication:

Leduc, Timothy B. *A Canadian Climate of Mind: Passages from Fur to Energy and Beyond.* Montreal: McGill-Queen's University Press, 2016.

If you downloaded an electronic version of the book from a library or a bookseller, include a description of the file (e.g., "PDF e-book." or "Kindle edition.") at the end. If you used an online version of the book, include the book's DOI or, if the book has not been assigned a DOI, the URL that will direct your reader to the book.

A Work by a Government Agency or a Corporate Author

Statistics Canada. *Career Decision-Making Patterns of Canadian Youth and Associated Postsecondary Educational Outcomes.* Ottawa: Statistics Canada, 2015.

A Book With an Editor in Place of an Author

Kilty, Jennifer M., Maritza Felices-Luna, and Sheryl C. Fabian, eds. *Demarginalizing Voices: Commitment, Emotion, and Action in Qualitative Research.* Vancouver: University of British Columbia Press, 2015.

A Book With a Translator or an Editor in Addition to the Author

Add the name of the translator (preceded by "Translated by") or the editor (preceded by "Edited by") after the title:

Charcot, Jean-Martin. *Charcot in Morocco.* Translated by Toby Gelfand. Ottawa: University of Ottawa Press, 2012.

An Edition Other Than the First

Bumsted, J. M., and Michael C. Bumsted. *A History of the Canadian Peoples.* 5th ed. Toronto: Oxford University Press, 2016.

A Work with No Identified Author

If the author is unknown, begin with the title:

"The Colors of Money." *Forbes,* November 23, 2015.

Author   *Title*   Publication information   Electronic source

When alphabetizing an entry that begins with a title, ignore an initial *A*, *An*, or *The*.

A Chapter or Article in an Edited Book

Macdonald, Laura, and Arne Ruckert. "Continental Shift? Rethinking Canadian Aid to the Americas." In *Rethinking Canadian Aid*, edited by Stephen Brown, Molly den Heyer, and David R. Black, 125–42. Ottawa: University of Ottawa Press, 2014.

Note that the number range following the names of the editors indicates the pages on which the entire chapter or article appears.

A Journal Article (Print)

Begin with the first author's name (inverted) followed by the title of the article (in quotation marks), the title of the journal (in italics), the volume and/or issue number(s), the year of publication, and the range of pages on which the article appears in the journal:

Kidd, Monica. "Shadows, Slicksters, and Soothsayers: Physicians in Canadian Poetry." *Canadian Literature* 221 (2014): 37–54.

A Journal Article (Electronic)

If the article has been assigned a DOI, include that identifier at the end of the entry:

Stockwell, Tim, M. Christopher Auld, Jinhui Zhao, and Gina Martin. "Does Minimum Pricing Reduce Alcohol Consumption? The Experience of a Canadian Province." *Addiction* 107, no. 5 (2012): 912–20. doi:10.1111/j.1360-0443.2011.03763.x.

If the article has not been assigned a DOI, include the URL that will direct the reader to the article:

Milne, Emily, and Janice Aurini. "Schools, Cultural Mobility, and Social Reproduction: The Case of Progressive Discipline." *Canadian Journal of Sociology* 40, no. 1 (2015): 69–70. https://ejournals.library.ualberta.ca/index.php/CJS/article/view/20891.

Author   *Title*   Publication information   Electronic source

A Magazine Article (Print and Electronic)

McLaren, Leah. "Workers of the World, Commute!" *Maclean's*, January 11, 2016.

Sorensen, Chris. "In Defence of Genetically Modified Food." *Maclean's*, March 13, 2016. http://www.macleans.ca/society/science/in-praise-of -genetically-modified-foods.

A Newspaper Article (Print and Electronic)

Parkinson, David. "Carbon-Tax Revenue Isn't Dirty Money." *Globe and Mail*, April 7, 2016.

Kenter, Peter. "Canadian Credit Card Holders Looking to Cool Down Overheated Debt." *National Post*, March 23, 2016. http://news .nationalpost.com/life/canadian-credit-card-holders-looking-to-cool -down-overheated-debt.

Note that you do not need to include newspaper articles in your bibliography if you have cited them in full in the text or in a note.

A Thesis or a Dissertation

De Riggi, Melissa. "Non-suicidal Self-Injury, Online Activity and Emotional Health Among Adolescents." Master's thesis, McGill University, 2015. Theses Canada (AMICUS No. 44230969).

For a dissertation, use the description "PhD diss." in place of "Master's thesis."

A Music Recording

Cohen, Leonard. "Born in Chains." On *Popular Problems*. Columbia, 2014. Audio file.

A Motion Picture

Baichwal, Jennifer. *Payback*. Montreal: National Film Board of Canada, 2010. DVD.

Author   *Title*   Publication information   Electronic source

A YouTube Video

Goodall, Jane. "Jane Goodall at Concordia: Sowing the Seeds of Hope." Filmed March 28, 2014. YouTube video, 55:01. Posted by Concordia University, June 19, 2014. https://www.youtube.com/watch?v=vibssrQKm60.

In this example, Jane Goodall has been credited as the main creator of the content. If you are not sure who created the content, begin with the title of the video.

A Podcast

Jensen, Katie. "Vice." *Canadaland* (podcast), 30:57. November 29, 2015. http://canadalandshow.com/podcast/vice.

A Blog Post

Hallam, Melany. "Volunteer Your Way into a Job." *Career Sense* (blog). April 4, 2016. https://careerlinkbc.wordpress.com/.

CHICAGO STYLE

Citing Material Published Informally on the Web

Usually, blog posts, tweets, social media updates, web pages, and similar web-based sources are cited only in the notes (see pages 463–464 for examples). However, you may choose to include them in your bibliography if you have referred to them multiple times, or if your professor requires you to do so. While *The Chicago Manual of Style* does not illustrate how to cite all such sources in a bibliography, the examples given here are consistent with its approach to documentation.

A Tweet

Garneau, Marc. Twitter post. January 25, 2016, 3:43 a.m. https://twitter.com/MarcGarneau.

Author   *Title*   Publication information   Electronic source

A Facebook Status Update

Trudeau, Justin. Facebook status update. Accessed May 4, 2016. https://www.facebook.com/JustinPJTrudeau/.

A Google+ Post

Hadfield, Chris. Google+ post. Accessed September 17, 2016. https://plus.google.com/+ChrisHadfield.

A Web Page or a Work Available Only on the Internet

While a note citation for a web page typically begins with the title of the page (see page 462), the corresponding bibliography entry begins with the author's name:

Canadian Parks and Wilderness Society. "About." Accessed March 31, 2016. http://www.cpaws.org/about.

As with note citations for web pages, you should provide the date on which you accessed the site only if the page does not list the date of publication or the date on which the content was last modified.

A Personal Email or Letter

Do not include in your bibliography emails, letters, and other forms of personal communication that your reader would not be able to access. Cite such sources directly in the body of your essay or in a note (see page 474 for an example).

The Number Method

The number method is used most often in the natural sciences. The following guidelines are based on those set out in the eighth edition of *Scientific Style and Format: The CSE Manual for Authors, Editors, and Publishers* (2014), which also outlines a name–year system and a citation–name system of documentation. In its number method, which the Council of Science Editors (CSE) calls the "citation–sequence system," superscript numbers in the text correspond to numbered references that appear at the end of the document.

Author   *Title*   **Publication information**   **Electronic source**

Note that there are many versions of this method, some of which use parenthetical or bracketed numbers instead of the superscript numerals recommended by the CSE, so you should always find out what version your instructor prefers before you submit your paper.

In-Text Citations

The citation numbers in the text most often appear as superscript numbers, directly following the information to which they correspond:

> **Hawking discusses black holes in great detail.[3]**

> **The study found no link between sugar consumption and chronic heart disease,[7] but more recent studies have brought this conclusion into question.[4,7,18–21]**

Note that when a citation number must be placed beside a punctuation mark, it appears *after* the punctuation mark. If the reference is to more than one source, as illustrated by the second example above, the items are listed in numerical order. Numbers that are not in sequence are separated by a comma, with no space following the comma; for a sequence of numbers—for example, 18, 19, 20, and 21—list the first and last number, separated by a hyphen.

A less common approach, which is not recommended by the CSE, involves enclosing the numbers in parentheses or square brackets:

> **Hawking discusses black holes in great detail (3).**

If you use this style, be sure to distinguish other parenthetical numbers from citation numbers by providing a description or a unit:

> **The distance the fluid travelled (27 mm) was shorter than the researchers had predicted (89).**

Reference List

The end references should begin on a new page titled "References." The works are listed in the order in which they are first cited in the text. Each entry begins with the note number followed by a period, then the name(s) of the author(s) (last name followed by first initials), the title of the work, and additional publication information, depending on the format. For works by up to ten authors, include the names of all authors; for works by more than ten authors, list the first ten followed by "et al." If no person or organization is listed as the author, begin the entry with the work's title.

The following are some examples of entries as they would appear in the "References" section of a document in CSE style.

A Book with an Author or Authors

1. Doern GB, Castle D, Phillips PWB. Canadian science, technology, and innovation policy: the innovation economy and society nexus. Montreal (QC): McGill-Queen's University Press; 2016.

An Edition Other Than the First

Add the edition number after the title:

2. Craig N, Green R, Greider C, Storz G, Wolberger C, Cohen-Fix O. Molecular biology: principles of genome function. 2nd ed. Oxford (England): Oxford University Press; 2014.

A Book with an Editor in Place of an Author

Begin with the name(s) of the editor(s), and include the label "editor" (for one editor) or "editors" (for two or more editors):

3. Fensome R, Williams G, Achab A, Clague J, Corrigan D, Monger J, Nowlan G, editors. Four billion years and counting: Canada's geological heritage. Halifax (NS): Nimbus Publishing; 2014.

A Book in Translation

Add the name(s) of the translator(s) followed by the label "translator" (for one translator) or "translators" (for two or more translators) after the title:

4. Rovelli C. Seven brief lessons on physics. Carnell S, Segre E, translators. New York (NY): Riverhead Books; 2016.

A Chapter or Article in an Edited Book

Begin with the name(s) of the article's author(s) followed by the title of the chapter or article. Next, add "In:" followed by a full description of the book. Conclude with the pages on which the chapter or article appeared:

5. Rasmussen P, Gardner D, Camus M. Toxins in the rocks. In: Fensome R, Williams G, Achab A, Clague J, Corrigan D, Monger J, Nowlan G, editors. Four billion years and counting: Canada's geological heritage. Halifax (NS): Nimbus Publishing; 2014. p. 346–353.

A Work by a Government Agency or a Corporate Author

Include the organization's name in place of the author's name:

6. Statistics Canada. Career decision-making patterns of Canadian youth and associated postsecondary educational outcomes. Ottawa (ON): Statistics Canada; 2015.

A Work by an Anonymous Author

If no author is listed, begin with the work's title:

7. The Colors of Money. Forbes. 2015;196(7):34.

An Article in a Journal (Print)

For a journal article, list the name(s) of the author(s), the title of the article, the title of the journal, the year of publication (followed by the month and day or the season of publication if the journal has no volume or issue number), the volume number, the issue number (enclosed in parentheses, if there is an issue number), and the pages on which the article appears:

8. Yosmanovich D, Rotter M, Aprelev A, Ferrone FA. Calibrating sickle cell disease. J Mol Biol. 2016;428(8):1506–1514.

Note that in the names of journals, all articles, conjunctions, and prepositions are omitted. In addition, all significant words are capitalized and abbreviated according to ISO 4, an international standard created by the International Organization for Standardization (ISO). The ISO's list of standard abbreviations can be found online at the following address: http://www.issn.org/services/online-services/access-to-the-ltwa.

Author   *Title*   Publication information   Electronic source

An Article in a Journal (Online)

Treat an article you accessed online—for example, through an online database—as you would treat a print article, but add the additional information required for online sources (see the box below).

9. Ogliari G, Mahinrad S, Stott DJ, Jukema JW, Mooijaart SP, Macfarlane PW, Clark EN, Kearney PM, Westendorp RGJ, de Craen AJM, et al. Resting heart rate, heart rate variability and functional decline in old age. CMAJ. 2015 [accessed 2015 Nov 13];187(15):E442–E449. http://www.cmaj.ca /content/187/15/1125.full. doi:10.1503/cmaj.141633.

THE NUMBER METHOD

Additional Information for Online Sources

When you cite an online source in CSE style, include as many of the details you would include for a similar print source as possible. In addition, provide the date the material was last updated (if known) and the date you accessed the material, separated by a semicolon; enclose these dates in a single set of square brackets and place them immediately after the publication date. Also provide the source's uniform resource locator (URL) following the final publication details. If the source has been assigned a digital object identifier (DOI), include this identifier after the URL. If you must break a URL or a DOI across two lines, do so *before* a punctuation mark; do not add a hyphen where the URL or DOI breaks.

A Newspaper or Magazine Article

Treat a newspaper or magazine article as you would treat a journal article, but do not abbreviate the title of a newspaper. Include the month and day of publication for newspapers and for magazines that do not use volume and issue numbers. For newspaper articles, also note the section number, the first page, and the first column of the article:

10. Parkinson D. Carbon-tax revenue isn't dirty money. The Globe and Mail. 2016 Apr 7;Sect. B:2 (col. 2).

11. Taylor PS. Rock and a hard place. Maclean's. 2016;129(10):46–47.

Author   *Title*   Publication information   Electronic source

A Thesis or a Dissertation

12. Berghout J. Identification of host genetic factors involved in cerebral malaria resistance: from mouse to human [dissertation]. Montreal (QC): McGill University; 2014.

For a master's thesis, replace "dissertation" with "master's thesis."

An Online Video

Provide the title of the video, a brief description of the format and the episode number (if available; separated by a comma and enclosed in square brackets), the title of the program (if applicable), the producer or the network, the date the video was posted, the length, the date you accessed the video (in square brackets), and the URL:

13. Moose: a year in the life of a twig eater [video]. The Nature of Things. CBC. 2015 Oct 15, 44:12 minutes. [accessed 2016 Jan 17]. http://www.cbc.ca/natureofthings/episodes/moose-a-year -in-the-life-of-a-twig-eater.

A Podcast

Treat a podcast as you would treat an online video, but begin with the narrator's name, and adjust the description of the format:

14. Schell, D. Artificial intelligence [podcast, episode 348]. Science for the People. Skepchick. 2015 Dec 18, 1:00:00 minutes. [accessed 2016 Jan 17]. http://www.scienceforthepeople.ca /episodes/artificial-intelligence.

A Blog Post

Begin with the author's name, then add the title of the post, a brief description of the format (in square brackets), the title of the blog, the date you accessed the post (in square brackets), and the URL:

15. Fournier, A. Beyond the numbers: what goes into estimating bird populations? [blog]. Borealis Blog. [accessed 2016 Jun 17]. http://blog.scienceborealis.ca/beyond-the-numbers-what -goes-into-estimating-bird-populations.

Author   Title   Publication information   Electronic source

A Status Update on Social Media

Begin with the full username (as it appears onscreen), then add the name of the social media site, a brief description of the page and the post (in square brackets), the date and time the message was posted, the date you accessed the message (in square brackets), and the URL:

16. Navdeep Bains. Facebook [timeline, user post]. 2016 Apr 21, 11:08 a.m. [accessed 2016 Apr 26]. https://www.facebook.com/NavdeepSinghBains.

A Website or Web Page

If you are citing an entire website, list the main title that appears on the website's homepage, the place of publication (usually the location of the publisher's main office), the name of the publisher, the website's publication date, the date the page was last updated (if available) and the date you accessed the page (separated by a semicolon and a space, in square brackets), and the URL:

17. Faculty of Health Sciences. Hamilton (ON): McMaster University; 2016 [accessed 2016 May 11]. http://fhs.mcmaster.ca/main/.

If you are citing a specific page other than the homepage, add the title of that page, the date that page was published, and the approximate length of the material (in square brackets), as follows:

18. Faculty of Health Sciences. Hamilton (ON): McMaster University; 2016. Canadian researchers pioneer next-generation therapy for prostate cancer; 2015 Sept 30 [accessed 2016 May 11]; [9 paragraphs]. http://fhs.mcmaster.ca/main/news/news_2015/prostate_cancer_treatment.html.

A Personal Email or Letter

Cite a personal email or letter in a parenthetical comment in the main text—for example, " . . . (2016 email from H Smith to me)."

Author *Title* Publication information Electronic source

Omnibus Checklist for Planning and Revising

The checklists presented below are designed to help you produce an appealing, complete, well-polished essay. The questions are based on the kinds of questions we ask ourselves in reading and evaluating students' writing. If you can answer all of the questions in the affirmative, your essay should be not just adequate, but very good.

1.   During and after planning the essay, ask yourself these questions:

Subject	❏ Have I chosen a subject that sustains my interest? (#9a)
	❏ If I am writing a research essay, have I formulated a researchable question? (#9a, #74)
	❏ Have I sufficiently *limited* my subject? (#9b)
Audience and Purpose	❏ Have I thought about audience and purpose? (#9c)
	❏ Have I written down a statement of purpose and a profile of my audience? (#9c)
Evidence	❏ Have I collected or generated more than enough material/evidence to develop and support my topic well? (#9d)
Organization and Plan	❏ Does my *thesis* offer a focused, substantive, analytical claim about the subject?
	❏ Is my *plan* or *outline* for the essay logical in its content and arrangement? (#9e–j)
	❏ Considering my plan or outline, do I have the right number of *main ideas*—neither too few nor too many—for the purpose of my essay?
	❏ Are my main ideas reasonably *parallel* in content and development?
	❏ Have I chosen the best *arrangement* for the main parts? Does it coincide with the arrangement of ideas in the thesis?

2. **During and after your revision of the essay, ask yourself these questions:**

Title	❑ Does the title of my essay clearly indicate the *subject* and *topic*? ❑ Is the title original? ❑ Does the title contain something to catch a reader's interest?
Structure	❑ Does my *beginning* engage a reader's curiosity or interest? ❑ Have I kept the beginning reasonably short and to the point? (#9-l) ❑ Have I clearly stated my subject (and my thesis as well) somewhere near the beginning? (#9-l.3) ❑ Does my *ending* bring the essay to a satisfying conclusion? (#8c, #11.9) ❑ Have I used the ending to do something other than re-hash ideas already well presented in the rest of the essay? ❑ Have I kept my ending short enough, without unnecessary repetition and summary?
Unity and Development	❑ Is my essay *unified*? Do all its parts contribute to the whole, and have I avoided digression? (#8a)
Emphasis	❑ Have I been sufficiently *particular* and *specific*, and not left any generalizations unsupported? (#66) ❑ Have I devoted an appropriate amount of space to each part? (#8c)
Paragraphs	❑ Does the *first sentence* of each paragraph (except perhaps the first and last) somehow mention the particular *subject* of the essay? (#4a.1, #8a) ❑ Do the early sentences of each body paragraph clearly state the topic, or part of the topic? Or, is the topic sentence, when it isn't among the first sentences, effective where it is placed? (#4a) ❑ Is each body paragraph long enough to develop its topic adequately? (#7b) ❑ Does each paragraph *end* adequately, but not too self-consciously? (#4c)

Coherence	❑ Do the sentences in each paragraph have sufficient coherence with each other? (#3–5)
	❑ Does the beginning of each new paragraph provide a clear *transition* from the preceding paragraph? (#4a.1, #8b)
	❑ Is the coherence between sentences and between paragraphs smooth? Do I need to revise any unnecessary or illogical transitional devices? (#5c–d)
Sentences	❑ Is each sentence (especially if it is compound, complex, or long) internally *coherent*? (#31)
	❑ Is each sentence *clear* and sufficiently *emphatic* in making its point? (#29)
	❑ Have I used a variety of *kinds*, *lengths*, and *structures* of sentences? (#28)
	❑ Have I *avoided the passive voice* except where it is clearly necessary or desirable? (#17-l, #29f)
Diction (Part VII)	❑ Have I used *words* whose meanings I am sure of or checked the *dictionary* for any whose meanings I am not sure of?
	❑ Is my diction sufficiently *concrete* and *specific*? (#66a)
	❑ Have I avoided *unidiomatic* usages? (#70)
	❑ Have I weeded out unnecessary repetitions and other *wordiness*? (#71a–c)
	❑ Have I avoided *jargon* and unnecessary *clichés* and *euphemisms*? (#71d–h, #68)
	❑ Have I avoided unintentional *slang* and *informal* diction, as well as *overly formal* diction? (#64)
	❑ Have I avoided inappropriate or confusing *figurative language*? (#65)
	❑ Have I avoided *gender-biased*, *sexist language*? (#15d, #72)
Grammar	❑ Are my sentences *grammatically* sound—that is, free of dangling modifiers, agreement errors, incorrect tenses, faulty verb forms, incorrect articles and prepositions, and the like? (Parts III and IV)
	❑ Have I avoided *run-on sentences* and unacceptable *fragments* and *comma splices*? (#54a, #12x, #54b)

Punctuation (Part V)	❑ Is the punctuation of each sentence *correct* and *effective*? ❑ Have I proofread sentences slowly with special attention to the punctuation?
Spelling (Part VI)	❑ Have I checked all my words—reading backwards if necessary—for possible spelling errors? ❑ Have I then used the spell-checker in my software package to check the essay?
Mechanics	❑ Have I carefully *proofread* my essay in hard copy and not just on the computer screen, and have I corrected all typographical errors? (#9-o) ❑ Is my manuscript *neat* and *legible*? Does it conform to all manuscript conventions (esp. spacing, margins, font size, pagination, and headers)? (#55) ❑ Have I introduced and handled all *quotations* and *references* properly? (#52, #78) ❑ Have I checked all quotations for accuracy? (#78)
Acknow-ledgement	❑ Have I acknowledged everything that requires acknowledgement according to the guidelines and rules of my university or college? (#77, #78) ❑ Have I double-checked my *documentation* for accuracy, consistency, and correct form? (#79a–d, Part VIII)
The Last Step	❑ Have I *read my essay aloud*—preferably to a colleague—as a final check on how it sounds and made adjustments for *clarity* and *emphasis*?

Specialized Checklist for Writers with English as an Additional Language

What follows is an additional checklist we hope will be of particular help to those of you who are bilingual or multilingual and working to achieve fluency in English as your second, third, or fourth language. The questions we have listed are meant to help you target your editing on those issues that are often problematic for a writer whose own first language differs significantly from English in its grammatical patterns. For example, English is a language with a complex set of tenses that inflect or change verbs to express actions and states of being. In contrast, other languages may express changes in time through adverbial expressions and not change or inflect verb forms at all.

When you take this targeted approach to checking a draft you have written, you need to re-read the draft several times, checking each time for patterns with which you have had difficulty in previous writing. In each reading (ideally a slow check of a hard copy you read aloud), you should focus on one or two patterns in a sentence-by-sentence and paragraph-by-paragraph review. Your short-term objective is to polish the paper itself; your long-term objective is to become a self-sufficient proofreader who will not have to rely on others to edit your work.

Next to each of the questions that follow, you will find references to the sections of this book in which we have treated these various patterns. You will also see, in a number of cases, the acronym *OALD*, our abbreviation for the *Oxford Advanced Learner's Dictionary*. This dictionary is an invaluable resource, and one we have used throughout our teaching careers in working with many students aiming to perfect their writing in their new language. The *OALD* can be of significant help to you in checking for verb forms, prepositional idioms, and accurate use of the indefinite articles *a* and *an*. You should take some time to read the introduction to the dictionary to learn how to use its specialized features.

Use the questions on this checklist and on the omnibus checklist preceding it *selectively*; that is, focus on the questions targeting problem areas you and your readers have identified in your recent writing. We hope that our cross-references here to particular sections of this book and to the *OALD* will help you to achieve mastery in your expression and confidence in your style.

Sentence Structure	❑ Have you checked your longer sentences for mixed constructions? (#37)
	❑ Have you checked your sentences for faulty predications? (#38)
	❑ Have you checked for ineffective fragments—especially at points where you are introducing examples and illustrations into your work? (#12x, #21e, #32)
	❑ Have you checked your compound sentences for faulty coordination? (#41)
	❑ Have you checked your complex sentences for faulty subordination? (#27b, #54-l)
	❑ Have you checked your longer and balanced sentences for faulty parallelism? (#40)
	❑ Have you checked your longer sentences for comma splices and misused semicolons? (#33, #54b, #54-l)
Grammatical Patterns Within Sentences	❑ Have you checked nouns for countability and uncountability, and have you then checked for correct number form (singular or plural) for these nouns? (#13a and *OALD*)
	❑ Have you checked that singular countable nouns in an indefinite context are preceded by an indefinite article? (#19c and *OALD*)
	❑ Have you checked that uncountable nouns are in singular form and unaccompanied by indefinite articles? (#19c and *OALD*)
	❑ Have you checked that nouns made specific by their context are modified by the definite article? (#19c)
	❑ Have you checked that verbs appear in their correct regular or irregular forms? (#17b–f and *OALD*)
	❑ Have you checked that you have used gerund and infinitive verbals correctly? (#21)
	❑ Have you checked that subjects and verbs in your sentences agree? (#18)
	❑ Have you checked that noun antecedents and pronouns referring to them agree? (#15)

Grammatical Patterns Within Sentences *(continued)*	❏ Have you checked that verbs used in the passive voice are transitive? (#17-l and *OALD*)
	❏ Have you checked that the tenses of your verbs are correct? (#17g–j)
	❏ Have you checked for correct sequence of tenses in sentences where you have used more than one tense? (#17h)
	❏ Have you checked that the prepositions you have used in combination with particular nouns or verbs are idiomatic? (#22d and *OALD*)
Diction	❏ Have you checked that the level of your diction fits your audience and purpose, and have you steered away from the kind of artificial diction created by overuse of a thesaurus? (#64)
	❏ Have you checked that you are using words new to your vocabulary in their correct parts of speech? (Part III and *OALD*)
Composing	❏ Have you checked that you have used transitions correctly and in moderation? (#5d)
	❏ Have you checked that your paragraphs position their core or topic sentences effectively and strategically? (#4a)

INDEX

Index

Index

Index

Index

Index

Index

Notes on Spelling and Other Issues

Notes on Spelling and Other Issues

Notes on Spelling and Other Issues

Notes on Spelling and Other Issues

Notes on Spelling and Other Issues

Notes on Spelling and Other Issues

Notes on Spelling and Other Issues

Notes on Spelling and Other Issues